D1576317

More Praise for *The Spym*

"Chris Whipple has become in recent years something of a Washington elite whisperer. In *The Spymasters*—as in his equally masterful book, *The Gatekeepers*—he gets almost everyone to spill their secrets."
—David Friend, *Vanity Fair*

"Riveting . . . a timely reminder of the outsize influence of our nation's intelligence bureaucracy—and the men and women who live in this wilderness of mirrors. 'They were all asked to do things they shouldn't do,' says Cynthia Helms, wife of the legendary CIA director Richard Helms. Whipple explores these ethical quandaries with nuance and fairness."
—Kai Bird, Pulitzer Prize–winning author
of *The Good Spy: The Life and Death of
Robert Ames*

"Astute . . . At a time when America's intelligence community is under attack from conspiracy theories and fake news, Whipple provides a real-world history of those who have held one of the most difficult posts in Washington. These portraits are accurate, fair, and informative."
—John W. Dean, Nixon administration White
House counsel and bestselling author of
Conservatives Without Conscience

"The job of CIA director is as difficult as it is important. He or she must predict the future while steering through a moral morass. No wonder the spymasters in Chris Whipple's engrossing story so often trip up. Whipple is at once clear-eyed and fair-minded while giving us a riveting read."
—Evan Thomas, *New York Times* bestselling
author of *The Very Best Men: The Daring
Early Years of the CIA*

"Chris Whipple has previously garnered wide acclaim for his history of the White House chiefs of staff. He now replicates that methodology with equal success in this history of CIA directors from Richard Helms to Gina Haspel. His group portrait of the DCIs offers a highly readable, fair, and well-researched history of the CIA over the past fifty years. He comes neither to pillory the CIA nor to praise it but, rather, to understand it—and he fully succeeds."

— Max Boot, *New York Times* bestselling author
of *The Road Not Taken: Edward Lansdale and the American Tragedy in Vietnam*

"*The Spymasters* will make you proud, and depressed. It will also cause you to lose sleep, not just because of the dangers we face, but because it's so damned riveting it will keep you up until all hours. How Whipple managed to pull so much history together, how he extracted such a wealth of detail from his principal sources—the CIA leaders themselves—is quite simply mind-boggling. This is an important book. And one hell of a story."

— Christopher Buckley, author of *The White House Mess* and *Thank You for Smoking*

THE SPYMASTERS

ALSO BY CHRIS WHIPPLE

The Gatekeepers:
How the White House Chiefs of Staff
Define Every Presidency

THE SPYMASTERS

HOW THE CIA DIRECTORS
SHAPE HISTORY AND THE FUTURE

CHRIS WHIPPLE

SIMON &
SCHUSTER

London · New York · Sydney · Toronto · New Delhi

First published in the United States by Scribner, an Imprint of Simon & Schuster, Inc., 2020
First published in Great Britain by Simon & Schuster UK Ltd, 2020

1 3 5 7 9 10 8 6 4 2

Simon & Schuster UK Ltd
1st Floor
222 Gray's Inn Road
London WC1X 8HB

www.simonandschuster.co.uk
www.simonandschuster.com.au
www.simonandschuster.co.in

Simon & Schuster Australia, Sydney
Simon & Schuster India, New Delhi

A CIP catalogue record for this book is available from the British Library

Hardback ISBN: 978-1-4711-8371-3
Trade Paperback ISBN: 978-1-4711-8372-0
eBook ISBN: 978-1-4711-8373-7

Interior design by Erich Hobbing

Printed in the UK by CPI Group (UK) Ltd, Croydon, CR0 4YY

MIX
Paper from
responsible sources
FSC
www.fsc.org   FSC® C020471

This one is for Ann.

Contents

Cast of Characters

RICHARD HELMS

Lyndon B. Johnson, president
Richard Nixon, president
General Vernon Walters, deputy CIA director
James Jesus Angleton, head of counterintelligence
Harold Adrian Russell "Kim" Philby, British Intelligence official
    and Russian mole
Cynthia Helms, second wife of Richard Helms
Robert McNamara, defense secretary
Charles Allen, National Intelligence Officer for Warning
Howard Hunt, ex-CIA member of "the Plumbers"
H. R. Haldeman, White House chief of staff
John Ehrlichman, White House domestic adviser
Henry Kissinger, secretary of state

JAMES SCHLESINGER

Richard Nixon, president
Mel Goodman, analyst
Leslie Gelb, Defense Dept. official
Cora Schlesinger, daughter of James Schlesinger
Brent Scowcroft, national security adviser
Fred Buzhardt, legal counsel to the president
Daniel Ellsberg, whistleblower, leaker of Pentagon Papers

WILLIAM COLBY

Gerald Ford, president
Ngo Dinh Diem, president of Vietnam
Seymour Hersh, reporter, *The New York Times*
Paul Colby, son of William Colby
Howard Hughes, billionaire
Donald Rumsfeld, White House chief of staff
Abe Rosenthal, executive editor, *The New York Times*
Daniel Schorr, CBS News correspondent
Cicely Angleton, wife of James Angleton
Salvador Allende, president of Chile, deposed in a military coup
Sally Colby, second wife of William Colby; diplomat
Carl Colby, son of William Colby; filmmaker

GEORGE H. W. BUSH

Gerald Ford, president
Barbara Bush, wife of George H.W. Bush
Elliot Richardson, former attorney general
James A. Baker III, Ford campaign official and Bush confidant
E. Henry Knoche, deputy CIA director
Richard Kerr, analyst
Jimmy Carter, president-elect
Stuart Eizenstat, domestic policy adviser
Theodore Sorensen, Carter's nominee as CIA director
Jack Watson, Carter's transition director
Hamilton Jordan, Carter's campaign manager

ADMIRAL STANSFIELD TURNER

Jimmy Carter, president
Walter Mondale, vice president
Charles Battaglia, military aide to Stansfield Turner

Thomas Twetten, veteran operative
Zbigniew Brzezinski, national security adviser
Mohammed Reza Pahlavi, the Shah of Iran
Bruce Riedel, Middle East analyst
Harold Brown, defense secretary
Ayatollah Ruhollah Khomeini, fundamentalist Shiite cleric, leader
    of Iranian revolution
Ernie Oney, Iran analyst
William Sullivan, U.S. ambassador to Tehran

WILLIAM CASEY

Ronald Reagan, president
Alexander Haig, secretary of state
Edwin Meese, counselor to the president
Robert Gates, executive assistant to William Casey
Admiral Bobby Ray Inman, deputy CIA director
Max Hugel, head of Directorate of Operations
Thomas Twetten, chief of Near East division
Howard Baker, Jr., Senate Majority Leader
Bob Woodward, *Washington Post* reporter
Imad Mughniyah, chief of operations, Hezbollah
William Buckley, chief of station, Beirut
Robert "Bud" McFarlane, national security adviser
Admiral John Poindexter, national security adviser
Oliver North, Marine Lt. Col., NSC official
Sheikh Mohammad Hussein Fadlallah, spiritual leader of Hezbollah
Prince Bandar Bin Sultan, Saudi ambassador to the U.S.
Sophia Casey, wife of William Casey

WILLIAM WEBSTER

Ronald Reagan, president
Mikhail Gorbachev, leader of the Soviet Union
Duane "Dewey" Clarridge, head of Latin American division

Charlie Wilson, Texas congressman
Dick Cheney, defense secretary
Brent Scowcroft, national security adviser

ROBERT GATES

George H. W. Bush, president
Mel Goodman, analyst
Boris Yeltsin, president of Russia
Jack Devine, operative, chief of Afghan Task Force
Aldrich Hazen "Rick" Ames, CIA mole

JAMES WOOLSEY

Bill Clinton, president
Warren Christopher, Clinton transition director
Anthony "Tony" Lake, national security adviser
Dee Dee Myers, campaign press secretary
Richard "Dick" Clarke, White House counterterrorism czar
Mir Aimal Kasi, Pakistani terrorist
Gina Bennett, senior counterterrorism analyst
Osama Bin Laden, head of Al Qaeda
Mohammed Farah Aideed, Somali warlord
Saddam Hussein, leader of Iraq

JOHN DEUTCH

Bill Clinton, president
Nora Slatkin, CIA executive director
Robert Baer, Middle East operative
General John Shalikashvili, chairman of the joint chiefs of staff
Admiral William Studeman, acting CIA director

GEORGE TENET

Bill Clinton, president
George W. Bush, president
Sandy Berger, national security adviser
Cofer Black, director, Counterterrorism Center
Richard Blee, head of Bin Laden Unit
Condoleezza Rice, national security adviser
Khalid al-Midhar and Nawaf al-Hazmi, 9/11 Al Qaeda hijackers
Jose Rodriguez, director, Counterterrorism Center
Gina Haspel, deputy to Jose Rodriguez
Abu Zubaydah, Al Qaeda terrorist
Ali Soufan, FBI interrogator
Khalid Sheik Mohammed (KSM), mastermind of 9/11 attacks
Colin Powell, secretary of state
I. Lewis "Scooter" Libby, adviser to V.P. Dick Cheney
Richard Armitage, deputy and confidant to Secretary of State Colin
    Powell
John McLaughlin, deputy CIA director

PORTER GOSS

George W. Bush, president
Kyle "Dusty" Foggo, executive director (ExDir)
Steve Kappes, deputy director of the Directorate of Operations (DO)
Mike Sulick, deputy to Steve Kappes
Joshua Bolten, White House chief of staff
John Negroponte, director of national intelligence

GENERAL MICHAEL HAYDEN

George W. Bush, president
Stephanie O' Sullivan, head of the Directorate of Science and
    Technology

Mark Mazzetti, reporter, *The New York Times*
John Durham, special counsel
Meir Dagan, head of Mossad, Israel's intelligence service
General Mohammed Suleiman, Syrian general
General Qassim Suleimani, head of Iran's Quds Force
Imad Mughniyah, chief of operations, Hezbollah

LEON PANETTA

Barack Obama, president
John Podesta, Obama's transition director
Michael Morell, deputy CIA director
Osama Bin Laden, head of Al Qaeda
Denis McDonough, deputy national security adviser
Jeremy Bash, chief of staff to Leon Panetta
Admiral Dennis Blair, director of national intelligence
Human Khalil al-Balawi, Al Qaeda triple agent
Jennifer Matthews, head of CIA base at Khost, Afghanistan
Elizabeth Hanson, CIA "targeter"
Ali bin Zeid, Jordanian intelligence captain
Rahm Emanuel, White House chief of staff
Nancy Pelosi, House Speaker
Dianne Feinstein, chair of the Senate Select Committee on
    Intelligence (SSCI)
Vice Admiral William "Bill" McRaven, head of Joint Special
    Operations Command (JSOC)
Bill Daley, White House chief of staff
Joseph Biden, vice president

GENERAL DAVID PETRAEUS

Barack Obama, president
Michael Morell, acting CIA director
Anwar al-Awlaki, radical jihadist cleric, and American citizen
Nasser al-Awlaki, father of Anwar al-Awlaki

Chris Stevens, U.S. ambassador to Libya
Paula Broadwell, Petraeus biographer and lover
Jill Kelley, Florida socialite
Nick Rasmussen, head of National Counterterrorism Center
   (NCTC)

JOHN BRENNAN

Barack Obama, president
Nick Shapiro, chief of staff to John Brennan
Avril Haines, CIA deputy director
David Axelrod, White House political adviser
James Clapper, director of national intelligence
General Valery Gerasimov, architect of Russia's "hybrid warfare"
Michael Daniel, White House cybersecurity coordinator
Lisa Monaco, Homeland Security adviser
Alexander Bortnikov, head of Russian Federal Security Service
   (FSB)
Vladimir Putin, president of Russia
Jeh Johnson, secretary of Homeland Security
Mitch McConnell, Senate Majority Leader
The CIA's Kremlin asset

MICHAEL POMPEO

Donald Trump, president
Reince Priebus, White House chief of staff
James Comey, FBI director
Meroe Park, acting CIA director
Steve Bannon, political strategist
Fiona Hill, NSC Russia expert
General James Mattis, defense secretary
Sergei Lavrov, Russian foreign minister
Sergey Kislyak, Russian ambassador to U.S.
Mohammad Bin Salman (MBS), Crown Prince of Saudi Arabia

Jared Kushner, senior White House adviser
Kim Jong Un, dictator of North Korea
Rex Tillerson, secretary of state

GINA HASPEL

Donald Trump, president
Dan Coats, director of national intelligence
Kamala Harris, Democratic senator, California
Steven Hall, retired head of CIA's Russia operations
Jamal Khashoggi, *Washington Post* columnist, murdered by Saudi
    hit team
Agnès Callamard, UN special rapporteur
Volodymyr Zelensky, president of Ukraine
Adam Schiff, chair, House Permanent Select Committee on
    Intelligence (HPSCI)
Courtney Ellwood, CIA general counsel
Michael Atkinson, inspector general of the intelligence community
Joseph Maguire, acting director of national intelligence
The whistleblower, anonymous CIA official assigned to NSC
John Michael "Mick" Mulvaney, acting White House chief of staff
General Qassim Suleimani, commander of Iranian IRGC Quds
    Force

INTRODUCTION

"There's *something going on.*"

In his seventh-floor office overlooking the wooded campus of Langley, Virginia, John Brennan sat at a conference table, hunched over his laptop. It was midnight, August 2, 2016, and the CIA director was surrounded by debris—black binders, white legal pads, a bowl of cold soup. It was not unusual for him to be there at all hours, poring over intelligence reports; in more than three years as head of the world's most powerful spy agency, Brennan often worked well into the night, trying to connect the dots of an imminent terrorist attack. But he'd never seen anything like the threat he was now confronting.

With his perpetual scowl, Brennan looked like an Old Testament prophet. At just over six feet, he was all elbows and knees; Barack Obama dubbed him "Jumping John"—a nod to Brennan's boast that in his youth he could dunk a basketball (before three hip replacements and multiple knee surgeries). More often, given the dire news the director usually brought him, the president called him "Dr. Doom."

A CIA insider, Brennan had joined the agency in 1980 on a whim and become a covert operative. But he was ill-suited to the clannish priesthood of the agency's clandestine service; within a year he'd left the Directorate of Operations (DO) to become an analyst. Introverted and soft-spoken, Brennan was the opposite of his mentor, George Tenet, the gregarious director who'd run the CIA under Bill Clinton and George W. Bush. The cigar-chomping Tenet had prowled the corridors of Langley, backslapping and cajoling the workforce.

The attacks of 9/11 had been preceded by a cacophony of warnings, "red lights flashing." But this threat, in the summer of 2016, was different—more like a gathering storm. "When you're CIA director

1

there are a lot of clouds up there," Brennan recalled. "You're looking out, and sometimes they're far off and they're forming. And you get the barometric readings. And sometimes there is that burning piece of intelligence that says: 'there's going to be an attack tomorrow.' Other times, you realize, there's *something going on*."

Something ominous had been going on throughout 2016, much of it in broad daylight. In March, the Russian intelligence agency, GRU, began hacking the email accounts of Clinton campaign officials, including chairman John Podesta. The following month hackers linked to Russia broke into the website of the Democratic National Committee (DNC); a huge cache of stolen emails was released on the eve of the Democratic National Convention. Equally troubling was the behavior of the eventual Republican nominee, Donald Trump, who seemed to echo Moscow's talking points. Members of his campaign staff had been in contact with officials linked to Russian intelligence. Then, in July 2016, Trump brazenly dared Moscow to illegally hack into Clinton's emails: "Russia, if you're listening, I hope you're able to find the 30,000 emails that are missing." That same day, the Russians made their first effort to break into servers used by Clinton's office.

In late July, Brennan told his experts to pull together everything they'd gathered on the Russian threat since the beginning of the year: SIGINT (signals intelligence, from electronic intercepts), HUMINT (human intelligence, from spies), and open-source analysis (public sources). No one was better than Brennan at sifting through and interpreting raw material from disparate sources—and he now realized it added up to one thing: The Russians were poised to launch a crippling cyberattack on the American electoral system. (Brennan and the CIA weren't yet aware of the extent of the social media disinformation campaign that would also be deployed.) The Russians' goal was not just to sow chaos and confusion but to tip the 2016 presidential election to Donald J. Trump.

And there was one other thing. According to a top secret source, a CIA asset inside the Kremlin, the order for this unprecedented assault had come from Russian president Vladimir Putin himself.

It was an intelligence bombshell, Brennan realized; the president would have to be informed. But how? Every morning, the CIA routed to the commander in chief a top secret digest of threat developments around the world: the President's Daily Brief (PDB). But Brennan thought this latest intelligence was too sensitive for the PDB, which was circulated to more than a dozen administration officials. This new information called for an urgent meeting with the president and his closest advisers. Brennan decided to send a note to the White House, an envelope hand-delivered by a courier. It would be marked "eyes only," restricted to just five people: President Obama; chief of staff Denis McDonough; National Security Adviser Susan Rice; her deputy, Avril Haines; and Homeland Security Adviser Lisa Monaco.

Every CIA director faces a defining crisis. Tenet had faced three: the attacks of 9/11; the brutal prisoner interrogation program known as "enhanced interrogation techniques" (EIT); and the CIA's botched intelligence on Iraq's weapons of mass destruction. Brennan, too, had grappled with formidable challenges: the unending civil war in Syria; the savage reign of the terrorist group ISIS; and the CIA's escalation of lethal drone warfare. But Brennan's ultimate test, the one that would define his directorship, was just now gathering critical mass.

Brennan was acutely conscious of his place in history. A few steps above Langley's soaring marble atrium, with the circular "CIA" insignia on the floor and the iconic Memorial Wall, is a long corridor lined with oil portraits of the CIA's directors. Although Brennan arrived at work in an armored car through an underground garage — and took a private elevator to his office — he often went out of his way to walk past this gallery of his predecessors.

They're some of Washington's most illustrious names: Allen Dulles, John McCone, Richard Helms, James Schlesinger, William Colby, George H. W. Bush, Admiral Stansfield Turner, William Casey, William Webster, Robert Gates, James Woolsey, John Deutch, George Tenet, Porter Goss, General Michael Hayden, Leon Panetta. (The portrait of Panetta's successor, General David Petraeus, wasn't yet finished.) Many had served in other powerful government posts: four-star general, FBI director, defense secretary — even president of the United States. But perhaps no job, except for commander in chief, is more consequential — and more politically perilous — than CIA director.

Petraeus, Brennan's predecessor, had suffered a precipitous fall from grace. The celebrated former commander of the International

Security Assistance Force (ISAF) in Afghanistan, and architect of the Iraq War "surge," Petraeus brought military acumen to the agency, but also a sense of entitlement that one CIA wag called "four-star general disease." Rumors of Petraeus's demands for special treatment while traveling became grist for Langley's gossip mill, and undermined his authority. Barely more than a year had elapsed, during which Petraeus had recovered from that rocky start, when he was caught sharing top secret information with his biographer and lover; within days he'd resigned.

Two directors who arrived on a mission to shake up the CIA— James Schlesinger, for Richard Nixon, and Stansfield Turner, for Jimmy Carter—also crashed and burned. Schlesinger, brilliant but condescending and arrogant, abruptly fired more than one thousand veteran operatives; after five months Nixon moved him to the Pentagon as secretary of defense. Schlesinger was so unpopular at the CIA that he was given extra security guards after a slew of death threats. Turner, a spit-and-polish former Navy admiral, was earnest but too straitlaced for the rough-and-tumble spy business, and no match in the bureaucratic wars for Carter's wily national security adviser, Zbigniew Brzezinski. Turner would preside over one of history's greatest intelligence debacles: the CIA's failure to anticipate the 1979 Iranian revolution.

Another cautionary tale comes from the tenure of John Deutch, Bill Clinton's director. A former deputy director of defense and MIT chemistry professor, Deutch was a visionary intellectual who helped usher in the era of unmanned drone warfare. Michael Morell, a two-time acting director, considered him the most intelligent person he'd ever met, followed by Barack Obama. But Deutch was politically tone-deaf. He insulted the CIA workforce, saying they weren't as smart as their Pentagon counterparts. And he assured Clinton that he'd get rid of Saddam Hussein through a CIA-sponsored coup; unfortunately, the covert operation was penetrated by the Iraqis and failed miserably, leaving Kurdish allies abandoned. (And not for the last time; decades later the Kurds in northern Syria would be abandoned again by Donald Trump.) Deutch resigned after seventeen months. Soon thereafter top secret classified material was found on his home computer, and he was stripped of his security clearance.

Other directors were towering figures who transformed the

CIA. Allen Dulles, who served Dwight Eisenhower, was a fierce Cold Warrior who ran the agency like a personal fiefdom; to combat the Soviets, he launched audacious covert operations that toppled governments in Iran and Guatemala. William Colby, who'd fought behind enemy lines as a young paratrooper for the Office of Strategic Services (OSS), the CIA's precursor, during World War II, made public the agency's darkest secrets—the so-called Family Jewels. In so doing he earned the enmity of the CIA's secretive old guard, but the respect of those who valued his transparency, and arguably saved the agency. Colby's death by drowning in 1996—at the age of seventy-six—while canoeing near his weekend house in Maryland, still strikes some of his colleagues as suspicious.

When George H. W. Bush, with no intelligence experience but with a stint as envoy to the People's Republic of China, became director, he was convinced it was the end of his political career. But Bush rescued the agency from scandal, restored its morale and reputation, and set the stage for his eventual presidency.

Few directors wielded more power than William Casey, who was empowered by Ronald Reagan to fight communism around the globe. A disheveled character who careened around CIA headquarters, mumbling unintelligibly, Casey waged covert wars against the Soviets and their proxies; on his watch, the mujahideen, armed with Stinger missiles by the CIA, turned the tide against the Soviet Red Army in Afghanistan. But later, in a bid to free American hostages in Lebanon, Casey spearheaded a harebrained plot to trade arms to Iran and illegally divert profits to the Central American guerrillas known as the contras. At the height of that scandal, Casey died of a brain tumor; he was so famously devious that one senator, unconvinced, asked to see the body as proof.

No one knew more about the CIA than Robert Gates, a suffer-no-fools analyst who rose through the ranks to become director under President George H. W. Bush. On his first bid for the top job, Gates withdrew his nomination after fierce criticism of his role in the Iran-contra scandal. He succeeded on his second attempt a few years later, though he was accused of exaggerating Soviet military capabilities, a charge he denied. As director, Gates helped President George H. W. Bush navigate the dangerous shoals of the post–Cold War world after the Soviets' collapse.

The most popular directors of the modern era were George Tenet and Leon Panetta. Charismatic, energetic, and down-to-earth, Tenet warned George W. Bush's White House of an imminent Al Qaeda attack in the summer of 2001, months before 9/11, a warning that went unheeded by the Bush administration. He also launched the CIA's lightning invasion of Afghanistan, routing the Taliban. But Tenet's promising directorship, the second-longest in history, would be marred by the controversy over enhanced interrogation techniques. And his most infamous mistake, which was sure to end up in the first paragraph of his obituary, was assuring Bush that the case for Saddam Hussein's weapons of mass destruction was a "slam dunk."

Panetta, the ex-congressman and White House chief of staff who served as President Obama's first CIA director, combined a common touch at Langley with political finesse in the corridors of power; no one was better at managing the president, bureaucracy, and Congress. He turned the page on the scandals of the Bush era while inspiring devotion among the agency's rank and file. Panetta's finest hour was helping to convince Obama, on uncertain circumstantial evidence, to launch the CIA-led mission that resulted in the death of Osama bin Laden.

Michael Hayden, an Air Force general (the only person to head both the CIA and National Security Agency), steadied the agency after the crisis over EITs, lifting its battered spirits. An eloquent defender of the CIA in public, Hayden secretly gave the go-ahead to one of the most audacious covert operations in CIA history, an operation still shrouded in secrecy: a joint CIA-Mossad mission to assassinate the infamous Hezbollah terrorist Imad Mughniyah. So elusive that he was called the "Scarlet Pimpernel" of terrorism, Mughniyah had been the agency's most wanted man for a quarter century. He was regarded as even more dangerous than his Iranian comrade-in-arms, General Qassim Suleimani, who would be killed in a drone strike ordered by Donald Trump in January 2020. In the late 1990s, under Bill Clinton, the CIA was poised to kidnap Mughniyah in Beirut, but the operation fell apart at the last minute. The story of that operation will be reported here for the first time.

Mike Pompeo, an ambitious former congressman and Tea Party member from Kansas, forged a close relationship with President Trump, thereby giving the CIA access to the forty-fifth president.

But Pompeo's slavish loyalty to Trump would tarnish him, and he couldn't defuse the president's visceral hatred of the intelligence community. Pompeo's successor, Gina Haspel, the first woman to become CIA director, stayed out of harm's way by keeping a low profile and tending to affairs at Langley. But on her watch a CIA whistleblower would plunge her into the middle of a scandal involving Ukraine and Trump that would trigger his impeachment.

All these directors, for better or worse, have shaped history. When the commander in chief confronts a crisis, the CIA director serves as his eyes and ears, providing the intelligence upon which decisions are made. The stakes range from starting unnecessary wars to averting Armageddon. During the Cuban Missile Crisis, Director John McCone ultimately advised JFK against an invasion that almost surely would have triggered a nuclear catastrophe. McCone was armed not only with U-2 aerial surveillance photos but also purloined Russian missile manuals, courtesy of a Soviet spy. Conversely, Director George Tenet provided George W. Bush with a faulty estimate of Saddam's weapons of mass destruction, helping to spur the invasion of Iraq in 2003. The consequences of decisions framed by CIA directors could scarcely be more fateful. "An intelligence failure like the one on WMDs changes history," said Bob Gates, the former director.

This book is about the men—and, currently, the woman—who have led the world's most powerful and storied intelligence agency. It's not a formal history of the CIA but rather a look at how its directors have helped shape a half century of world events, and how they'll affect the future. I've interviewed nearly every living director, and many of their colleagues, but the judgments are, of course, mine, not theirs.

By this book's finish I hope to have answered the following questions: Who succeeds and fails as CIA director? What is the proper relationship between the director and the president? What is the CIA's mission? Is the world's most powerful intelligence agency a force for good or evil in the world?

The notion that the CIA has bungled its way through the last fifty years—missing real threats and ginning up false evidence for fake ones—is a common belief. It's a version of history culminating in the agency's botched estimate of Iraq's WMDs. And Iraq has hardly been the agency's only debacle. The CIA has had its share of intelligence failures—from missing Iran's 1979 revolution to misjudging Russia's social media assault on the 2016 U.S. presidential election.

But that is a skewed version of history. The CIA has succeeded in disrupting terrorist plots and saving lives. It has also sounded alarms that politicians chose not to hear. Contrary to conventional wisdom, in the months before 9/11, though it could not specify the target, the agency repeatedly warned of an imminent attack by Al Qaeda; it was the Bush White House, not the CIA, that was asleep at the switch. More than an intelligence failure, the 9/11 attacks represented a dereliction of duty by policymakers. As Director Helms observed, "It's not enough to ring the bell; you have to make sure the other guy hears it."

But how much are CIA directors swayed by political pressure? The official myth is that they gather intelligence and call it as they see it, regardless of who occupies the Oval Office. And yet the CIA reports to the president. So as the writer Thomas Powers has noted, if you know what the CIA is doing you know what the president wants; and if you know what the president wants you know what the CIA is doing.

What's wrong with this? Nothing—except that presidents sometimes try to get the CIA to go along with dubious or downright dangerous ventures: to create false reasons to go to war, as George W. Bush did before the Iraq invasion; to do in secret what they can't do in public, as Ronald Reagan did when he traded arms to Iran for hostages; and to save their own skin, as Richard Nixon did during Watergate and Donald Trump did when he repeatedly obstructed the investigation into his alleged collusion with Russia. At such times the CIA isn't an imagined deep state trying to bring down the president; it's the thin line between the president and a potentially disastrous outcome for America's citizens. That's why congressional oversight is essential to ensure that the CIA isn't misused.

Sometimes what the president wants is so clearly illegal or inappropriate that the CIA director must draw the line. But nothing is guaranteed. Richard Helms defied an illegal order to obstruct justice in the Watergate scandal and thereby upheld the rule of law and saved the CIA. Bill Casey, on the other hand, broke the law in the Iran-contra scandal and almost destroyed the Reagan presidency and the CIA. It's easy to say that the CIA director should defy improper presidential orders and speak truth to power. But by what authority does he or she do so? Helms refused to cover up Watergate for Nixon. But he was willing to bend the law on domestic surveillance for Lyndon Johnson. How much does a director's personality, or character, have to do with it?

This book will examine those questions. In January of 2020, a complaint brought by a CIA whistleblower resulted in a Senate trial of Donald Trump for high crimes and misdemeanors. It is up to CIA director Haspel—and the acting Director of National Intelligence, her nominal superior—to protect that whistleblower from reprisal. And it's up to Congress to strengthen the whistleblower statute so that future complaints aren't bottled up in the White House or Department of Justice.

How outspoken should directors be? John Brennan has publicly questioned the loyalty of Donald Trump, who once compared the behavior of the intelligence community to that of "Nazi Germany." Many of Brennan's fellow directors, who believe that ex-intelligence officials should not criticize sitting presidents, think Brennan's criticism has been out of bounds. It's hard to imagine Helms calling a president's behavior "treasonous," as Brennan did after Trump's 2018 summit with Putin in Helsinki. But Helms would have been appalled by Trump's venomous attacks on the intelligence community, and his refusal to accept its findings of fact—from global warming to the Russian assault on the 2016 U.S. presidential election.

This book is also a look at the challenges facing the U.S. and its allies in the years ahead. What are the threats that keep the directors up at night? What new forms will terrorism take? Should the CIA devote more of its time and resources to detecting emerging pandemics?

Astonishingly, the United States had no intelligence service prior to World War II. The U.S. got into the spying business two and a half millennia after China, and Sun Tzu's *The Art of War.* Founded in 1947 to prevent a repetition of the attack on Pearl Harbor, the CIA mostly met that challenge during the Cold War: It was never blindsided by a Soviet attack, or surprised by a military advance that altered the balance of power. But at moments of crisis the CIA has been caught flat-footed: Why was it surprised by the Soviet Union's collapse? How did it miss the Arab Spring? Was the agency late to recognize the peril of the Russian social media threat?

Too often the CIA has been stunningly ignorant about America's adversaries. "As a country we just don't have good intelligence," said Stuart Eizenstat, former domestic policy adviser to Jimmy Carter. In 1979, the CIA couldn't conceive of a theological revolution, much less the Shiite-inspired revolt that toppled the Shah of Iran, the leader the U.S. had helped to install. The overthrow was a seismic shock, triggering a struggle between the West and militant Islam that continues to this day. The agency hasn't fared much better with Iraq, Syria, or Afghanistan. "Did we understand Iraq?" asked Eizenstat. "If we had, would we have gotten rid of Saddam Hussein? My God, the lives and treasure lost—there and in Afghanistan!"

After the Iranian revolution, Helms, the former director, observed: "We must develop a far deeper knowledge of people's culture, religion, and politics. . . . Believe it or not, we are still essentially a provincial nation." The CIA's officers are less provincial and more diverse now, but for decades they were all too "white, male, and Yale"—homogenous and conformist. "It wasn't that they weren't articulate and they didn't dress well," said Leslie Gelb, who spent years dealing with CIA officers as a Defense Department official. "But in terms of the quality of their reports? You wouldn't believe how bad they were. I knew a lot of these guys. I wouldn't have hired them."

The CIA is useless without access to one person: the president of the United States. The director commands an army of analysts, an air force of lethal drones, and a covert paramilitary force that can kill terrorists in any corner of the globe. But if he or she does not have the ear of the president, the whole enterprise is for naught. "The CIA has one protector and one customer, and if you can't get that relationship right then the agency is screwed," said Gates. In the age of Trump, that challenge has been more difficult than ever.

How should CIA directors deal with presidents who can't handle the truth? Trump is uniquely resistant to facts he doesn't want to hear. But he's not the first president to dismiss the CIA's views. During the Vietnam War, Lyndon Johnson demanded evidence that the bombing of North Vietnam was sapping enemy morale. But Helms told him the bombing was having *no* effect; he even commissioned a study that questioned why the U.S. was fighting in the first place.

The director must tell the president hard truths—even when they're the last thing he wants to hear. LBJ was typically blunt when summing up his attitude toward CIA briefers: "When I was growing up in Texas we had a cow named Bessie. I'd seat myself and squeeze out a fresh pail of milk, but I wasn't paying attention and old Bessie swung her tail through that bucket of milk. That's what these intelligence guys do. You work hard and develop a good program and they swing a shit-smeared tail through it."

The CIA director is the president's favorite scapegoat. "Victory has a thousand fathers, but defeat is an orphan," President Kennedy famously said after the disastrous CIA invasion at Cuba's Bay of Pigs. In fact, while publicly accepting blame, Kennedy privately excoriated the agency and threatened to "scatter it to the winds." He ended up sacking Director Allen Dulles and demanding that the agency eliminate Cuban dictator Fidel Castro, by fair means or foul. The agency was, of course, used to taking heat. Richard Nixon had blamed the "clowns out at Langley," for his loss in the 1960 presidential election, convinced the CIA had given ammunition to his opponent, JFK, by telling him that Eisenhower and Nixon had let the Soviets get ahead in missiles. "A president would never abolish the CIA," says one former director, "because then he would have no one to blame." It's an attitude reflected in a common lament at Langley: "There are only policy successes—and intelligence failures."

And intelligence scandals. The directors have had their share—from the Bay of Pigs to assassination plots on foreign leaders to illegal domestic surveillance to testing drugs on unwitting subjects to overthrowing governments. And yes, meddling in elections: From 1946 to 2001, the CIA pumped propaganda and money into some eighty-one elections, from Western Europe to South America. During the 1970s, congressional investigations flung open a Pandora's box of CIA abuses.

Yet the CIA has never been a "rogue elephant," despite lurid headlines. Scandalous or not, virtually every covert operation the agency has carried out was done at the direction of the president of the United States. And those operations that were truly beyond the pale it tried to slow-walk. Helms endured so much hectoring from Bobby Kennedy about the need to "get rid of" Fidel Castro, he complained he had lash marks on his back. Helms ignored the attorney general's orders as long as he could before delegating the Castro murder plots to subordinates; he thought Operation ZR/RIFLE, with its poisoned cigars and exploding seashells, was absurd and impractical—but he didn't call it off.

Presidents have often asked directors to break the law. "They were all asked to do things they shouldn't do," said Cynthia Helms, widow of the legendary director. Helms reluctantly succumbed to Johnson's demand that he do something—*anything*—to find evidence of communist involvement in the anti–Vietnam War movement; so he approved Operation MHCHAOS, a domestic surveillance program that was both illegal and a violation of the CIA's charter. Helms reasoned that the alternative was getting fired—and that only he could keep the damn thing under wraps. The CIA found no trace of foreign subversion and ultimately MHCHAOS was exposed.

Arguably more harmful than its scandals has been the CIA's inability to ferret out enemies in its midst: moles. An intelligence agency is useless if it can't keep secrets from the enemy. And yet for more than a decade Harold Adrian Russell "Kim" Philby, a British intelligence official who was also a Soviet agent, carried on a close friendship with the CIA's head of counterintelligence, James Angleton. Philby's betrayals sent dozens of CIA agents to their deaths in the Soviet Union. Angleton—who exemplified the CIA's tendency to venerate eccentric, Ivy League intellectuals—was obsessed with a so-called Master Plot; critics dubbed it "the Monster Plot." In his paranoid "wilderness of mirrors," every Soviet defector was a KGB plant; CIA colleagues were guilty until proven innocent; and many careers were ruined.

Decades later, an agency spy named Aldrich Ames managed, despite certain habits that should have aroused suspicion—among them, driving a flashy Jaguar and a penchant for binge drinking—to feed the Soviets a steady diet of secrets, including the names of CIA agents, many of whom were subsequently arrested and executed. During Barack Obama's first term, more than a dozen CIA assets in China were compromised; most disappeared. Counterintelligence— the detection of enemy spies—is a perennial CIA weakness that has at times paralyzed the agency. And given the sheer number of people with access to secrets, ferreting out moles may be a futile enterprise. "It's an actuarial certainty that at almost any given moment the agency has been penetrated," said the CIA's chief historian David Robarge.

Yet for all the agency's flaws, presidents can't resist the quick fix of CIA covert action. "It was always predictable," explained Bob Gates. "The State Department would recommend the use of military force. The Defense Department would recommend diplomacy. And when they couldn't agree, everybody would decide, 'let CIA do a covert action.'" Often that way lies disaster—as in 1970, when Nixon ordered the CIA at the eleventh hour to keep Chile's leftist Salvador Allende out of power. As a rule, presidents have no grasp on what the CIA can and can't do. Perhaps the only president who understood the agency's capabilities was George H. W. Bush, a former director. Another exception, arguably, was Dwight Eisenhower, who knew something about intelligence from his stint as D-Day commander.

The mystique of CIA covert action stems from the storied exploits of William "Wild Bill" Donovan of the OSS, the CIA's forerunner, who sent spies and saboteurs into action against the Nazis during World War II. Future CIA directors Dulles, Helms, Colby, and Casey cut their teeth as OSS officers. The myth of covert action as a panacea persisted in the postwar period, thanks to two successful operations. A CIA-led coup in 1953 kept the pro-Western Mohammed Reza Shah Pahlavi on the throne in Iran, preserving U.S. and British oil interests. A year later, in Guatemala, a CIA clandestine operation drove the democratically-elected, left-leaning president Jacobo Árbenz from power through a barrage of propaganda and disinformation.

Heartened by these relatively bloodless victories against communism, President Dwight Eisenhower became a believer in the magic bullet of covert action. A few decades later, a ragtag band of Afghan rebels, supplied with Stinger missiles by the CIA, bloodied the Soviet Union's Red Army and sent it limping out of Afghanistan; it was the most successful covert operation in modern history.

And yet covert operations are much more likely to fail. (The Bay of Pigs, Iran-contra, the anti-Castro Operation MONGOOSE, the revolt against Sukarno in Indonesia, the Kurdish rebellion against Saddam—the list goes on.) Helms warned his successors to beware the seductive allure of clandestine operations; he believed they rarely worked and almost always brought unintended consequences, often

referred to as "blowback." Many "successful" operations have ultimately come back to bite the U.S.—in Guatemala, where the CIA-led
coup was followed by decades of bloody dictatorship; in Afghanistan, where the American-allied mujahideen eventually formed the
basis of Al Qaeda; and in Iran, where hatred of the Shah inspired
the Islamic Revolution of 1979 and a generation of terrorism against
the West. What will the fallout be from Trump's latest covert operations against Iran's Islamic Revolutionary Guard Corps (IRGC)?
That remains to be seen.

For directors, having the ear of the president is one thing; earn-
ing the confidence of the workforce is another. Insular and fiercely
tribal, Langley's denizens can devour outsiders "like white blood
cells attacking alien tissue," said one ex-spy. "It's like Scottish tribes
waiting for the English king," explained Cofer Black, a legendary
operative. The CIA is a collection of spies, geeks, scientists, tech-
nocrats, lawyers, linguists, fixers, and paramilitary warriors. But it
consists mainly of two camps: the analysts, of the Directorate of
Intelligence (DI), and the operatives, of the Directorate of Operations (DO). They live in such different worlds and speak such different languages that their working areas were once literally walled off
and they ate in separate cafeterias.

Analysts tend to be intellectual and introverted (and often sun-
deprived). "What's the difference between an introverted and an
extroverted analyst?" goes a joke at Langley. "An extroverted analyst
stares at *your* shoes." They master such arcana as the throw weight of
nuclear missiles, and are expected to decipher enemy war plans, read
the minds of foreign leaders, and predict the future. During a legendary forty-year CIA career, Charles Allen, now eighty-three, served
many roles, including the National Intelligence Officer (NIO) for
Warning, charged with detecting imminent threats. Renowned as the
agency's "Cassandra," Allen is still haunted by the prediction that
got away: his failure to sound a timely warning of the 1973 Arab-
Israeli (Yom Kippur) War. "It still bothers you?" I asked him, sitting
in his Washington office in the summer of 2018. "Deeply," he replied.
He sighed. "Awful. It's deep inside me."

CIA analysts aren't perfect and they often pay the price. John
McLaughlin, a courtly intellectual who served twice as acting director, is also an accomplished magician; on a visit to Moscow he daz-

zled his Russian intelligence counterparts with feats of sleight of hand, turning a 10,000 ruble note into 100,000. But when McLaughlin and his fellow analysts botch an intelligence estimate—as with Iraq's WMDs—their mistakes do not magically vanish. "Analysts write things down, venturing assessment and prediction on issues that are contentious, sometimes unknowable," he said. "They are hanging out there in words that never go away. Very few others in government do that. No one understands any of this."

CIA operatives are a different breed; brash and outgoing, they practice deception and seduction, enticing strangers to betray their countries. Breaking the laws of foreign countries is their modus operandi. Members of this tribe are dismissive of the pampered life of analysts. As Cofer Black put it: "It's like being a weatherman in the Navy. There's a difference between being a pilot that flies an F-14 off an aircraft carrier in the North Atlantic in the winter with snow blowing across it, and the ship is going up and down—and a guy who runs the Officer's Club in Idaho. They are not the same."

Morell, the former acting director, described the ideal characteristics of an "ops guy"—or woman: "incredibly strong interpersonal and emotional intelligence skills. And self-confidence to the point of over-confidence—because asking another human being to commit espionage against their own country is one of the hardest conversations you will ever have." Successful directors know that analysts and operatives require different care and feeding. "The analysts will do whatever you tell them to do," said a former senior intelligence official. "If you tell them to walk off a cliff, they'll walk off a cliff. The ops guys will only do what you ask them to do if they believe that you love them—if you believe that they are as great as they think they are."

Operating in a world of shadows, CIA directors need a strong moral compass but they can't be saints. "At CIA you get into moral ambiguities more than you do in other agencies," said Charlie Allen. "Hard decisions are made. And there are high-risk stakes, particularly as you move into covert action."

Theodore "Ted" Sorensen, John Kennedy's former aide and confidant, was Jimmy Carter's first choice to become director in 1977. But Sorensen withdrew his nomination when it was revealed that he'd been a conscientious objector during World War II. After his defeat, Sorensen seemed conflicted—bitter and simultaneously relieved. "Now you won't have to do those things you didn't want to do," his twelve-year-old son told him.

Years later, Sorensen reflected: "Could I, as a lawyer, oversee employees constantly breaking the laws of other nations? Could I, as a moralist, direct operations widely condemned as immoral? With my insistence on candor and truthfulness, could I head the most secretive and deceptive agency in government?" For Sorensen, who was averse to covert operations, the answer was no. "Clandestine operations and covert intelligence are a critical and essential part of intelligence gathering," said Jack Watson, Carter's transition director and later his White House chief of staff. "I'm not suggesting that you abandon the values of the nation or ignore moral considerations. But if you're going to be in that world, as I think you have to be as director, then you can't be too pure."

For CIA directors, ethical issues abound. Obvious transgressions—assassination plots, coups against elected governments, harsh interrogation techniques, domestic surveillance—are now constrained by law and congressional oversight. Yet the goalposts for what's acceptable keep moving, depending on who's in power and the vicissitudes of national security threats. "CIA directors and deputies make some of the toughest decisions in government," said McLaughlin. "Operators are authorized to play near the edge of the law, knowing the view of the law may change with the next election. Intelligence law is frontier law—with few cases and few settled precedents."

Indeed, Leon Panetta was shocked to discover that he faced life-and-death decisions as director every day. When it came to authorizing lethal drone strikes—when innocent civilians were in the crosshairs—the devoutly Catholic director lamented: "You have to be true to yourself—and just hope that ultimately God agrees with you." In the aftermath of 9/11, when prisoners were subjected to enhanced interrogation techniques, Director Tenet and his defenders insisted the methods prevented attacks and saved innocent lives. But McLaughlin, one of those defenders, concedes, "There's an answer to that, which is: Slavery worked too but it was still wrong."

In the late summer of 2016, John Brennan faced his own dilemma. Confronted with an imminent Russian threat against American democracy, what should he do?

In the months before the election, the options were unappealing: Should the U.S. strike back at Moscow, "rattling its cages" with a cyber offensive that might bring its economy to its knees? That would risk retaliation that could spiral out of control. Should the U.S. release embarrassing information about Putin and his oligarchs? That would be stooping to their level. The Russian threat was "orders of magnitude more complicated than counterterrorism or weapons of mass destruction," said Brennan, "because it is dealing with this ubiquitous digital domain."

And then there was an equally sensitive question: how to respond to Donald Trump. As CIA director, Brennan was almost obsessively apolitical, determined to be Obama's honest broker, a stickler for process. But underneath that dispassionate exterior, he was a moralist, an "Irish cop," as political strategist David Axelrod dubbed him. Every time Trump said something reckless (for example: "I would bring back waterboarding, . . . and a hell of a lot worse") the Irish in Brennan would rise up; he considered the Republican nominee a con man and a fraud. "That's where you see his anger and frustration," said a close friend. "John just can't fathom someone with no moral compass or ethics as president of the United States."

Beyond his personal feelings, Brennan was convinced that Trump posed a threat to American interests. The Republican nominee was a "useful idiot," Brennan believed, unwittingly serving Moscow's purposes. How else to explain the sudden change in the Republican Party platform, in favor of disarming Ukraine? What about Trump's gushing admiration for the Russian leader, and his contempt for NATO and American alliances?

Putin's meddling on behalf of Trump was a matter of urgent public interest. But Obama, ever cautious, was loath to speak out; in the hyper-partisan climate of 2016, any presidential statement would cause a firestorm, fueling Trump's cynical narrative that the election was rigged. And there was another factor that weighed on Brennan and Obama: No one imagined that the Republican nominee had a real chance of winning.

So as the election approached, Obama held his fire in public. In private, he and his advisers tried to get Republican congressional leaders to join in a warning about Russian election interference. They failed, and the backroom wrangling was partisan and ugly. "It's the hardest thing about my entire time in government to defend," said one adviser. "I feel like we choked."

John Brennan's anger only deepened when, on January 20, 2017, Donald J. Trump took the oath of office as president of the United States.

Brennan was not alone in his alarm. A few months after the election, a retired agency operative, with decades of experience in the Near East Division, paid a visit to Gina Haspel at CIA headquarters. Haspel had risen through the ranks of the Directorate of Operations and was now deputy to CIA director Mike Pompeo.

The veteran spy sipped coffee outside Haspel's office—and thought about how to broach his subject: What if, on Haspel's watch, the CIA learned that Trump was involved in wrongdoing?

Finally, Haspel waved him into her office. They exchanged pleasantries, and then her visitor got to his point. "You gotta think, Gina," he told her. "You've got this Russian thing going on—and you could have a moment when information arrives from a source that you might ordinarily share with the president. But to do so would be illegal—because it's *law enforcement* intelligence." He underscored the point to make sure she got it. "It needs to go somewhere else. *Not* to the White House."

Haspel listened intently. Just then the door opened and Director Pompeo walked in. The veteran spy stood up and introduced himself. Then he said his goodbyes, and departed.

In September 2019, the CIA's general counsel, Courtney Elwood, received an urgent message: A CIA officer had important information from a colleague, a whistleblower who wished to remain anonymous. The information involved a troubling conversation between Trump and the president of Ukraine. This was almost exactly what the veteran CIA operative had tried to warn Haspel about. It would not be long before Donald Trump accused the whistleblower of treason.

It was not the first time a president had declared war on the CIA. Back in 1972, convinced that its spies were out to get him, Richard Nixon tried to blackmail the agency, hoping to obstruct the investigation into Watergate. He hadn't bargained on running up against a director named Richard Helms.

CHAPTER ONE

"Stay the hell away
from the whole damned thing."

Richard Helms, Lyndon Johnson, and Richard Nixon

At his transition headquarters on the thirty-ninth floor of New York City's Pierre Hotel, in a suite with a panoramic view of Central Park, Richard M. Nixon was preparing to become president of the United States. It was Friday, November 15, 1968, and Nixon had been huddling with his closest advisers, meeting with candidates for his cabinet, plotting to bend the Washington establishment to his will. The president-elect was "in the mood of a general about to occupy an enemy town," wrote author Thomas Powers, "bringing with him a visceral dislike and suspicion of the federal bureaucracy . . . because it was in his character to see himself always as surrounded by enemies, obstructionists and saboteurs." Oddly enough, in Nixon's mind, no one exemplified the Washington elite—those enemies, obstructionists, and saboteurs—more than the man he'd summoned to meet with him, CIA director Richard Helms.

It would be hard to imagine a partnership less likely to end well, more riven with intrigue and mutual suspicion, than Helms and Nixon. Helms personified the CIA, rising through the ranks of the agency to become Lyndon Johnson's director for the previous two years. Nixon was still seething about the CIA's role in his 1960 election loss, convinced the agency had helped JFK invent a Soviet-American "missile gap." He wasn't about to let Helms forget it. Worse, in Nixon's mind, Helms was a member of the "Georgetown set," a tony cabal that spent its evenings sipping martinis and making fun of the president-elect. (Helms *did* frequent the living rooms of

19

Washington's high-society doyennes, but he was quick to point out that he'd never lived in Georgetown.)

In their manner and dress the two men were polar opposites. Helms wore Savile Row suits with kerchiefs and was an avid tennis player and ballroom dancer. (Born with nine toes, Helms had shoes specially designed for him in London when he lived there in the 1930s.) Nixon was fumbling and socially inept, and so sartorially clueless he wore dress shoes while walking on the beach.

Helms arrived at the hotel and was shown into Nixon's suite. He was greeted there by the president-elect and John Mitchell. Jowly and overweight, Mitchell, who'd been Nixon's law partner and was most recently serving as the president-elect's confidant, was about to become attorney general—and would later go to prison for his role in the Watergate scandal. After some pleasantries, the president-elect told Helms he wanted him to stay on as CIA director. Helms thanked him and left, promising not to tell anyone until the decision was made public. A month later, on December 18, 1968, Richard Nixon announced Helms's reappointment as director of Central Intelligence.

Nixon must have had his reasons. Possibly, he'd been swayed by LBJ's urging him to keep Helms around as an honest broker. "I've no idea how he voted in any election and I have never asked him what his political views are," Johnson told the president-elect. "He's always been correct with me and has done a good job as director. I commend him to you." But beyond Helms's bona fides, other considerations were undoubtedly at work in Nixon's conspiratorial mind. It was a mind that Helms could never fathom. "He couldn't figure out Nixon," recalled his widow, and second wife, Cynthia Helms. "He just could never figure out what Nixon was up to." What Nixon was up to, it does not seem far-fetched to conclude, was choosing a CIA director who could be blackmailed into doing his bidding.

Surely, anyone who'd been in the spy business as long as Helms must have something to hide, must be malleable, or vulnerable to exposure. "We protected Helms from one hell of a lot of things," Nixon would say later, as the White House tapes rolled, implying that he'd kept damaging information from coming to light, that Helms owed him, and it was time to collect the debt. Did Nixon and his henchmen have something on Helms, a secret that would make him do their dirty work on Watergate? The fate of Nixon's presidency would hinge on the answer to that question.

Richard Helms hadn't set out to become a spy. Born on Philadelphia's Main Line, he was sent to a Swiss boarding school and then attended college at Williams. In 1936, as a twenty-three-year-old reporter for United Press, speaking passable French and German, Helms found himself at the Nazi Party Congress in Nuremberg, standing next to the German führer, Adolf Hitler. "At arm's length, Hitler appeared shorter and less impressive than at a distance," Helms reported in his UP dispatch. "Fine, dark brown hair, rusty in front, slightly graying along the crown; bright blue eyes, coarse skin, with a pinkish tinge." Helms was appalled by Hitler's demagogic narcissism. By contrast he was impressed by the quiet modesty of American track star Jesse Owens, whom he met while crossing the Atlantic on the *Queen Mary* after his dominant performance at the Olympic Games.

After Pearl Harbor, Helms joined the Naval Reserve. Then, two years before the Nazi surrender, he was summoned to the Office of Strategic Services (OSS) in Washington, D.C. The wartime intelligence service, precursor to the CIA, wanted someone who spoke French and German, had lived in Europe, and worked as a journalist.

The OSS was the creation of William "Wild Bill" Donovan, a dashing figure who led an eclectic band of intellectuals and paramilitary adventurers, running spies and saboteurs behind Nazi lines from its headquarters in London. Helms was sent to Maryland for training (knife fighting, hand-to-hand combat, maintaining a cover)—and finally dispatched to London. There, he reported to a rumpled Navy lieutenant named William J. Casey, the chief for secret intelligence collection in Europe.

Restless, indefatigable, and brilliant, Casey, who would later become Ronald Reagan's CIA director, was as rough around the edges as Helms was silky smooth; he was so excitable during meals, and his table manners such an afterthought, that he often ended up chewing on his tie. The two young OSS recruits became roommates and sent spies into occupied Europe right up until the Nazi surrender.

By 1943 Helms had given up his journalistic ambitions (he'd wanted to own a newspaper) in favor of a career as a spy. "I now realized that I was hooked on intelligence," Helms wrote years later in his memoir, *A Look over My Shoulder*. And he intuited that the OSS, or something like it, would still be necessary after the war: "The need for an effective intelligence service in the turbulent and anything but benign postwar world seemed obvious." But Helms wasn't done with Hitler yet. At war's end, as the Third Reich lay in ruins, while he was on a reconnaissance mission in Berlin, Helms seized a chance to sneak into Hitler's chancellery. He helped himself to the few pieces of crockery that hadn't been shattered—and Hitler's personal note cards. On one, Helms penned a note to his toddler son, back in Virginia.

Dear Dennis,

   The man who might have written on this card once controlled Europe—three short years ago when you were born. Today he is dead, his memory despised, his country in ruins. He had a thirst for power, a low opinion of man as an individual, and a fear of intellectual honesty. He was a force for evil in the world. His passing, his defeat—a boon to mankind. Thousands died that it might be so. The price for ridding society of bad is always high.

                                                                     Love,
                                                                     Daddy

By then both Helms and Casey were focused on a new force for evil, one they considered as threatening as the Third Reich. The struggle against Soviet communism, starting in Eastern Europe and extending across the globe, would shape the ethical choices they made while working for, and later running, the CIA. They believed the morality of their methods shouldn't be judged in a vacuum, but against those of the KGB. (Helms disliked John le Carré's classic novel *The Spy Who Came in from the Cold*, with its gray compromises and cynical, world-weary protagonist.) Helms's world was black-and-white: The CIA's spies were honorable men in a fight against evil.

   It was while they were in London that Casey told Helms about an idea hatched by Bill Donovan: the creation of a peacetime intelligence service that would be assembled from the remnants of the OSS. Upon the disbanding of OSS in 1945, several halfhearted iterations were tried—the Strategic Services Unit (SSU), the Office of Special

Operations (OSO), and the Central Intelligence Group (CIG). Then, in 1947, the Central Intelligence Agency (CIA) was born, created by President Harry Truman's National Security Act.

The first Director of Central Intelligence (DCI) was appointed two years earlier. Rear Admiral Sidney Souers became the first man to hold the title; to commemorate the occasion, Truman threw a lunch—and presented each guest with a black cloak, black hat, and wooden dagger. Souers was the first of four mostly forgettable CIA directors plucked from the military; he was followed in rapid succession by Army Lieutenant General Hoyt Vandenberg, Navy Admiral Roscoe Hillenkoetter, and Army General Walter Bedell Smith. Then, in February 1953, Eisenhower appointed the first civilian CIA director, Allen Dulles.

For the next eight years, allied with his influential brother, Secretary of State John Foster Dulles, Allen Dulles transformed the CIA into a powerful cudgel against communism, overthrowing governments in Iran and Guatemala, and serving as Ike's covert army general in the Cold War struggle.

Present at the creation, Helms would be at the center of the CIA for the next three decades, privy to its secrets, triumphs, and disasters. It was a time when the agency largely did what it wanted and Congress looked the other way. When it was time to renew the CIA's budget, the director would pay a visit to Senator Richard Russell, chairman of the Appropriations and Armed Services Committees. As one veteran operative recalled: "Russell would say, 'How much do you need?' [The director] would say, 'Well, here's my number.' And Russell would say, 'Well, how about this number?' And that was it." It was accepted that spies were mysterious figures who moved in the shadows. All of this would change soon enough.

Few were better than Helms at navigating the corridors of power in Washington, D.C. "He understood how to operate at the policy level as bravely and as ably as anybody I've ever seen," said veteran CIA analyst Charles Allen. An agency legend who joined the CIA in 1958, Allen would become the National Intelligence Officer (NIO) for Warning, and later the Assistant Director for Collection (ADCI). (This is probably a good place to explain some CIA terminology: "Agents" or "assets" are by definition foreigners who are recruited overseas to spy for the agency; CIA employees, by contrast, are called "officers." Officers in turn may be "operatives" or "analysts," depending on the division they belong to.) Allen had never seen anyone with a better survival instinct than Helms. During his steady rise through the Directorate of Plans (DP), as the covert operations division was then called, the paperwork for most clandestine missions crossed his desk, but Helms avoided blame for operations that went sour. "Ducky Dickie," he was called, for his ability to evade responsibility for ill-fated ventures; like a good covert operative, Helms seldom left fingerprints behind.

Operation ZAPATA, the CIA debacle that came to be known as the Bay of Pigs, was a classic example of Helms's dodging a bullet that might have ended his career. He was aided by a fortuitous turn of events. In 1958 Helms was the odds-on favorite to be named Deputy Director of Plans (DDP). (This was the CIA's covert arm, later renamed the Directorate of Operations, or DO.) But Helms was passed over by Director Allen Dulles in favor of Richard Bissell. Bissell, a brilliant technocrat, had spearheaded the groundbreaking development of the U-2 surveillance plane. His promotion was a shattering blow to Helms, but it would turn out to be a blessing in disguise—because it would fall to Bissell, as DDP, to plan the ill-fated invasion that would become the CIA's worst disaster. Sensing a fiasco-in-the-making, Helms, instead of warning against the operation, made sure that he wasn't in the loop. An office betting pool was started: How long would it take Helms to attend a planning meeting for the Cuba invasion? He never attended a session.

Helms kept a low profile. He drove old, conservative black cars that wouldn't be noticed. Not even his son knew what he did for a living. "There is nobody who was more artful at dodging questions than my father," said Dennis Helms, now seventy-seven, a patent attorney in Princeton, New Jersey. "If you asked him the time, he'd give you the weather. He was guided by the principle that if you don't say anything, then you can't say anything wrong." The stories of Helms's laconic nature are legion. His second wife, Cynthia, recalled that on the eve of their marriage in 1968 she got a phone call from Alice Acheson, wife of former secretary of state Dean Acheson. "She said, 'You can't possibly marry him!' And I said, 'Why not?' And she said, 'He *doesn't talk!*'"

Despite being the soul of discretion, Helms moved effortlessly from watering holes to embassies to the living rooms of high-society hostesses like Katharine Graham, *The Washington Post*'s publisher. "He was almost a James Bondian figure," said Robert Gates, a young CIA analyst who would later become director. "In those days people still smoked. He was a smoker and he drank martinis; he was very suave and clearly was a player in town." Helms smoked two packs of Chesterfields a day but limited himself to a single, very dry martini. Washington's literati, among them James "Scotty" Reston of *The New York Times* and columnist Stewart Alsop, gathered round when the spymaster worked the room, martini in hand. "Run it by Dick," a *New York Times* editor once told his star investigative reporter, Seymour Hersh (to Hersh's dismay). But Helms seldom stayed long at the party. "He knew exactly where the exit was in every embassy in Washington," said Cynthia.

At his modest suburban house in Chevy Chase, Maryland, Helms threw his own parties: eclectic gatherings of spies, professors, journalists, and diplomats (but rarely politicians). "They used to come on New Year's Eve, a lot of the old guys in black tie, and we'd play charades," recalled Dennis, referring to the parlor game in which contestants acted out well-known phrases which the other team tried to guess. "Dad's friends were a pretty smart crowd: two Williams College presidents, all kinds of people from Yale."

One regular at these affairs was a CIA legend, a lean, angular, bespectacled Yale grad with a mischievous grin and a mysterious manner. A chain-smoker, he bred rare orchids and designed elaborate fishing flies. At Yale he'd published a literary magazine and befriended the poet Ezra Pound. The phrase he chose for charades, recalls Dennis, was from T. S. Eliot: "garlic and sapphires in the mud, clot the bedded axle-tree." "So needless to say *nobody* guessed that, and my mother said, 'Time out!' " The man she banned from future charades games was the CIA's head of counterintelligence, James Jesus Angleton.

Angleton would cause Helms and the CIA no end of grief in the postwar years. But in the immediate aftermath of the Bay of Pigs, Helms had more pressing problems. For his role in the debacle, Director Allen Dulles had been sacked by Kennedy, who appointed John McCone in his stead; Bissell was gone, too. But there'd still be hell to pay because the attorney general, Bobby Kennedy, was furious, out to avenge the president for his embarrassing humiliation at the hands of his generals and spies. "After the Bay of Pigs, Bobby Kennedy became obsessed, which means Jack Kennedy became obsessed, with killing Castro," said Burton Gerber, an operative who served in the Middle East and Russia. The marching orders, for Helms and his colleagues, were to get rid of Fidel Castro—immediately, by any means necessary.

This was not a new command. The CIA's murder plots against Castro had begun under Dwight Eisenhower. The schemes had been delegated to the CIA Security Staff, a shadowy division for off-the-radar operations, and a colorful character named William Harvey. Harvey, a rotund ex-FBI agent who'd had a falling-out with Director J. Edgar Hoover, was a bullheaded operative who seldom let rules interfere with a mission; Harvey almost always carried a loaded pistol in his belt. While stationed in Germany, he'd run an ambitious covert operation: Workers burrowed a tunnel under the Berlin Wall, tapping into Soviet cables; unfortunately, the operation was compromised by a Russian mole. At one point Harvey was taken to the Oval Office to meet John Kennedy, who loved pulp spy novels. "They tell me you're the closest thing we have to James Bond," quipped the president.

Not that close, in Helms's opinion. Anyone who thought so "had either never read Ian Fleming's books, seen a Bond movie, or caught a glimpse of Harvey . . . who would never win the battle with his waistline." Harvey was also "deliberately blunt and loudly outspoken, qualities that, with his heavy drinking, were eventually to catch up to him." In short, the CIA had chosen a gun-toting, hair-triggered loudmouth with a heavy drinking habit to carry out the assassination of a foreign leader. What could possibly go wrong?

Harvey pursued an out-of-the-box idea: Why not reach out to people who did this kind of thing for a living—the Mafia mob boss Sam Giancana and his lieutenant Johnny Roselli? (Giancana's mistress Judith Exner was having an affair with JFK, though Harvey was probably unaware of this.) Would the mobsters be interested in teaming up with the CIA to knock off Fidel Castro? No gadgets were too outlandish for ZR/RIFLE, as Harvey's project was called, including poisoned cigars, deadly scuba diving gear, and exploding seashells. (Most of these never got beyond the CIA laboratory.) Roselli managed to have a jar of poison pills smuggled into Havana. But in the end, ZR/RIFLE was a case of life imitating farce, a Peter Sellers and Monty Python movie rolled into one: No would-be assassin got anywhere near Castro.

Helms insisted he knew nothing about ZR/RIFLE until he replaced Bissell as DDP in 1962. "After checking into it I told Bill Harvey—who agreed entirely—to close it down," he wrote later. But the evidence suggests that Helms approved Harvey's project and kept it secret from those who didn't need to know. That was the way assassination plots were handled in the agency's early days; presidents—and even CIA directors—maintained plausible deniability. Helms evidently kept his boss, Director John McCone, out of the loop. McCone, a devout Catholic, professed to be appalled when he learned about the Castro plots years later.

"There is no easy answer to the question of assassination," Helms would write later. "Clearly, boundless misery would have been avoided if Hitler had been struck down. . . . That said, in peacetime the assassination of troublesome persons is morally and operationally indefensible." But though the Mafia hit men were now gone, the pressure on Helms to "get rid of Castro" only intensified. Bobby Kennedy was relentless. "[Robert] Kennedy wanting Mr. Castro killed was a huge issue," recalled Cynthia Helms, who got an earful about it years later from her husband. "Robert Kennedy was out at the agency and he was obsessed by it. Dick said, 'you can't see the lashes on my back but they are there.'"

Bobby Kennedy never stopped demanding that the CIA eliminate Castro. Helms would nod dutifully, and then go about his business of trying to topple the Cuban government by other means. It wasn't the first or last time that Helms, faced with an arguably illegal order, would pretend to go along while dragging his heels. "When people wanted to invade Cuba or kill Castro, his attitude was, '*Oh, God,*'" said Thomas Powers, author of the Helms biography, *The Man Who Kept the Secrets*. "He just was so against it all," said Cynthia of the plots to kill Castro. "He said to me one day, 'I was never going to do it. We were never going to do it.' But they made his life miserable over it."

ZR/RIFLE was part of Operation MONGOOSE (so named by presidential assistant Richard Goodwin). Its objective was to overthrow Castro—through sabotage, propaganda, and efforts to spark an insurrection. The operation involved six hundred CIA personnel and five hundred contract personnel, as well as elite counterinsurgency experts General Maxwell Taylor and Edward Lansdale. "The Kennedys were enchanted by those guys," said Frank Wisner Jr., son and namesake of a legendary Helms CIA colleague. "The Green Berets, John Wayne: 'Send in a few good men.' The music plays in the background, the natives are rallied and deal with the hated communists." But it was mostly a show by Helms; he knew the enterprise was a fool's errand. MONGOOSE only confirmed Helms's skepticism toward presidents (and attorneys general) who were clueless about the CIA's capabilities.

It also clinched Helms's belief that covert operations were a dangerous gamble. It wasn't just the "perfect failure" of the Bay of Pigs. In Helms's view, even the successful CIA coups in Iran and Guatemala—AJAX and PBSUCCESS, respectively—had been flukes, unique situations: they'd depended on ideal circumstances, and on everything going right. "Most of the best clandestine service officers that I've ever known thought that way," said Bob Gates. "I'm not sure that any careers got destroyed by a failure on the espionage side, but many were destroyed by covert action." Covert action, Helms wrote, should not be "wielded about like an all-purpose chainsaw. It should be used like a well-honed scalpel, infrequently, and with discretion lest the blade lose its edge."

In 1962 the CIA would find out if it was equal to the ultimate challenge: averting Armageddon. The CIA's new director, John McCone, in Helms's opinion, was "exactly the right man" to replace Dulles. A rich conservative who'd run the Atomic Energy Commission, McCone was intelligent and aggressive, not afraid to give the president his unvarnished advice. In the late summer of 1962, JFK would need it. Something strange was going on in Cuba: Eight Soviet ships had docked there; thousands of Russian military specialists were on the island; and a CIA-run U-2 flight showed a Soviet construction site with two surface-to-air (SAM) missiles protecting it.

The foreign policy establishment was unanimous: Soviet premier Nikita Khrushchev wouldn't risk installing offensive nuclear missiles so close to Florida. Such a move would be rash, provocative; it could start World War III. But McCone, alone in the administration, was convinced the Soviets were doing just that. From the south of France, honeymooning with his second wife, he pressed his case with the president. U-2 photos showed that McCone's hunch was right. In the end, armed with eyewitness accounts from the island and stolen manuals of Russian intercontinental missiles (provided by a Soviet defector named Oleg Penkovsky), McCone gave Kennedy a decisive edge in his showdown with Khrushchev. The CIA helped to avert a nuclear war.

On November 22, 1963, Helms was having lunch with McCone in a small room adjoining the director's office when the door flew open: An aide burst in with news that President Kennedy had been shot in Dallas. McCone grabbed his hat and raced to meet Bobby Kennedy at his home in nearby Hickory Hill, Virginia. Helms headed to his office to hold down the fort.

Helms later wrote, "I have not seen anything, no matter how far-fetched or grossly imagined, that in any way changes my conviction that Lee Harvey Oswald assassinated Kennedy, and that there were no co-conspirators." But Helms was being disingenuous. The truth is, he was deeply concerned that Oswald might have been sent to kill Kennedy by a foreign power.

The Kennedys had tried mightily to have Castro killed. Did Castro get Kennedy first? "Dick thought, and I don't think I'm exaggerating," said Cynthia, "that Robert Kennedy suffered from guilt after Kennedy was assassinated, from this relationship with the Castro murder plots. Because Bobby never quite knew . . . he never quite knew how the thing had played out." If Bobby Kennedy felt guilty about the Castro plots, it might explain why the first question he asked McCone at Hickory Hill was whether Castro was involved in JFK's assassination. McCone told him the CIA had no evidence of that.

Helms dismissed the idea of a Cuba-Oswald plot as a figment of conspiratorial imaginations, the tinfoil hat brigade. But Russia was another story. "A much better case can be made that Oswald was put up to it by the Russians," Helms told a CIA historian, without elaboration. Helms, it seems, was worried about Moscow's possible involvement.

In the early 1990s, Helms invited a retired head of the KGB, Vadim Bakatin, to dinner at his house in Northwest Washington. "My job was to keep his wife busy," recalled Cynthia. While the women chatted, Helms took the former Russian spymaster into his study. "Dick obviously wanted to check some things," said Cynthia, who strained to overhear their conversation. "I noticed he went through some things that he really wanted to know. One was Alger Hiss, he got confirmation of that." Bakatin confirmed that Hiss, a former State Department star, had in fact been a spy for the Soviet GRU. "And another thing . . .was Oswald." Alas, what the ex-KGB head told Helms about the Soviets and Oswald is not known. And Helms never wrote or spoke about this encounter.

The possibility of Oswald's having been a tool of the Russians triggered a decade of soul-searching at the CIA: a bitter struggle that would almost paralyze the agency and destroy promising careers. And the man at the center of this drama was the mysterious head of counterintelligence, James Angleton. In his book *Wilderness of Mirrors*, David Martin described his aura: "Angleton. Even the name suggested labyrinthine conspiracies. His body seemed stooped and cocked to one side in a way that hinted of both deformity—as if his very frame had been twisted out of shape by machinations—and conspiracy, as if he were perpetually bending toward someone's ear to whisper a secret."

Angleton had an office on the second floor of CIA headquarters, where he sat at his desk, enveloped in cigarette smoke, the blinds closed, barely illuminated by a green desk lamp. Once a bright light of the CIA, Angleton in his later years would become a kind of Death Star, pulling people into his orbit and ruining careers. And Helms, blinded by admiration and loyalty, was at a loss for how to deal with him.

The trouble began with the defection of a Russian major named Anatoliy Golitsyn. Assigned to the Soviet embassy in Helsinki, Finland, Golitsyn escaped to the United States on December 15, 1961, in a dramatic dash with his wife and daughter by train across the Finnish-Swedish border. He was flown to the United States, where Angleton and his counterintelligence (CI) staff were waiting for him.

Golitsyn told Angleton that the CIA had been penetrated at the highest level by Russian spies. Be on the lookout for CIA officers with the letter "K" in their surname, he warned. Moreover, Russian defectors were actually KGB plants, Trojan horses sent to deceive the West with disinformation. It was all part of a sophisticated and diabolical Soviet deception campaign. As Angleton weaved Golitsyn's warnings into the web of his Master Plot, he would henceforth consider every defector, and many CIA officers, guilty until proven innocent of spying for the Soviets.

"We used to call it Sick Think," said Gerber, the veteran operative whose friendship with Helms was strained by the Angleton affair. Critics within the CIA dubbed Angleton's conspiratorial musings "the Monster Plot." There was no arguing with the byzantine logic of the counterintelligence chief, said Gerber. "I'd say, 'Here we have this and that and I think such and such.' And he'd say, 'Well, I understand, based on what you know, but *if you only knew what I know.*' I'd say, 'Well, tell me.' He'd say, 'Well, I *can't* tell you.' I became convinced he was the Wizard of Oz; there was nothing there except a curtain."

But Angleton's authority was almost impossible to challenge. And he used that authority to mount a campaign against one of the CIA's most valuable informants, a Soviet defector named Yuri Nosenko. After Kennedy's assassination, Nosenko, a KGB lieutenant colonel still working for the Soviets, met secretly with his CIA handlers while on leave in Geneva and assured them that the Russians weren't involved with Oswald. But Angleton was having none of it; he insisted that Nosenko was lying—he was a KGB plant. Hadn't Golitsyn warned them about just such a thing?

After he defected to the U.S., Nosenko was put in solitary confinement at Angleton's insistence—verbally abused and harshly interrogated for nearly two years. Angleton's suspicions were never confirmed, and Nosenko was later relocated in the U.S. But it was just the beginning of Angleton's reign of paranoia: More than a dozen CIA officers were fired, or their careers derailed, based on unfounded accusations of spying for the Russians. "He destroyed some agency career people's lives, there's no question about it," said Richard Kerr, a veteran CIA analyst who would become deputy director. "The suspicion of everything, of everybody, was nearly a disease, an infection."

While the agency was in the grip of Angleton's infection, Helms, now the DDP, was loath to rein in his old friend; he had Angleton's back. "It was a question of loyalty there," said Burton Gerber, the Russia expert who was Helms's contemporary. "These old boys knew each other. When he writes about Angleton in his memoir, you can see he's queasy about the whole thing." No intelligence service, Helms wrote, "can for very long be any better than its counterintelligence component." And no one was better at counterintelligence than Angleton. Helms's wife, Cynthia, recalled a pointed conversation about their odd, idiosyncratic friend: "Dick sat me down one day—he didn't often do this—and he said, 'I want you to understand something. You are going to have to defend my stance on Angleton, and I want you to understand that I have made up my mind—because I will never have a mole with Angleton there, and that is more important to me than anything.' "

No doubt, Angleton had an eye for moles and a mind for counterintelligence. The only trouble was, in an almost unbelievably ironic twist, Angleton himself had been betrayed by the most notorious Russian mole of all.

Harold Adrian Russell Philby, better known as "Kim," was a rising star in the British intelligence service, MI6, a smooth-talking bon vivant who charmed his way into the nerve center of American intelligence. Philby had met Angleton at Bletchley Park in England, the headquarters of the British wartime decoding effort, and saw him again in Rome. While serving as Britain's chief liaison to the CIA and FBI in Washington, the British spy struck up an intimate, boozy friendship with the American counterintelligence chief over long, martini-soaked lunches. Angleton and his wife, Cicely, often flew to London, where they babysat Philby's children while he gallivanted around Europe.

But all along Philby was a Soviet spy; he'd been recruited at Cambridge University in his early twenties. When the CIA finally put two and two together and Philby was exposed in 1951, the disgraced British intelligence official was recalled to England at the insistence of the CIA. Philby quit MI6 but was not arrested by the British (no one wanted to face the embarrassment of such a scandalous intelligence breach); he joined *The Economist* as a foreign correspondent. In 1963, at an apartment in Beirut, an MI6 officer confronted him with evidence of his treason. The next day Philby fled to Moscow, where he spent his remaining years gloating about his betrayal of the West. He died, a hero of the Soviet Union, in 1988.

Angleton was crushed. His friend and intelligence soul mate had not only made a fool of him; he'd given up to his Soviet masters scores of CIA and British agents who were summarily tried and executed. Angleton was never the same after Philby's betrayal; he drank more and more heavily, and receded deeper into his wilderness of mirrors. But as long as Helms had anything to say about it, Angleton would remain the head of counterintelligence at the CIA. (Decades later, in 2007, at a dinner party at Washington's Willard Hotel, this author found himself seated next to an elegant, diminutive woman in her nineties. "Mrs. *James Jesus Angleton*," she replied proudly when I asked her name. "My God, you must have known Kim Philby!" I said. Cicely Angleton paused for a beat, and then said: "Well, evidently not well *enough*!")

One day in 1965, President Lyndon Johnson summoned Helms, then the CIA's Deputy Director of Plans (DDP), to the Oval Office. Since Kennedy's assassination, LBJ hadn't given much thought to the CIA. But now he was ready to make some changes. "John McCone has resigned," he told Helms, "and I've decided to appoint Admiral William Raborn as the new DCI. Do you know him?" "No, sir," replied Helms. "Well, you will. You'll be named deputy director at the same time. I want you to go to every meeting with the admiral whether here or around town. You know the agency. Red doesn't."

Vice Admiral William "Red" Raborn was evidently chosen to run the CIA because LBJ loved the way he ran the Polaris Missile program. But the agency wasn't the only thing Raborn didn't know. Geography was also not his strong suit. At one meeting that became grist for the CIA gossip mill, the new director asked his briefer about Libya: "Is that a land-locked country?" The briefer replied: "Well, mostly." After just fourteen months, Raborn resigned. On June 30, 1966, LBJ appointed Richard Helms as his new Director of Central Intelligence.

During the two years he served as Johnson's CIA director, Helms would regard his boss with a mixture of fond admiration and complete exasperation. Helms admired LBJ's determination to achieve his dream of a Great Society; he was exasperated by his obstinacy over Vietnam. "He really admired Johnson," said Cynthia. "And he really thought that Johnson suffered so over Vietnam. He said it was agony to see him sitting with his head in his hands." Helms was not an agonizer; when it came to Vietnam, he was "the coolest of advocates," as his biographer Powers put it, "presenting his agency's views on paper, defending them on paper, a paper general in a paper war." Nonetheless Vietnam was a flesh-and-blood debacle, and it became for Helms "my nightmare for a good ten years. Like an incubus . . . it seemed I would never be free of it."

The war had gone from bad to worse after an American-backed coup toppled South Vietnam president Ngo Dinh Diem in 1963. Barely three weeks before Kennedy's assassination, an aide barged into the Roosevelt Room, where the president was meeting with aides, and announced that Diem had been killed; a cabal of generals had seized power. Kennedy turned ashen and abruptly left the room.

Whether he felt responsible for the death of Diem—whom the U.S. considered an impediment to the war effort—is anyone's guess, but Kennedy knew that he'd given the generals the green light to proceed. For his part, Helms insisted his conscience was clear. "We were following orders and we were doing what we were supposed to do," he said later. "But we had no role in this. . . . It was the Vietnamese who got together and chopped up Diem. . . . It simply is not true that the agency had anything to do with [it]." There's no evidence that the CIA conspired in Diem's murder—but, also, no doubt that the U.S. encouraged the rebellious generals to stage their coup.

In the beginning, Helms was excluded from LBJ's inner circle. After briefings with the president and his advisers, at Johnson's request he'd gather his papers and excuse himself. That was fine with Helms, who considered himself a neutral broker of intelligence, content to keep his opinions on policy to himself. "My role was to keep the game honest," he said. But Helms's standing with LBJ improved markedly after war broke out in the Middle East in 1967.

In the fall of that year, the Israelis warned the U.S. that without American help they faced defeat at the hands of their Arab enemies. Helms assured LBJ of the contrary. The CIA estimated that not only would Israel defeat her Arab neighbors but that the war would last no more than seven days. That prediction looked prescient after Israel's lightning victory in the Six-Day War. Helms proudly called it "the intelligence bingo of my time." Shortly thereafter, newly impressed with his CIA director, LBJ invited Helms to stay behind for lunch. From that day forward, he was a regular guest at Johnson's famous Tuesday lunches where the inescapable subject was Vietnam.

While Helms was preoccupied professionally by the war, his personal life took a fateful turn. He and his first wife, Julia, had been drifting apart. "She wanted a little more from him, and he didn't have a lot to give," said their son, Dennis. "His job was 8:15 in the morning till 7:15 at night, half a day on Saturday." Helms was restless, too, and in 1965, at a dinner party, he met Cynthia McKelvie, a British expatriate also on the verge of divorce. She was opinionated, curious, and adventurous; as an eighteen-year-old during World War II she'd joined the "Wrens," Women's Royal Naval Service, and ran naval harbor craft, often under Nazi bombardment. With LBJ's permission (he felt compelled to ask for it) Helms divorced Julia. He and Cynthia were married in 1968.

Helms now had a partner who shared his passion for tennis and ballroom dancing. Years later, during Nixon's presidency, they found themselves on the White House dance floor, waltzing next to Fred Astaire and his partner, Farah Pahlavi, the glamorous *Shahbanou*, or empress, of Iran. "Dick on the same dance floor with Fred Astaire was his idea of heaven," recalled Cynthia. Tight-lipped with everyone else, Helms confided nearly everything that was not classified to his new wife—especially his frustrations with LBJ over Vietnam.

By 1966, when Helms became DCI, 200,000 American troops were fighting in Vietnam out of more than two million who would join that losing cause. LBJ was desperate to give them good news and kept calling Helms in search of it. "You've got to give them some hope," the president pleaded. "Just like a football team: You call them at the half and they are 21–0 behind and say, 'Goddamnit boys, you can do it, now here's how to do it. Let's go!' That's what I've got to do. So I've got to rely on you to get this stuff."

In an attempt to force the North Vietnamese to the bargaining table, LBJ launched Operation Rolling Thunder, a massive campaign of B-52 bombardments over North Vietnam. Had it intimidated Hanoi and changed hearts and minds? The answer, Helms told him emphatically, was no. In fact, the CIA concluded: "We see no signs that the air attack has shaken the confidence of the regime. . . . North

Vietnam in the short term at least, will apparently take no positive step toward a negotiated settlement." Analyst Richard Kerr recalled: "Our reporting was consistently negative, in terms of the effectiveness of the bombing and the question of whether the people were being won over."

If anything, Helms told Johnson, the enemy's will to fight was stronger. CIA analysts reported that North Vietnam's ability to move troops and supplies down the Ho Chi Minh Trail, its main supply route to the South, had increased *fivefold*. In a 250-page study, "The Vietnamese Communists' Will to Persist," they concluded: "Nothing happening to the Vietnamese Communists as of mid-1966 is bad enough to make them stop fighting." By defending the CIA's relentlessly pessimistic estimates, Helms, who'd come up through the ranks as an operative, won the respect of the agency's analysts.

He had to play referee between the CIA's rival camps, who held diametrically opposed views on the conflict. The operatives on the ground in Saigon—including a future director named William Colby—were mostly convinced the war was winnable; they were by nature aggressive, can-do, optimistic—or if not, willing to suspend disbelief. By contrast, the analysts at Langley were deeply pessimistic, convinced there was no light at the end of the tunnel, in the metaphor of the day (or that the light was a freight train coming toward them). Helms chose a different metaphor. Trying to corral his feuding camps, he was "a circus rider standing astride two horses, each . . . going its own way."

The third horse was the Pentagon and its Military Assistance Command, Vietnam, or MACV. While American troops were dying at a rate of nearly three hundred per week, the CIA and MACV engaged in a fierce argument over the size of the enemy they were facing. The bone of contention was the Order of Battle, the estimate of enemy troop strength. MACV calculated that the North Vietnamese troops were approximately 250,000 strong. The CIA counted "irregulars"—part-time fighters, guerrillas, and such—and put the number at twice that: about 500,000.

Helms's special assistant for Vietnam affairs, George Carver, reported that General William Westmoreland, the commander in Vietnam, had simply ordered MACV to ignore the CIA's estimate.

So far, our mission frustratingly unproductive since MACV stone-walling, obviously under orders. . . . [The] inescapable conclusion [is] that General Westmoreland . . . has given instruction tantamount to direct order that [enemy] total strength will not exceed 300,000 ceiling. Rationale seems to be that any higher figure would generate unacceptable level of criticism from the press. This order obviously makes it impossible for MACV to engage in serious or meaningful discussion of evidence.

In the end Helms hammered out a compromise with MACV; he knew that the CIA couldn't win an argument with the Pentagon over enemy troop strength. But he felt he hadn't pulled his punches with LBJ. "I was honest about my point of view and stood up to him, I didn't take a lot of backtalk from him."

Still, eventually it became clear that the president wasn't listening. Helms never gave in to Johnson's hectoring for good news—but he did not pile on with bad news either. "Helms reached a point where, in the morning briefings and the president's daily brief, we just slacked off on providing information on Vietnam," said analyst Kerr. "We did not do the aggressive pieces that were negative, because they were counterproductive." Helms knew that bad news simply got LBJ's back up. The president was fixated on the Pentagon's ever-mounting toll of enemy casualties: "the body count." Cynthia recalled her husband's frustration: "The body count was a huge issue—who you count, and who it is that goes into that. But it was just endless, and he felt it was focused on the wrong thing."

Helms thought it was time to reconsider the fundamental assumptions behind the war. It was an article of faith among LBJ's advisers that allowing South Vietnam to fall would trigger the toppling of one neighboring country after another until all of Southeast Asia succumbed to communism. It was called "the domino theory." But was there anything to that theory? At a pivotal meeting of LBJ's senior advisers back in 1965, the war's controversial architect, Defense Secretary Robert McNamara, made an impassioned argument: "Our national honor is at stake. Our withdrawal would start further probing by the communists. We would lose all of Southeast Asia." In August 1967, on his own authority, Helms asked one of his analysts to examine what might happen if the U.S. acknowledged that the war was lost and simply packed up and went home.

The resulting thirty-three-page memorandum, on September 11, 1967, was titled "Implications of an Unfavorable Outcome in Vietnam." It considered what might happen after the U.S. made a "reasonably orderly" withdrawal from Vietnam.

At some stage in most debates about the Vietnam war, questions like the following emerge: What would it actually mean for the U.S. if it failed to achieve its stated objectives in Vietnam? Are our vital interests in fact involved? Would abandonment of the effort really generate other serious dangers?

The memo conceded some risks.

There could be a spectacle of panic[ked] flight from the country, suicidal resistance by isolated groups, and Communist terror and vengeance. Clearly if this worst case came about, the discredit the U.S. would earn, which would be seen by many as not merely political but also a moral discredit, would be far greater.

. . . if one or more states in Southeast Asia did in fact fall under Communist control . . . the region could be in a turbulent and regressive condition for a long time. This would mean a major frustration of U.S. policy aims, but we think would not bring any major threats to U.S. security.

It concluded:

. . . If the analysis here advances the discussion at all, it is in the direction of suggesting that such risks are probably more limited and controllable than most present argument has indicated.

The memo was full of caveats, but Helms knew it was damning; given the bitterly contentious debate over the war, just its *existence* would be politically explosive. Cynthia recalled her husband's trepidation about showing it to LBJ: "He told me that he was going to stay behind after the Tuesday lunch and talk to Johnson, and give him the memo. He said it's a little risky because I shouldn't really be doing that. But he really felt so involved in LBJ's trauma. He really thought that Johnson should get out of Vietnam."

Helms gave Johnson the memo in a sealed envelope. And then he waited. Helms would later write that the president never said a word about it: "President Johnson never mentioned the document to me; nor, to my knowledge, did he raise it with anyone else." But it's hard not to suspect that Helms was dissembling here, perhaps keeping a presidential confidence. "Did LBJ read it?" I asked Cynthia. "Oh, yes," she said. "And they talked about it. Dick was saying that there'd be no domestic repercussions if he got out of Vietnam. I suppose you could say that's advocating. But he really wanted to help him." Mrs. Helms did not know what LBJ said in reply.

Did any of LBJ's advisers, or his war cabinet, read the memo? It was addressed to both LBJ and his national security aide, Walt Rostow. Rostow never acknowledged seeing it, but Cynthia believed he read the memo—and destroyed it, realizing how dangerous it would be to the war effort if revealed. Rostow "deep-sixed it," she said.

Years later, Cynthia was at home alone. The phone rang and she answered it. It was McNamara, who at the time was researching his forthcoming memoir, *In Retrospect: The Tragedy and Lessons of Vietnam*. When published in 1995, the book would become a sensation with its dramatic mea culpa. More than 58,000 Americans and countless Vietnamese, McNamara now believed, had died in an ill-conceived cause.

Over the phone, more than twenty years after the American defeat, McNamara told Mrs. Helms that he'd just read "Implications of an Unfavorable Outcome" for the first time. He'd found the memo, declassified in 1993, in the archives of the LBJ Library. McNamara was shocked that he hadn't seen it before. "Why wasn't I shown this?" he demanded. "This would have helped me! I should have known!" "He was screaming over the phone at me," said Cynthia. "He was just furious."

In his memoir, McNamara wrote: "Having a senior adviser submit a memo questioning the fundamental premise underlying our involvement in a war, and not allowing him to discuss it with his colleagues, is certainly no way to run a government." Helms shared McNamara's vexation with LBJ's decision-making process—the keeping of secrets from colleagues, the pitting of advisers against one another, the cajoling and bullying. But Helms also knew that you couldn't change a president, and that CIA directors shouldn't try.

"Every president is going to do business the way he wants to do it," Helms reflected years later. "You say, well, he should discipline himself—but they never do. They do it exactly the way they want to do it. Even if you convince them that they ought to do it differently, they'll never do it more than twice . . . and then they go back to the way they wanted to do it before."

Helms almost never raised his voice, rarely betraying annoyance or satisfaction. But one day a CIA analyst named Jack Smith barged into his office and got a rise out of him. Why, Smith demanded, had the president just approved a war initiative that the CIA had trashed in a recent study? "Dick fixed me with a sulfurous look," recalled Smith. "How do I know how he made up his mind?" Helms snapped. "How does any president make his decisions? Maybe Lynda Bird was in favor of it. Maybe one of his old friends urged him. Maybe it was something he read. Don't ask me to explain the workings of a president's mind!"

Yet Helms came to believe he understood Johnson. Why didn't LBJ cut his losses and extricate the U.S. from the quagmire of Vietnam? Helms thought it was for just one reason: He couldn't bear to be the first American president to lose a war.

In the summer of 1967, Johnson pushed Helms to go after his enemies at home. LBJ and his inner circle were convinced, despite no discernible evidence, that the leaders of the antiwar movement were controlled and directed by foreign communist powers. The president wanted Helms and the CIA to confirm this supposition—by any means necessary. Specifically, the president wanted the agency to conduct domestic surveillance of anti-Vietnam protesters.

One might have expected Helms, of all people, to refuse point-blank: The CIA was forbidden by its charter to engage in domestic police activities; surveillance of U.S. citizens required court-ordered search warrants. But when Helms tried to object, Johnson cut him short: "I'm quite aware of that. What I want is for you to pursue this matter, and to do what is necessary." The next day, Helms set up a Special Operations Group (SOG) and MHCHAOS was born. (The prefix MH was for projects with worldwide reach.) Under the program, which ran from 1966 to 1973, the CIA would illegally compile files on 7,200 Americans and infiltrate antiwar groups and even unrelated organizations—from the women's liberation movement to the Jewish service organization B'nai B'rith.

Why did Helms succumb to LBJ's pressure? He had a soft spot for Johnson; Helms sympathized with his anguish over the war. He also thought he had little choice but to go along. "Johnson never said to me, 'do X, Y, Z,'" Helms explained. "He said, 'I need this.' So MHCHAOS was an effort to put in real life terms the solution to his problem." I asked Cynthia why her husband didn't draw a line. "Why not simply say, 'Mr. President. I'm sorry, that's illegal. We can't do that?'" "Well, I think he did," she replied. "He said he didn't want to do it. He tried not to, he tried not to break the law. But he did it. He just felt that LBJ needed help."

As with MONGOOSE, which targeted Castro, Helms reasoned that the way to minimize the danger, and keep it under wraps, was to put the operation under his thumb. As he later explained: "Because the president had directed us to sail so closely to the wind, I wanted to keep this activity compartmented from other operational activity and firmly under my control." The truth was, Helms was sailing not close to the wind but right up on the rocks: Later, MHCHAOS would be exposed by *New York Times* reporter Seymour Hersh.

Helms had allowed his sympathy for a president to distort his judgment as director; he'd violated the law and the CIA's charter. He would face a similar test, and even bigger stakes, with Richard Nixon.

Johnson's announcement in March 1968 that he wouldn't run for reelection shocked almost everyone. But it didn't surprise Helms; he'd seen the war—and LBJ's heart condition—take a heavy toll on the man he "had thought to be indefatigable." Helms was worn out, too, but he wanted to stay on as director—and got his wish when Nixon reappointed him. Over the next few years, he'd have ample opportunity to wonder whether he should have retired with LBJ.

In the beginning, Helms barely saw the president. "Nixon just didn't like to deal with people individually the way Johnson did," Helms recalled. "They're just different personalities. He liked to deal through his staff." The director was told to go through Henry Kissinger, Nixon's imperious, domineering national security adviser, who would give summaries of his views to Nixon as he saw fit. Moreover, the President's Daily Brief (PDB)—traditionally the agency's conduit to the president—would go first to Kissinger and the national security team. Nixon wasn't reading it. Adding insult to injury, Nixon installed two loyalists as Helms's deputy directors: General Robert E. Cushman, who'd been Nixon's military aide when he was vice president, and Vernon Walters, a retired Army general, who'd worked as his interpreter. Helms soon realized they were sent to spy on him.

Nixon didn't hide his disdain for his CIA director. At NSC meetings, he interrupted Helms frequently—sometimes gratuitously, often correcting him on some niggling point of fact or geography. Nixon's low opinion of the CIA's workforce was also on display. "What are those idiots out in McLean doing?" Nixon wondered aloud. "There are forty thousand people out there, reading newspapers." Helms shrugged off the slights; he worked for one president at a time, and he'd take whatever indignities came his way. "Get on with it!" was his favorite rallying cry (and his advice to beleaguered successors). But he found Nixon puzzling—and bizarre. He told Cynthia he felt sorry for the president's wife, Pat Nixon. One day he watched as Mrs. Nixon stepped out of a car and stumbled, landing on her face on the pavement. The president didn't move a muscle to help her.

Nixon was convinced that the CIA's past was full of skeletons, particularly involving the Kennedys; he surmised that Helms and his ilk must be covering up for them. The president's close aide and domestic adviser, John Ehrlichman, had assembled a team of oddball investigators known as "the Plumbers," so named because their original mission was plugging national security leaks. They were told to find dirt on Nixon's enemies and political opponents—and if that failed, to manufacture it.

One of the plumbers, a veteran ex-CIA operative named Howard Hunt, created a bogus White House cable tying President Kennedy to the Diem assassination. Then, one day in 1971, Ehrlichman called Helms with a request: Would he send over the CIA's documents on the Bay of Pigs and the Diem assassination? Helms replied that such a request would have to come from the president himself. Ehrlichman arranged a meeting with Helms and Richard Nixon.

Just before the meeting, Nixon and Ehrlichman engaged in a

giddy conversation, caught on the White House tapes; they chatted excitedly about all the skeletons they imagined must be hidden in the CIA's closets. "Helms is scared to death of this guy Hunt that we've got working for us—because he knows where a lot of the bodies are buried," Ehrlichman told Nixon. "Supposing we get all the Diem stuff, and suppose we get something that we can really hang Teddy or the Kennedy clan with . . . we're going to want to run with it." Nixon enthusiastically agreed.

But it was an exercise in wishful thinking; there was no secret cudgel to bring down on the Kennedys—or any hammer involving Helms and the Bay of Pigs. It was all a figment of Nixon's imagination. (Much like another president's delusion, more than forty years later, that a computer server from the Democratic National Committee was spirited away to the Ukraine.)

When Helms arrived for his appointment at the Oval Office, he was carrying an assortment of files, apparently innocuous, related to the Bay of Pigs. "I said, 'Now do you want these papers? Here are the problems and so forth,'" Helms recalled telling the president. "Nixon said, 'these things didn't happen on your watch' . . . and gave me certain assurances that while he wanted the papers, he would not use them to damage the agency or anything." Helms agreed to give him the files. Nixon later complained that the Bay of Pigs file was "incomplete."

A few years later, a congressional report criticized Helms for having given *anything* to Nixon; future CIA directors, it said, should have their own political base or independent means by which to withstand presidential arm-twisting. Helms was infuriated. "It's just baloney that you have to have a personal fortune or a big political base to have the guts to stand up to a president," he fumed. "I stood up to Nixon, I stood up to Johnson—and if anybody can tell me any time when I failed to do so I'd appreciate knowing it."

As the Vietnam War raged on, Helms had many opportunities to stand up to Nixon. The president had promised a "secret plan" to end the Vietnam War, but Nixon had no plan, only the vaguest notion of getting out without appearing to have lost. Helms thought Nixon's chances of success were no better than Johnson's, but he stayed in his lane, continuing to deliver news the president didn't want to hear. "He would do it in a way that's polished but that would not pull his punches," recalled Charlie Allen, the veteran analyst. "Maybe it was his years in journalism, in policy circles, in Europe, his understanding of other cultures and language." But while Helms was polished around the cabinet table, he would let his hair down with Cynthia. "We were at a dinner party," she recalled. "I can remember it so clearly. Kissinger got up and said, 'Peace is at hand.' And he made this speech. Well, we got going out through the passageway, and Dick said to me, '*Bloody hell!* You haven't gotten any peace at all.'"

Yet the crisis that would make Richard Helms a household name, and cause him the most personal anguish, would unfold closer to home. In 1970 a leftist candidate named Salvador Allende was poised to win Chile's presidential election, threatening to nationalize industry and confiscate foreign-owned property. This unexpected development was anathema to Nixon, who feared that all of South America, from Cuba to Chile, would become a "red sandwich." Since 1960, the CIA had been disseminating anti-Soviet propaganda and pouring money into the campaigns of Chile's centrist candidates. It did the same in the run-up to the 1970 election.

Even in the context of the Cold War, Allende was hardly a serious threat to American national security; Kissinger would later quip, "Chile is like a dagger pointing to the heart of Antarctica." But the possibility of Allende gaining power alarmed American corporations, including International Telephone & Telegraph (ITT) and Pepsi-Cola. "There was really no heavy U.S. interest except business interest," said Burton Gerber, the Russia hand. "That's what was driving it." That and one other factor. As Helms put it: "Truman had lost China. Kennedy had lost Cuba. Nixon was not about to lose Chile."

The CIA predicted that a centrist candidate would win the election. Instead, Allende squeaked out a victory in a plurality; when approved by the Chilean Congress he would assume the presidency in a little over a month. The reaction in the White House was apoplectic. At a hastily called meeting with Kissinger and Helms, Nixon was furious with his director, convinced the CIA had failed him again. Helms was to do whatever it took to prevent Allende from taking office, Nixon demanded. As the president fumed, Helms scribbled notes:

One 10 chance perhaps, but save Chile
worth spending
not concerned risks involved
no involvement of Embassy
$10,000,000 available, more if necessary
Full-time job—best men we have
game plan
make the economy scream
48 hours for a plan of action

Helms understood exactly what this meant: "President Nixon had ordered me to instigate a military coup in Chile, a heretofore democratic country." And he saw no possibility of ignoring, or slow-walking, this command. As Helms later wrote, defensively: "By what superior judgment was I to leave the White House and then decide that the President did not mean what he said?" Yet more troubling to Helms than his marching orders was the impossibility of carrying them out; preventing Allende from taking office would take time, and the CIA didn't have enough of it.

Ultimately, Allende *would* take office, only to be overthrown in a military coup that had the CIA's fingerprints all over it. Allende was an apparent suicide. And an oppressive military regime would rule Chile for a generation.

Helms's day of reckoning would come a few years later, in testimony before Congress. Asked under oath if the CIA had tried to overthrow the Chilean government, Helms would find himself caught between his oath of secrecy as director and his obligation to answer truthfully. (The story of Chile's military coup, and Helms's fateful testimony about it, is told in chapter 2.)

Chile and all the other challenges were about to be overshadowed by the central drama of Nixon's presidency. As his campaign for reelection began, the thirty-seventh president was overwhelmingly favored to defeat his potential Democratic opponents. But Nixon was taking no chances. His political enemies would stop at nothing to beat him, he believed. Nixon would do whatever was necessary to win.

Early in the morning on June 17, 1972, Helms was awakened by a phone call. It was the CIA's chief of security. Five men, he reported, had been arrested at the Watergate Complex, planting bugs in the Democratic National Committee headquarters. Helms took a deep breath. "Yes," he said. The security chief went on:

"Four Cubans and Jim McCord."

"McCord? Retired out of your shop?"

"Two years ago."

"What about the Cubans. . . . Do we know them?"

"As of now I can't say."

"Is that all of it?"

"No, not half. Howard Hunt also seems to be involved in some way."

As far as Helms knew, the Watergate break-in wasn't a CIA operation. But Hunt had worked for the CIA in Guatemala, Mexico, and Europe—and on the task force of the Bay of Pigs operation. Helms also knew that Hunt had worked as a "security consultant" at the White House. What Helms did *not* know was that in July 1971, Ehrlichman had telephoned Helms's deputy Robert Cushman to tell him that Hunt needed some assistance and wanted to come by the CIA.

Without informing Helms, Cushman had said yes to Hunt and given him some "operational gear": a wig, a voice-altering device, and some fake IDs. When Hunt came back a few months later with more demands—for telephone answering services and a secretary—Cushman got cold feet. He said no—and informed Helms. (The CIA gear Hunt borrowed was used in another botched break-in: at the Los Angeles office of the psychiatrist for Daniel Ellsberg, who had leaked the secret Pentagon Papers.)

As his security chief talked about the incident at the Watergate, Helms took another deep breath. "Is there any indication that we could be involved in this?" he asked.

"None whatsoever," the chief replied.

Helms told him to stay on top of the matter; he would see him Monday morning.

For the next two weeks, as the break-in dominated Washington's news cycles and political gossip mills, Helms's instructions to his staff were, in effect: "Keep cool, do not get lured into any speculation, don't volunteer any information, and just stay the hell away from the whole damned thing."

But the damned thing was closing in on Helms.

Nixon and his henchmen had hit on a plan: If the break-in could be portrayed as a CIA covert operation, instead of a Nixon campaign plot, the White House could escape scot-free. After all, three of the Watergate burglars—James McCord, Frank Sturgis, and Bernard Barker—had once worked for the CIA. And FBI director Patrick Gray had suspected agency involvement from the start.

H. R. Haldeman, Nixon's White House chief of staff, kept calling Helms at home. Cynthia had never known her husband to raise his voice, much less shout, but "he and Haldeman had words, definitely." Haldeman kept pressing Helms to help the White House out of its jam. There was the thorny problem of coming up with hush money for the Watergate burglars. Couldn't Helms pay it from the CIA's "unvouchered funds"? Helms emphatically could not. "If the president wants that done, he'll have to call me himself!" he shouted into the receiver. "I'm NOT doing it!"

Less than a week after the break-in, on June 23, Haldeman summoned Helms and his deputy Vernon Walters to the White House. When they arrived, Ehrlichman, the president's other close adviser, was there. A moment later, Haldeman walked in.

"What connection did the CIA have with the break-in?" Haldeman asked the director. "The CIA had no connection whatsoever with the Watergate break-in," Helms replied coolly. Haldeman ignored this and then got to his point. "The [FBI's] investigation of certain Mexican leads," he told Helms and Walters, "might jeopardize CIA activity there. Therefore it has been decided to have General Walters go to see [FBI director] Pat Gray and tell him that further investigation in Mexico could lead to the exposure of certain agency assets and channels for handling money."

Then Haldeman made a bald threat. Even worse things might be exposed, he said darkly. "The President asked me to tell you this entire affair may be connected to the Bay of Pigs, and if it opens up, the Bay of Pigs may be blown . . ."

Helms leaned forward in his chair. His eyes narrowed as he looked straight at Haldeman. "The Bay of Pigs hasn't got a *damned* thing to do with this," he said. "And, what's more, there's nothing about the Bay of Pigs that's not already in the public domain." Ehrlichman thought Helms reacted "like a scalded cat." Haldeman suspected the CIA director's outraged reaction meant he was hiding something.

Helms's recollection was different: "I did not shout in the White House, and cannot even remember having shouted in my own office."

Cynthia recalled that Helms was mystified by Haldeman's talk of CIA operations in Mexico; nor did he have any idea what Nixon's men were alluding to about the Bay of Pigs. "What the heck's the president talking about?" he vented to his wife when he got home. Helms telephoned his security chief. "What are they *talking* about?" he said. "I don't think we have any other operation in South America. I want you to search the whole agency, because I can't think what the president's talking about. He's threatening me. And I don't think there's anything there."

Threatening him *with what*? In his references to the Bay of Pigs, Haldeman later wrote that Nixon "might have been reminding Helms, not so gently, of the cover-up of . . . [plots against] Fidel Castro—a CIA operation which might have triggered the Kennedy tragedy and which Helms desperately wanted to hide." But the truth was Nixon and Haldeman had nothing on Helms beyond idle suspicions about skullduggery.

Haldeman had completely misread the CIA director. This was the hill Helms was prepared to die on. One thing was clear: If he obeyed the order to block Gray's investigation, both he and the CIA would be at risk. Helms could end up in prison. Just paying the Watergate burglars might be enough to jeopardize the CIA's existence: "We could get the money," Helms reflected. "But the end result would have been the end of the agency. Not only would I have gone to jail if I had gone along with what the White House wanted us to do but the agency's credibility would have been ruined forever."

In an intelligence career that spanned three decades, Helms had approved some dubious operations; looked the other way on others; violated the CIA's charter; and broken the law. But he would not let Nixon make the CIA a scapegoat for White House crimes; nor would he commit obstruction of justice to save his presidency.

But what about Walters? The White House thought Helms's deputy could be counted on to follow orders. "Walters is a big weapon," Nixon said to Haldeman on the Oval Office tapes. "Walters is a total loyalist. He is a total believer in the president. Don't you agree?" In fact, Walters did meet with FBI director Gray, though he stopped short of telling him to end the investigation.

Helms was scheduled to depart on a trip to Australia, and he was taking no chances. As Cynthia recalled: "He was calling Walters and saying, 'You are not to make a single decision while I'm gone.' He was yelling at him, like a two-year-old child. He said, 'I don't want you doing anything the president or Haldeman asks you to do while I'm out of the country. You understand? Nothing! No decision is to be made!'"

The FBI investigation continued. And as prosecutors closed in, Nixon decided to act on the hunch he had expressed to Haldeman two years earlier: "Maybe the lesson is: Just get rid of Helms."

On February 2, 1973, Helms was summoned to meet with the president at Camp David, the presidential retreat. Helms assumed Nixon wanted to talk about the CIA budget. When he arrived at Aspen Lodge, the president was in the sitting room, flanked by Haldeman, and motioned Helms to sit down. Then Nixon got to his point. It was time for "new blood": He planned to appoint a new DCI. While Helms digested the news of his firing, Nixon asked him if he'd like to be an ambassador: "What about Moscow?" Still stunned, Helms said that the home of the KGB might be a stretch for an ex-CIA director; perhaps Tehran would be more suitable.

When Helms got home and broke the news to Cynthia, she went into the bedroom and cried. It wasn't just her husband's firing that upset her; it was the prospect of leaving friends behind. I asked Helms's son Dennis if he ever spoke to his father about that day. "No, no, no," he said. "Wouldn't have been like him to talk about it. He *never* talked about any conversation with the president."

Two years later, on August 5, 1974, following an 8–0 decision of the Supreme Court, transcripts of Nixon's tape-recorded White House conversations were released to the public. Among them was a talk between the president and Haldeman, six days after the break-in, and just hours before Helms and Walters came to the White House.

> *Haldeman: The only way to solve this . . . is for us to have Walters call Pat Gray and just say, "Stay the hell out of this . . . this is, ah, business here we don't want you to go any further on it" . . . it's got to be Helms and what's his name? Walters?*
> *President Nixon: Walters.*

Haldeman: And the proposal would be that Ehrlichman and I call him.

President Nixon: All right, fine. . . . How do you call him in, I mean you just—well, we protected Helms from one hell of a lot of things.

Haldeman: That's what Ehrlichman says.

President Nixon: Of course this . . . Hunt . . . that will uncover a lot, a lot of—you open that scab and there's a hell of a lot of things in it that we feel that this would be very detrimental to have this thing go any further. This involves those Cubans, Hunt and a lot of hanky-panky that we have nothing to do with ourselves. . . .

The conversation continued:

President Nixon: When you get in these people . . . say "Look, the problem is that this will open the whole, the whole Bay of Pigs thing, and the President just feels that . . . they should call the FBI in and say that we wish for the country, don't go any further into this case." Period.

In the case for Nixon's impeachment and removal from office, this conversation was the "smoking gun," proof that the president had obstructed justice. Almost overnight, Nixon's staunchest supporters abandoned him; impeachment and conviction were inevitable. A delegation of senior senators, led by Arizona's Barry Goldwater, paid a visit to the Oval Office. It was time, they told the president, to resign.

In the end, what struck Helms was Nixon's arrogance, and contempt for the government that served him. He "constantly disparaged everyone. . . . He would describe the State Department people as a bunch of pin-striped cookie-pushers who really didn't have America's interests at heart . . . the implication being the only smart fellow in town was Nixon. . . . But along comes Watergate, where he uses the most terrible judgment in the world and this to me is the crowning irony of his administration. That here he thought he was such a bright guy and he pulls the dumbest trick that anybody could pull and loses the presidency."

It wouldn't be the last time a president's obsession with enemies brought him to the brink of disaster. More than four decades later, Donald Trump's delusion that he'd been the victim of a plot hatched in Ukraine would lead him to withhold foreign aid in return for bogus investigations into mythical Democratic servers and dirt on a political opponent.

Helms had sacrificed his job to protect the CIA. But the agency's troubles were just beginning; its doors were about to be thrown open and many of its secrets revealed. The intelligence world would change forever, bound by new rules and congressional oversight. And Helms himself would be hauled before Congress to testify about what the CIA had done in Chile.

The people Helms blamed for all this weren't the press or the Congress or the KGB, but rather, his successors as CIA director: James Schlesinger and William Colby.

CHAPTER TWO

"You know he's one of *them*,

don't you?"

James Schlesinger, William Colby, and Gerald Ford

The CIA's refusal to do Richard Nixon's bidding on Watergate confirmed his worst suspicions about the agency. Helms was gone, but in the president's mind the place was still a den of Nixon-hating peaceniks who opposed his conservative agenda and wanted to see him run out of town. It wasn't even clear what anyone *did* out at Langley: A lot of spies came in from the cold, he said—paraphrasing John le Carré—to take nice, cushy jobs. What the CIA needed, Nixon was convinced, was an outsider who could grab the place by the heels, turn it upside down, and shake it until the rotten apples fell out. The president thought he knew just the person for that job: James R. Schlesinger.

One of the administration's brightest stars, Schlesinger had served as deputy head of the Bureau of the Budget. In 1971 he joined the Atomic Energy Commission, where he served as chairman for a year and a half. Brilliant and professorial, Schlesinger wore tweed jackets with patched elbows and constantly puffed on a pipe; he loved to pontificate and suffered no fools, presidents included: Gerald Ford would complain that he spoke to him as to a not-very-bright child. But Schlesinger wasn't above serving presidents' agendas. At the Bureau of the Budget, at Nixon's request, he'd agreed to do a cost/benefit analysis of the intelligence community—and pronounced the CIA bloated and inefficient. Helms had balked at Nixon's request that he cut a billion dollars from the CIA budget. But with Schlesinger at the helm, on February 2, 1973, it was a new day.

Out at Langley, the workforce braced themselves. Few events are as wrenching at the CIA as the transition to a new director. "No alien penetration or treachery of double agents has ever done nearly as much damage to the CIA as the infighting consequent upon the arrival of each new director," wrote Alexander Cockburn years later. That's an overstatement, but it's true that a new director often arrives with an agenda, "charged by his White House master with cleaning house and settling accounts with the bad guys installed by the previous White House incumbent."

The unease at Langley is magnified when the new director is not one of their own. "The agency has always been suspicious of outsiders," said David Robarge, the CIA's chief historian, who has been at the agency for thirty years. "They're always brought in after periods of problems and difficulties. So you kind of get your hair up, watching for signs that this person is not your friend." In Schlesinger's case, no one had to watch for long.

From the moment he set foot on the CIA's campus, the new director was in constant motion—shirttail flapping, reading everyone the riot act. "He made it clear that Nixon didn't like the intelligence he was getting from the CIA and we had better clean up our act," recalled Mel Goodman, then a young analyst. "And, of course, we knew Nixon hated the CIA, hated intelligence analysts." Under Helms, the standard for CIA analysts had been to present dispassionate intelligence, interpreted without fear or favor. Now there'd be a new standard. Schlesinger ended his first full day by summoning senior analysts to a meeting. "The Agency," he pronounced, "is going to stop fucking Richard Nixon."

Everything about the CIA bothered Schlesinger. "He was very suspicious of the agency's culture of secrecy," said Robarge. That cult of secrecy was symbolized, in Schlesinger's view, by the fact that CIA headquarters did not even have a sign marking its location; he had one installed on the George Washington Parkway. That was just the beginning. "He thought the agency was overstaffed, too many Vietnam-era holdovers, nobody ever got fired, it was inefficient," said Robarge. "The analysis was too academic, the operations were sort of irrelevant, we were not really doing our core missions." Schlesinger vowed to change all that.

"He was a first-rate defense intellectual with the stress on the word 'intellectual,'" recalled Leslie Gelb. A plainspoken veteran of both the Defense and State departments who would later become a Pulitzer Prize–winning *New York Times* columnist, Gelb admired Schlesinger's expertise on defense, military strategy, and energy. But his intellect came with a heavy dose of condescension. "Anybody who didn't have very high horsepower and know a lot, he didn't have time for," said Gelb. "He told me on several occasions, 'Well, these people just don't know what they're doing.' He had no particular background in intelligence, but he knew better than all of them. And he set about to reorganize the place. But he didn't understand that you couldn't do that without the participation of the people who worked there."

The bloodletting that followed was swift and unceremonious. "He walked in and he started firing people," recalled Charlie Allen, the legendary National Intelligence Officer (NIO) for Warning, who was a young analyst at the time. Not only people but entire departments were axed. "He fired one of our most brilliant officers, who came out of the OSS. After talking to him for fifteen minutes, he said, 'You and your staff are fired. You're abolished, it's gone.' He came in for the jugular. He made decisions that were just impulsive and without merit. And he took out some good people. Perhaps they needed to be gradually eased out, but he handled it in a brutal style, a sledgehammer."

Schlesinger believed that the agency had become bloated because of Vietnam, and that the workforce was getting old. "So I said that the three deputy directors should begin to find out who was the deadwood and move them out, and that was not exactly popular." Most of the people Schlesinger fired were in covert operations. "His attitude was, use a meat cleaver," said the historian Robarge. "So he just antagonized everybody." Before the downsizing was finished, the new director had terminated one thousand officers from the newly named Directorate of Operations (DO). (Before Schlesinger's arrival, the division had been called the Directorate of Plans, DP.) The cuts represented seven percent of the CIA's personnel.

Schlesinger's daughter Cora, who was twenty at the time, recalled her father's carping about the workforce: "Nixon sent him to clean the CIA up—they weren't doing their jobs. They'd be in London and would take each other to lunch all the time. They would all chase the same intelligence." Schlesinger took an axe to the London CIA station, firing much of its staff. Afterward, Cora recalled, her father's security detail suddenly grew larger; this was reportedly because of death threats against the new director. Cora remembered a vivid story her mother told her: "Dad had a chair in the living room by the window, and they told him to move it away from the window because someone could shoot him." This was probably just bluster from an overzealous security guard, but it left an impression on the director's daughter.

Nixon had another assignment in mind for his new director. With Watergate investigators closing in, he wanted Schlesinger to do what Helms had balked at—cover up the president's involvement in the scandal. But while Schlesinger was ambitious, there were limits to what he'd do for Nixon. He wouldn't be the president's fall guy. As the White House tapes rolled, the president's attorney, Fred Buzhardt, warned Nixon that his CIA director was uneasy about "memcons," or notes, made by Vernon Walters—notes that captured Haldeman's orders to obstruct the FBI investigation.

> Buzhardt: Jim was a little worried about the . . .
> President Nixon: Walters memorandum.
> Buzhardt: Walters thing . . .
> President Nixon: Yeah.
> Buzhardt: And so I . . .
> President Nixon: Was he worried about presidential involvement?
> Buzhardt: Yes . . .

Walters's memcons weren't the only thing that worried Schlesinger. The press was now doggedly pursuing the CIA's involvement in Watergate; the story soon broke that the agency had supplied Hunt with spy gear used in the break-in at Ellsberg's psychiatrist's office. Moreover, the CIA had done a psychological profile of Ellsberg for the White House—also in violation of the agency's charter. Blindsided by these revelations, Schlesinger went ballistic. "His anger over this had to be experienced to be believed," recalled William Colby, his deputy. "And I experienced it, both barrels." For Schlesinger, this was the last straw, according to Robarge: "He kind of blew up at that, because he did have a strong moral streak and he thought that the agency simply was doing too many shady things. And when this came up, that's when he launched the 'tell me everything you know' campaign."

Prodded by Colby, Schlesinger prepared a memo to the entire CIA staff. Addressing the disclosures about the CIA, Hunt, and Ellsberg, he vowed to "do everything in my power" to prevent the agency from violating its charter again. To help him do so, he was issuing a "standing order":

I have ordered all the senior operating officials of this Agency to report to me immediately on any activities now going on, or that have gone on in the past, which might be construed to be outside the legislative charter of this Agency.

I hereby direct every person presently employed by CIA to report to me on any such activities of which he has knowledge. I invite all ex-employees to do the same. . . .

Any CIA employee who believes that he has received any instructions which in any way appear inconsistent with the CIA legislative charter shall inform the Director of Central Intelligence immediately.

"Very few human institutions in this world," one CIA veteran would later grumble, "from the American Civil Liberties Union to the Boy Scouts, could survive in good working order after suffering such an instruction." Indeed, in ensuing months the floodgates opened, and reports of shady or just plain questionable CIA deeds poured into the director's office.

Both Schlesinger and Colby signed the memo—because on the day it was sent out, they received startling news: Schlesinger was leaving. His unpopularity at Langley had nothing to do with it; the cause was a shake-up of Nixon's cabinet: Defense Secretary Elliot Richardson was leaving the Pentagon to become attorney general, and Nixon needed Schlesinger to replace him. On July 2, 1973, after just five months as director, he was gone. Secretary of defense was the job Schlesinger had wanted in the first place—but the CIA workforce was even happier to see him go. "I was attending a conference with CIA officers, and it was announced that he would be leaving as DCI," recalled Charlie Allen. "And there was applause in the room. People actually cheered his departure, and there was a great relief throughout the building."

Schlesinger's scorched-earth management and his imperial style took a toll. So much so that when his oil portrait was finished and hung in its place of honor with the other directors, a security camera was installed just in case employees tried to vandalize it. To this day, when CIA insiders bemoan a sitting director for some grievance, they often begin: "You know how we used to say that *Schlesinger* was the worst director . . . ?"

But the relief over his departure was short-lived. A storm was coming: The CIA's secrets would soon be revealed, touching off a firestorm in Congress and the press, and sparking outrage among the public. The person responsible for this existential crisis wasn't a Russian mole or a muckraking journalist or a vengeful ex-spy. It was the CIA's new director, William Colby.

Like Helms, Colby was a CIA insider; he'd worked his way up through the clandestine service to become one of Schlesinger's top deputies. But he'd never aspired to become director; when Colby got the news that he'd been chosen, in a phone call from Nixon's new chief of staff, Alexander Haig, he was momentarily at a loss for words. Now he would lead the CIA through the most tumultuous, and revolutionary, period in its history.

William E. Colby seemed the least likely person to turn the intelligence world upside down. He'd joined the OSS at the age of twenty-four; but whereas Helms had fought the war mostly from a desk in London, Colby had seen it up close. A member of the Jedburghs, an elite paratrooper team, he'd parachuted into Nazi-occupied Norway and France, blown up trains and bridges, and rallied the resistance. The Jedburghs' motto was "surprise, kill, vanish." Colby had slept in trenches and killed enemy soldiers. He rarely talked about such things.

Colby was the last person you'd notice, much less picture as a war hero. Slightly built, he wore gray suits and spectacles and spoke softly. "He was the quietest voice in the room," recalled Allen, the veteran analyst. "Absolutely ice cubes. Never raised his voice." If Helms was hard to read, he was practically transparent next to Colby. Years later, in a documentary film made by his son Carl Colby, the CIA director was portrayed as a figure who was almost impossible to know. If poker players are an open book compared to CIA directors, as Thomas Powers has observed, Bill Colby was unreadable, opaque.

Born in St. Paul, Minnesota, and raised an Army brat, Colby went to Princeton at age sixteen; after his wartime OSS exploits, he enrolled in Columbia Law School and got his degree in 1947. Intent on a career as a lawyer and liberal activist, he became a union organizer and took a job at the National Labor Relations Board in Washington, D.C. But when Colby was offered a position at the newly created CIA, he couldn't resist, and joined the agency in 1950. He was sent to Italy, where he ran covert operations against the Italian Communist Party—and got to know another OSS veteran, and future CIA nemesis, James Angleton. Colby was poised to become head of the agency's Far East Division when Lyndon Johnson abruptly told Helms that he had someone else in mind for that job: his CIA station chief in Saigon. Helms asked Colby to pack his bags and go to Vietnam.

Colby and his wife, Barbara, thought Saigon in 1959 was a French colonial paradise, as enchanting as Rome and more exotic. Vietnam seemed perfectly safe; the Colbys and their children—there were four, with a fifth on the way—moved into a comfortable mansion with whirling ceiling fans and live-in servants. They ate lunch around the pool of the Le Cercle Sportif, a private club across the road. Fluent in French, Colby struck up a rapport with South Vietnamese president Ngo Dinh Diem and his brother Ngo Dinh Nhu. Despite violent demonstrations against the Catholic regime—Buddhist monks were setting themselves on fire in protest—Colby was convinced the CIA could work with Diem. (Ngo was his family name but Americans erroneously referred to him by his given name, Diem.) The station chief opposed the U.S.-supported coup against him (though there was no talking President Kennedy, Ambassador Henry Cabot Lodge, and the State Department out of it). Indeed, Colby traced the whole downward spiral of the Vietnam War to Diem's assassination.

Vietnam was one—but far from the only—issue on which Colby and Richard Helms would disagree. Whereas Helms was a skeptic when it came to covert action, Colby was a true believer. He was convinced that sending hundreds of thousands of American troops to fight and die in Vietnam was a grave mistake. The way to win was to covertly help the Vietnamese fight the war themselves. Colby believed in securing one village at a time through a program known as rural pacification. Later, he was put in charge of one of the war's most controversial operations: the Phoenix Program, a campaign to root out Vietcong infiltrators among the population. But the program, which Colby ran out of the State Department, was bloody. An estimated twenty thousand people were killed, many of them civilians. Critics denounced Phoenix as an "assassination" program. Colby vehemently denied that, insisting that he explicitly forbade it; indeed, he considered Phoenix one of his great accomplishments.

Yet others insist that Colby's eyes were wide open about the brutality of Phoenix. "Well, we killed people," said Charlie Allen. "We tried to earn reconciliation, pacification in the countryside and the villages, and Colby began that process. And part of the process was capturing and killing the Vietcong. It was a pretty cold-blooded way of operating—but remember, he fought with the French partisans. And the Germans, when they captured partisans, tortured them and killed them."

In the late 1960s, the Colby household was no different from other American families when it came to Vietnam: The war was a flashpoint, a trigger for bitter debates. Colby's son Paul, then a college student, recalled one evening around the dinner table after his father had returned from Vietnam in 1971. (Colby's daughter Catherine suffered from anorexia and epilepsy, and the CIA man had come home to get her treatment; she died two years later.) "We were expressing all this antiwar stuff to him, and being really aggressive," said Paul, now a government attorney. In the heat of the argument, someone— he couldn't remember who—told his father he had blood on his hands. Paul never forgot what happened next. The ghosts of Colby's OSS experience came flooding back. "He said, 'I *do* have blood on my hands. I have blood on my hands from World War II.' And he was getting emotional. I'd never seen him get emotional before."

The Vietnam War was still raging when Colby was nominated as CIA director in September 1973. His confirmation hearings were roiled by controversy over Phoenix; antiwar activists plastered Capitol Hill corridors with posters showing Colby's face, a skull-and-crossbones, and the ace of spades, an omen of death. Within two years, on Colby's watch, Saigon would fall to the communists. But the ignominious American defeat in Vietnam was just one of many challenges the new director faced, including a hostile Congress and press, a president on the verge of resignation, a demoralized workforce, and a closetful of agency skeletons. And there was one other problem: James Angleton.

During Schlesinger's brief tenure, Colby had tried to talk him into firing Angleton; with the departure of his ally Helms, surely the increasingly paranoid counterintelligence chief would have to go. But despite the damage Angleton had done with his mole hunt, Schlesinger had dragged his feet; he was "clearly fascinated by Angleton's undoubted brilliance," Colby recalled, "and couldn't help wondering if there just might not be something to his complicated theories that deserved further exploration."

But Angleton's behavior had gotten worse; he was losing his grip. In addition to his Master Plot, the CI chief now preached that the Sino-Soviet split was a hoax, more Russian disinformation. And he continued to smear innocent colleagues as Soviet dupes. While Helms was still director, Angleton had flown to Paris to meet with his French counterparts; he informed them that the newly installed CIA station chief was a Russian spy. Another career was derailed when a defector told Angleton about a Soviet-compromised CIA officer—he did not know his name, only the city where he was stationed. That was enough to send a clandestine officer who was based there to a remote, dead-end assignment.

In Angleton's mind, no one was above suspicion—not even the new director. He made no secret of his disdain for Colby, openly bad-mouthing him to his colleagues; he told Colby to his face that he should be sued by taxpayers for inefficiency. Angleton spread a rumor that while in Vietnam, Colby had met with a Frenchman with ties to the Soviet KGB and had failed to report the encounter.

One day, Angleton summoned a young CIA analyst to his office. The younger man found the legendary counterintelligence chief seated at his desk in the dark, puffing on a cigarette. Angleton motioned for his visitor to sit down. Then, pointing at the ceiling (toward Colby's office, on the seventh floor), he said: "You know he's one of *them*, don't you?" The young officer nervously replied: "No, sir, I don't believe he is. And I'm afraid I will have to report what you just said." Angleton took a drag on his cigarette, and then replied: "Well, then, I guess *you're* one of them, too."

The story undoubtedly got back to Colby. Yet even now, as director, he hesitated to fire Angleton. Instead, Colby tried to clip his wings, hoping he'd take the hint and retire. In addition to heading counterintelligence, Angleton had for decades been the CIA's chief liaison to the Israelis. Colby called him to his office and suggested he give up the Israeli "account." But Angleton resisted furiously, and Colby backed off. "My father honestly thought that Angleton was so wrapped up in the job, that if he had been fired, he might have committed suicide," recalled his son Paul. "So he just kept shelving this issue; he kept putting it off."

Leslie Gelb, the Defense and State Department veteran, thought Angleton's longevity spoke volumes about the CIA's dysfunction. "It tells you what kind of place the CIA was that people like that can be so powerful for—what, twenty-five years? Where else can that happen? They would never have someone like that at the Pentagon or the State Department. But the CIA was a palace of intrigues. And Angleton was the great intriguer. And it was too dangerous to go after him because he'd unload on you."

While Angleton was causing turmoil from within, Colby had his hands full fending off threats from without. The press was in hot pursuit of the agency; years of official lies about Vietnam and Watergate had put it in reporters' crosshairs. Anything CIA-related promised headlines. And the most dogged reporter of all was on the verge of jeopardizing one of the most audacious covert operations in CIA history.

Seymour Hersh, a brash, irascible investigative reporter, had won a Pulitzer Prize in 1970 for his exposé of the My Lai massacre, a mass murder by U.S. troops of women and children in South Vietnam. Now, four years later, working for *The New York Times*, Hersh had a sensational tip: In 1968 a Soviet Golf-class submarine (the K-129), carrying a crew of ninety-eight and three nuclear-tipped missiles, had sunk in the Pacific after a catastrophic accident. The Soviets had given up their rescue search. But the U.S. Navy had found the doomed sub on the ocean floor 1,500 miles east of Oahu, Hawaii. In a daring clandestine mission, the CIA was attempting to raise it, from almost 17,000 feet below the surface. The deepest previous ocean salvage of a ship had been from 245 feet.

Project AZORIAN, as it was known, was so preposterous and technically outlandish it seemed like something out of pulp science fiction. It had begun six years earlier when hydrophones monitored by the Air Force Technical Applications Center (AFTAC) pinpointed the sub's location; Naval Intelligence brought back remarkably detailed underwater photographs. They revealed a treasure trove: one still intact missile with a nuclear warhead; launching codebooks; and, morbidly, remains of the ill-fated Russian crew. Retrieving these items would be an extraordinary intelligence coup; through reverse engineering, experts could learn all about Soviet missile capabilities. Briefed by Naval Intelligence on the discovery in the Oval Office, then Director Helms had persuaded President Johnson to let the CIA take over the daunting project.

By the time Hersh got wind of it, Nixon was president and AZORIAN was well under way; an enormous, state-of-the-art salvage ship, the *Glomar Explorer*, was on the site, using a gigantic underwater claw in an attempt to raise the several-thousand-ton sub from the floor. It was the most implausible CIA operation of the Cold War, carried out under the noses of its adversary; the enormous ship and its crew were being watched, and harassed, by Soviet craft in the area. And yet the Russians evidently never figured out what the ship was up to. They bought the ingenious cover story: The *Glomar Explorer*, owned by the reclusive billionaire Howard Hughes, was on a deep-sea mining mission, digging minerals from the seabed.

Colby was alerted that Hersh was sniffing around the story; the director decided to pay a visit to him at the *Times*'s Washington Bureau. Colby offered Hersh a deal. AZORIAN, he pleaded, had been under way for six years; exposing it would foil the agency's most important covert operation. But if Hersh would hold off on publishing the story, Colby would give him a thorough briefing when the operation was completed. Hersh, who didn't have enough information to publish, reluctantly agreed. (The story would eventually be broken in 1975 by the investigative reporter Jack Anderson.)

On August 9, 1974, eleven months into Colby's directorship, Nixon resigned, and Gerald Ford assumed the presidency. That same morning, by coincidence, the *Glomar Explorer* finished raising the crippled Soviet sub. But the mission had suffered a horrible malfunction: While lifting its enormous quarry, the crew felt a sudden, violent shudder; the giant claw had nearly broken—and two thirds of the sub, including the missile, its codebooks, and fire-control system, had tumbled back to the ocean floor.

The next day, Ford's first as president, Colby briefed him in the Oval Office. "What did *Glomar* recover?" Ford asked him, no doubt wondering what the CIA had to show for its $250 million covert operation. "It's very hard to tell what they have," replied Colby. "We think that at least one of the missiles was loose and it may have fallen free. . . . It is too bad that, with the whole mission having gone so well, we lost the section that we did."

The operation recovered two nuclear torpedoes, some code-books, and the remains of six of the crew. The CIA team buried the Soviet sailors at sea in a solemn service conducted in Russian and recorded on videotape. Soon Ford would have to decide whether to send the *Glomar Explorer* back to sea in an effort to retrieve the lost section. (He chose not to do so.) But with the apparent failure of AZORIAN, Colby was off to an inauspicious start with the Ford White House. Soon Kissinger would complain: "Colby is a disaster and really should be replaced."

Making matters worse, Colby hadn't heard the last of Seymour Hersh. On December 18, 1974, the phone rang at Colby's home. It was Hersh again. "I've got a story bigger than My-Lai," he barked. It had nothing to do with AZORIAN. This was massive, Hersh said, and involved illegal CIA domestic activities. As he kept talking, Colby had a sinking feeling. Though his information was exaggerated, Hersh had the goods: It was Operation MHCHAOS, the domestic surveil-lance program ordered by LBJ and continued under Nixon. Hersh also mentioned illegal wiretapping and unauthorized mail-opening. Colby felt he owed Hersh for his restraint with AZORIAN. He also thought the only way to minimize the damage from this new story was to talk to him and put MHCHAOS in context. The director agreed to meet Hersh for an interview at his Langley office.

A few days after their phone call, Hersh came to Colby's office at Langley. "Look, Sy," Colby began, "what you're onto here are two very separate and distinct matters that you've gotten mixed up and distorted." Colby tried to argue, misleadingly, that MHCHAOS was somehow within the CIA's charter because it was aimed at *foreign* powers, not the antiwar movement. The mail intercepts and wire-taps were something else entirely, he said—and, yes, sometimes the agency had overstepped, but it was now on the straight-and-narrow. All this was music to Hersh's ears: confirmation of his story.

Two days later, *The New York Times* landed on the nation's door-steps with a page-one headline splashed across three columns: HUGE CIA OPERATION REPORTED IN U.S. AGAINST ANTI-WAR FORCES, OTHER DISSIDENTS IN NIXON YEARS. Colby's son Paul remembered going with his father to the newsstand in that pre-internet era to pick up the paper and was struck by how unfazed he seemed while reading it; the director didn't bat an eyelash.

But Hersh's story hit with the force of a ten-megaton bomb. Colby would write later: "A press and political firestorm immediately erupted. The charge that the agency had engaged in domestic spying, the inference that it had become a Gestapo, proved the fatal spark. All the tensions and suspicions and hostilities that had been building about the agency since the Bay of Pigs, and had risen to a combustible level during the Vietnam and Watergate years, now exploded." But the cat was not yet out of the bag. Indeed, MHCHAOS was far from the most shocking revelation among many that were about to be exposed.

While he didn't know it yet, Hersh had stumbled into the inner sanctum of CIA secrets. Colby referred to them as "our family skeletons." Someone else at the agency came up with a phrase that stuck: "the Family Jewels." They were the litany of agency abuses that had poured in as a result of Schlesinger's memo to the CIA workforce, asking for violations of the agency's charter. Compiled into a highly classified, 693-page document, they were a compendium of CIA misdeeds and skullduggery.

They were listed in a memo from Howard Osborn, the CIA's director of security. It was marked EYES ONLY and included activities that had "flap potential." The first item was redacted. The rest were in black-and-white:

2) *Johnny Roselli - The use of a member of the Mafia in an attempt to assassinate Fidel Castro.*

3) *Project MOCKINGBIRD - During the period from 12 March 1963 to 15 June 1963, this office installed telephone taps on two Washington-based newsmen who were suspected of disclosing classified information. . . .*

4) *Yuriy Ivanovich Nosenko - A KGB defector who from the period 13 August 1965 to 27 October 1967 was confined in a specially*

constructed "jail" at [REDACTED]. He was literally confined
in a cell behind bars with nothing but a cot in it for this period.

The memo went on, item after item. You couldn't make this stuff
up: unauthorized wiretapping of journalists; illegal mail-opening;
administering LSD and other drugs to unwitting subjects; approving
a plan to bug subjects and entrap them with prostitutes; supplying
unauthorized equipment to local police departments; making contact
with the Watergate burglars; and more.

Some of the Family Jewels read like an Elmore Leonard novel:
a Mafia hoodlum recruited for the Castro plot asked the agency to
place a listening device in the Las Vegas hotel room of the television comedian Dan Rowan; he thought his girlfriend was cheating
with the *Laugh-In* star, and he wanted to catch them in flagrante
delicto. When the technician planting the bug got caught, the CIA
appealed to the attorney general, Bobby Kennedy, and he quashed
the case.

But most of the items were deadly serious. And the worst came
last—four cases of alleged assassination attempts against foreign
leaders: Castro, Diem, Patrice Lumumba of the Congo, and Rafael
Trujillo of the Dominican Republic. All of this would become public
in congressional hearings to come.

Meanwhile, at the White House, heads were exploding over
Hersh's exposé, which almost no one had seen coming. While Colby
had given National Security Adviser Brent Scowcroft a cursory
heads-up, he hadn't prepared Ford, Kissinger, and his national security team for the magnitude of the story; they didn't even know that
the Family Jewels existed. The president was on his way to Vail for
Christmas; Colby reached him on Air Force One for a brief conversation. He then prepared a memo on Hersh and MHCHAOS, attached
an abbreviated list of the Family Jewels, and gave it to Kissinger to
take to Vail. A week went by, and Colby heard nothing.

When Ford returned to Washington, he summoned his CIA
director to an Oval Office meeting with Kissinger and White House
chief of staff Donald Rumsfeld. The president told Colby he was
considering the appointment of a blue-ribbon commission on CIA
abuses in an effort to head off congressional investigations. Ford,
who was no innocent, had been briefed on the Family Jewels and

seemed shocked by them. "Frankly, we are in a mess," Ford would later tell Helms.

Then, on January 16, 1975, Ford hosted a small off-the-record meeting with the publisher and top editors of *The New York Times*. The president told them about his plan for a commission, led by Nelson Rockefeller; he'd chosen the members with care because some CIA activities were so sensitive they had to remain secret. "Like what?" asked Abe Rosenthal, the *Times*'s executive editor. Ford replied: "Like assassinations." Then, evidently realizing whom he was talking to, he added: "That's off-the-record!"

Remarkably, the *Times* kept its promise and didn't publish Ford's secret. But Hersh, who hadn't been invited to the Oval Office meeting, learned about Ford's gaffe, and passed it to Daniel Schorr of CBS News. On February 28, Schorr reported: "President Ford has reportedly warned associates that if current investigations go too far they could uncover several assassinations of foreign officials involving the CIA."

Bedlam ensued. The press went into overdrive, and reporting about the Family Jewels, along with every other rumor of CIA malfeasance, filled newspapers and the airwaves. Ford's Rockefeller Commission was already in the works. Now Congress joined the stampede to investigate CIA abuses: It formed the Select Committee to Study Governmental Operations with Respect to Intelligence Activities, headed by Senator Frank Church, on January 27; and the House Select Committee on Intelligence, headed by Representative Otis Pike, on February 19.

With Congress and the media in full pursuit, Colby faced a quandary. The Family Jewels memos were locked in his office safe. What should he do with them? Should he inform the Department of Justice? He placed a call to the deputy attorney general, Laurence Silberman, and then paid him a visit. Was the CIA compelled to refer the Family Jewels to DOJ? "Come on, Bill," replied Silberman. "You're a lawyer. You know better than that." In this day and age, Silberman said, there was no way the CIA could decide for itself which Family Jewels might call for prosecution, and which wouldn't. In a later meeting, Silberman raised the stakes: "In withholding that evidence for a year and a half, Bill, you may have committed a crime yourself." Colby arranged for a copy of the report to be delivered to the Justice Department.

What about Congress? Should the CIA reveal its litany of past misdeeds to the country's elected representatives? It was a question that would sorely divide the agency; indeed, it would touch off a virtual civil war. On one side were those, including Dick Helms and his friend Angleton, who believed their oath to protect the agency's secrets and safeguard sources and methods trumped any need to cooperate with Congress, or to be transparent with the public. On the other side were those who believed the CIA must be accountable to Congress and the American people, admit its mistakes, and clean up its act.

The lawyer in Colby came down squarely in the latter camp (he carried a miniature copy of the Constitution in his coat pocket). "I believed that the Congress was within its constitutional rights to undertake a long-overdue and thoroughgoing review of the Agency and the Intelligence Community," he wrote later. Colby also believed that Helms's handling of the Watergate scandal—admitting nothing, shielding the agency at all costs—was a relic of the past. "The traditional role of intelligence [that] allowed it to operate in almost total secrecy, had to collapse in the new times where no one, not even a president, was allowed to put himself above the law." Colby made the Family Jewels available to the heads of the intelligence committees. And he told Senator Church to expect the full cooperation of the CIA.

Over the next twelve months—dubbed the Year of Intelligence—CIA abuses became a national fixation. A parade of witnesses—CIA directors, officers, operatives, even Mafia hit men—testified on live television about agency horrors; Colby appeared before Congress fifty-six times. Helms made the seventeen-and-a-half-hour trip from Tehran to Washington, D.C., thirteen times in a three-month period.

CIA officers around the world watched, heads in hands. And they blamed Colby for the whole sorry spectacle. Not only had he ignited the scandal but he was exposing agency secrets and methods—even things that were demonstrably untrue. At one point, senators brandished a CIA "poison gun" that was said to be loaded with lethal shellfish toxin and cobra venom. In fact, it was a never-used dart gun. Helms dryly observed: "The pistol would be more effective if thrown rather than fired at the prospective victim." Charlie Allen recalled: "I remember being overseas and saying, why are we doing this? I was with our chief of station, and we were both really upset. Colby was standing there holding the poisonous fish gun—which was never used." (Actually, the senators held the gun, not Colby, but Allen and his colleagues saw Colby everywhere.) "We called him 'the soldier priest' because he confessed to things we hadn't done."

The White House shared that view; Colby had run amok, jeopardizing state secrets and national security. They considered his actions heresy, or worse. "Colby made a decision, wise or unwise, that I'm going to make the agency a lot more open in order to make it clear we've turned ourselves away from the past," recalled Frank Wisner Jr., son of a top CIA official who served in the State Department when Colby was in Vietnam. "Well, let me tell you, the shitheads in the administration saw that and said, 'There's Bill out there, trying to look nice.' And they cut him down. They didn't plunge a dagger in Colby's back, but they certainly made it clear they thought he was . . . a cuckoo."

If there was any upside to this scandal for Colby, it was an opportunity, at long last, to do something about Angleton. MHCHAOS had been in the master spy's bailiwick, the counterintelligence division, and although he hadn't been in charge of it, Angleton would inevitably be blamed. Colby called him. "Jim, go. You are finished," he said. He could stay and write a history of CI, Colby offered, but Angleton declined.

Now that he was outside the tent, Angleton started lobbing stones back in. He gave rambling, apparently inebriated interviews, lambasting Colby for his naïveté. One Sunday morning, he called Hersh at his home. "Do you know what you have done?" he asked. "You've blown my cover. My wife, in thirty-one years of marriage, was never aware of my activity until your story. Now she's left me." In fact, Cicely Angleton *had* left him to go live in Arizona, but it had nothing to do with Hersh—and she knew exactly what her husband did for a living. The master spy seemed a lost soul. Leslie Gelb, who'd left the Defense Department to become one of Hersh's colleagues at the *Times*, remembered seeing Angleton on a Georgetown street corner. "He was the scariest-looking thing, slouched against the window of a store with his feet out in front of him, smoking a cigarette, just looking up at the sky."

• • •

Exposing the Family Jewels had made Colby a pariah among the CIA's old guard, but things were about to get worse. Because Colby was now faced with a momentous decision about one of the agency's most infamous scandals: its repeated interventions against Salvador Allende in Chile.

It had begun on Richard Helms's watch. Back in 1970, under orders from Nixon to prevent the leftist Allende from taking office, Helms had launched a secret "Track II" covert operation. There was nothing ambiguous about the project, also known as FUBELT. "It is firm and continuing policy that Allende be overthrown by a coup," wrote CIA officer Thomas Karamessines in a secret cable to the agency's station in Santiago. "We are to continue to generate maximum pressure toward this end utilizing every appropriate resource." Those resources included $10 million of CIA money—and weapons and tear gas that were air-dropped to coup plotters led by Chilean General Camilo Valenzuela. The plan called for "neutralizing" a powerful general named René Schneider, who opposed removing Allende.

But on October 22, 1970, another military faction staged an abortive coup, killing Schneider in a botched kidnap attempt. At the eleventh hour, the CIA had tried to call off this group, fearing they would fail; the agency had originally encouraged them before backing a different horse.

The issue now before Colby was Helms's testimony to Congress. On February 7, 1973, during confirmation hearings to become ambassador to Iran before the Senate Foreign Relations Committee, Helms was questioned under oath by Senator Stuart Symington of Missouri:

> *Did you try in the Central Intelligence Agency to overthrow the government of Chile?*
> *No, sir.*
> *Did you have any money passed to opponents of Allende?*
> *No, sir.*
> *So the stories you were in that war [sic] are wrong?*
> *Yes, sir.*

Did Helms lie about the CIA's activities? Immediately afterward, Helms had reviewed his testimony with the CIA general counsel, who said there might be a problem. Helms begged to differ. In the old days, he would never be expected to divulge classified information to congressmen who weren't cleared to hear it. What other answers could he give?

This allegation against Helms, brought by a mid-level CIA officer, "was about as welcome on my desk as a cobra, and as hard to handle," Colby said. "Here I was in the middle of another conflict between the past and the future. Helms did nothing wrong for which he could or should be condemned." Or did he? Three midlevel CIA officers had examined the case, and recommended referral to the Justice Department. Colby concluded that the decision wasn't his to make. Reluctantly, he reported the accusation. To the Helms faithful, this was an unthinkable betrayal. "[Many] would say that I had turned against my friend, benefactor and predecessor," Colby admitted later. "But I am satisfied that I did what I had to do."

Making matters worse, on Colby's watch as CIA director Allende was finally overthrown in a violent coup. The Chilean leader was dead, an apparent suicide. The country was now ruled by a brutal authoritarian, General Augusto Pinochet. During his first three weeks in power, Pinochet's secret police force, the National Intelligence Directorate (DINA), executed 320 citizens suspected of leftist sympathies. And teams of his assassins roamed South America and beyond. One of their victims was a former Chilean diplomat, Orlando Letelier, blown up by a car bomb in Washington, D.C.

Helms was furious with Colby for referring his case to DOJ. Yet even worse, Helms thought, was Colby's surrender of the Family Jewels—lock, stock, and barrel—to people who couldn't understand them or be trusted to keep them safe. "I recall only two instances in history in which the intelligence files were as thoroughly ransacked as those of the Agency during these investigations," Helms complained. Those instances occurred during the reigns of the Russian tsars and the Third Reich. His friend Angleton emphatically agreed: The CIA was being "pillaged by a foreign power, only we have been occupied by the Congress, with our files rifled, our officials humiliated, and our agents exposed."

Charlie Allen said the animosity between the directors ran deep. "The Family Jewels contributed to the tremendous antipathy that

Helms had towards Colby in his latter years." In Helms's view, Colby could do nothing right. There was something else that rankled, petty as it might seem: Colby's decision to install, outside Langley headquarters, a statue of Nathan Hale. A spy who managed to get himself hanged, for God's sake.

Meanwhile Congress continued to broadcast CIA transgressions to the television cameras. What was the truth about the CIA's "assassinations"? The Rockefeller Commission and Pike Committee punted on this issue; it fell to the Church Committee to examine whether the CIA had been "Murder Incorporated," as LBJ once called it, referring to Jack Kennedy's alleged plots against Diem and Castro. The committee looked at the agency's alleged involvement in plots on four foreign leaders:

> *Fidel Castro (Cuba). United States personnel plotted to kill Castro from 1960 to 1965. American underworld figures and Cubans hostile to Castro were used in these plots and were provided encouragement and material support by the United States.*
>
> *Ngo Dinh Diem (South Vietnam). Diem and his brother, Nhu, were killed on November 2, 1963, in the course of a South Vietnamese generals' coup. Although the United States government supported the coup, there is no evidence that American officials favored the assassination. . . .*
>
> *Patrice Lumumba (Congo/Zaire). In the fall of 1960, two CIA officials were asked by superiors to assassinate Lumumba. Poisons were sent to the Congo, and some exploratory steps were taken toward gaining access to Lumumba. Subsequently, in early 1961, Lumumba was killed by Congolese rivals. It does not appear from the evidence that the United States was involved in any way in the killing.*
>
> *Rafael Trujillo (Dominican Republic). Trujillo was shot by Dominican dissidents on May 31, 1961. From early in 1960 and continuing to the time of the assassination, the United States government generally supported these dissidents . . . three pistols and three carbines were furnished by American officials . . . there is conflicting evidence concerning whether the weapons were knowingly supplied for use in the assassination and whether any were present at the scene.*

The Church Committee also examined a fifth case, the killing of Chilean General Schneider during the attempted overthrow of Allende; it concluded that the CIA couldn't have foreseen the killing and didn't supply the weapons. In short, Congress ruled that the CIA hadn't succeeded in killing anyone, though it had repeatedly tried. Burton Gerber, who served the agency for thirty-nine years as a case officer and station chief, pointed out: "The CIA was charged by different presidents to kill somebody and they failed all three times. Don't ask us to kill."

Public revulsion over the murder plots contributed to lasting changes. On February 18, 1976, Gerald Ford signed Executive Order (EO) 11905, prohibiting the U.S. from engaging in assassination. Later updated by Jimmy Carter in EO 12036 and then Ronald Reagan in EO 12333, the order would constrain presidents, and the CIA, in the decades to follow. But the orders wouldn't end the debate. Should the prohibition apply to lethal drone warfare? Should it prevent the CIA from participating in operations with Israel's Mossad, which has no such rule? And what about the targeted killing of General Qassim Suleimani by Donald Trump in January 2020? These questions are explored in the chapters to come.

Still, the disclosure of the Family Jewels led to important and lasting changes: Senate Resolution 400, in 1976, and House Resolution 658, in 1977, would establish permanent congressional intelligence committees; the CIA would be required to brief the heads of those committees in advance on all covert operations. Equally important, no CIA covert action could take place without a "finding" signed by the president. The era of "plausible deniability" was over. It was a tectonic shift in the landscape of intelligence, signaling a new world.

It is remarkable how rarely CIA directors know when they're about to be fired. They may be able to predict the duration of the Six-Day War to within twenty-four hours. But when their necks are on the chopping block they're usually the last to realize it. On November 2, 1975, Colby received a message to report to the Oval Office the next morning. He thought Ford wanted to talk about the Kurdish rebels in Iraq. The Kurds weren't on his agenda.

"Good morning, Mr. President, you wanted to see me?" Colby asked. Ford, seated at the Resolute Desk, didn't stand or offer to shake hands. "Yes," he replied. "We are going to do some re-organizing of the national security structure." Colby knew instantly that he'd been fired. In fact, the CIA director was just one casualty in a cabinet shake-up dubbed "the Halloween Massacre." Schlesinger was being replaced at the Pentagon by Rumsfeld; Rockefeller was removed from the Ford ticket as VP in the next election; and Kissinger replaced as national security adviser by Brent Scowcroft (Kissinger would remain as secretary of state). Dick Cheney was taking Rumsfeld's place as White House chief of staff. Finally, Colby would be replaced as CIA director by George H. W. Bush.

Trying to make the news more palatable, Ford asked Colby if he'd like to be ambassador to NATO. "I should have been shattered," Colby said later, "but my old discipline of thinking of the next step ahead took over." After talking it over with his wife, Barbara, he declined the NATO offer. Colby was under no illusion about why he'd been fired: It was his handling of the Family Jewels. "I had not played the game during that turbulent year as a loyal member of the White House 'team.' "

With his intelligence career behind him, Colby returned to his law firm. He picked up where he'd left off before joining the CIA in 1950: fighting for liberal causes. He lobbied to cut defense spending by fifty percent and invest the savings in education and poverty programs. In 1984 he divorced Barbara and married Sally Shelton, an accomplished diplomat and former ambassador to Grenada and Barbados. It was a happy second marriage; she was convinced her husband was content with his new career.

Bill Colby never dwelled on past triumphs or failures; he moved on. After the Soviet Union's collapse, in the early 1990s, Colby took his expertise overseas. "He was working with the spy agencies in newly democratic Eastern Europe," recalled Sally, "helping them figure out how to function in a newly democratic system."

Early on the evening of April 27, 1996, Colby was alone at his weekend retreat in Rock Point, Maryland, sixty miles south of Washington, D.C. It was a modest two-bedroom cottage on a peninsula, with a small dock and a canoe. Colby, now seventy-six, had spent all day at a nearby boatyard on his hands and knees, getting his sailboat ready for the season, sanding the hull and repairing a torn sail. On his way home he stopped to pick up some clams and a bottle of wine.

On weekends, Colby liked to go canoeing, and he had a routine: He took an aluminum ladder out of the garage and put it in the water next to the dock, so that he could step into the canoe. When he returned from a paddle around the inlet, he took the ladder out and put it back in the garage. But on this evening, Colby wasn't planning to go anywhere. At 7:00 p.m., he called Sally, who was visiting her mother in Houston, and told her he was tired. He was going to have dinner, and then go to bed.

Less than twenty-four hours later, on Sunday afternoon, Colby's next-door neighbor noticed that his red Fiat was still in his driveway. The canoe was gone, and the ladder was still in the water. That seemed odd; she knew that Colby, a creature of meticulous habit, would never leave the ladder there. The neighbor picked up the phone and dialed 911.

Over the next forty-eight hours, police rescue workers and Coast Guard divers thoroughly searched the area but found no trace of Colby. Reporters and television crews descended; there was speculation that the ex-CIA director might have committed suicide. Then, two days after his disappearance, the canoe was found, half-filled with sand and washed up on the shore.

Finally, nine days after he vanished, Colby's body was discovered; it was more than a hundred yards from where the canoe was found. As far as anyone knew, Colby didn't have a heart condition. But the Maryland medical examiner found that he'd most likely suffered a "cardiovascular incident" that caused him to black out; he toppled into the water and drowned. With that, the media packed up their equipment and went home.

But not everyone believed Colby's death was an accident. Zalin Grant, a freelance journalist, was in Paris when he picked up the *International Herald Tribune* and read that Colby had died while paddling his canoe after dark. He'd gotten to know and admire Colby in Vietnam, on assignment for *Life* magazine and CBS. Grant didn't believe the official story for a second.

It was a month before Grant could get to Maryland and do some digging on his own. What he found alarmed him. To begin with, there was the timeline of that evening. Based on eyewitness accounts of a gardener and neighbor who'd seen Colby that evening, if the former DCI had prepared and eaten his dinner, it would have been nearly pitch-black outside by the time he set out, impulsively, for his canoe trip. Colby wasn't impulsive about anything, much less canoeing in total darkness. And he was compulsively neat, putting everything in its place; and yet plates were left on the counter, along with an uncorked bottle of wine.

Then there was the timeline of when key evidence was found. Since the same area had been thoroughly searched, why didn't the canoe turn up until two days later, and why was it half-filled with sand (which seemed unlikely to accumulate in just two tide cycles)? It looked to Grant as though someone wanted the canoe to be found there. And what about the discovery of Colby's body—*nine days* later? This was strange, given how comprehensive the search had been. But there was something else, Grant thought, that was telling: A body that has been submerged for any length of time is likely to be grotesquely bloated. But autopsy photos showed Colby's body was in remarkably good condition, as though he'd been in the water for a day. Grant became convinced that Colby had been killed, and the crime scene made to look like an accident.

Colby's family dismissed Grant and his murder theory; Colby's widow, Sally, spoke with the journalist initially, but never called him back. "The coroner ruled it an accidental death," said his son Paul, the government lawyer. "And how often do people get rubbed out like that? I'm sorry. It's just ludicrous, I think." Suicide seemed less far-fetched, and some who knew Colby wondered about that possibility. "Why he took it upon himself to reveal the Family Jewels, expose his lifetime's love, the CIA, just bewildered me," said one veteran CIA observer. "I never had the chance to sit down with him and ask him why. And yes, I think he killed himself. I think there was just too much on his conscience."

Frank Wisner Jr. thought the former DCI had undergone a profound disillusionment with government. "He was a really devout Catholic, and being a devout Catholic, he believed in God, King, and country," he said. "When the king's clothes began to shred, it was hard for him. I watched Colby unravel. He would invite me to lunch, and each time it was almost as if another layer of scales had fallen from his eyes. So I'm perfectly prepared to believe—though I do not know anything about this—that he took his life in the end."

But most of Colby's family dismissed the talk of suicide; the notion that he was haunted by Vietnam's demons seemed absurd. "This is a guy that did not have one ounce of regret," said his son Paul. Indeed, Colby was proud of his role in the Phoenix Program— and wrote a book, *Lost Victory*, arguing the war might have been won, if only it had been fought as a counterinsurgency. "He *loved* Vietnam," said Sally. "Every fall, I had to plant red and yellow tulips, 'cause those were the colors of the old Vietnam flag."

But there is one family member for whom Bill Colby, in life and death, is still a mystery. A few years after his father's death, film-maker Carl Colby, Paul's younger brother, made a documentary, *The Man Nobody Knew: In Search of My Father, CIA Spymaster William Colby*. The film drove a wedge between Carl and the rest of the family; Paul and Sally stopped speaking with him. On one level, the film is a straightforward, even admiring account of Colby's journey from the OSS to the pinnacle of the intelligence world. On another, it suggests Colby's complicity in the atrocities of Phoenix, implying that his father endured a kind of dark night of the soul. One sequence ends with the famous photograph of a South Vietnamese police chief pressing a pistol against the ear of a Vietcong prisoner, about to pull the trigger. "Nothing to do with Phoenix," complained Paul. "But it was portrayed that this was what [it] was all about."

Phoenix is a sore subject in the family, and so is the possibility that Bill Colby's death wasn't an accident. Toward the film's end, Carl suggests that his father might have taken his life because of guilt over not having done enough to care for his dying daughter, Catherine. "Foul play was suspected, but I knew otherwise," Carl pronounced. "I think he'd had enough of his life."

William Colby had shaken the world of intelligence to its core. After the release of the Family Jewels and the advent of congressional oversight, nothing would be the same. To his admirers, Colby was as great a CIA director as he was a war hero. To Helms and the old guard, by contrast, Colby was the man who gave away the secrets, who flung open the doors of the CIA and let in the barbarians.

Not long after her husband's death, Sally went to pick up the mail. Among the condolence cards and flowers were a half dozen envelopes addressed to her, handwritten, with no return address. She opened them. The letters were all variations on the same message: "It's about time. He had it coming to him."

CHAPTER THREE

"We were just plain asleep."

George H. W. Bush, Stansfield Turner, and Jimmy Carter

George H. W. Bush bobbed above a sea of pedestrians and pedicabs as he pedaled his bicycle down a dirt road in Beijing, glancing over his shoulder to make sure Barbara Bush was still behind him. It was Sunday, November 2, 1975, and Bush, the U.S. envoy to the People's Republic of China, had been here for more than a year: an earnest, gangly American better known to the Chinese for these conspicuous bicycle jaunts than for any diplomatic prowess. To the U.S. political establishment, Bush was out of sight and out of mind, stationed half a world away from the capital's political wars. But that was about to change.

This morning a courier from the U.S. Liaison Office had caught up with Bush; there was an urgent message for him at his house. The lanky diplomat wheeled his bicycle around and raced home. When he got there, a State Department cable was waiting.

The "eyes only" message was from Henry Kissinger, Ford's national security adviser.

> THE PRESIDENT IS PLANNING TO ANNOUNCE SOME MAJOR PERSONNEL SHIFTS ON MONDAY, NOVEMBER 3 AT 7:30 P.M., WASHINGTON TIME. AMONG THOSE SHIFTS WILL BE THE TRANSFER OF BILL COLBY FROM THE CIA.
>
> THE PRESIDENT ASKS THAT YOU CONSENT TO HIS NOMINATING YOU AS THE NEW DIRECTOR OF THE CENTRAL INTELLIGENCE AGENCY.

Bush's reaction was "total and complete shock." He handed the cable to Barbara. "From the expression on her face," he later wrote,

"I could tell we shared the same thought: New York, 1973." Two years earlier, at the height of Watergate, Richard Nixon had asked Bush to become chairman of the Republican National Committee, to act as a kind of political heat shield for the embattled president. Bush thought that job was radioactive, but he'd learned from his father, Prescott Bush, the patrician Connecticut senator, that when the president asks you to do something, the only answer is "yes, sir." So Bush, who'd been a congressman and U.N. ambassador, had taken the job and survived it. Now both he and Barbara thought Bush was being given another thankless task, asked to "take charge of an agency battered by a decade of hostile Congressional investigations, exposés, and charges that ran from law breaking to simple incompetence."

Bush's second thought was that he was being had. Was this a plot to end his political career? It wasn't just that Bush considered the CIA directorship a dead end politically; as he said in his reply to Kissinger, "I see this as the total end of any political future." The timing also seemed suspicious. As part of the so-called Halloween Massacre—the wholesale shuffle of Ford's cabinet officials—Vice President Rockefeller was being removed from the 1976 presidential ticket. If Bush were offered that VP slot, it could be a springboard toward the presidency. Running the CIA would be a different story—"serving as point man for a controversial agency being investigated by two major Congressional committees. The scars left by that experience would put me out of contention." But who would want to take him out of contention through such a scheme? Some of Bush's friends thought they knew: Donald Rumsfeld.

God knows Rumsfeld, Bush's fierce political rival, was ruthless enough. As Ford's outgoing White House chief of staff (he was replacing James Schlesinger as defense secretary), Rumsfeld had ample opportunity to orchestrate such a plot. He, too, could still be a candidate for the VP slot, and Rumsfeld's ambition was never in doubt. "From the moment his feet touched the floor in the morning until his head hit the pillow at night," said a close friend of forty years, "Rumsfeld thought about one thing: how to become president." Bush's friend Rogers Morton, the outgoing commerce secretary, told him that "Rummy" had enlisted the president in his plan to send Bush into political exile. "I think you ought to know what people up here are saying about your going to CIA," another friend told Bush. "Rumsfeld set you up, and you were a damn fool to say yes."

In truth, the evidence suggests that Rumsfeld did not orchestrate Bush's selection. According to Dick Cheney, Ford's first choice for CIA director had been Elliot Richardson, the former attorney general. But Kissinger couldn't stand Richardson, and so at the last minute Ford sent Bush to the CIA. Still, for almost forty years, Bush believed he'd been the pawn in a grand Rumsfeld chess maneuver. Indeed, when George W. Bush made Rumsfeld his defense secretary twenty-five years later, it was practically an act of defiance toward his father. Bush 41's friend James Baker warned Bush 43: "Don't forget what he did to your daddy."

For all his reservations about the CIA job, George H. W. Bush believed in his father's commandment, and more than a year of sipping tea and learning Mandarin had made him restless. "After thirteen months of duty in China," he reflected, "I liked the idea of having a worldwide organization, a job that would require 110 percent effort from early morning to late night." Still, Bush was conflicted. And Barbara was opposed to the move. "I WISH I HAD SOME TIME TO TALK TO ONE OR TWO CLOSE FRIENDS ABOUT THIS MATTER," he cabled back to Washington. But Kissinger's original message had said, "REGRETTABLY, WE HAVE ONLY THE MOST LIMITED TIME BEFORE AN ANNOUNCEMENT, AND THE PRESIDENT WOULD THEREFORE APPRECIATE A MOST URGENT RESPONSE." Bush reasoned that "as long as what he'd asked me to do wasn't illegal or immoral, and I felt I could handle the job, there was only one answer I could give." He said yes.

The notion that heading the CIA would be a political death sentence spoke volumes about the agency. Bush returned to Washington the following month to a flurry of terrible headlines. On November 20, the Church Committee had released its report detailing the CIA's involvement in attempted assassinations of foreign leaders. On December 4, the committee alleged that the agency had overthrown Allende's government in Chile. The Pike Committee demanded that the Ford White House explain the CIA's covert involvement in the civil war in Angola, and the Senate soon cut off funds to the American-backed rebels there.

The press and Congress were pummeling the agency, and some former agency officers had taken aim as well: Philip Agee and Victor Marchetti had written scathing exposés. Then, on December 23, the CIA station chief in Greece, Richard S. Welch, was assassinated outside his house in Athens. In Washington, there was serious talk, for the first time since the Bay of Pigs, about disbanding the agency, putting it out of its misery.

How could Bush, with no background in spycraft, run the world's most powerful intelligence service at a time of existential crisis? Ford wasn't sure, but he was willing to gamble. What Bush lacked in intelligence experience, the president reasoned, he made up for in political savvy. After the scandalous Year of Intelligence, and the constant hemorrhaging of secrets, the CIA needed someone who could perform triage: stop the bleeding, restore morale, and resuscitate the agency's reputation.

Still, choosing an outsider involved considerable risk. Schlesinger's toxic directorship was a fresh memory. Bush would be starting cold, knowing almost nothing about the clandestine service. And he would have to gain the respect of its covert operatives, those "Scottish tribes waiting for the English King," as Cofer Black, the veteran operative, had described them. Frank Wisner Jr. summed up Bush's challenge in his own colorful way: "He had to master the spies, find a way to live with them, and direct them to be successful—or be hung up by his balls."

At 7:30 a.m. on January 30, 1976, an armor-plated gray Chevrolet, with a chauffeur and CIA security officer, picked up Bush at his home in Northwest Washington and wound through traffic toward CIA headquarters at Langley. Bush hated having a security entourage, and as director would ditch it whenever he could in the days to come; he and *Life* photographer Dick Swanson enjoyed going for jaunts on the Capitol subway with no bodyguards in tow.

Just before starting at the agency, Bush had been pitched the idea of setting up his office in the Old Executive Office Building (OEOB), the grand, ornate edifice right across from the White House, in order to have easy access to the president. But the new director rejected the idea, sensing that symbolism mattered: "It would send a message that the new director was a politician more interested in playing the power game than running the agency." When it rained, Bush was driven into Langley's underground garage to the private elevator that went to his seventh-floor office. But most days he hopped out at the main entrance and walked through the lobby, past the Memorial Wall, and flashed his badge as he went through security, like everyone else.

The new director understood the importance of preserving the CIA's senior ranks. As his deputy he chose an agency veteran, E. Henry Knoche, to replace the outgoing Vernon Walters. And though he changed eleven of fourteen top administrators, many through promotion or retirement, Bush delivered the news to them in person, as he later wrote, "not by impersonal notices or pink slips." Those words were a direct slap at Schlesinger, whose ham-handed ruthlessness Bush was determined not to repeat. As for the rank and file, the truth was, the CIA *was* bloated and inefficient, as Schlesinger charged. The Vietnam War had swelled the ranks of the Directorate of Operations (DO); an internal report concluded that there were 1,350 unnecessary positions. But Bush, who hated firing people, ignored it. He would not throw spics under the bus at the expense of the agency's morale. Bush's message was the opposite of Schlesinger's warning about Nixon: People are going to *stop fucking the CIA.*

Not that they wouldn't keep trying. Appearing at the Overseas Press Club shortly after his appointment, Bush was heckled by reporters, many of them drunk, unhappy about allegations that the CIA had hired journalists as spies. (Which was true, Bush admitted.) It was a "disastrous" appearance—"I really bombed . . . it's tough to talk to a group of press people after two hours of cocktails," he said. But Bush kept on accepting invitations from all quarters to defend the agency and its spies, whom he'd come to respect and admire. In a speech marking the commemoration of the Revolutionary War Battle of Guilford Courthouse, he declared:

> *Intelligence is a demanding craft. I have not been in this business very long, but already I can tell you a few things. . . . I am impressed with the competence and dedication of the people in our intelligence community. They are professionals in the finest sense of the word. I might add that the spread of academic skills is remarkable. The CIA alone has enough PhDs to stock a university faculty with everything from historians to economists to mathematicians to aeronautical engineers. . . . Let me tell you another thing I have*

learned about the CIA. Its employees have very deeply ingrained pride and loyalty. . . .

Our intelligence people have suffered a vicious battering. Their families have been put under great pressure. Many of the charges have not been true. . . . I wish you could all have the chance to feel the spirit and pride I feel in the intelligence community. . . . I wish you could talk to some of our employees whose heads are high after a couple of years of enormous attack. They are as vigorously opposed to the mistakes of the past as our strongest critics, but they have retained a perspective, they know the need for strong intelligence, and they are prepared to withstand the attacks, if that is necessary, to work for a cause they believe in.

It was vintage Bush, corny but sincere and 180 degrees removed from the prevailing cynicism on Capitol Hill. The Yale-educated Yankee struck some at Langley as a Brahmin, to-the-manor-born, but he was genial and approachable, and hard to dislike. Bush was a great listener; he loved hearing stories about covert ops and dead drops and daring missions to tap into Soviet cables at the bottom of the sea. "I've never worked so hard in my life," Bush wrote to his friend Jack Mohler after three months at the agency. "I conclude this is the most interesting job I've ever had. That includes Congress, the UN, Peking, and the RNC. There are great people, fascinating subjects to get into, but just not enough time." For their part, the Langley workforce appreciated a director who listened, tried to understand their problems, and had their backs.

Bush was also blessed by a run of good luck: after Vietnam, Watergate, and the Family Jewels, his tenure as DCI was practically a walk in the park. There was a bureaucratic dispute over the Soviet "backfire bomber"—the CIA and the Air Force disagreed about its capabilities—and resistance to Bush's creation of "red teams" to challenge the CIA analysts' assessment of Soviet military capabilities. But there were mercifully few real crises. In June of 1976, the U.S. ambassador to Lebanon was assassinated; the CIA recommended that Americans leave the country and helped to execute an evacuation by land and sea. Yet Bush's real test as director came not against foreign enemies but against the CIA's domestic foes: Congress, the White House, and the press.

The new director received a crash course in public relations. "It is still almost impossible to have a speech containing positive things about CIA given prominent coverage," he complained. A friendly reporter explained, "George, your problem is that our profession thinks you are all lying bastards." Given recent history, the press had good reason to think so.

The CIA, unlike the FBI, was unaccustomed to pleading its case to the public. There was no agency equivalent of the hagiographic hit television show, *The F.B.I.*, starring Efrem Zimbalist Jr. "Intelligence has no constituency," explained Richard Kerr, an analyst who spent thirty-two years at the agency, rising to deputy director. "The bureau has always had a constituency, they've been very good at PR. The Marines have always been really good at it. The CIA has no people out there who say, 'Oh yeah, it's a great organization,' except the people who work there." Bush filled that void with a flurry of appearances, speeches, and interviews. By August 1976, he'd testified thirty times on Capitol Hill, met with thirty-three members of Congress or their staff, and made twenty-one public appearances. In a memo to President Ford, he reported:

> *Morale at CIA is improving. . . . Our recruitment is up. Our people are willing to serve abroad and take the risks involved. . . . Things are moving in the right direction. There are an infinite number of problems stemming, some from the excesses of the investigations and some from the abuses of the past—real and alleged. Somehow the problems, however, seem more manageable. Our organization is good, our product is sound though it can always be improved. Some of our assets have been diminished, but the CIA is intact, and functioning pretty darn well.*

Gradually, the CIA regained its footing under Bush's no-drama leadership. "He found us at a dark hour when all you heard were these 'rogue elephant' charges," said Charles Allen. "He defended the ramparts carefully, thoughtfully. He achieved a great reconciliation with Congress, by constantly courting its leaders, talking about the greatness of the Central Intelligence Agency—its people, its mission."

But the agency soon came under attack from an unexpected quarter. As Ford geared up to run for reelection in 1976, he faced a

determined opponent in an unlikely Democratic challenger: a pea-
nut farmer from Georgia named Jimmy Carter. Brilliant, pious, and
moralistic, Carter vowed to banish the illegality of the Watergate era;
he promised voters he would never lie and lambasted the CIA, accusing it of "plotting murder and other crimes." Carter also took a direct
shot at Bush, accusing Ford of using government posts as "dumping grounds for unsuccessful candidates, faithful political partisans."
Then, in June 1976, before he'd even clinched the Democratic nomination, Carter made an unprecedented request to Ford: He asked
that he be given classified CIA briefings on intelligence issues. Ford
agreed. It fell to George H. W. Bush to conduct them.

Carter's first meeting with Bush took place in Hershey, Pennsylvania, on July 5, 1976. While it was meant to be about the logistics
of future briefings, "the conversation ranged over virtually the entire
field of intelligence," recalled Richard Lehman, Bush's deputy for
national intelligence. They talked about everything from the future
of white-ruled Rhodesia (now Zimbabwe) to morale at the agency.
Subsequent meetings, continuing after the election, took place at his
home in Plains, Georgia. Unable to land a Gulfstream jet on the rudimentary air strip, Bush and his intelligence entourage had to be heli-
coptered in from an Air Force base. Carter was tireless and insatiable,
asking detailed questions about arms control talks with the Soviets,
Lebanon, Iraqi-Syria relations, strains between Egypt and Libya, the
Taiwan Strait, the Cuban presence in Angola, and developments in
Uganda.

But when it came to covert operations, Bush found Carter attentive but opaque, hard to fathom. As he wrote in his diary, "the
President-Elect never indicated that he thought these operations
were good or bad, that he was surprised or unsurprised." In fact,
Carter disapproved of what he learned about some of the CIA's clandestine relationships, including the fact that the agency was paying
Jordan's King Hussein millions of dollars every year.

As the sessions continued, Stuart Eizenstat, a young Carter aide
who would become his White House domestic policy adviser, noticed
that the president-elect seemed to be warming up to the director.
"They were good briefings," he recalled. "And Carter joked afterward
that he thought H.W. was trying to audition for a reappointment."

Keeping Bush on as CIA director would not have been a novel idea.

In fact, it would have been the norm: The last time an incoming president had appointed his own director was when Dwight Eisenhower picked Allen Dulles twenty-four years earlier. And Carter appeared to be considering the notion: Despite his attacks on the Bush-led CIA during the campaign, he surprised the press corps before his second briefing by hinting that Bush might continue as DCI. He'd "brought the CIA a good background as former United Nations Ambassador and U.S. representative to China," Carter noted.

Bush wanted to stay on, to finish the job he'd found so rewarding. So on November 19, 1976, the director asked the president-elect for a few minutes to discuss "personal matters." Bush met privately with Carter, Walter Mondale, soon to be vice president, and Bush's personal assistant Jennifer Fitzgerald. Bush proposed that by keeping him as director, Carter could avoid charges that he was politicizing the agency, the same charges Bush himself had faced when appointed by Ford. But his pitch was rambling and conflicted, arguing both sides of the issue—and he ended it by saying: "The president-elect should put his own man in the organization in whom he has confidence."

After listening to this monologue, Carter simply said, "Okay." He would appoint a new director. It was one of those moments when history could have taken a sharp turn, when a different decision by Carter would have profoundly changed the next fifty years of American politics and the course of world events. If Carter had kept him as CIA director, George H. W. Bush wouldn't have run for president in 1980; Ronald Reagan wouldn't have made him his running mate; and neither Bush nor his son George W. would have occupied the Oval Office. "If I had agreed to that," Carter reflected, "Bush never would have become president. His career would have gone off on a whole different track." But a second tour as director was not to be. Carter turned him down, and the hinge of history swung shut.

The name Theodore Sorensen never appears in Carter's exhaustive memoir, *Keeping Faith*; how he became his nominee to run the CIA is something of a mystery. Perhaps it was because Sorensen, Jack Kennedy's eloquent wordsmith, alter ego, and confidant, was, as Eizenstat recalled, "an early campaign supporter, adviser, and validator for suspicious New York liberals." (Sorensen was Carter's second choice; Thomas L. Hughes, who'd run the State Department's

Bureau of Intelligence and Research, turned him down.) Jack Watson, a young Atlanta lawyer who ran Carter's transition team, said Sorensen seemed at first glance to be a good fit for Carter's agenda. "The president's number one goal was bringing the CIA back into compliance with the law," Watson explained. "He wanted it not to be involved in assassinations, in underhanded regime change, in the surveillance and wiretapping of American citizens. On those subjects, Ted would have been a good reformer." The problem was, on second or third glance, Sorensen was completely ill-suited to run the CIA.

"No, that's not the job for me," Sorensen recalled telling Watson, when Carter's aide called to tell him that he was being considered for the post. But Sorensen was eager to land a big job in the Carter administration, and when the president-elect invited him to meet in Georgia, he agreed. At that session, after a perfunctory question about conflicts of interest, Carter asked Sorensen to be his CIA director. "I was surprised that he had not taken more time to review my background and suitability," Sorensen admitted later. But he said yes.

The trouble began on December 23, 1976, in a phone call to the nominee from Carter's closest adviser, Hamilton Jordan. Was it true that Sorensen had been a conscientious objector during the Korean War? It was true, and it was a problem. The biographical detail had been flagged by Jack Kennedy's former aide Kenneth O'Donnell, who warned the incoming administration that a conscientious objector would be in an untenable position dealing with military officers in the intelligence agencies: "They're not going to stand for it. . . . I don't want to see Carter get hurt by this."

O'Donnell was right. At Langley, the reaction to Sorensen's nomination was visceral: He wasn't just an outsider but a threat to the CIA's whole way of operating. And you didn't have to be a military officer to suspect that a pacifist might be the wrong person to send CIA paramilitary teams into harm's way. Sorensen himself later declared that "as a moralist" he would have been unable to authorize covert operations. But Sorensen resented O'Donnell's shot across his bow—he bitterly referred to his ex-colleague as "my own personal Inspector Javert." His belief that O'Donnell's warning was somehow disloyal spoke to Sorensen's egotism; in his mind this was about him, not the president-elect or the CIA.

The conscientious objector revelation was just the first in a barrage of attacks on Sorensen from other quarters. As JFK's most powerful adviser, he'd been arrogant dealing with members of Congress; years of resentment now came spilling out. He antagonized the powerful Democratic Senate majority leader Robert C. Byrd. Soon other charges swirled around the nominee: He didn't understand the Soviet menace; he couldn't keep secrets; he must have known about JFK's orders to kill Castro. "No one checked to see how he would be received by the Senate," recalled Eizenstat, Carter's campaign staffer and future domestic policy adviser. A brilliant, bespectacled Harvard Law School grad (and former high school All-America basketball star), Eizenstat, now seventy-six, blamed the inexperience of Carter's team. "It's sort of an obvious question. But nothing was obvious to this crowd, our crowd, at the beginning."

The failure to vet Sorensen's nomination was caused partly by disarray over who had the lead responsibility for appointments in the transition: Watson or Jordan. "No one doubted for a moment how smart or how capable Ted Sorensen was," said Watson, a fellow Harvard Law grad and ex-Marine. "When it came time to vet him thoroughly for this specific job, we failed. But the fact of the matter is that I don't see how a man who was opposed to covert operations could possibly be confirmed as director of the CIA. Nor should he be."

Sorensen had expected flak from "a few right-wing activists and conservative senators," but the groundswell of opposition to his nomination took him by surprise. For weeks, he rejected pressure from Carter and his aides to withdraw, demanding a hearing where he could be exonerated of all the charges against him. But finally, and bitterly, Sorensen bowed out, declaring: "I return to private life with a clear conscience." At a press conference afterward, with typical hubris, Sorensen made a prediction about his replacement: "I think it's clear from the statements by the mourners . . . that in their consideration of the next director, they could do worse—and they probably will."

On paper, Jimmy Carter, who was trained as a nuclear engineer, was possibly the most intelligent American president of the twentieth century. His next choice for CIA director, Stansfield Turner, was arguably even smarter: A classmate at the Naval Academy, Turner had outranked Carter in his graduating class, gone to Oxford as a Rhodes Scholar, and become a four-star admiral and Commander of Allied Forces Southern Europe. "You couldn't have a résumé of a naval or a military officer that was superior to that of Stan Turner," recalled Watson.

Yet when Carter invited the naval officer to his home in Plains to talk about the job, Turner was reluctant; he'd hoped to become Chief of Naval Operations (CNO). "I saw my career in the United States Navy flash before my eyes," he said. Carter made an impassioned argument about the importance of the position, and promised Turner he'd be not just CIA director but truly the Director of Central Intelligence—in charge of all fifteen agencies (authority that his predecessors had on paper, but almost never in practice). "Mr. President," Turner replied, "I appreciate that, but I'd really rather continue to serve for the military." At that, Carter turned to Mondale and said: "Fritz, I've just narrowed down the field of candidates for director of Central Intelligence from two to one. Please swear Stan in." Turner relented, replying: "Aye. Aye." After the Sorensen debacle, the decorated admiral sailed through his Senate hearings, and was confirmed by a unanimous vote.

Square-jawed and handsome, with a chestful of medals, Turner had won high marks for his leadership as president of the Naval War College, and he seemed well equipped to succeed as director. But Turner was entering treacherous waters he'd never navigated before. Carter would later write: "The DCI job must be depoliticized. Bush was too political. That is why I selected Stan Turner." But Carter completely misunderstood that it was Bush's political skills that had made him effective, both in restoring the CIA's reputation and rebuilding its morale. Turner was apolitical all right, but it made him tone-deaf to the nuances of leading the world's most powerful intelligence agency.

The new director stumbled right out of the gate by bringing in a coterie of naval officers as his principal deputies. "That just sent a message to the entire agency that this guy doesn't trust us," said Bob Gates, the future director. Word spread that Turner had wanted to be CNO, not CIA director. And there was a more fundamental, philosophical clash over Turner's belief in technology over human intelligence.

"The guts of the CIA at that time was human intelligence," recalled Charles Battaglia, a naval officer who became Turner's military aide. "Stan didn't think highly of it. He just thought that we had these other sources of intelligence, which were far more credible and timely." It was true that technology was revolutionizing spycraft. But in the eyes of the operatives, Turner valued toys over spies. Thomas Twetten, a case officer who rose to become Deputy Director of Operations (DDO), summed up the prevailing attitude: "Turner was one of these military engineers who came in intent on doing more technology—more sensors in the ocean like the Navy had. But the Navy doesn't do spying. He didn't understand anything about the spy business, and he didn't care about it."

Along with spit-and-polish military discipline, Turner had a strong moral streak that rivaled his boss Carter's. "He was a real, straight-shooting, Black Shoe Navy guy," recalled John Deutch, a Defense Department official and future CIA director. ("Black Shoe" distinguished Surface Officers from the "Brown Shoe" Aviators.) Turner got along well with the CIA analysts; he read almost all of their reports and made copious notes with his red pen in the margins. But he was squeamish about the darker code of the covert operatives. Unable to imagine committing treason himself, Turner disapproved of recruiting Soviet military officers to betray their country. "He was sort of an Eagle Scout," said Charlie Allen. "You know, 'We don't read other people's mail.' Well, yes, we do. We read other people's mail, and we turn them, and make them serve the interests of the United States."

A teetotaler and devout Christian Scientist, the new director was determined to root out sinners. "One of the things Turner came with was a mandate to find immoralities in the Directorate of Operations," recalled Twetten, a thirty-four-year CIA veteran. "So he had an aide that he sent overseas—who would go into stations and talk to everybody and try to find some dirt." Extramarital affairs, excessive drinking, all were considered firing offenses. Turner's aide found what he was looking for in Zaire: The married CIA station chief was enjoying a biweekly tryst with a Scandinavian flight attendant, at an agency safe house. The chief was brought home, and dismissed.

Turner's vice squad approach to management didn't win him many friends, which he would sorely need in the days ahead. Because Carter's new director now faced the problem that Bush had adroitly sidestepped: what to do about all those veteran CIA officers—more than a thousand—who'd outlived their usefulness. Bruce Riedel spent three decades as a top analyst at the agency, specializing in counterterrorism and the Middle East. "Because of Vietnam, the DO had grown enormously with people who were good at working in the military, in a war zone, doing things that normal DO officers never do," he explained. "The problem was you had this huge cohort of people, many of whom were a decade away from being able to retire, and you needed to get rid of them." Turner's aide Battaglia thought there was plenty of deadwood to be cut: "I tell you, I met some of them. People would be assigned overseas and hadn't recruited a person in twenty years, just enjoying the good life. When George Bush was up there, he didn't want to be bothered with it."

Turner plunged ahead; he launched a purge that rivaled the bloodletting carried out by Schlesinger. The new director called in officers without notice and fired them on the spot. According to Battaglia, he justified all this with a naval metaphor: "We used to call it a 'bottom blow.' You clean out the boilers by doing a bottom blow and get rid of all the slag that builds up." By the time he was finished, Turner had fired 820 CIA officers.

"Firing so many people right out of the starting blocks was a grave mistake," said Watson, who became Carter's White House cabinet secretary. "It couldn't have gotten Stan off to a worse start." To make matters worse, in an interview with *Newsweek*, Turner called his critics "crybabies." Battaglia said Turner tried but failed to cushion the impact of the pink slips. "Stan wanted to send a personal letter to each of them explaining why they were being cut back," he recalled. "He got talked out of it by the CIA lawyers, and that was a big mistake."

Once again, as with Schlesinger, there were rumors that the director feared reprisals. Charlie Allen, then a young analyst, recalled: "I came in the northwest entrance and there was a guard walking along with a big German shepherd. I said, 'Why do we have German shepherds?' And he said, 'Well, we think the director doesn't trust us. He's scared he might be assassinated.'" In his memoir, Turner said nothing about that, but he admitted: "In retrospect, I probably should not have effected the reduction of 820 positions at all. . . . [Bush] simply let it sit, which was far more politically astute than my action."

Meanwhile, the new director was getting little respect at the White House. His relationship with Carter was formal and stiff. "There was no warmth between them," recalled Eizenstat, the domestic policy adviser. "It was not, 'He's my buddy from the Naval Academy.'" At meetings Turner bored Carter, and seemed more comfortable saluting the president than telling him hard truths. Leslie Gelb, then a State Department official, renowned for speaking his mind, recalled watching Turner at National Security Council meetings: "I saw him there, sitting silently throughout, and waiting for Carter to ask him something, which he would answer all too briefly. If he spoke twenty-five words, I was surprised."

There was friction between Turner and Carter's defense secretary, Harold Brown, a brilliant technocrat. Turner might have been a Rhodes Scholar, but he was no intellectual match for Brown, whose brain power was intimidating. "He absolutely could not get along with Brown," said Gelb. "There were fifty to a hundred IQ points between them." But Turner's most formidable rival was Carter's pugnacious national security adviser, Zbigniew Brzezinski.

A trusted Carter confidant, Brzezinski, a Polish immigrant and former Columbia Law professor, modeled himself after Kissinger: He was determined to control the flow of intelligence to the president. Like Kissinger, he would read the PDB and summarize it for Carter as he saw fit. Brzezinski was also a skilled bureaucratic infighter who reveled in finding demeaning ways to put Turner in his place.

On his first visit to the White House, the new director noticed an entry on the president's calendar at 6:30 every morning; it was marked "intelligence briefing." Turner hadn't been invited—and called Brzezinski to complain. "If there's an intelligence briefing," he insisted, "I should be doing it." Brzezinski replied, "Stan, you're absolutely right." The next morning the calendar entry had been changed to read: "national security briefing."

In 1977, as Turner struggled to get his footing as director, the CIA was rocked by the return of an old scandal: the 1970 coup against Chile's Salvador Allende. In testimony before the Senate in 1973, Richard Helms's denial of CIA involvement had raised eyebrows— and caused Bill Colby to refer the matter to the attorney general.

Now Jimmy Carter's Justice Department was poised to prosecute Helms, who was serving as American ambassador to Iran.

Visiting Helms in Tehran, an American friend told him: "You'd better get yourself a good lawyer." Helms was appalled by the thought. When Burton Gerber, who was serving in Tehran's CIA station at the time, brought Helms a telegram containing a court summons, something in the ambassador snapped. "You son of a bitch!" he screamed. "Why did you bring this thing over?"

For making two false statements to Congress, Helms faced a potential prison sentence of ten years. He was incredulous. What kind of catch-22 was this? Helms had been ordered by the president never to discuss the Track II covert operation with *anyone*— not the State Department, the Defense Department, or even the U.S. ambassador to Chile. Now he was being asked about it by Congress. Answering truthfully—even in secret session—would have violated not only his oath as a CIA officer but also a presidential directive. Moreover, the questioner, Senator Stuart Symington, already knew the answer; he'd been briefed on CIA activity in Chile as a member of the Senate Armed Services Committee. "I maintain that it was a setup," said Gerber.

But Helms's attorneys persuaded him that no jury would understand the nuances of a CIA director's duty, or the importance of his oath to protect the agency's secrets. The only sensible thing was to plead nolo contendere to two misdemeanor counts. On November 4, 1977, Helms appeared in the Washington, D.C., courtroom of the Honorable Barrington Parker, and received a tongue-lashing. "You stand before this court in disgrace and shame," the judge berated him. "Public officials at every level, whatever their position, like any other person, must respect and honor the Constitution and the laws of the United States." For one count of lying to Congress, he slapped Helms with a $2,000 fine and a two-year sentence, suspended.

On the courthouse steps immediately afterward, Helms's lawyer, Edward Bennett Williams, told a throng of reporters: "Helms will wear this conviction like a badge of honor." Keeping a previous commitment, Helms went to a nearby country club for lunch. Waiting for him was a crowd of several hundred, many of them CIA colleagues. When the beleaguered ex-director walked in, they stood and applauded. Someone produced two wicker baskets and passed them around; within ten minutes, Helms's entire fine was raised.

As Bob Gates, the future director, saw it, the old spymaster was trapped between two eras of intelligence. "Helms was playing by the old rules and got caught by the new rules," he said. "Directors in those days rarely testified. And there was a kind of an unwritten pact that if you ask me a question about a covert action, I may just deny it because that's what we do. And that's what trapped Helms. That's why he wore the plea bargain as a badge of honor." A few years later, Helms's dilemma would become a subject for scholars. A course at Harvard's John F. Kennedy School was titled "The Two Oaths of Richard Helms."

Jimmy Carter had an ambitious foreign policy agenda, and he needed timely intelligence to implement it: the return of the Panama Canal; arms control with the Soviets; promotion of human rights; normalization of relations with China; and the historic Middle East peace accord between Israel's Menachem Begin and Egypt's Anwar Sadat. These were thorny, complex challenges, but Carter's last two years would be dominated by another crisis: the militant fundamentalist revolution that toppled the Shah of Iran, and the seizure of American hostages.

Support for Mohammed Reza Pahlavi had been a bedrock of American foreign policy since 1953, when a CIA-led coup overthrew the government of Mohammed Mossadegh, a nationalist who threatened American and British oil interests, and restored the young Shah to the Peacock Throne. For decades the U.S. had showered his authoritarian regime with sales of advanced weapons and billions of dollars in foreign aid and helped train his brutal secret police force, SAVAK. In return, the U.S. and its allies were guaranteed a steady supply of oil and a staunch ally in the volatile Middle East. As with Vietnam a decade earlier, it was an article of faith among the U.S. foreign policy establishment that if Iran fell to communism, so would the entire region—with dire consequences for U.S. interests.

Flush with oil money and American largesse, the Shah turned from constitutional monarch to authoritarian ruler. Cultured and silver-tongued, he dazzled his American friends. "He was glamorous," recalled Carter's aide Eizenstat. (As was his elegant wife, the empress, or *Shahbanou*.) "He spoke beautiful English and French and was cultured. He was not a one-dimensional dictator." The Shah launched a program to modernize Iran and lift it out of poverty, building schools and hospitals, giving women the vote, and breaking up private estates.

But what made the Shah attractive to Westerners was a liability at home. "He was trying to reform too quickly," said Eizenstat. "He did land reform, basically prohibited veils, empowered women in all sorts of ways, tried to reform education. It was a very conservative society, and he was imposing Western-style reforms on it." The forced modernization brought disparate groups together in opposition to him: the religious clerics, landowners, and the merchant class, who were subject to heavy fines. Telltale cracks in the foundation of the Shah's splendid edifice were spreading, becoming the fault lines of a massive upheaval to come. Almost anyone who was speaking to the opposition, or the religious clerics, would have found these fissures impossible to miss.

But no one in the American foreign policy establishment, least of all the CIA, saw them.

"It was one of those moments when no one really knows what the hell is going on," wrote author George Packer. He was referring to the ignorance of American officials before the fall of Ngo Dinh Diem in South Vietnam, but he could have been describing American decision-making before the Shah's demise. "It's comforting to believe that a group of powerful people sit around a table . . . and decide on a course of action—which then unfolds according to their design," Packer wrote. "More often, we can't say why events of the most momentous consequence even happen. The people in charge make decisions . . . in sheer ignorance compounded by wishful thinking— on anything but solid information." Those words, true enough about the tragedy in Vietnam, apply equally to the catastrophe that loomed before the Carter White House in late 1977 and early 1978.

When Carter came into office, foreign policy experts agreed unanimously that nothing threatened the stability of the Shah. Bipartisan American support for the autocrat was so automatic that Carter wasn't asked, and didn't say a word, about Iran during the campaign. Nor did anyone worry when, during a state visit to Washington in November 1977, the Shah was greeted by massive protests on the capital's Ellipse, by the Washington Monument, organized by the Iran Student Movement. When tear gas fired by riot police wafted over during a ceremony on the White House South Lawn, causing both Carter and the Shah to cough and wipe their eyes, the president shrugged it off. "One thing I can say about the Shah," Carter joked at a dinner that night. "He knows how to draw a crowd." At the end of his first year, Carter paid a visit to Tehran and toasted his excellency the *Shahanshah* (King of Kings), pronouncing him "an island of stability in one of the more troubled areas of the world."

But opposition to the Shah was coalescing around a charismatic, fundamentalist religious figure. Since 1963, Ruhollah Khomeini, a grand ayatollah, or high-ranking Shiite cleric, had preached fiery jeremiads against Iran's autocratic monarch, calling for the establishment of an Islamic Republic and touching off widespread protests. Exiled to Iraq the following year, Khomeini spent the next decade and a half inveighing against the Shah's corruption and his ties to Israel and the United States.

A week after a visit by Carter to Tehran in 1978, a government-controlled newspaper, *Ettela'at*, accused the ayatollah of being a foreign agent, setting off a spiral of demonstrations across the country. In a move that would backfire disastrously, the Shah persuaded Saddam Hussein to expel the Ayatollah from Iraq; Khomeini decamped for a town outside Paris, France. It put him within easy reach of the world's media and gave him a stage from which to preach his revolutionary gospel.

All of this went almost unnoticed by the CIA. "It was one of the most massive intelligence failures in history," said Stuart Eizenstat. Jack Watson, who was Carter's White House chief of staff during his final year, could hardly believe how little the CIA knew about the unfolding disaster. "The abysmal failure of our intelligence community with respect to Iran is hard to imagine and impossible to justify," he said. "We didn't have a clue," said Leslie Gelb, who was then a Defense Department official. "I was reading reports every week. We didn't have any inkling if a coup was about to occur, or whether the Shah was in any serious trouble. Not one word. This was horrific. And we had a shitload of guys there." There were thousands of Americans in Iran, and the CIA had an active station there.

There were many reasons for the CIA's Iran debacle: incompetence, wishful thinking, a failure of imagination, deception by the Shah himself—and secret deals that rendered the agency blind. Iran was virtually the only major country in which the CIA had no contact with the government's opposition. How could that be? Because the Shah wanted it that way. Everyone—including, ironically, the ambassador to Tehran, Richard Helms—was willing to wear blinders to keep the Shah happy. Even more than his oil, the U.S. needed access to listening sites on Iran's border with the Soviet Union. Helms's old friend Burton Gerber, then an operative stationed in Tehran, recalled: "Everyone in the leadership gang—that includes Helms and my station chief—was very nervous about doing anything that could upset the Iranians because of the importance of the sites."

An agreement had been struck between Henry Kissinger and the Shah before Carter took office. "The Shah was really pissed off that the State Department was in touch with some dissidents inside Iran," explained Bob Gates. "And so the Shah confronted Kissinger and Nixon. And Kissinger cut the deal." In return for access to its listening sites along the Soviet border, the U.S. would stop talking to the Shah's opponents. Instead, the Americans would rely on intelligence provided by SAVAK. "We put all our eggs in the Shah basket in ways that were unseemly," said Charlie Allen. "I met people from SAVAK. It was a cruel, despotic group of torturers. It was like an inquisition." Robert Jervis did a postmortem study for the agency on the Iranian fiasco. In *Why Intelligence Fails*, he concluded that the CIA in the end learned nothing from SAVAK about the Shah's opposition.

Blinded to developments, the CIA also did not understand the region. The agency's Iran desk consisted of two people. "They consistently said through the spring and summer of 1978, this'll fade away, this'll go away," recalled Bruce Riedel, the Middle East analyst. The "Weekly Summary" of November 1977 reported: "There is no serious domestic threat or political opposition to the Shah's rule. At 58 he is in good health and protected by an elaborate security apparatus: He would seem to have an excellent chance to rule into the next decade." Every one of those assertions was false. In fact, opposition to the Shah was growing and deadly serious; he was gravely ill (though he kept this a secret from almost everyone); and he lacked the resolve to use SAVAK or his military to crack down on his opponents. Another CIA assessment in August 1978, "Iran After the Shah," concluded: "Iran is not in a revolutionary or even a 'pre-revolutionary' situation."

Part of the problem, said Bob Gates, who was then an analyst, was a mind-set that hardened over time. "If you've got the same people working on the problem for so long," he pointed out, "they may be the ones least likely to see a discontinuity coming." The CIA's top Iran expert was a highly respected analyst named Ernie Oney. "In an era when the agency did not do a lot of long, in-depth papers, Ernie was one of the few who did," said Riedel. "He captured all the complexities and contradictions of Iranian society in the mid-1970s." But Oney's view of the Shah was static. "He had been there so long that he just couldn't imagine the Shah's collapse. . . . He just thought, the Shah will tough it out."

There was something else that neither Oney nor anyone else on the Iran desk could imagine. "He could not conceive of a world in which there was an Islamic republic," said Riedel, who joined a CIA Iran task force that was formed during the crisis. "He just thought it was impossible. And when the new team came in, we immediately said, yeah, not only can it happen, it's going to happen. Because they're the only part of the opposition that has real mass support and armed support."

During the Middle East peace talks at Camp David, Carter was given detailed psychological profiles of Israeli prime minister Menachem Begin and Egyptian president Anwar Sadat. But the CIA never did a profile of the Shah, who, unbeknownst to the Americans, was suffering from cancer. "Here's our principal ally, getting hundreds of billions of dollars in military assistance, F-14 fighter jets, and everything else—and we don't know the guy is getting secret treatments?" asked Stuart Eizenstat, still incredulous almost forty years later. Instead, the agency portrayed the Shah as a picture of health, waterskiing and hitting tennis balls at his retreat on the Caspian Sea.

In the summer of 1978, William Sullivan, who'd replaced Helms as the U.S. ambassador to Iran, assured the Carter White House that the worst of the unrest was over. In fact, it was just beginning. On September 8, violence flared in Tehran after the Shah declared martial law; his troops opened fire on a demonstration, killing scores of protesters. On November 6, the Shah announced that he was forming a military government, and addressed the nation, promising democratization as soon as order was restored.

After an emergency meeting with senior aides, National Security Adviser Zbigniew Brzezinski noted, "I was really appalled by how inept and vague Stan Turner's comments on the crisis in Iran were. This reinforces my strong view that we need much better political intelligence." Brzezinski urged Carter to reprimand Turner and demand that he fix the problem. Carter did so, but included his national security adviser and secretary of state on the memo:

> To Cy, Zbig, Stan—
> I am not satisfied with the quality of our political intelligence. Assess our assets, and as soon as possible, give me a report concerning our abilities in the most important areas of the world. Make a joint recommendation on what we should do to improve your ability to give me political information and advice.

But of course it was too late.

On November 9, Ambassador Sullivan did a complete about-face; he sent an urgent cable to the White House, titled "Thinking the Unthinkable." Conditions were so dire, he warned, that the Shah might be forced to resign. Carter was furious that he'd been blindsided. As Iran's security deteriorated and the Shah vacillated, the administration gave him mixed signals. In meetings with the Shah, Sullivan, backed up by Cyrus Vance, urged him to implement democratization; Brzezinski, on the other hand, kept calling the Shah directly and telling him to use military force to stem the unrest. At the White House, Carter and his advisers debated whether to give the Iranian military a signal to mount a coup. Brzezinski was for it, but Carter concluded that Iranian armed forces were hopelessly divided; a repeat of the successful CIA-led coup that installed the Shah in 1953 was not in the cards.

On January 16, 1979, with his country in open revolt, vowing that "a sovereign may not save his throne by shedding his countrymen's blood," the Shah fled Iran in humiliation. His handpicked prime minister would leave for France after just thirty-seven days in power. The stage was set for the triumphant return of the Ayatollah Khomeini, and a bloody purge of everyone associated with the ancien régime.

The Shah took refuge at first in Egypt, then spent the next month bouncing from there to Morocco to Panama to the Bahamas, desperately seeking permission to enter the U.S. Now another intelligence lapse became evident: The Carter White House learned—not from the CIA but from David Rockefeller, the American banker and the Shah's close friend—that the monarch was dying of cancer. The diagnosis had been kept secret even from his wife and family. He'd kept his condition under control for a while with medication, but it had progressed into an aggressive form of lymphoma. To survive, the Shah needed state-of-the-art care from a top-notch medical facility in the United States. Or did he?

Everyone knew that allowing the Shah to set foot on American soil risked touching off an explosion in Iran. But Kissinger, the former secretary of state, furiously lobbied Carter not to turn the Shah away, threatening to withdraw his support for SALT II, an arms control treaty with the Soviets. Carter was wary—and prescient. "What do you propose to do," he asked, "if they take our diplomats hostage?" No one had an answer. Yet Carter ultimately agreed to let the Shah enter the U.S. The ailing monarch was taken to New York Hospital-Cornell Medical Center in Manhattan. Even this fateful decision was based on yet another intelligence failure: Carter and his aides would later learn that the Shah's treatment could have been performed in Mexico, with American surgeons flown in.

On Valentine's Day 1979, CIA director Turner was awakened at 5:30 a.m. by a phone call from the agency duty officer: The American embassy in Tehran had been overrun by Iranian students, he was told, and Langley had lost all communication with it. Within hours, the Ayatollah's government had intervened and ordered the students to leave. "We got the false impression—it was accurate at the time—that the government was going to support the sovereignty of our embassy," recalled Eizenstat. "But the students during the first seizure were communists. And when the second one happened, the fatal one, they were fundamentalists."

The seeds of that second seizure were sown months later when, on November 1, Brzezinski met with officials of Iran's new Islamic government in Algiers. As Bob Gates, who accompanied him, recalled it: "He went through his litany of, 'we'll recognize your government, we'll sell you all the weapons that we contracted to sell the Shah, we want to have a good relationship with you because we have a common enemy to your north, the Soviet Union.' And they said, 'Give us the Shah.' Brzezinski finally stood up and said, 'For us to give you the Shah would be incompatible with our national honor.' And that ended the meeting."

The crisis that would consume Carter's presidency began three days later. Director Turner received a call almost exactly like the one on Valentine's Day, and thought he was dreaming: The American embassy had been overrun—again. Sixty-six Americans had been taken captive.

Carter's advisers, along with Turner, met that Monday morning. The CIA had almost no information about the "students" who were holding the Americans. All Turner knew was that they were hard-line Islamic militants—and this time the Ayatollah gave his blessing to their siege. "There were small indications that this group in November was a different ilk, but our intelligence team inside Iraq was very limited," Turner wrote later. "After all, the shah was our trusted friend and you are careful about spying on friends, so before his fall we had few trusted assets in place—and not much chance of acquiring them once his regime crumbled." In the end, Turner admitted with stunning frankness: "We were just plain asleep."

Nearly forty years later, Stuart Eizenstat, seventy-six, was still baffled by the CIA's botched response to the crisis, beginning with the Ayatollah's move to a village outside Paris: "Why didn't we bug the villa, or get the French intelligence to bug the villa? I mean, that's just unimaginable. Why didn't we say to the French, don't let him come back? Why didn't we give clearer direction to the Shah to use military force against the demonstrators who were advancing? And then not telling the president he could get treated just as effectively in Mexico with Houston doctors? We can fly them in." It was a stunning succession of missed opportunities to head off disaster.

Amid this intelligence nightmare, there was one bright spot: Several hostages had managed to escape and hole up in the Canadian embassy. Turner approved an ingenious and outlandish covert operation to rescue them. Posing as the advance man for a Hollywood production company, scouting locations for a film called *Argo*, CIA officer Tony Mendez flew into Tehran and met secretly with the hostages-in-hiding. Disguised as members of his production team, they finagled their way through the Tehran airport—equipped with bogus passports and bios—and escaped on a flight to Switzerland. One reason for the operation's success was that it was planned and executed by the CIA, without the intricacy of a joint military operation. Alas, that would not be true of the hostage rescue mission to come, named Operation EAGLE CLAW.

The hostage siege would last 444 days, an excruciating period marked by frantic, round-the-clock diplomatic efforts to free the captives—and a barrage of media coverage. Blindfolded Americans paraded before television cameras. ABC News created a nightly program, *The Iran Crisis: America Held Hostage.* In the debate over diplomatic and military options, Turner bounced back and forth between the hawkish Brzezinski and the dovish Vance, who advocated diplomacy at all costs. White House aide Eizenstat argued for a naval blockade of Kharg Island, from which sixty percent of Iran's oil was shipped. Carter refused, saying: "We'll get the hostages back, but they'll come back in coffins." The president, who vowed that he wouldn't leave the White House until the crisis was resolved, would risk no harm to the hostages.

But Carter's patience wasn't infinite. Remarkably, when the president and his inner circle began to consider military action, they didn't bother to inform Turner. The CIA director's first inkling that there was a rescue plan in the works came when he noticed military aides heading to Brzezinski's office after NSC meetings. When Turner got back to Langley, he called Carter's national security adviser to complain. "I was then admitted to this tight-knit rescue-planning group and met with it regularly thereafter."

The challenge of extracting hostages from a busy city like Tehran was herculean, and it fell to Turner and the CIA to come up with a plan. In an effort to exploit U.S. racial tensions, the militants voluntarily released thirteen African American hostages—but the remaining fifty-three were in two locations: fifty in the embassy, and three in the Iranian Ministry of Foreign Affairs. Moreover, rescue helicopters would have to travel hundreds of miles from an aircraft carrier outside the Strait of Hormuz. Because of the Israelis' successful 1976 rescue mission at Entebbe, where commandos freed 102 hostages held captive by Palestinian terrorists at an airport in Uganda, they were asked their opinion. They said the American plan wouldn't work—the U.S. embassy was in the middle of a city, not an isolated airport.

The military planners, and Turner, persisted. Because there was as yet no Special Operations Command (this elite, specialized military unit was created afterward), the mission would involve elements of the Army, Navy, Air Force, Marines, and CIA—with all of the potential for mix-ups, rivalries, and petty jealousies. CIA operatives scouted the locations in Tehran, and reported back that a rescue and evacuation were feasible. The military insisted on sending its own undercover team, which almost got caught. Oddly, no one at the CIA bothered to consult Helms, the former ambassador, who knew every square inch of the embassy: "Nobody, not even the assistant pencil sharpener in the State Department or in the White House, called me to ask about that situation," he groused to his son Dennis.

The initial plan called for landing heavy transport planes at a staging area, a remote site in the Iranian desert; from there, five helicopters would ferry rescuers, Army Rangers, to Tehran. "I felt that it was a well-planned rescue operation," Jimmy Carter, the former president, told me. He'd prepared for every eventuality. "As a safety precaution, the Army chief of staff and my defense secretary said, 'let's send one extra helicopter along.' And I said, 'No, why don't we send eight?'" So on Carter's orders eight helicopters were sent, three more than necessary.

Still, Bruce Riedel, of the CIA's Iran Task Force, wasn't sanguine about the desert staging plan. "We were asked very, very late in the game: If you landed an airplane at this location, what are the chances you'd be found? And all you had to do was look at the map and see there was a major highway at that location. You will be found." But Carter and CIA director Turner were satisfied. "It was one of the most difficult decisions I ever made," Turner said. "It meant putting lives on the line and one doesn't do that casually. But I looked at it and said, 'We don't have many choices here, we've got to take this risk.'" Among Carter's top advisers, only Secretary of State Cyrus Vance opposed the mission; afterward he would resign. "What I remember most," recalled Turner, "is telling the president just before this took place that I knew this was a very difficult decision for him, but I felt like we were going to make it."

The operation was launched on April 24, 1980. At the desert

landing site, the first C-130 encountered a pickup truck coming down the road, just as Riedel had predicted; the Rangers disabled it with an antitank missile, sending the passengers fleeing on foot. The rescue team then encountered a bus full of Iranians on their way to a religious pilgrimage. They were taken into captivity and released later.

Then the real trouble began. The pilot of the first helicopter, alarmed by a warning light on a gauge, returned to the carrier. Sandstorms erupted, obscuring visibility, and a second chopper underwent navigation and instrument failure and also turned back. Almost incredibly, a third chopper experienced a partial hydraulic failure. At that point the commander on the ground asked Defense Secretary Harold Brown for permission to abort the operation, which he granted. Then things got even worse. During refueling, one helicopter crashed into a C-130, igniting a blaze that lit up the desert sky. Eight crew members died, and five other team members were injured. Turner now had to decide whether to send another helicopter team back—to destroy the C-130 and its cargo of classified documents. He decided not to risk it.

The rescue mission was an unmitigated failure. And the Ayatollah Khomeini's humiliation of America wasn't yet complete. Despite Carter's exhaustive negotiations with Iranian officials, the American hostages wouldn't be released until January 20, 1981. They were flown to freedom minutes after Ronald Reagan took the oath of office.

Almost four decades later, at his presidential library in Atlanta, Carter told me he didn't regret approving the mission. "Obviously, I regret we didn't send nine helicopters instead of eight," he said, "and I regret that the helicopters went down in unanticipated accidents, but at that moment it was the right thing to do." We spoke just a year after the successful CIA-led raid that killed Osama bin Laden; Carter suggested it was *his* experience that led Obama to add two more helicopters to the raiding party—which made all the difference when the first crashed into the compound's wall; a replacement for the crashed chopper swooped in from its position nearby. "I've just surmised that they probably doubled up on the margin of error so that they wouldn't make the same mistake I made," he said.

When I spoke with Stansfield Turner, he was eighty-nine, suffering from dementia, and struggled to communicate. He could remember little about his time as CIA director. But he was crystal clear about the moment he learned that the Iranian rescue mission had failed. "I was devastated," he said softly. He stared into the distance, his bright eyes clouded by the terrible memory. "I just didn't know what to do."

Did it matter in the end that the CIA couldn't predict the Iranian revolution? Would accurate intelligence have made a difference to the course of history? "I can't tell you sitting here that if we'd had perfect intelligence, the Shah would still be on the throne or his son would be on the throne, or that there wouldn't have been an Islamic Revolution," said Stuart Eizenstat. "I do think there was a *chance* there wouldn't have been."

A chance, perhaps. But that assumes that men in suits around a table in the White House Situation Room have real influence over the course of fast-moving events—in this case, a fundamentalist revolution that had been building over decades. If the CIA failed to forecast that revolution, Carter's advisers weren't any clearer about what to do about it. What is clear, in Eizenstat's view, is that without accurate information, policymakers have no chance: "Good intelligence doesn't assure a good policy decision, let alone a policy outcome. But bad intelligence inevitably leads to failure."

It was hardly the first, nor the last foreign policy disaster born of American ignorance. The best minds of the JFK and LBJ eras were as deluded about South Vietnam as Carter's advisers were about Iran. The architects of the 2003 American invasion of Iraq were equally misinformed. Indeed, intelligence failures such as the Iranian revolution and the botched estimate of Iraq's WMDs may in the end be impossible to prevent. "They are not rare events," wrote Robert Jervis, who conducted official postmortems of both the Iranian and Iraqi disasters. And "there is no reason to believe that they have become less frequent over time."

Eizenstat cautioned against blaming the Iranian fiasco on Turner—or Carter: "This is an endemic problem of American intelligence. It is not some isolated incident, where we knew what was happening, and then suddenly intelligence went to hell. It was a continuum of not knowing anything about a key leader, our key ally, and a key country."

The Iran debacle is also a warning to presidents who overlook an ally's unsavory behavior. In this respect, some at the CIA see a parallel between the Shah of Iran and Saudi Arabia's Crown Prince Mohammed bin Salman (MBS), whose brutal authoritarianism is well known, and whose henchmen rival SAVAK in their murderous conduct.

In January 1981, a new administration swept into office, promising that it knew better than to be humiliated by a bunch of Iranian mullahs. Then Americans began to be snatched off the streets of Beirut by Iranian-backed kidnappers—and Ronald Reagan demanded that something be done. In one of the great ironies of history, his CIA director devised a plan to free them: The U.S. would sell arms to the same Iranian mullahs. Another hostage crisis was born, one that would almost end the Reagan presidency. The mastermind of the scheme was William Casey.

CHAPTER FOUR

"That's the most frightening thing
I've ever heard."

William Casey and Ronald Reagan

At 716 Jackson Place, a townhouse near the White House, Ronald Reagan was huddling with his advisers, planning his new cabinet. It was late November 1980, and the president-elect was wrestling with a thorny decision: what to do with William Casey. The eccentric former chairman of the Securities and Exchange Commission had been brought in to manage Reagan's campaign when it was flat broke, and rallied wealthy contributors to his cause. Casey had wanted to become secretary of state. But "Mumbles," as he was known, was no one's idea of America's top diplomat—least of all, Nancy Reagan's; not only was Casey's speech unintelligible but he was perpetually disheveled and his table manners were abysmal. Alexander Haig Jr., the charismatic, blue-eyed former NATO commander, looked much more the part. But if Casey couldn't be secretary of state, what about CIA director?

Reagan's inner circle, the so-called California Mafia, was divided. Michael Deaver, a close aide, considered Casey unqualified, a "political hack." Stuart Spencer, the political strategist and confidant to both Reagans, thought he was devious, untrustworthy. But Edwin Meese, the president-elect's counselor, believed the Wall Street mogul shared Reagan's fierce anticommunism and his experience in the wartime OSS made him a natural spymaster. That was fine with Reagan, who called Casey in New York and offered him the job. Casey politely stalled, saying that he wanted to talk it over with his wife, Sophia.

A week later, with a promise of cabinet rank and direct access to the president, Casey called Reagan back and accepted his offer. He would become the most powerful CIA director since Allen Dulles, fighting covert wars against the Soviets in every corner of the globe. But Casey's determination to run the CIA like an off-the-books enterprise, and his flouting of rules, would trigger the most serious political crisis since Watergate.

The new director was sixty-seven, with oversized, square-rimmed glasses, and just a wisp of gray hair. When Casey walked, recalled Bob Gates, who'd become his executive assistant, he resembled "a committee of bones and muscles all trying to amble more or less in the right direction." Yet Casey was always in motion, restless and impatient. Gates remembered his first visit to the director's office three weeks into his tenure. Suddenly the door to Casey's office flew open. "Two vodka martinis!" the director barked, to no one in particular, before slamming the door shut. Befuddled aides, accustomed to running a dry establishment under Turner, scrambled to find liquor for Casey and his guest, the former director John McCone. It was a telling glimpse of the director's modus operandi. "He would demand something be done immediately which the agency no longer had the capability to do," Gates recalled. "He would fire instructions at the closest person regardless of whether that person had anything to do with the matter at hand. And he would not wait around even for confirmation that anyone heard him."

Casey barely slept and regarded meals as pit stops, to be raced through. "It was very hard to understand what he said, particularly when he was eating a sandwich," recalled Bruce Riedel, a young analyst who'd later become one of the agency's top Middle East experts. Instead of reaching for a napkin, Casey "would grab his tie and wipe his lips with it." One CIA wag noted that Casey was the first director who didn't need a voice scrambler to encrypt his phone conversations. Tom Twetten, a longtime case officer and Russia hand, recalled the time he was summoned to the director's office early in the morning: "He was eating eggs—and he said, '*Mmmph.*' And I said, 'I'm sorry, sir, I didn't quite catch that.' And he said, '*Mmmph.*' After a couple more bites, I said, 'Yes sir, I'm honored and I will do my best.' Because luckily someone had told me beforehand that he was appointing me chief of the Near East Division."

To Casey, the CIA directorship was a chance to revive his glory days as a young OSS officer. Under "Wild Bill" Donovan, he and Helms—and a band of "bankers and tycoons, safecrackers and forgers, printers and playwrights, athletes and circus men," as Casey described them—had helped save the world from Hitler. The new director hung an oil portrait of Donovan on his office wall, where no one could miss it. In Casey's view, the struggle against the Soviet Union was a continuation of his covert campaign against the Nazis; the enemy had changed, but not the rules or the stakes. "Casey's approach to the job was very much shaped by his experience in the OSS," said Gates. "World War II was no-holds-barred. This is life and death. We will do whatever it takes to win. That was his attitude toward the Soviet Union."

Because there were no rules, in Casey's view, congressional oversight was an annoyance. "He just couldn't understand the power that Congress had acquired in the interval to second-guess him," said Gates. "As far as he was concerned, they were just insects biting at his ankles and trying to keep him from doing what needed to be done." Bruce Riedel explained: "His basic view on law and regulation was, that's what you hire lawyers for to get around. And if you read his books on how to cheat on your income taxes, you could see that this had been his career." Casey wrote about evading New Deal regulations and exploiting tax loopholes. (He was also the author of *The Secret War Against Hitler*, about his experience in the OSS.) "He was a little short on morals," explained Twetten. "Hell, he was a New York City businessman."

Casey's view of the Soviets meshed perfectly with Reagan's philosophy, which was: "We win, they lose." Stuart Spencer, Reagan's campaign manager, was struck by how deeply he believed in a day of reckoning with the Soviet Union. "I turned to him early on and said, 'Why do you want to be president?' And he gave me a detailed plan on the nuclear buildup and how he was going to change it. And I'm sitting there, and I thought, 'This guy believes in Armageddon.'" Averting Armageddon, in Reagan's view, meant pressuring the Soviets on every front: economically, militarily, diplomatically—and through covert warfare. "Reagan said to me, 'I'll break the sons of bitches,'" said Spencer. "He knew where he was going, he knew how he could get there, and he didn't need a bunch of stuffed shirts in the middle."

Under Casey, the CIA would be totally dedicated to Reagan's agenda. Traditionally, the CIA director dealt with the outside world—tending to the president, Congress, and the intelligence community—while the deputy director managed the internal affairs of the agency. "That wasn't what Casey wanted to do at all," said Admiral Bobby Ray Inman, who came over from the National Security Agency (NSA) to become Casey's deputy director. "He wanted to run everything related to covert operations and analysis and he didn't want to deal with any of the rest of it. He didn't want to deal with Congress if he could possibly avoid it." That would be Inman's job, as long as he lasted.

In his first seventeen months Casey didn't attend a single National Security Council meeting; he preferred to meet one-on-one with Reagan in the Oval Office. He was one of a few cabinet officials who didn't have to go through James A. Baker III, Reagan's powerful White House chief of staff; but afterward, Mike Deaver, the deputy chief and Reagan confidant, would drop by and ask the president what they had talked about. Contrary to conventional wisdom, Casey and Reagan weren't close. "He never had the influence with Reagan that he liked to convey and that some others thought," said Gates. "I always thought it was one of the dirty little secrets." The CIA director chafed at being excluded by Nancy from state dinners, and he was frustrated by Reagan's detachment and indifference to detail. Yet Casey wrote the president letters about anything that was on his mind. "They ranged from who he should appoint as ambassador to the Vatican," said Inman, "to things going on in the intelligence community."

"Casey arrived appalled at what had happened under Carter," said Twetten, "and immediately found a friendly Congress to help him put it back together." Casey's first priority was to revitalize the clandestine service, which he believed had been gutted under Schlesinger and Turner. With Reagan's help, he squeezed hundreds of millions of dollars out of Congress for covert programs, and used some of those funds to hire nearly two thousand operatives.

Casey chose an unlikely person as his Deputy Director of Operations (DDO): a streetwise entrepreneur named Max Hugel. Hugel (pronounced *Who*-gull) had made a fortune selling sewing machines and investing on Wall Street; as a businessman, he was even less

scrupulous than Casey. Five-foot-two inches tall, sporting a toupee, a shirt open to his navel, and gold chains, Hugel cut a ridiculous figure amid the gray suits of Langley. He knew nothing about
spycraft. This didn't faze Casey; he thought Hugel was exactly the
kind of unorthodox, idiosyncratic thinker the Directorate of Operations needed.

In truth, the DO *was* a shambles. Battered by years of scandals,
budget-cutting, and second-guessing, operatives had become timid.
Their ranks had been gutted by Schlesinger and Turner, and those
who remained were mostly white, Anglo-Saxon males, many killing time until retirement. The DO needed a shot in the arm. But in
Hugel, Casey had found a cure that was worse than the disease.

The new DDO quickly became a laughingstock. One day, when
Hugel was walking with Casey, a gust of wind blew the director's
papers in one direction and Hugel's toupee in the other; Hugel fran-
tically chased after both, to the amusement of onlookers. Almost
immediately, damaging leaks about his incompetence appeared
in *The Washington Post*. By the summer they included allegations
of impropriety: It turned out that while on Wall Street Hugel had
engaged in insider trading. (These are the kind of things clandestine
operatives know how to dig up.) By July 1981, just seventy days
after his appointment, Hugel was forced to resign and was replaced
by a career operative, John Stein. For Casey the experience was not
only an embarrassment but a lesson: If he couldn't bend the clandestine service to his will, he'd go outside it to get big things done. That
would prove to be a dangerous epiphany.

In Casey's view, the Directorate of Intelligence (DI) also needed
shaking up; the agency's analysts had become intellectually flabby,
academic, and cautious. "This is a bunch of crap," Casey would often
write on papers he considered boring, badly written, or unimaginative. He was intellectually voracious, relentlessly seeking an edge
over the Soviets, no matter how esoteric or dubious the source.
When traveling, Twetten recalled, Casey would suddenly shout out:
" 'Come on, we've got to go to a bookstore.' He'd plow into that
store and pick out about ten books that he hadn't seen before. He'd
read them before we finished the trip." But when it came to his analysts, Casey wasn't interested in learning for its own sake; he wanted
them to tee up action against the Soviet Union and its proxies.

Casey believed the world's major terrorist organizations were controlled and directed by Moscow. Exhibit A, in his view, was a book by a journalist, Claire Sterling, called *The Terror Network: The Secret War of International Terrorism.* It argued that murderous groups such as Italy's Red Brigades, Germany's Baader-Meinhof gang, and Northern Ireland's Irish Republican Army (IRA) took their orders from Soviet spymasters. The book's evidence was thin, but Casey demanded to know why his analysts hadn't confirmed it; he was furious when they came back and punched holes in Sterling's thesis. Go back and look again, he demanded. "I paid $13.95 for this book, and it told me more than you bastards whom I pay $50,000 a year!" In the end, the analysts reported that while the Soviets supported and encouraged some terrorist groups, they had little control over them.

As his executive assistant, Casey chose Gates, thirty-eight, an ambitious, tough-minded analyst and one of the agency's rising stars. Gates shared Casey's view of the Directorate of Operations. The DO, he thought, was "unimaginative, a blindered fraternity living on the legends and achievements of their forebears of the 1950s and 1960s." In a memo to Casey and Inman, he wrote:

How is the health of CIA? I would say that at the present time it has a case of advanced arteriosclerosis: the arteries are clogging up with careerist bureaucrats who have lost the spark. It is my opinion that [this] has led to the decline of the quality of our intelligence collection and analysis. . . . CIA is slowly turning into the Department of Agriculture.

Gates, who had been Stansfield Turner's executive assistant and was the agency's senior Soviet expert, was as brutal as Casey on the analysts. "It wasn't like I would just mark the paper an 'F' and send it back," he said, "or as the rumor once had it that I stapled a paper to a burn bag and sent it back. I never did that. Another one was that I put a knife through a paper. I never did any of those things. But my attitude with them was, 'You're a CIA officer. You're not working in some frickin' university somewhere and if you feel strongly enough about what you've written, and you disagree with what I said, you've got to have the guts to come talk to me about it.'"

Gates's meteoric rise created detractors, including some who claimed that he deliberately exaggerated the Soviet military threat, enabling Casey's prejudices. "Reagan wanted the highest defense increases in peacetime, and he needed an enemy to do that," said Mel Goodman, an analyst who became Gates's nemesis. "The exaggeration of the Soviet threat is what the White House called for—and that is what Casey and Gates worked so hard to give the president."

In May of 1981, a Turk named Mehmet Ali Agca shot and wounded Pope John Paul II in a botched assassination attempt. Casey insisted that the Soviets must be involved. He rejected initial reports on the episode, demanding evidence of Russian complicity. "The big question was, 'Who was behind the shooting?'" recalled an operative based in Italy at the time. Gates, according to this operative, made sure Casey got the answer he was looking for. "Gates wrote at the bottom of one of the papers that the Soviets were behind it, which corresponded with Casey's view. It's something that I would never do because we didn't have the evidence." Gates insisted that the paper he signed off on was inconclusive. "The paper basically said you couldn't prove [the Soviets] did it," he said. "But because it adduced all the evidence we had that they did, some of the analysts who were involved were pissed off."

Casey believed the showdown over Soviet expansionism would come in America's backyard. Alan Fiers, who ran the CIA's Central American Task Force, recalled a conversation with the director: "Alan, you know the Soviet Union is tremendously overextended and they're vulnerable. If America challenges the Soviets at every turn and ultimately defeats them in one place, that will shatter the mythology . . . and it will all start to unravel. Nicaragua is that place."

During the 1980 election campaign, the head of French intelligence had made a prediction to Reagan. As Admiral Inman recalled: "He told Governor Reagan, 'You are going to be tested, militarily, by the Soviets in your first year in office. And that will probably take place in Central America.'" A leftist faction known as the Sandinistas had taken power in Nicaragua and they were supplying arms to a guerrilla insurgency fighting a rightist government in El Salvador. This was the threat Reagan and Casey had been expecting. During the final days of his presidency, Carter had approved covert operations to thwart this communist menace. At Casey's urging, Reagan accelerated those programs.

Intelligence showed that arms shipments from Castro's Cuba were ending up in Nicaragua. Haig, now secretary of state, wanted to go to the source of the problem, and blockade or even bomb the island. But military action of any kind was anathema to the Reagan administration's pragmatists, led by White House chief of staff James Baker, who wanted the president to focus on domestic policy. A shooting war was equally unwelcome to Reagan. For all his fiery anticommunist rhetoric, the fortieth president was loath to use military force. John Negroponte, who served as his ambassador to Honduras, said Reagan feared reviving memories of Yankee imperialists. "His constant refrain was, 'We just can't afford to look like the big brother coming down there to fix things again,' " he recalled.

So the stage was set for covert warfare. As chief of the Latin American Division, Casey had installed Duane "Dewey" Clarridge, a hard-charging operative who spoke no Spanish but shared his boss's scorched-earth attitude toward the enemy. "Make war in Nicaragua and start killing Cubans," Clarridge replied when Casey asked him for a covert action plan. In March of 1981, Reagan had authorized the CIA to supply guns and money to counter subversion and terrorism in Central America. The purpose, Casey told Congress, was to stop arms shipments to the leftist guerrillas in El Salvador. That was not true; Casey's real aim was to overthrow the government of Nicaragua. Toward that end, the CIA would train and arm a band of right-wing thugs and mercenaries known as the contras.

Casey's formula for winning in Central America was straight out of the OSS playbook. As the writer Thomas Powers noted, his idea of a secret war meant "brave men with cork-blackened faces blowing up power lines in enemy territory." That worked as a supporting act before the Allied invasion of Nazi-occupied Europe; it was less suited to winning a guerrilla war against a superior Sandinista force. And Casey had no political strategy to go along with "bang and boom." When, in March of 1982, the contras blew up bridges connecting Nicaragua to Honduras, it was mostly an annoyance. And when saboteurs detonated bombs at the airport in Managua, the Nicaraguan capital, the stunt served no discernible purpose. (The bombs missed Senators Gary Hart of Colorado and William Cohen of Maine, unintended targets whose plane landed several hours later.) The following year, the CIA was caught red-handed mining the harbors of Nicaragua.

By October 1984 the Democratic Congress, fearing another Vietnam-like quagmire, had had enough; it passed a law prohibiting the CIA from using funds to topple the Sandinista regime. Money was to be spent only on interdicting the flow of weapons to El Salvador.

But Casey regarded Congress as meddlers and obstructionists, to be ignored or circumvented. "Casey was guilty of contempt of Congress from the day he took the oath of office," said Gates. When testifying, the director would bob and weave and obfuscate, often with his trademark mumble. Deputy Director Inman, who was respected by Congress, sat next to Casey during many of his appearances. "If I got nervous, I'd tug at my socks," Inman recalled. "It became folklore that that was my sign to the members that Casey was lying. When that came out in the press, I said, 'That's not true, I don't do that.' And Casey said, 'Oh, yes, you *do* tug at your socks.' "

Casey had become persona non grata on Capitol Hill. At one point, Tennessee senator Howard Baker Jr., the majority leader, and Bob Michel, the House minority leader, were having lunch with Reagan in the White House Diplomatic Room. "Don't send Casey to the Hill anymore to testify," pleaded Michel, "because nobody can understand a word he says." Reagan smiled. "To be honest, I don't understand him half the time either," he replied. "Mr. President," said Baker, "that's the most frightening thing I've ever heard."

Casey and Inman clashed over the ethics of clandestine operations. "His broad view was, anything not explicitly prohibited by law, you could do," said Inman. "My view was that endangered the profession, you had to follow the spirit as well as the letter." Inman had become a believer in congressional oversight while working with the Church and Pike committees. "I had become absolutely persuaded that you needed clarity in legislation which authorized what you could do. I'd been involved in writing Executive Order 11905 [the prohibition on assassination]. And then in doing the rewrite, under Reagan [EO 12333]. We had a conversation after that and Casey told me, 'You're too damn legalistic.' At that point, I discovered that he made his fortune writing books on how to avoid paying taxes."

Casey's deceptions took their toll on Inman. "Candidly, our relationship became very chilly—because I'd catch him lying to me," said his deputy. One bone of contention was Casey's friendship with *The Washington Post*'s Bob Woodward; for all his secretiveness, Casey couldn't resist talking to the legendary reporter. "He had Woodward at his house for breakfast fairly frequently," said Inman. "I would then get a call from the *Post*'s managing editor—with questions which seemed to be based on knowledge of what we were saying back and forth. So I asked Casey about it. He said, 'Oh, no, I rarely see him.'" After less than a year and a half, Inman grew tired of Casey's lying and resigned.

Central America wasn't the only battleground where Casey intended to fight. Under sweeping authorities signed by Reagan, the director launched covert operations in Poland, Lebanon, Ethiopia, Chad, and Angola. Almost no country was too insignificant to contest. At one point, Casey argued to Reagan that the CIA should back a rightist coup in the tiny South American republic of Suriname. George Shultz, who had replaced Haig as secretary of state, thought the idea was absurd, and the director backed off. But a much more promising opportunity was presenting itself on the other side of the world, in Afghanistan.

On Christmas Day 1979, as Jimmy Carter headed into his last year as president, the Soviet Union's Red Army had invaded and occupied the mountain kingdom. The CIA was caught flat-footed, failing to issue a warning. Carter was furious. The invasion had poisoned his entire agenda—nuclear arms control, deploying missiles in Western Europe, promoting human rights. He felt personally betrayed by the Soviets, and for the first time concluded that they might be truly evil.

Carter was ready to unleash the CIA to bloody the Red Army in its backyard. He signed a series of presidential findings authorizing clandestine operations to assist the Afghan mujahideen. Ironically, the president whose proudest achievement was avoiding a single American death in combat had launched a secret war that would eventually kill as many as fifteen thousand Soviet soldiers. The brutal nine-year conflict would claim the lives of nearly ninety thousand mujahideen fighters and an estimated one million civilians.

In the beginning, no one thought the Afghan rebels had a chance.

Although they were fierce warriors, the ragtag tribes, armed with World War I–vintage rifles, seemed no match for the Russians and their lethal helicopter gunships. They were also hampered by the CIA's reluctance to go all in.

Part of the problem was the agency's aversion to taking risks: Decades of investigations, firings, and armchair quarterbacking had sapped the clandestine service of its initiative and fighting spirit. It had been a long time since the swashbuckling CIA-backed coups in Iran and Guatemala. By the early 1980s, aggressive operatives risked being hauled before a congressional committee and reprimanded or worse. As George Crile wrote in *Charlie Wilson's War*: "It had almost become the trademark of the CIA's Operations Division to fight and lose and finally be exposed and then mocked and vilified in the press, in Congress, and even at home by their children." Casey was a risk-taker but even he was slow to realize the potential of the CIA's secret war in Afghanistan. Over dinner with the director on October 23, 1983, at his house in Northwest Washington, author Bob Woodward noted: "On Afghanistan he said that he thinks the Soviets will over power and wear down the rebels."

Compounding the problem was the CIA's bureaucratic inertia. The mujahideen desperately needed antiaircraft missiles that could knock Soviet helicopters out of the sky. But as a rule the CIA never provided weapons that could be traced back to the U.S. This was supposed to be a *secret* war; why needlessly provoke the Soviets? Howard Hart, chief of the CIA's Islamabad station in neighboring Pakistan, believed the idea of defeating the Russians was fanciful— and dangerous. What if the Soviets upped the ante and sent in a half million troops, instead of its current force of 120,000? The Russians might crush the rebels and then even invade Pakistan.

While the mujahideen fought the Soviets in Afghanistan, the fuse of another jihad was being lit in the Middle East. Ground zero was the U.S. embassy in Beirut, Lebanon, where, unbeknownst to the CIA, Islamic fundamentalism's visceral hatred of the West was about to explode. The looming catastrophe would avenge the American-led coup that put the Shah of Iran on the Peacock Throne in 1953 and trigger a decades-long war between the West and Islam.

In the spring of 1982, the Israeli army, led by General Ariel Sharon, invaded and occupied Lebanon. The pretext was to clear out strongholds of Yasser Arafat's Palestinian Liberation Organization (PLO), but the incursion turned into a bloody siege. When Israeli troops finally withdrew, Reagan sent a contingent of Marines to Lebanon as peacekeepers; they were dug into a compound outside Beirut's airport. The Marines weren't the only Americans in Lebanon; a few miles south, on the corniche facing the Mediterranean, was the U.S. embassy, an eight-story structure on the Rue de Paris. It was the home of the CIA's Beirut station, the nerve center of American intelligence in the Middle East.

The morning of April 18, 1983, had been stormy. But by noon the sun was out, and the waterfront near the embassy was crowded with pedestrians. Just after 1 p.m., a GMC pickup truck draped with canvas drove down the corniche, weaving slowly through traffic. The vehicle rode low on its springs, and its tires were nearly flat under the weight of its concealed cargo. Suddenly the truck veered left into the embassy's circular driveway, rolled under the portico, and lurched up the steps.

The detonation was instantaneous. The shock wave could be felt by U.S. sailors on a ship ten miles offshore. A black cloud of debris blotted out the sun. The entire front of the embassy collapsed, leaving a skeletal shell. Sixty-three people were killed, including seventeen Americans, thirty-two Lebanese employees, and fourteen visitors or passersby. Of the Americans who were killed, eight were CIA officers. The station chief, Kenneth Haas, who had been conducting a meeting, was crushed under the weight of falling concrete. Robert Ames, a renowned Arabist who'd briefed Reagan and Secretary of State George Shultz on the intricacies of the region, just happened to be visiting Beirut that day; he was killed instantly.

It was the worst day in the CIA's history, measured not only by the number of dead but by the incalculable loss of the station's regional expertise. "Beirut was the listening post for the United States in the Middle East," said Robert Baer, a CIA officer and Middle East hand who would become obsessed with the embassy bombing. "That's where we got all our information. And it was gone in a split second."

Gone, too, was the illusion that terrorists could be deterred by conventional defenses such as armed Marine guards. The method of the attack was something the CIA had never experienced before. "A suicide car bomber: That was the first time we'd seen it," said Baer. "We didn't even know what that was; that somebody was willing to give his life to kill us was something brand-new." Indeed, a new kind of warfare had been born, or at least a kind Americans hadn't seen since the Japanese kamikazes of World War II. And then there was the technical sophistication of the attack. "The planner of the embassy bombing was a genius," said Baer. "In tactics. Explosives. Ability to keep quiet. Discipline. There had been nobody like this. Period. You name any terrorist in the twentieth, twenty-first century, and no one was as good as this guy."

The CIA knew that Iran was behind the bombing; beforehand it had intercepted SIGINT (signals intelligence) indicating an imminent attack against Americans, but not the exact target. Back at Langley, Casey was furious. He was even more animated and restless than usual, mumbling and barking at everyone within earshot. He ordered an investigation.

But the carnage had only begun. Six months later, on October 23, another vehicle loaded with concealed explosives drove into the U.S. Marine barracks and detonated its cargo. This explosion was even more devastating, an earth-shattering blast with force just short of a nuclear weapon. Minutes later, a French military garrison was struck by another massive truck bomb. Two hundred forty-one Marines died in the first blast, and sixty-four French soldiers in the second. The Marine barracks bombing was, prior to 9/11, the largest loss of American life ever suffered in peacetime.

At one point Lebanese intelligence officers arrested and questioned a suspect, who confessed to carrying out the embassy bombing under orders from Syria. But the suspect had been tortured, and Casey dismissed the confession as bogus. (He also fired a CIA officer who'd participated in the brutal interrogation.) The truth was the CIA knew who'd ordered both the embassy and Marine barracks bombings: It was Hezbollah, backed by Iran. And slowly a picture emerged of the mastermind suspected of orchestrating the attacks. It was a young Shiite operative who would become the most deadly and elusive terrorist in history, more cunning than his Sunni counterpart, Osama bin Laden. His name was Imad Mughniyah.

Born in a poor neighborhood south of Beirut in 1962, Mughniyah was described by Israeli intelligence as "an extremist, uninhibited psychopath." In the name of enforcing Islamic law, he liked to maim prostitutes and drug dealers by shooting them in their knee-caps. Mughniyah became a member of Force 17, Yasser Arafat's elite security detail. (Though he was a Lebanese Shiite, he was accepted by these Palestinian Sunnis.) But after the PLO evacuated Beirut, Mughniyah and his brother joined Lebanon's rising force, Hezbollah, or the Party of God. For the next thirty years, the Iranian-backed Hezbollah would become Israel's, and the CIA's, implacable enemy, responsible for killing hundreds of Israelis and Americans. And Mughniyah was its operational genius. The young Hezbollah terrorist was closely allied with Iran's Islamic Revolutionary Guard Corps (IRGC). He reported to a rising star in the Quds Force who'd become famous decades later when he was assassinated by a U.S. military drone outside Baghdad Airport. His name was Qassim Suleimani.

Remarkably, Reagan didn't retaliate militarily for the Beirut bombings. Neither Reagan nor Shultz had any appetite for a bloody entanglement in the Middle East. Instead, two days after the Marine barracks bombing, to remove a Cuban-backed regime, Reagan ordered an invasion of the tiny Caribbean island of Grenada, which distracted attention from his troubles in the Middle East. But Hezbollah and Mughniyah weren't done tormenting the United States.

In early 1984, Islamic militants opened a new front in their war against the West. On March 7, CNN's Beirut bureau chief, Jeremy Levin, was accosted at gunpoint on the street, forced into a car, and driven away. Two months later, an American Presbyterian minister, Benjamin Weir, was abducted in West Beirut. In December, another American, Peter Kilburn, a librarian at the American University of Beirut, was kidnapped. A caller again claimed responsibility in the name of Islamic Jihad, a terrorist group.

Ronald Reagan wasn't interested in abstractions like foreign policy or strategic doctrine, but he was touched by the misfortunes of human beings. As Americans continued to be kidnapped, Reagan met with their families and tried to console them. The president repeatedly asked Casey what he was doing to find the hostages. What good was an intelligence agency if it couldn't find abducted Americans? Reagan never raised his voice, but that made his plaintive queries all the more effective.

Tom Twetten, head of the Near East Division, watched his boss become consumed by Reagan's anguish over the hostages. "Every time Bill Casey went over to the White House to talk about the Cold War and how things were going in Afghanistan, the president would say, 'Okay, let's talk about what's important: the hostages.'" And there was another, cold-eyed reason for Reagan's concern. "Jimmy Carter lost the election because of American hostages," said Twetten. "The last thing Bill Casey and Ronald Reagan wanted was to lose an election because of American hostages. They were going crazy. It was, 'Somebody rid me of this Lebanese hostage mess.'"

The CIA formed a task force, and a paramilitary unit was dispatched to Lebanon to find and free the hostages. But their captors moved them constantly, maintaining radio silence, leaving few traces. "We ran so many operations trying to find those people," recalled Bob Gates. "And there were times when we were literally an hour behind them. But the closer we would get the more frustrating it would be."

At the end of 1984, five Americans were being held in Lebanon by Hezbollah. Casey was getting desperate. On March 16, William Buckley had been ambushed outside his home in West Beirut and taken captive. Buckley wasn't just another American hostage: He was the new Beirut station chief, chosen by Casey to rebuild the CIA's capabilities in the Middle East. There was no telling how much Buckley, under torture, might reveal to his captors, including the names of officers and CIA assets. Soon the CIA received a chilling message that confirmed Casey's worst suspicions: It was a package delivered to the agency. Inside was a videotape showing Buckley being tortured by his captors.

In late 1984, Bill Casey had two urgent priorities: freeing the hostages and funding the contras. But he was faced with two inconvenient truths. The first was that the United States didn't pay ransom for hostages; that would only encourage terrorists to capture more Americans. The second was that, because of a law passed by Congress known as the Boland Amendment, the CIA was prohibited from providing any money to the contras.

But Casey had never played by the rules and wouldn't be constrained by them now. In the months to come, working with the National Security Council, he would devise a scheme to free the hostages *and* fund his beloved contras. It was an extraordinary, off-the-books, covert operation, involving gullible NSC officials, crooked Iranian middlemen, radical mullahs, and a president who wouldn't admit (perhaps even to himself) that he was paying ransom for hostages. To do Reagan's bidding Casey constructed a Hall of Mirrors, where no one could see the disaster that was just around the corner.

Casey found a willing partner in the NSC, which in 1984 had been decimated by turnover. Robert "Bud" McFarlane, Reagan's third national security adviser, was ambitious but insecure. Admiral John Poindexter, McFarlane's deputy, a pipe-smoking introvert, had little political or legal savvy. Oliver North, a marine lieutenant colonel, was a zealot: all throttle, no brakes. Along with Casey, they'd bring Reagan to the verge of impeachment.

In July of 1985 McFarlane had been approached by an Israeli official who told him there were moderates within the Iranian leadership who wanted better relations with the United States. Regaining American influence in Iran, McFarlane thought, would be a diplomatic coup. But the so-called moderates were offering something even more valuable: As a goodwill gesture, they'd use their influence with Hezbollah to release the American hostages. In return they wanted the U.S. to ship antitank weapons to Iran, which was at war with its bitter enemy Iraq.

From the outset, the scheme was doomed: The CIA assessed that there were no moderates among Iran's leadership; they'd all been killed during the bloody purges of the 1979 revolution. Moreover, the Iranian middleman who was peddling the deal, Manucher Ghorbanifar, was known to the CIA as a notorious liar; on polygraph tests he flunked everything except his name and nationality. Tom Twetten, head of the Near East Division, was astonished by Casey's willingness to deal with such a con man: "His attitude was, 'Okay, Ghorbanifar failed the polygraph worse than anybody in history; let's work with him anyway.'" Deputy director John McMahon opposed the plan: "McMahon was almost violently against the idea and was just overruled," said Riedel, who was then head of the Syria/Lebanon desk. "It was a stupid idea. You didn't have to be a rocket scientist to see that you were only going to get more people taken once you pay a ransom."

Yet Casey couldn't resist the prospect of freeing the hostages. And if the NSC took the lead, he could keep the CIA out of it (or, at least, keep its role secret). The Israelis, including Prime Minister Shimon Peres, were enthusiastic, envisioning a return to the good old days of doing business with the Shah. Edwin Meese, who was Reagan's attorney general when the affair came to light, explained the scheme's tortured logic: "The Boland Amendment prohibited the State Department, Pentagon, and CIA from being involved [in funding the contras]. And so Ollie North took it over because the only place it could be implemented was through the White House [the NSC]. And hence this dumb idea of trying to combine these two very different things: the Iranian initiative and the support of freedom fighters. You put 'em together and it was kind of like a match and gasoline."

Casey made sure that no one had a complete picture of what was going on. "Within the agency, this was an incredibly compartmented program," said Riedel. "Compartmented within compartment within compartment. And the operation was run out of a miniature Situation Room, which was set up on the seventh floor and you had to have a special badge to get in there. And even when you got in there, you got access to parts of it but not all of it." It was Casey's way, said Gates, his executive assistant, of keeping his colleagues in the dark. "He knew this thing was risky and unsanctioned and maybe illegal because he always played right on the baseline. I think he didn't tell anybody at CIA and played along to protect the agency." There was only one reason, said Riedel, for Casey's elaborate shell game. "You don't really need compartments within compartments, unless you're breaking the law."

While the operation was run by Lieutenant Colonel North out of the NSC, there were certain things only the CIA could do—such as transferring weapons. It fell to Tom Twetten to authorize the first arms shipment: "So I'm given the name of a person to call in the Pentagon who will put me in touch with the logistics Army base down in Alabama. The man's name is Colin Powell. I've never heard of him. He didn't want any part of it any more than I did."

But Casey also created a series of entities, or cutouts, with no links to the agency. "For everything that he did there was a cutout," said Riedel. "The people who knew the whereabouts of the hostages were cut off from the Iranians; who were cut off from the people who knew that the arms were coming from Israel; who were cut off from the people who knew that the money was going to the contras. All of those boxes were separate. And only Casey and a handful of people knew that all the connections came together."

It was McFarlane who first pitched the plan to Reagan in July of 1985, while the president was hospitalized for a cancer operation. Reagan noted in his diary the day before: "Some strange soundings are coming from the Iranians. Bud [McFarlane] will be here tomorrow to talk about it. It could be a breakthrough on getting our seven kidnap victims back." The next day, White House chief of staff Donald Regan noted: "The president after asking quite a few questions . . . assented and said yes, go ahead. Open it up."

In the months that followed, Reagan wrote about the "highly secret convoluted process" in his diary: "[Israel sells] Iran some 'Tow' anti-tank weapons. We in turn sell Israel replacements & the Hisballah [sic] free our five hostages. Iran also pledges there will be no more kidnappings. We sit quietly by & never reveal how we got them back." By January of 1986, the U.S. had removed Israel as the middleman and was selling arms directly to the Iranians, with the president's approval. The irony of Reagan capitulating to hostage-takers wasn't lost on Bruce Riedel. "Carter for all his faults never contemplated trading something for the hostages whereas Reagan and Casey knew exactly what they were doing."

Meanwhile, Hezbollah and Mughniyah, backed by Iran, continued to launch attacks against Israel and the West. In September of 1984, in East Beirut, a suicide bomber drove a truck into the U.S. embassy annex, killing twenty-four people, including two Americans. In June of 1985, Palestinian terrorists hijacked TWA Flight 847, bound from Athens to Rome, and flew the plane back and forth between Algiers and Beirut, holding passengers and crew at gunpoint. While Americans watched on television, the body of a passenger, Navy diver Robert Stethem, twenty-three—shot by the hijackers—was dumped on the Beirut airport tarmac.

The siege ended after secret negotiations between the White House and the governments of Syria and Iran. But the hijacking was thought to be the handiwork of Mughniyah. (He'd left a calling card; his fingerprints were found inside the plane.) "The idea that Mughniyah could hijack an American airplane full of Americans and begin to execute them was an absolute nightmare in Washington," said Middle East hand Bob Baer. But in the months and years to come, neither the CIA nor Israeli intelligence could get close enough to Mughni-yah to capture or kill him. All they had were two faded photographs of the man they nicknamed "Maurice." "He was totally elusive," said Baer. "He *lived* secrecy. He never left by the door he came in. He never used cell phones or high-frequency radio. If you caught his voice on a walkie-talkie, it was always encoded. People around him never talked. There was never a defector from his ranks. He was the Scarlet Pimpernel of terrorism."

Casey was determined to strike back at Hezbollah. According to Bob Woodward, who continued to meet with him frequently, the director wanted to create paramilitary teams of foreign nationals: five-man units that could strike preemptively at terrorists. Secretary of Defense Caspar Weinberger objected, and McMahon was also opposed; surely these hit squads would violate Executive Order 12333, prohibiting assassinations. But Casey persuaded Reagan to sign a finding authorizing the teams.

Meanwhile, the director was eyeing another target: Sheikh Mohammad Hussein Fadlallah, the spiritual head of Hezbollah. Casey thought he knew just the person who could help eliminate him. And this time he'd be sure to hide the CIA's fingerprints.

No one had been more generous to the CIA than Saudi Arabia's ambassador to the United States, Prince Bandar bin Sultan. The Saudis had secretly financed many of the agency's causes—including the contras at a rate of $1 million a month. In defiance of Congress, Casey had secretly solicited contributions to the contras from U.S. citizens and foreign donors, including Israel, China, and the Sultan of Brunei.

After lunch at Prince Bandar's sprawling estate in Virginia, Casey and Bandar went for a walk outside. Would Bandar consider financing a covert operation to kill Fadlallah? Yes, he would. Not only would the Saudis finance the operation but they'd also carry it out; Lebanese intelligence would participate. Casey wanted to be sure the mission couldn't be traced to the CIA. In this case, he wouldn't even have to lie to Congress; liaison with foreign intelligence services was one area not covered by congressional oversight.

On March 8, 1985, a car packed with explosives drove into the West Beirut suburb known as Bir al-Abed and stopped about fifty yards from Fadlallah's high-rise residence. As Fadlallah's SUV came driving by, the car exploded. The detonation collapsed a seven-story building. Eighty people were killed, all innocent civilians, many worshippers at a mosque. Imad Mughniyah's brother, who served as a bodyguard for Fadlallah, also died. But Fadlallah wasn't in the vehicle and escaped unharmed; he'd been delayed and his SUV had gone ahead without him. Afterward, residents suspected who was responsible: A white sheet fluttered over the bombed-out site with a message scrawled in black letters: "MADE IN USA."

The Iran-contra affair began to unravel in 1986. On November 3, a Lebanese magazine, *Al-Shiraa*, broke the story of a strange American diplomatic mission: An American emissary had flown into Tehran on a C-130 cargo aircraft, bearing a Bible signed by Reagan, a key-shaped cake, and a cargo of TOW missiles. (The cake was described as a key to open Iran-U.S. relations.) The emissary was McFarlane, the former national security adviser, and he was accompanied by North. It was the first of ten shipments of arms to Tehran. The news broke as Reagan was presiding over a Rose Garden news conference welcoming home David Jacobsen, released after seventeen months of captivity in Lebanon. Reagan swatted away reporters' questions about the story, denying any connection between Jacobsen's release and the arms sales.

As details of the affair became public, the president refused to concede that he'd authorized trading arms for hostages. "Those charges are utterly false," he declared in a televised speech. "The United States has not made concessions to those who hold our people in Lebanon. And we will not." At another appearance, a reporter asked: "What would be wrong in saying that a mistake was made on a very high-risk gamble so that you can get on with the next two years?" Reagan replied: "Because I don't think a mistake was made."

But trading arms for hostages with a sworn enemy of the United States was only half the story.

Troubled by Reagan's public misstatements about the scandal, Edwin Meese, now the attorney general, began a review of the Iran arms deal. On Saturday, November 22, over lunch at a restaurant near the White House, one of his aides told Meese of an unexpected discovery: Among North's papers was a memo describing a plan to send profits from the arms sales to the Nicaraguan freedom fighters.

Out of "residual funds" from the arms sales, it said, "$12 million will be used to purchase critically needed supplies." Meese had a sinking feeling. Trading arms to Iran was one thing; it was another thing entirely to funnel the profits to a secret army prohibited by law from receiving U.S. funds.

On Monday, Meese told chief of staff Donald Regan that he had to see the president right away. Regan accompanied Meese and recalled the president's reaction to news of the diversion: "The color drained from his face, leaving his skin pasty white. . . . The president wore a stern, drawn expression that was new to me—and just as new, I suspect, to Meese, who has known him for twenty years." But if he was shocked by the discovery, Reagan noted it matter-of-factly in his diary: "On one of the arms shipments the Iranians paid Israel a higher purchase price than we were getting. The Israelis put the difference in a secret bank account. Then our Col. North (NSC) gave the money to the Contras."

The next day, November 25, appearing in the White House press briefing room, Reagan made a brief statement and then turned the proceedings over to Meese. "Certain monies," the attorney general told the press corps, "were made available to the forces of Central America, which are opposing the Sandinista government there." The affair, now dubbed the Iran-contra scandal, was a full-blown crisis.

The pointed question, from Watergate, was suddenly relevant again: What did the president know and when did he know it? Almost as important: Was his CIA director aware of the illegal diversion? Casey's colleagues had learned about the overcharging scheme well before Meese. This was thanks to Charles Allen, the veteran analyst who became known as the agency's Cassandra. Allen's responsibilities had grown under Casey; by now he was the National Intelligence Officer (NIO) for both Counterterrorism and Warning. Allen had been going over ledgers of the transactions with Iran, and noticed something was amiss. Millions of dollars were missing or unaccounted for: $3.5 million from the first 1985 shipment; $24 million from one Swiss account. The same people were involved shipping arms to the Iranians and the contras. He couldn't prove it, but Allen suspected the money was ending up with the contras—and went to see Bob Gates. But Gates didn't want to hear the details. It would be illegal for the agency to be involved, he said. Allen should inform Casey.

A week later, Allen wrote a memo to Casey and hand-delivered it to the director. "This is spinning out of control and you'd better do something," Allen told him. Gates was also present. Both he and Allen thought Casey looked surprised to learn that money from the arms sales had been diverted to the contras.

But others were convinced that Casey knew exactly what North was up to. Tom Twetten, head of the Near East Division, was summoned by the director right after Allen gave Casey his memo. According to Twetten, Casey referred to Allen's write-up and said, "What do you know? Did you know about this?" Twetten insisted he didn't but he was virtually certain Casey knew about the diversion to the contras: "Oh, I think almost a hundred percent. 99.4 percent. Casey was playing his cards very close to his vest. It was institutional protection. He was going to handle the politicians. He was going to take the blame." Admiral Inman also believed that Casey was well aware of North's creative bookkeeping: "I will tell you my personal conviction: He was Ollie North's case officer. I think he was fully informed."

Not one but three investigations were launched: one by Congress, another by Independent Counsel Lawrence Walsh, and a third, the Tower Commission, appointed by the president. Testifying before Congress, Casey was defiant, obfuscating, and denied everything. But there was something wrong with the director. "He was having trouble with sentences, lost his train of thought," said Twetten. "He was really sick during the hearings, and we didn't know what it was." At one point, Casey was standing next to Twetten, berating him for sharing too much information with Congress. Suddenly, in mid-sentence, Casey's head slumped onto Twetten's shoulder; he'd fallen sound asleep.

The White House was in total disarray, paralyzed by murderous infighting. Poindexter and North had been fired, and chief of staff Regan soon followed; the Tower Report concluded that Regan had been responsible for letting the NSC run amok. (His fate had been sealed by Nancy Reagan after Regan hung up on her during a shouting match over the phone.) Secretary of State George Shultz, who'd bitterly opposed the Iran initiative, offered to resign—and Casey tried to push him; he wrote a scathing letter to Reagan, urging him to fire Shultz and "hire a new pitcher." Reagan burned the letter in the Oval Office fireplace.

The president was in political free fall. For the first time, polls showed that Americans didn't trust Reagan to tell the truth; his approval rating dropped from 63 percent to 47 percent. Impeachment was a real possibility. "Reagan wasn't just a lame duck, he was a dead duck," said an aide.

As his new White House chief of staff, the president appointed Howard Baker Jr., the Tennessee senator who'd become a household name during Watergate. Fueled by Reagan's confused, halting performance during press conferences, rumors had spread that the president was mentally unfit, perhaps in the early stages of Alzheimer's. Baker and Reagan's deputy chief, Kenneth Duberstein, made a pact: They'd sit the president down and ask him to come clean about Iran-contra. If they concluded that he was lying to them, they'd resign. After more than a dozen interviews, accompanied by White House counsel A. B. Culvahouse, they concluded that while Reagan could not remember much about the arms deal, he was being honest. For his investigation, Culvahouse employed a staff of sixty-seven people, and reviewed twelve thousand documents and Reagan's personal diaries.

Still, Reagan's political survival hung by a thread. No one knew if North and Poindexter might implicate the president, and Casey's testimony could be even more dangerous: God knows what he might have told Reagan about the diversion in their private Oval Office meetings. If Casey said the president was aware of the scheme, impeachment and would likely follow. But Casey had made his last public appearance. On December 15, as he was preparing to go before the Senate Intelligence Committee, the CIA director collapsed from a seizure while having his blood pressure taken in his seventh-floor office. He was wheeled out of Langley on a gurney. At Georgetown Hospital he suffered another seizure.

Three days later Casey underwent surgery for a cancerous tumor on his brain. It was a lymphoma, on the inner left side of the brain, which controls movement on the right side of the body. He was moved to Room C6316 at Georgetown Hospital, registered under the alias "Lacey," and put under round-the-clock guard by the CIA's security division.

His recovery was slow, and Bob Gates, who was now acting director, visited him frequently. Reagan's inner circle, led by his wife, Nancy, was emphatic that Casey should resign, and Gates resisted their pressure. But on January 29, Gates arrived at Casey's hospital room with a letter of resignation ready for the CIA director's signature. Sophia was at his bedside. As Gates later recalled:

> *We moved to the side of Casey's bed to give him a chance to try to sign the letter with his left hand (his right was paralyzed) or at least initial the letter.... Finally, impatiently, he handed the letter to her, and she signed it. At that point she was crying, and he lay back on the pillow with tears in his eyes and said, "Well, that's the end of a career." And I said, "It was never supposed to end like this." I held his hand for a few minutes and then I left.*

Later, Casey would be visited by one more guest, an encounter that would trigger one final controversy in the spymaster's eventful life. The visitor was Bob Woodward.

On his first attempt to gain access to Casey's bedside, Woodward said he followed a CIA security guard into a new wing of the hospital and took the elevator to the sixth floor. Casey's door was closed and the lone guard on duty turned him away. But Woodward was persistent. Several days later he made a second attempt. This time the door to Casey's room was open—and Woodward slipped in. "Scars from the craniotomy were still healing," he wrote of Casey, who was groggy but alert. "You finished yet?" the director asked him, referring to his book. Woodward said he'd never finish with so many questions still unanswered. And then he cut to the heart of the matter:

> *"You knew, didn't you?" I said. The Contra diversion had to be the first question: you knew all along.*
> *His head jerked up hard. He stared, and finally nodded yes.*
> *"Why?" I asked.*
> *"I believed."*
> *"What?"*
> *"I believed."*
> *Then he was asleep, and I didn't get to ask another question.*

When his account was first published in his book, *Veil,* in late 1987, some CIA veterans accused Woodward of inventing it out of whole cloth; the dramatic visit, they insisted, never happened. Their argument was threefold: Casey's room was guarded round-the-clock by CIA security; the director never would have talked to a reporter; after his brain surgery he was non compos mentis. In a television interview, broadcast live shortly after Woodward's book was published, Sophia insisted that the author had *never* spoken with her husband. Woodward, who was a guest on the same show, listening on a split screen, interjected: "Sophia, don't you remember when you cooked breakfast for us?"

More than three decades later, opinions about this encounter seem only to have hardened. "That's bullshit," said Charlie Allen, the octogenarian CIA veteran, of Woodward's account. "I know the people that ran the team of security around him at Georgetown Hospital. There was never a second that we didn't have officers there in the room. And all the staff at the hospital and all the doctors knew that the CIA controlled this patient." Tom Twetten, the veteran case officer, insisted Casey was too incapacitated to speak coherently: "Everybody who knew Casey at that time knows he was not capable of that." David Robarge, the CIA historian, concluded: "It just seems totally fanciful, whatever Woodward's motivation."

Woodward was unfazed. In a telephone interview, he insisted it was only natural for Casey's handlers to let down their guard; he spent so much time with Casey he was practically part of his entourage. "Have you ever interviewed someone forty-three times?" he asked me. "I was in his home. I was on his plane. I was a regular, and I gave copies of my earlier books to the security guards. I got to know them."

I went to see Woodward at his townhouse in Georgetown, where he showed me meticulously organized, typed notes of several interviews he did with Casey. Sitting at a table in his den, switching on a 1980s-vintage microcassette recorder, Woodward played the tape of a conversation he had with Sophia Casey after her husband's death in which they chat with the familiarity of old friends:

> *Woodward: As you always knew, he was willing to talk to me and deal with me, and it certainly wasn't always pleasant for him but he did it and I admired him for that.*
> *Mrs. Casey: Yeah, I know.*
> *Woodward: He had a lot of strength.*

Mrs. Casey: He did. He really did.

Woodward: . . . The book is finished and will be out in the fall. And I just wonder is there anything — this is an awfully broad question — but is there anything else I need to know?

Mrs. Casey: I don't think I could tell you anything, Bob. You know everything. [Laughs]

Notes from Woodward's interviews with Casey suggested a similar familiarity with the spymaster. "You know who wrote that?" Casey said to Woodward as they sat in the director's den, watching Reagan give a speech. "Ronald Reagan. His greatest skill is as a writer. . . . I've never seen anyone talk quite so fast, say so much without stumbling." Britt Snider, general counsel to the Senate Select Committee on Intelligence, confirmed that Woodward had indeed spoken with Casey in person or by phone forty-three times. And William Donnelly, head of CIA administration, conceded: "Woodward probably found a way to sneak in." Yet for all his careful archiving of interviews, Woodward said he wasn't sure he'd made any notes of his fateful bedside encounter.

In the spring of 1987, Sophia took her husband home to Maryknoll, his sprawling estate on Long Island, New York. Shortly thereafter Casey contracted pneumonia and was hospitalized again. On May 6, 1987, the day after Congress began public hearings into the Iran-contra affair, Casey died. He was seventy-four.

Given the timing, and his history of deception, some wondered if this was one last trick, a vanishing act by the old spymaster. "Many people in the agency at the time did not believe Casey died," said Bruce Riedel. "They thought it was an elaborate cover story and that he lived for many years after." When Senator Barry Goldwater learned of the director's death, he asked if he could see the body.

On Saturday, May 9, 1987, a throng of Washington power brokers traveled to St. Mary's Roman Catholic Church in Roslyn Harbor, Long Island, for Casey's funeral mass. Ken Duberstein, Reagan's last White House chief of staff, and Frank Carlucci, his final national security adviser, watched as the pallbearers came by, carrying the closed casket. Carlucci leaned over and whispered: "How do we know he's in there?"

In some respects, Casey had left the CIA stronger than he found it: He'd reinvigorated the clandestine service, now numbering nearly six thousand officers; banished the timidity of the Carter era; fought the Soviets in covert wars around the globe. In Afghanistan, he'd waged the most successful covert operation in history. When it came to illegally trading arms for hostages, he'd protected Reagan, taking the secret of what the president knew to the grave. "I think history has to give Casey his due," said Woodward, reflecting on the president who barely escaped impeachment for the Iran-contra affair. "Who made sure that Reagan did not have a Nixon problem? Bill Casey. Because he took it on himself. What Dick Helms would not do for Nixon, Bill Casey did for Reagan."

True enough. But what Casey did for Reagan was lie, obfuscate, evade, and break the law. He politicized intelligence when it suited his purposes. He fought secret wars without accountability. He believed the president's power—and the communist threat—trumped congressional meddlers and the rule of law. In the end, the CIA was corrupted—and weakened—on Casey's watch.

In the aftermath of the Iran-contra scandal, the agency needed a director with unquestioned integrity and moral rectitude, a squeaky-clean reputation, and a devotion to the rule of law. There was just such a person in Washington, D.C. Everyone called him "Judge."

CHAPTER FIVE

"Never go home at night without wondering where the mole is."

William Webster, Robert Gates, and George H. W. Bush

Bill Casey's bungled Iran-contra scheme almost sank Ronald Reagan's presidency. In early 1987 the scandal threatened to scuttle the CIA. Casey was gone, but there'd still be hell to pay for the agency and its next nominee as director. The morning after Casey's resignation, Bob Gates, then the acting CIA director, was summoned to see President Reagan in the Oval Office. "I have a decision to make about the director of the CIA," Reagan told him. "Are you interested?" Gates said yes, he would be honored. Later Gates reflected that he'd just accepted "a job no one else seemed to want at the end of January 1987. No wonder."

When his confirmation hearings began in February, Gates walked into a political free-fire zone. "Congress was outraged over Iran-contra," he recalled, "and I was a great target." In a scrum of more than fifty photographers and cameramen, during a break on the second day, Gates was asked: "How do you like the job so far?" He replied: "Remember that country and western song, 'Take This Job and Shove It'?" The comment, caught on an open microphone, led all three evening network news programs.

It wasn't just the Iran-contra scandal that threatened to derail Gates's nomination; he'd made enemies and they were gunning for him. One charge was that Gates had exaggerated the Soviet threat to appease his old boss Casey. Michael Morell, a young analyst and future acting director, recalled: "There were questions about his views on Russia, particularly on Russia's involvement in the potential assassination of the pope." Morell thought the criticism was triggered not by any effort on Gates's part to skew analysis but by his abrasive management style. "Gates was a very, very, very tough head of analysis at CIA," Morell said. "And when he challenged people, they interpreted it as politicization."

But it was Gates's role in the CIA's trading of arms for hostages that dominated the hearings. He was eviscerated—first, for failing as deputy director to object to the scheme; second, for failing to notify the intelligence committees; and third, for not acting more decisively when he learned about the illegal diversion of funds to the contras. Upon being told about the diversion by Charles Allen, Gates had informed Casey, the CIA general counsel, and John Poindexter, the national security adviser. "I felt, at the time, that I'd done what I was supposed to," Gates told me, more than thirty years later. But in retrospect he wished he'd done more. "I hadn't done anything wrong, but I hadn't done enough right. If I had it all to do over again, I probably would have told the White House counsel. And perhaps even gone to the Justice Department. Those are the two things that I probably should have done."

After two days of combative questioning by Congress, it was clear to Gates that his nomination to head the CIA was doomed. It was Howard Baker's first day as White House chief of staff, and Gates went to see him. With Casey in his grave, Gates told him, Congress would demand his scalp. "Howard, I'm the last guy standing here," he said. "And I think everybody would be best served if I withdrew." Gates offered to stay on as deputy CIA director. Baker readily agreed.

William H. Webster, the FBI director, was on his way to Capitol Hill for a hearing on the bureau's budget when he got a phone call from Ronald Reagan. Would he consider becoming the new CIA director? Webster, sixty-three, a former U.S. attorney and federal judge, was about to retire and take a lucrative job at a law firm, but he promised to consider the president's request and get back to him soon.

If you set out to create the antithesis of Bill Casey, you might end up with William Webster. Tall, slim, and patrician, with impeccable manners, Webster, born in St. Louis, personified Washington's establishment right down to his bespoke suits, monogrammed shirts, and gold cuff links. Recently widowed, he was known for dating beautiful women and playing tennis with the powerful and well connected; one of his regular opponents was the septuagenarian William "Wild Bill" Donovan. Webster noted that the legendary OSS founder wasn't fast on his feet but had an uncanny sense of where the ball was going. "He never had to move more than about two feet because he had the best anticipation of anybody I ever knew. And that is a good trait for an intelligence director."

Earnest and meticulous, Webster personified devotion to the rule of law; his words were literally engraved on a conference center wall at FBI headquarters: "We will do the work the American people will expect of us in the way the Constitution demands of us." That was a far cry from Casey's anything-goes credo, but Webster had been personally fond of his CIA counterpart, whom he regarded as a charming rapscallion. Once, after a conference in New Zealand, Casey offered Webster a ride home on his military plane. The subject, Webster recalled, turned to covert operations "and Casey said, 'Bill, we gotta get these lawyers out of the picture.'" Webster replied, "Well, I work for the Department of Justice, Bill. I don't think I can accommodate you."

As CIA director, Webster would be venturing into uncharted, possibly hostile territory. Could he really lead the nation's spies while being faithful to his own legal and ethical standards? Would the CIA's covert operatives rebel against his principles? Webster wanted to be sure. "I think there were people who didn't feel they should be bothered by legal restrictions," he said. Before giving the president an answer, Webster phoned Admiral Bobby Inman, Casey's ex-deputy. "He said, 'I've been debating this all day,'" recalled Inman. "'Can I do the job for the country that it needs as director, being a man of the law?' And I told him, 'Absolutely.'" With that assurance, Webster called Reagan back and accepted the position.

Unlike Casey, who loved wading into the trenches, Webster floated above the fray. Tom Twetten, the veteran case officer and head of the Near East Division, recalled how different Webster's style was from his predecessor's. "He didn't do like Casey and call the Italian desk and say, 'Give me somebody who speaks Italian, *right now!*' Webster was less hands-on. He delegated day-to-day operations to his deputies. In a gesture of respect for the agency, Webster shrewdly brought an old CIA hand, and Amherst classmate, Richard Stolz, out of retirement to become his Deputy Director of Operations (DDO).

The new director had a lot to learn, including world geography. Soon after he arrived, Twetten was summoned to brief Webster on his areas of responsibility. "So we start running through what's going on," recalled Twetten. "And he said, 'Do you have a map? You keep mentioning Baghdad and Cairo, and I can't quite place them.'" At an interagency meeting on Panama, Webster referred to the country's new president as "a good man. . . . He's somebody we can work with." Unfortunately, the U.S. didn't recognize this president, who was considered a flunky for strongman Manuel Noriega, indicted for drug trafficking.

At one point, Charlie Allen and another officer briefed the new director on a weapon known as the electromagnetic pulse (EMP). It's a nuclear device that, when detonated in the atmosphere high above an enemy's territory, can virtually destroy that country's electrical grid. "We had spent two hours trying to explain EMP to Judge Webster, who had a legal mind but not necessarily a technical mind," Allen recalled. "And we were trying to explain that the device could shut down operations of electronically driven machines and could have a huge, devastating effect on our grid and so forth. And finally, Judge Webster looked at us and said, 'All right, if we had an EMP attack, would my watch stop working?' And we said, 'No, your watch would probably continue to work.' We struggled to explain it."

The idea of answering to a lawyer was anathema to some covert operatives. The last thing they needed was another moralistic do-gooder like Stan Turner. Duane "Dewey" Clarridge, the notoriously sharp-tongued head of the Latin America Division, was scathing about the new director: "We probably could have overcome Webster's ego, his lack of experience in foreign affairs, his small-town America world perspective, and even his yuppier-than-thou arrogance. What we couldn't overcome was that he was a lawyer. All of his training as a lawyer and as a judge was that you didn't do illegal things. He couldn't accept that this is exactly what the CIA does when it operates abroad. Webster had an insurmountable problem with the raison d'être of the organization he was brought in to run."

But Clarridge's was a minority view; in the wake of Casey's scandals, most operatives welcomed Webster. "The majority opinion was: I don't want to go to jail; I don't want to be sued; I can't afford a lawyer," explained Bruce Riedel. "Let's clean this place up. No more of these shenanigans." And Webster took pains to reassure the Directorate of Operations that he had not come to clip its wings. "I did have some Ops guys who were used to being freewheelers," he recalled. "I told them we could still be imaginative and courageous, and daring—as long as we did not forget that we were citizens of the United States and obliged to do our work consistent with the Constitution." Fortunately, there was nothing in the Constitution about breaking the law in foreign countries.

While Gates, who stayed on as deputy director, took care of things at Langley, Webster managed Congress and the president. Under Casey, Webster recalled, Reagan was receiving his President's Daily Brief every morning at eight but barely read it. The president's inner circle cut him plenty of slack. "They'd say, 'Mr. President, you can get by with reading pages two, six, and twelve.'" Webster asked for, and got, regular briefings with the president. "They reserved half an hour for me to meet on anything I wanted to present. I was grateful for that, and he was a good listener and very attentive. But it was not enough, and the president asked for more time, so we doubled it."

In March of 1987, Reagan had apologized for the Iran-contra scandal, declaring in a nationally televised speech: "A few months ago I told the American people I did not trade arms for hostages. My heart and my best intentions still tell me that's true, but the facts and the evidence tell me it's not. . . . It was a mistake." His approval ratings immediately rebounded. But Reagan's close brush with political death had an unforeseen consequence: It made him determined to become a peacemaker with the Soviet Union.

Nancy Reagan and the president's inner circle were convinced that only a historic breakthrough on arms control could remove the stain of scandal. Reagan had a potential partner in the form of an extraordinary new Soviet leader, Mikhail Sergeyevich Gorbachev. Gorbachev had dreamed of transforming the Soviet state through his ambitious programs of transparency and economic reform, glasnost and perestroika. But it was a futile dream. By 1987, the Soviet Union was coming apart—economically, militarily, and socially. Hastening its dissolution was the ruinous Soviet adventure in Afghanistan.

The Afghan rebels had turned the tide of the conflict. Part of it was the infusion of millions of dollars of funding freed up by Texas congressman Charlie Wilson and his allies on Capitol Hill. But the main factor was the rebels' deadly use of Stinger missiles supplied by the CIA. Webster decided to travel to Pakistan to inspect the progress of his clients firsthand. Traveling through the Khyber Pass, the director and his entourage ended up in a tent near the Afghan border. Webster, dressed in smartly pressed khakis, mingled with the warlords he'd been directing from half a world away. "I never saw so many disparate-looking people," Webster recalled. "They brought them all together and we had lunch. There was Burhanuddin Rabbani, who was a university president, very scholarly, and ultimately became president of Afghanistan. Gulbuddin Hekmatyar, a warrior who became prime minister. There was another tribal leader who was chewing the bones along with the chicken while he was eating." Webster noted that their fierce tribal rivalries were exceeded only by their hatred of the Russians. "They didn't really like each other that much, but they had one common goal and that was to get the Soviets out of their country."

With their Stingers, the rebels now controlled the skies. "Morale just plummeted among the Soviet pilots," said Webster. "They were angry. They were humiliated. They were forced out of positions. They didn't want to be there and they seemed to have trouble understanding why they were there." Not only was the Red Army in retreat but restive Muslims in the Soviet Union were rising up in solidarity with the rebels. The long war had proved to be a geopolitical disaster for the USSR, and a triumph for the CIA. Never before had the agency had such success arming a large-scale insurgency without putting its own people in harm's way. "If I had to pick the half dozen most significant steps in the dissolution of the Soviet Union," Webster concluded, "I would certainly put that there at the top—the fact that they could not hold on to Afghanistan."

On February 15, 1988, Colonel General Boris Gromov of the Soviet 40th Army followed the last Russian soldier across the "Bridge of Friendship," in a final retreat from Afghanistan to the USSR. "There is not a single Soviet soldier or officer left behind me," he said. When word of the Red Army's withdrawal reached Langley, Webster pulled out all the stops; he ordered champagne and threw a party, inviting the congressman who'd been so instrumental in the rebels' cause, Charlie Wilson. Amid the revelry, few gave any thought to what would now become of the mujahideen. In the soil of Afghanistan's militant fundamentalism, the roots of Al Qaeda had been planted, but no one knew it yet.

The dissolution of the Soviet Union, of course, would come not on Reagan's but on George H. W. Bush's watch. After his election in November 1988, the first president-elect to have served as CIA director knew just what he wanted in his Director of Central Intelligence. "As Ford's DCI I learned the proper role for the director in the national security structure," Bush wrote. "He is not, and should not be, a policy-maker or implementer, and should remain above politics, dealing solely in intelligence." Bush also believed that CIA directors should stay on from one presidency to the next; replacing them only politicized the position. "Treating the DCI just as presidents usually treat the chairman of the Joint Chiefs of Staff—continuing through changes in administration—is, under all but the most unusual circumstances, a good formulation." After all, Carter had replaced Bush at the CIA with Turner, and look how badly *that* turned out. Bush asked Webster to remain as CIA director.

The world's attention now turned to Eastern Europe, where the Iron Curtain was crumbling. The Soviet Union and its satellites were coming apart—and yet the CIA was caught off guard. Charles Allen, still the National Intelligence Officer for Warning, conceded that the agency was slow to grasp that the Soviet Union was imploding. "They could see it coming," he said. "But the speed with which that collapse came—no one in the West that I know of, certainly not the British, saw it coming." As the agency's top Soviet analyst, Bob Gates had been skeptical about the prospects of change, predicting that Gorbachev's promises were a chimera. As the historian Jonathan Alter wrote, "Gates had received his Ph.D. for studying the Soviet Union, but he managed to miss the signs of its impending demise, calling Mikhail Gorbachev a 'phony' and discounting his reforms as meaningless."

Gates did not entirely deny that charge. He confessed there was truth to a line in a May 28, 1989, article in *The Washington Post*: "Gates has become to the world of Sovietology what Eeyore is to Pooh Corner—someone capable of finding a dark lining in even the brightest cloud." Gates observed that, along with Bush's defense secretary Dick Cheney and national security adviser Brent Scowcroft, "we believed that no matter how much Gorbachev did, many of his actions could be reversed and the USSR could continue to be a major potential security problem for the United States."

By October of 1989, the collapse was well under way. Civil unrest in Poland and Hungary spread to East Germany, its capital divided for thirty years by the infamous Berlin Wall. Webster alerted the president to the popular groundswell for German reunification. "I sent a back-channel message to President Bush in which I recall using the terms 'it's bubbling to the surface.' And three weeks later the wall was breached. They opened the doors and they never closed."

As the Cold War was ending, Bush touted a "new world order" based on international law. But the new order was quickly shattered. On August 1, 1990, Saddam Hussein dispatched tanks and troops toward the border of his tiny, oil-rich neighbor, Kuwait. Sensing an imminent invasion, the CIA sounded the alarm. But no one would listen.

The warning came from the agency's veteran analyst, Charlie Allen. Poring over satellite imagery, Allen was alarmed. "The tanks had aligned themselves," he recalled. "Iraqi T-72s were about a hundred yards apart at points of entry into Kuwait. So I tried to raise the roof. I issued a warning of attack because it struck me that it would occur within twelve hours." The day before the invasion, the lead sentence of the CIA's President's Daily Brief was: "Kuwait thinks the Iraqis are bluffing. We don't." But Bush wasn't buying the warning. Middle Eastern intelligence services—and his friends, Egypt's Hosni Mubarak and Jordan's King Hussein—assured him that Saddam wouldn't invade. "I went home rather angry that night at about 1700," said Allen. "About 1800 I called the CIA ops center and I said, 'What's going on?' And they said, 'Nothing.' Well, soon the ambassador in Kuwait City called and said tanks are knocking down custom booths." Saddam's invasion of Kuwait was under way.

Blindsided by the Iraqi invasion, policymakers wrongly blamed the CIA for missing it. "It's pretty clear that we were clanging the bell pretty loud," said David Robarge, the CIA's chief historian. "We said that based on everything that's going on, this doesn't seem to be a military exercise or bluff. And that's what we told the president. Webster was wrongly blamed for a failure. The perception was that we were surprised when we weren't."

For Allen, who sounded the alarm, it seemed no good deed would go unpunished. "A story broke in *The New York Times*, which said, 'the CIA is getting rid of its Cassandra, Charlie Allen,'" he recalled. But then Allen's phone rang. It was the director of the Senate Select Committee on Intelligence, an ambitious young man named George Tenet. "He said, 'What is this? There are rumors that people are abolishing your job. Is that true?' He took me to lunch and assured me that this was crazy." When Allen got back to the office, his job security suddenly improved. "Judge Webster called me in and said, 'I have no intention of abolishing the NIO for Warning.' Clearly, George Tenet had gotten through to Webster." Tenet, the future director, was already making his influence felt at Langley. (The position of NIO for Warning would be eliminated in the late 1990s; Allen considered that decision a grave mistake.)

After three years and ten months in the job, in the spring of 1991, Judge Webster was ready to retire. "He was really out of his element," said Bruce Riedel, "and that became more apparent to Bush and his team as time went on." As a case in point, Riedel recalled riding with Webster to the White House for a critical NSC meeting the day after Saddam's forces overran Kuwait. Iraqi tanks were now massing on Kuwait's border with Saudi Arabia; an invasion of the desert kingdom could be imminent. "Webster said, 'Well, how can you tell they're massing?'" Riedel recalled. "I said, 'Well, their tanks are all lined up and the turrets and the guns are pointed south, and they have all these vehicles loaded with petroleum and gas and ammunition immediately behind them.' And he said, 'Show me the picture.' And I showed him the picture. It just struck me: He's not really well prepared for what he's about to do."

Yet "the Judge" had made a lasting impact on the CIA. Much as George H. W. Bush had cleansed the agency of the taint of the Family Jewels, Webster had removed the cloud of Iran-contra. "We were in a trauma," recalled Tom Twetten. "The trauma was Casey: He was the best director we've ever had, he was also the worst director we ever had. Judge Webster restored congressional confidence in the agency after Casey had given them the finger for those many years." Now, with Webster's departure, Bob Gates was about to get his second chance at the brass ring.

On May 14, 1991, Bush nominated Gates to become director of the CIA. The choice was a gamble; the factors that had sunk Gates's nomination the first time hadn't changed: his alleged politicization of intelligence under Casey; his failure to act decisively when he learned of the Iran-contra diversion; his unpopularity among those he'd leap-frogged on his way up the ladder. "There are a whole bunch of analysts who can't stand the little twerp, and they're out to get him," said one veteran. "He wasn't well liked in the building." But Gates was *respected*; he was a survivor; he had earned points by soldiering on as Webster's deputy when he could have walked away; he'd carefully cultivated allies in Congress, including the chair of the Senate Select Committee for Intelligence, David Boren. And Bush considered Gates a friend.

The charge that Gates had exaggerated Soviet military capability dated back to the Carter years. One of those who believed it was Leslie Gelb, the straight-talking defense intellectual who was Secretary of State Cyrus Vance's deputy at the time. "When Gates was running the Soviet desk, they exaggerated the goddamn Soviet missile capability," said Gelb. "The truth was Russia's military was the exaggerated strong right arm of a dying creature. But Gates made it look as if a missile gap made them superior to us. It was a bunch of crap—which I knew, because that was my main business." Gates was a gifted infighter, and Gelb thought exaggerating Soviet strength was his way of currying favor with Zbigniew Brzezinski. Later, the argument went, Gates became Casey's chief enabler, catering to his anti-Soviet views. But some CIA colleagues insisted that Gates was perfectly willing to tell Casey what he didn't want to hear.

Riedel recalled the time he produced a paper predicting that the Marines in Lebanon were sitting ducks. "The draft we produced said, 'Not only is the current mission of the Marines in Lebanon hopeless; it's going to end in disaster,'" he said. "The draft went up to Casey and Gates intercepted it. He said, 'You know, Casey's not going to like delivering this message to the president, because it's a really hard, negative message.' So Gates came down to my office and said, 'Are you really sure about this? What's the evidence?' And for forty-five minutes he grilled me about the whole thing. And at the end he said, 'Okay. I'm convinced.' Gates did the right thing. He queried the evidence. He wanted to know: Was there really unanimity about this? Once he was certain on those things, he put his signature on it and persuaded Casey." Alas, if the CIA's warning ever got as far as Reagan, it evidently was ignored; the Marine Corps barracks was blown up a month later.

Gates's most serious obstacle to confirmation turned out to be someone he once considered a friend. Mel Goodman, a CIA analyst, had been working in the Soviet Foreign Policy branch of the agency's Office of Current Intelligence when Gates arrived in 1968. "I knew from that first lunch that [we] would one day be working for Gates," Goodman later wrote. "I had never met anyone so ambitious, who seemed to have no interests outside work, who was prepared to work beyond any reasonable call of duty." Goodman had taken Gates under his wing but later turned against him, and was now an avowed enemy. He accused Gates of pandering to Casey. "For accommodating Casey, we began to refer to Gates as the 'windsock,'" he wrote. At Gates's confirmation hearing, Goodman hammered home alleged examples of his slanting of intelligence, including the controversial paper on the pope's attempted assassination.

Gates was stunned by his old friend's animosity. "I think there was an element of personal jealousy," he said. "But I did have problems with some of the analysis that came out of his shop that basically said the Soviets aren't doing anything in the Third World." Gates disputed the notion that CIA analysts were so easily manipulated. It was as though "everybody in the agency had prostituted themselves, and nobody did anything honestly and so on and so forth. I commented that he probably worked at the agency for twenty years. 'You know, it's an amazing thing how a guy can live twenty years in a whorehouse and come out a virgin.'"

This time, in his second bid to become director, Gates fought back. That weekend President and Mrs. Bush traveled to St. Simons Island, Georgia, and Gates went along. "I took with me five boxes of classified estimates and assessments and I hand-wrote a point-by-point refutation of everything Goodman had ever said. And quoting from estimates and from the documents, because I knew everybody would parse every word." When the hearings resumed, Gates delivered his detailed rebuttal. He pledged to form a task force to study the issue of politicizing intelligence. On November 5, 1991, he was confirmed by the Senate by a vote of 64–31.

There would be no shakedown cruise for Gates as CIA director. Just six weeks after he was sworn in, on December 26, 1991, the Soviet Union officially collapsed. "I had two challenges, Gates said. "The immediate problem was what the hell's going to happen in the Soviet Union as it falls apart? Would there be famine? Would there be riots? You had a country dissolving itself. I was worried about what was going to happen to forty thousand Soviet nuclear warheads. How do we know where they are? How many [locations of warheads] do we *think* we know? How many do the Soviets think they know, and how do you get them out of Belarus, Kazakhstan, and Ukraine? The Soviets themselves didn't know where they all were—and so the potential for theft of one of those or of a rogue government getting hold of some of them was a matter of very great concern."

One of the new director's first overseas trips was to Moscow; it would be the first-ever visit by a CIA director to his counterparts in Russian intelligence. Gates would also meet with the new Russian president, Boris Yeltsin. As a token of American goodwill, Gates decided to bring Yeltsin something that was truly one-of-a-kind: a memento of Operation AZORIAN, the daring 1970s covert operation that had partially raised a sunken Soviet submarine from the Pacific Ocean. During the retrieval, two thirds of the sub had broken off and plunged back to the ocean floor. But the CIA had recovered the remains of Russian submariners and some missile codebooks. That much Yeltsin and the Russians knew. What they did *not* know was that CIA officers had buried the sailors at sea in a ceremony that was recorded on videotape. Gates was bringing that videotape with him, along with the Soviet flag that covered the remains of the ill-fated crew.

Yeltsin asked for a television console to be installed in the room where he and Gates met. "I gave him the flag and the videotape of the funeral ceremony and told him what had happened," Gates recalled. Then Yeltsin, a huge bear of a man, watched the video. And he wept. Later, the burial was shown on Soviet national television, where families of the sailors learned the fate of their loved ones for the first time.

Gates, at forty-eight, was the youngest CIA director, and the first to have risen to the top job from an entry-level position (a group that now includes John Brennan and Gina Haspel). Like Helms and Colby, he knew the agency intimately. "He was the ultimate insider," said Charlie Allen. "And he was incredibly smart. He was quick, bright, and he had deep foresight about what was occurring. He could put things in larger context." Jack Devine, a veteran operative who'd worked under every director since Richard Helms, thought no one topped Gates at working the levers of power in the intelligence community, the White House, and Capitol Hill. "Pound for pound, he was the best bureaucrat we ever had. He knew how to run the U.S. government."

But for many the new director was an acquired taste. On overseas trips Gates liked his creature comforts, which caused some eye-rolling in the DO. "Bob and I went to Algeria and we were given the royal treatment," recalled one longtime operative. "We were put into a swanky military guest house and fed really well, and we each had a suite. It was as nice as any place I've stayed in my overseas career. Bob comes to breakfast the next morning and he says, 'Did you breathe in the shower?' And I said, 'Yeah, did you have a problem?' And he said, 'Well, yeah. I didn't. I was worried about the water.' "

If Webster was cordial and collegial, Gates could be arrogant and aloof. "Bob Gates never said hello to me, never acknowledged my presence," said a case officer who met with him frequently. "And I didn't know whether that was because I was from the clandestine service, but I mean: Good God!" Others dismissed the longtime analyst as another "suit." "We were in very dangerous territory when Bob Gates became the director because he hated the DO," said one. "It was a personal thing. He's a little guy. He didn't like flashy, so-called dangerous stuff."

Gates was more comfortable cracking the whip on his analysts. "I thought he was pushing us to higher levels," said Charlie Allen. "He wanted us to do more critical thinking. He pushed the NIOs and challenged them. In fact, he conspired with me. He'd call me up and say, 'I want you this morning to pick a fight with the NIO for the USSR, and see what happens.' So I'd pick a fight with him. And then we'd get in a big debate. Gates got very bored with 'administrivia'; he had no interest in that. He was interested in substance and implications and context. And he was always pushing and demanding more. He didn't spend time working on nonessential things as director of Central Intelligence."

Beyond picking up the pieces after the Soviet collapse, Gates's biggest challenge was adapting the agency to a new world. "The long-term problem was, how do you reorient this American intelligence juggernaut that for forty-five years had been focused on primarily the Soviet Union, the Cold War, and the threat of communism?" he said. "How do you reorient that entire operation to problems around the world that were becoming more serious? At one point I had twenty-four different task forces working simultaneously. At the same time we were dealing with the fact that after the Cold War the budgets for defense and intelligence were being slashed. How do you take on all these new problems in the world? So that's the kind of thing that occupied my days."

But while Gates was scanning the horizon for threats, an enemy was at work within, right in the heart of the CIA's clandestine service. Looking back, Gates was struck by the prescience of an old colleague who tried to warn him.

Upon becoming director, Gates had reached out to his old boss, Richard Helms, the iconic CIA director, then retired for twenty years. The old spymaster and the new director had lunch alone in the private dining room high above the woods of Langley. They surveyed the state of the world and compared notes on intelligence-gathering and covert operations. Then Helms paused. He looked his young protégé in the eye to make sure he had his attention. Helms had one more bit of wisdom to impart. "I just have one piece of advice for you," Helms said. "Never go home at night without wondering where the mole is."

Gates was stunned. Was it possible that the CIA, at that moment, was compromised by a Russian mole? As Gates recalled more than thirty years later, "He did not say not *whether*, he said *where*."

The search for traitors within the CIA had been a low priority since Angleton's ill-fated mole hunt back in the 1960s and early 1970s. Angleton's paranoid reign as chief of counterintelligence had ruined Soviet assets and derailed many CIA officers' careers on flimsy to nonexistent evidence. Helms's successors were in no hurry to repeat the Angleton experience; CIA officers shouldn't be labeled traitors just because they acted oddly. But as early as the mid-1980s it was clear that something was terribly wrong: The CIA's Soviet assets were disappearing.

The first signs had come in May of 1985, later known as "the Year of the Spy." One of the CIA's Russian assets, Sergey Ivanovich Bokhan, a GRU officer in Athens, was recalled to Moscow. The CIA concluded he was under suspicion by the Soviets and advised him to defect. The next month Moscow station officer Paul Stombaugh was arrested by the KGB as he was attempting to meet with Adolf Tolkachev, a CIA asset since 1977. Tolkachev would later be arrested and executed by the Soviets. In October KGB officer Leonid Poleshchuk was arrested while trying to retrieve a dead drop from an undercover CIA officer in Moscow. That same month GRU officer Gennady Smetanin, a CIA agent in Lisbon, did not return after taking home leave in the Soviet Union. The agency never heard from him again. But it would get much worse: In the years to come, the CIA would learn that at least nine of their missing Soviet agents had been arrested and executed. And dozens of CIA covert operations had been detected and rolled up.

There were only two possibilities: either the CIA's secret communications had been breached—or the agency had been penetrated by a Russian mole. If it was the latter, the CIA had some suspects. In May, U.S. Navy senior warrant officer John Walker was arrested by the FBI; it turned out he and his family had been spying for the Soviets for more than twenty years. In September, Edward Lee Howard, a former CIA case officer, defected to the Soviets in Helsinki; he'd fled before being arrested for spying for the KGB. Both traitors caused enormous damage to U.S. national security. But they weren't privy to information about all of the missing agents, and couldn't have betrayed them to their Soviet handlers.

So a new mole hunt began. One of the people who came under suspicion was a disgruntled CIA case officer named Aldrich Ames.

Aldrich Hazen "Rick" Ames was a second-generation CIA officer from Wisconsin. He'd joined the clandestine service in 1962 and worked his way up to chief of counterintelligence for the Soviet Union. A chain-smoker and heavy drinker, he'd behaved badly and performed erratically but had always found superiors who'd cover for him. While stationed in Italy, "Ames would binge drink," recalled Charlie Allen. "And the police, *polizia*, found him asleep on the streets. And so they asked him who he was and Rick said, 'I'm American.' They asked who's his boss—and they delivered Ames to the CIA station chief's residence in Rome. But [the chief] never reported him back to headquarters."

Nor did alarms go off when Ames flaunted a lifestyle that seemed well beyond his financial means; back at Langley he drove a Jaguar to work every day. The car, and a large house for which he put down $650,000 in cash, were the fruits of his lucrative career as a spy for the KGB. For a decade, beginning in 1985, Ames had passed thousands of CIA secrets to the Soviets. It was the most devastating betrayal since Kim Philby gave the crown jewels of Western intelligence to the KGB in the 1950s and 1960s.

Charlie Allen had attended Ames's wedding years earlier, to a CIA employee named Nancy, a good friend of Allen's wife. In retrospect he was struck by his wife's intuition. "We were driving home and she said, 'I don't know. The word God wasn't mentioned in that service.' I said, 'Well, they're Unitarians. You've got to live with that.' She said, 'I don't like Rick Ames.' And I said, 'Why? He seemed like a nice enough guy to me.' She said, 'I just don't like him. He's not the right guy for Nancy.'"

In retrospect, the CIA's Cassandra wished he'd paid more attention to his wife's premonition.

But neither George H. W. Bush nor Bob Gates would have to deal with the problem of Rick Ames. It would take almost a decade for the CIA to ferret out the spy in its midst. Ames's arrest would come on Bill Clinton's watch—and lead to the demise of Clinton's new CIA director.

CHAPTER SIX

"A jungle full of poisonous snakes."

James Woolsey, John Deutch, and Bill Clinton

James Woolsey was at his home in Washington, D.C., packing for a family trip to California, when the telephone rang. It was just before Christmas 1992, and Warren Christopher, Bill Clinton's transition director, was calling: "Jim, you don't suppose you could come to Little Rock and talk to the president-elect about the CIA job?" he said. Woolsey, a conservative Democrat and former undersecretary of the Navy, knew Al Gore, the vice-president-elect, but had only met Clinton once. The idea that he was being considered to run the world's most powerful intelligence agency seemed far-fetched, but Woolsey agreed to fly down to Arkansas.

Arriving at Clinton's house that evening, Woolsey was ushered in to see the president-elect after midnight. The two men chatted for an hour about fishing and Arkansas and Oklahoma football. (Woolsey had grown up in Tulsa, across the state line.) Then, out of the blue, Clinton asked: "Do you think the CIA director ought to express positions on policy?" Woolsey replied: "The only way he ought to do it is in a handwritten note to you—because if he says what he thinks ought to be done in National Security Council meetings, people are going to think he's skewing intelligence to match his objectives." Clinton digested this. Then he said, "I agree with that. I think that's right."

The next morning, Woolsey was checking out of his hotel when he got another phone call from Warren Christopher. "Jim, we're going to need you over here for this press conference at 12:30," he said. Woolsey wondered what for. "Does the president want me to be director of Central Intelligence?" he asked. "Well, I'll tell you what," Christopher replied. "Come on over to the press conference and we'll get it sorted out." Woolsey said, "I think I'd like to know *before* the press conference." "Well, okay. Just a minute," Christopher replied. Then, returning to the phone, he said: "I stuck my head in his office and asked him and he said, 'Yeah, sure.'"

Minutes before Woolsey was announced as Clinton's nominee to run the CIA, Dee Dee Myers, the press secretary, took him aside. She'd evidently just read Woolsey's CV. "Admiral Woolsey, I didn't know you served in the Reagan administration," she said. "Dee Dee, I'm not an admiral," Woolsey replied. "I was undersecretary of the Navy but I never got above captain in the Army." "Oops," she said. "We'd better change the press release." For Woolsey, it was a preview of the seat-of-the-pants governing style of Bill Clinton: "I came within five minutes of being announced as Admiral Woolsey."

The truth was Clinton had given almost no thought to who'd be his CIA director. He'd spent an enormous amount of time picking candidates for his domestic cabinet, but when it came to national security, Clinton had deferred to his running mate. Gore's recommendation had evidently carried the day. In a recent appearance, Woolsey had likened the United States after the Cold War to someone who'd slain a dragon, the Soviet Union, only to find himself in a jungle full of poisonous snakes. Woolsey had no idea how apt that metaphor would be for his tenure as CIA director.

R. James Woolsey, fifty-two, was a brilliant technocrat who, while working for the Bush administration, had mastered the arcana of the NATO–Warsaw Pact arms talks in Vienna. "If you had a technical problem that was really hard to solve, you could throw him at it and he could do it," said Richard "Dick" Clarke, the White House counterterrorism adviser. (Clarke's official title at the NSC was national coordinator for security, infrastructure, and counterterrorism.) "He'd piss everybody off but he would get it done." Anthony "Tony" Lake, Clinton's national security adviser, thought Woolsey possessed "a strange intelligence; it wasn't linear—so we would have these meetings and I could not figure out, at least at first, how he had arrived at his conclusions."

"Intense" was a word often used to describe Woolsey. With his receding hairline and beady eyes, he resembled a hammerhead shark. Back in the late 1960s, Woolsey had been a Rhodes Scholar and anti–Vietnam War activist, just like Clinton. He found it amusing that the former head of Yale Citizens for Eugene McCarthy for President could grow up to become CIA director. But unlike Clinton, Woolsey had opposed the Vietnam War not because it was wrong but because he thought LBJ wasn't doing enough to win it. Since then Woolsey had become even more hawkish and he had a predilection for woolly right-wing conspiracy theories.

Right from the start, as CIA director, Woolsey drove Clinton up the wall. They were "oil and water," recalled John Podesta, who was then the White House staff secretary. "Clinton just did not like the guy." Especially grating was Woolsey's apparent belief that he was the smartest guy in the room. Early on the new director went to the White House and gave the president a briefing on Iran. It turned into a forty-minute lecture. Clinton fidgeted and tapped his pencil. Finally Woolsey departed. Clinton turned to an aide and said: "I don't *ever* want to see that man again."

Clinton hardly ever did, at least one-on-one. But according to Lake, it was nothing personal: "I don't think Clinton hated him because I don't think Clinton paid that much attention to him." A few years later, in a freak accident, a small plane crashed on the South Lawn of the White House, killing its pilot. Woolsey, who had a self-deprecating sense of humor, enjoyed telling people, "That was me, trying to get a meeting with the president."

Part of Woolsey's problem was Clinton's work habits; it wasn't that the president was uninterested in intelligence, he just liked to receive it in writing and read it at his leisure. Clinton hadn't changed much since his days as a Yale Law School student when he pulled all-nighters before exams. "He read prodigiously and would mark things up and send them back to the NSC," recalled Bruce Riedel, the longtime Middle East analyst. "He would also send obscure articles from things like *The Journal of Slavic Military Studies* that he had marked up with question marks. I always wondered: A, where does he get the time to do this? And B, how does he *find* this stuff?" Clinton had an eclectic circle of friends who sent him obscure material.

According to Dick Clarke, his counterterrorism czar, the president had a near-eidetic memory; he could repeat verbatim words on a page that he'd read years earlier. "He would mark up the PDB every day in his incomprehensible left-handed scroll and then rip it up and send it to you with a question," he said. But Woolsey wasn't getting

Clinton's queries. They were going to Clarke, Lake, and his deputy Sandy Berger.

Ideally, the CIA director and national security adviser mesh, as Bob Gates and Brent Scowcroft did under George H. W. Bush. "I always regarded it as a symbiotic relationship," observed Gates. "The CIA director has assets and troops but no access. The national security adviser has access but no troops. And so if you've got a good relationship between those two, the agency is miles ahead." But Woolsey didn't click with Lake. At NSC meetings, when the CIA director opined on policy, Lake would interject: "Jim, is there an *intelligence briefing* that goes along with that?" Tom Twetten, the longtime operative and head of the Near East Division, observed: "So he fails at two of the most important things—working with the president and the national security adviser. How can he do his job?"

Woolsey would soon be tested by a series of crises. At 7:50 a.m. on January 25, 1993, five days after Clinton was sworn in, a line of cars was waiting at a stop light on Route 123, just outside the Langley entrance gate. Suddenly a man stepped out of his vehicle and opened fire with an AK-47 assault rifle. Two CIA officers were killed and three grievously injured. The shooter, a Pakistani terrorist named Mir Aimal Kasi, climbed back into his car and drove away. Hours later, he boarded a flight and escaped to Pakistan. When a memorial service for the fallen officers was held at Langley a few weeks later, President Clinton was a no-show, sending the first lady in his place. It was a slight that further soured relations between the White House and the CIA.

Just a month after the shootings, on February 26, 1993, the secure phone rang in Clarke's office. It was Lake. "Did the Serbs do it?" he barked. "Did the Serbs bomb it? Was it a bomb?" Clarke, who had no idea what Lake was talking about, said he'd find out—and turned on the television. CNN was reporting on a chaotic scene in New York City; in an underground garage of the World Trade Center, a van packed with explosives had detonated. The explosion had killed six people and injured more than a thousand.

It would turn out to be the precursor of the attacks of 9/11, a foreshadowing of the deadly assault by Al Qaeda. But Woolsey and the CIA were flying blind. The FBI took the lead in investigating the bombing, and eventually traced it to Omar Abdel Rahman, a blind

Egyptian cleric, and his cell of militant followers. By June the plotters had been rounded up and imprisoned. But Woolsey and the CIA had no idea who they were or what was going on. "All of that was run by the bureau and by NYPD," said Woolsey. "We were told we could not be given access to the documents that were picked up from the blind cleric's holdings. There was a closetful of Arabic materials that would've been extremely valuable that stayed locked and we could not look at it." Woolsey didn't dare challenge the FBI's dominion; it would take the attacks of 9/11, nearly a decade later, to breach the almost impenetrable wall between the CIA and FBI.

But not everyone at the CIA was in the dark. On the morning of the bombing, Gina Bennett, a CIA senior counterterrorism analyst, had just given birth to a son in an emergency C-section at George Washington Hospital when her cell phone went off. "I heard my boss screaming on the other end, '*Your people* did this, *your people* did this,'" she recalled. "And I had no idea what she was talking about." Bennett had been connecting the dots of a shadowy network of jihadists based in Afghanistan. Once dedicated to defeating the Soviet infidels, "her people" were now bent on attacking the United States; these were the poisonous snakes that Woolsey had warned about.

In the months to come, Bennett would follow the trail from the World Trade Center bombing to a group known as Al Qaeda and a charismatic Saudi multimillionaire named Osama bin Laden. At the time he was considered an eccentric "terrorist financier." Bennett got the attention of her CIA colleagues when she compared him to a flamboyant New York businessman. "I had likened Osama bin Laden at the time—I know this is horrible to say—to Donald Trump," she told me, well before the real estate tycoon ran for president. She laughed at the thought. "Osama bin Laden was like the Donald Trump of the terrorism underworld. He had the wherewithal and a vision that was clearly controversial and different from everybody else, and the tenacity to follow it. I definitely drew a lot of snickers from my colleagues, who thought I was blowing bin Laden out of proportion."

In truth, she was one of the first to take bin Laden seriously. The first World Trade Center bombing, carried out by his acolytes, signaled a tectonic shift in the struggle with Islamic terrorism. John

McLaughlin, the analyst and future deputy director, admitted that the CIA was slow to grasp the significance of the attack. "The big message that comes out of the 1993 Trade Center bombing is that a threshold has been crossed. They've hit us here. But that message was not as powerfully absorbed as we can see it in retrospect."

Half a world away, Al Qaeda was plotting another attack, though it was well disguised at the time. In the waning days of his presidency, George H. W. Bush had dispatched American troops to the East African nation of Somalia, where 700,000 people faced starvation due to famine. On Clinton's watch, the humanitarian mission morphed into a campaign to kill a Somali warlord, Mohammed Farah Aidid, after his militants slaughtered two dozen Pakistani peacekeepers and three Americans. In response, Clinton sent U.S. commandos to capture or kill the warlord.

On October 3, the mission devolved into a bloody fiasco, chronicled in Mark Bowden's book *Black Hawk Down*. Aidid's militia ambushed the American Special Forces, shooting down two helicopters. Eighteen Americans were killed, and several of their corpses dragged through the muddy streets of Mogadishu; some 1,200 Somalis also died. Dick Clarke, the White House counterterrorism adviser, repeatedly pressed Woolsey and his team for intelligence: Were Aidid and his fighters aided by terrorists? The CIA had no idea but discounted the idea. "How the shit would CIA know?" complained one of Clarke's friends who'd been based in Somalia. "They had nobody in the country when the Marines landed." It was another place where the CIA was flying blind. As it turned out, unbeknown to the CIA, Al Qaeda operatives had been on the ground assisting Aidid's militia. The subsequent American retreat from Somalia sent a message to Osama bin Laden: The United States was a paper tiger.

Meanwhile, Iraq's Saddam Hussein continued to torment Clinton and his national security team. The dictator's crushing defeat in the Gulf War hadn't deterred him from murderous behavior. In April 1993, George H. W. Bush, the former president, traveled to Kuwait on a goodwill visit, where terrorists linked to Iraqi intelligence tried to blow up him and his entourage with a bomb-laden pickup truck. The assassination plot was foiled when the truck was involved in a fender-bender. In retaliation, Clinton launched twenty-three cruise missiles at the Iraqi intelligence headquarters in Baghdad.

The strike, launched on a Saturday night to minimize casualties, wound up killing a few janitors as well as some innocent civilians nearby. The American reprisal was designed to be "proportional." But Clinton's action was criticized as feckless in the press, and Woolsey regarded it as a pinprick. It was effective, he muttered to colleagues, against "Iraqi cleaning women and night watchmen but not especially effective against Saddam Hussein." Clinton was sensitive about the perception that he wasn't serious about Saddam, and Woolsey's words almost certainly got back to him.

Another crisis would turn out to be an opportunity for Woolsey and the CIA. After the disaster in Somalia, Clinton was determined to avoid foreign military adventures. But by 1993 he could no longer ignore a bloody conflict on European soil: the civil war in Bosnia and Herzegovina. The breakup of Yugoslavia after the Soviet Union's collapse had unleashed decades of suppressed animosity among Serbs, Croats, and Muslims; the result was a seemingly intractable war, the worst in Europe since 1945. In early 1993 appalling Serbian atrocities against Muslim communities took place: a massacre in a town called Srebrenica and the shelling of civilians in Sarajevo's marketplace.

After months of indecision, Clinton resolved to act. But he was frustrated by his inability to see anything on the ground; orbiting satellites, obscured by clouds, were inadequate and the Serbs were adept at hiding their big guns. To act, the U.S. needed better intelligence. Woolsey thought he knew the answer to Clinton's problem: unmanned aerial vehicles (UAVs), or drones.

Woolsey had no background in spycraft, but he was a natural at integrating technology and human intelligence. And so was a man who'd become his partner in the nascent drone program: a brilliant chemical engineer named John Deutch. The new deputy for acquisitions and technology at DOD, Deutch was a former MIT chemistry professor and knew Woolsey from defense circles. Their shared fascination with unmanned aerial vehicles would help usher in a revolutionary new field of intelligence-gathering and warfare.

Tom Twetten, then the CIA operations director, had been trying to develop a drone capability within the agency. "I went to Woolsey one day and said, 'My little Air Force has come to me and said we're done with drones.'" The CIA pilots, products of a macho,

"Top Gun" culture, wanted nothing to do with unmanned gadgets operated with joysticks. But Twetten was undeterred. He told the director he wanted to explore piggybacking on commercial ventures. Woolsey lit up at the idea. "He said, 'I know the guy!'" recalled Twetten. "It was an Israeli who had been kicked out of their military program and he was out in California. Two weeks later I'm in the desert in California with this Israeli and he flies this thing over that sounds like a lawn mower at a thousand feet, and I say 'I can't see it, but I can sure hear it.' And he said 'piece of cake, no problem,' and he put a silencer on it. And that was the prototype for the Predator."

With backing from Woolsey and Deutch, the unmanned prototype, known as the GNAT-750, would evolve into a formidable eye in the sky. Launched from a military air base in Albania, the first drones began flying over Bosnia in late 1993, sending back video of artillery, decoys, surface-to-air missiles, tanks, gun movements, checkpoints, and mass graves. Generals and admirals were mesmerized by the images; they began peppering ground control stations with requests: "Can you go back and take another look at that barn?" The drone operators joked that they'd created "Predator crack" and "Predator porn." At one point Woolsey couldn't believe his eyes as he watched footage of pedestrians crossing a bridge in Mostar, Bosnia.

Drones represented a miraculous new tool of spycraft but also something more lethal and troubling: Once armed with missiles, they'd become remote-controlled killing machines, raising legal and ethical quandaries well into the next century. Those challenges would fall to Woolsey's successors.

By 1994 the CIA was adrift, an agency without a mission. The Soviet Union, which had defined its existence, was gone. Budgets were shrinking as Congress capitalized on the so-called peace dividend. Recruitment was at an all-time low, morale at rock bottom. The agency seemed unable to perform basic tasks. Dick Clarke and a blunt-talking, ambitious White House staffer named George Tenet, Clinton's special assistant to the president for intelligence, sat next to each other in the West Wing basement and compared notes on CIA fecklessness. "They were the gang that couldn't shoot straight," Clarke said. "Every time we poked them, they couldn't do something, or they were doing something they shouldn't have done. They were clueless about everything: information we wanted on terrorism, things that we wanted done on narcotics. We were constantly running into poor agency performance."

It was worse than that: The agency's inner sanctum was compromised. Ever since its Soviet assets started disappearing mysteriously in 1985, it was clear that a mole was at work, exposing the CIA's operations and unmasking its agents. But the agency had been oblivious, looking the other way; it didn't begin a serious investigation of the security breach until 1991. And then it took nearly three years to find and arrest the mole, Aldrich Ames. Ames got away with it for so long "not because he was careful and crafty," in the words of a CIA Inspector General's report, "but because the agency effort was inadequate."

The CIA's paralysis was partly the legacy of James Jesus Angleton, the infamous counterintelligence chief. Because agency employees who'd suffered from Angleton's paranoia had come to recoil at the idea of accusations of spying being leveled on the flimsiest of evidence, a culture of credulity had arisen. Officers' explanations for what they were doing were accepted without the necessary questions being asked. The result: A would-be Soviet spy didn't have to worry much about being caught. Officers misbehaved and colleagues looked the other way. The Inspector General's report would conclude that senior CIA officials gave Ames "significant access to highly sensitive information despite strong evidence of performance and suitability problems" and "substantial suspicion regarding his trustworthiness." Ames was a spy hiding in plain sight.

The son of a CIA analyst and schoolteacher, Ames at first seemed normal enough; Jeanne Vertefeuille, a fellow CIA officer (and one of the investigators who eventually tracked him down), recalled: "Rick was just Rick—a gentle sort whose company his fellow officers enjoyed while silently laughing at his goofy physical appearance." He was "mildly unkempt, with hair that badly needed styling, teeth stained from his cigarette habit" but also "an interesting conversationalist, full of ideas." Nevertheless, the station chief in Turkey, Duane "Dewey" Clarridge, had his doubts. When Ames arrived there as a junior operative, Clarridge reported, he "lacked the necessary, fundamental personality skills.... He was in the wrong business." Yet despite his binge drinking and habitual laziness, Ames ascended the CIA ladder, failing upward until he ultimately became chief of counterintelligence for the Soviet Union.

In 1981, Ames was sent to the CIA station in Mexico City, where he began a romance with María del Rosario Casas Dupuy, a cultural attaché at the Colombian embassy. When he returned to Langley two years later, María joined him; after divorcing his first wife, Ames married María in August of 1983. Ames boasted that his new wife came from an elite Colombian family (true) and that she had plenty of money (false). The truth was she ran up huge shopping bills on Ames's modest CIA salary. But when investigators finally started asking questions about Ames's lavish lifestyle, they bought his story about María's supposed fortune hook, line, and sinker.

In the spring of 1985 Ames embarked on his secret career as a Soviet agent. He bought an expensive house with cash and began driving a flashy sports car to work every day. "I saw that damn Jaguar," Charlie Allen recalled. "It was up in the west parking lot. He used to park it next to the fence because he was afraid it'd get scratches on it."

It's said that people betray their countries for reasons having to do with "MICE" (money, ideology, compromise, ego). In Ames's case, it was money and ego: By 1985 he was deeply in debt, supporting María's expensive habits; he was also a narcissist who evidently never felt a twinge of conscience about sending Soviet agents to their deaths. As Vertefeuille later wrote, "the psychological studies of Americans who have committed this crime show that . . . what is important is self-gratification or self-interest. . . . That they are betraying their colleagues, their organization, the lives of other people, and their country as a whole seems not to weigh in the balance."

In April, Ames arranged a meeting with a Soviet intelligence official from the Russian embassy in Washington. It was the kind of "sanctioned contact" CIA officers use to entice potential Soviet recruits. Ames told both Langley and the FBI about it in advance. What they did not know was that Ames was offering himself as a recruit to the Soviet cause.

The two men agreed to meet for a drink at the Mayflower Hotel. But the Soviet spy was a no-show. After draining several vodka martinis, Ames marched over to the Russian embassy and presented an envelope to the startled receptionist. Inside was a second envelope

for the KGB rezidentura, or station chief, addressed to his operational pseudonym (something only a KGB or highly placed CIA
officer would know). This envelope contained information on two
or three cases that were being handled by the CIA's Moscow station.
Also included was a telephone list with the names of CIA personnel.
Ames circled his own. The message asked for a payment of $50,000.

For Ames it was the beginning of a lucrative second career. On
June 13, he delivered a package detailing every major case the CIA
and FBI were running against the Soviet Union, a treasure trove that
became known as "the big dump." A message arrived from his grateful Soviet handlers: "Congratulations, you are now a millionaire!"
Twice over, in fact: The KGB had set aside $2 million for him.

A joint CIA-FBI task force was formed to search for the mole.
But constant bickering and turf battles ensued, and it wasn't until
1993 that investigators finally homed in on Ames. Some at the CIA
discount the official story that he was tracked down by dogged
agency investigators; they insist that Ames was betrayed by a mysterious Soviet defector. In any event, at one point, Ames was scheduled
to leave the country—so he was summoned to a meeting at Langley,
a ruse designed to keep him in town. George Tenet, then an NSC
staffer, attended the meeting, unaware of who the mole was. Tenet
made a bet with a friend that he could identify the traitor. When they
sat down, he looked under the table and noticed a pair of expensive
Bruno Magli shoes. It was Ames. Tenet jotted down the name and
sealed it in an envelope; months later, he collected on his bet.

In early 1994 a search of Ames's trash turned up an "operational
note" between him and the KGB. On February 21, 1994, Ames was
arrested in his Jaguar after leaving his house; he was on his way to
meet an FBI agent who was posing as his Soviet handler.

Ames's arrest touched off pandemonium in the press. Director
Woolsey had recently returned from a four-country tour of the Middle East. Congress had been caught off guard by the scandal. Testifying before the House Intelligence Committee about the catastrophic
intelligence breach, Woolsey was drawn and quartered. Senators
demanded that he fire the CIA officers who'd enabled Ames's treason. But Woolsey refused to single out scapegoats. "There were four
intelligence officers during Ames's career who had made it easier for
him to continue his spying for nearly a decade," Woolsey conceded.

But those officers had retired. "So I wrote a letter to each one, saying, 'You made some very serious errors here and they had very terrible consequences to the U.S.'"

Woolsey had been on thin ice at the White House from the beginning; now his support in Congress was ebbing away. If he wanted to survive politically, heads would have to roll. "I was continually told by senators and congressmen, 'Woolsey, you have got to fire somebody,'" he recalled. "One of my favorite members of the Senate came to me and said, 'Just fire the first three people through the door.' Another senator said, 'Woolsey is acting like a civil rights lawyer, not like a DCI.'" But Woolsey wouldn't budge.

Dick Clarke could tell the end was near when Tenet kept barging into his office to vent about the director. "George would say, 'This is not working. This is not working.' Whether he was channeling the president or not, I think George had a lot to do with the decision to get rid of him." Woolsey was ready to quit but needed a nudge. He and his wife flew out to Colorado for a visit with Admiral Bobby Ray Inman, the former CIA deputy director under Bill Casey. "He looked terrible, he'd gained a lot of weight," recalled Inman. "He wanted my concurrence for him to resign. I said, 'If you're not happy, if you don't feel like you're being effective, and it's clearly impacting your health, get out.'"

On December 28, 1994, Woolsey sent a letter of resignation to the White House by courier. "It gets hard to do a job if everybody knows you can't talk to your boss," he said. "So I decided that I'd just go back to being a lawyer."

Bill Clinton had a replacement in mind: John Deutch, now deputy secretary of defense, who had been Woolsey's partner in creating the drone program. Deutch loved nothing more than brainstorming energy systems and weapons designs. He was even smarter than Woolsey and let everyone know it; his condescension could be withering: "Well, I could explain that to you but it would take too long." But Clinton was drawn to his wonky intellect and outsized, garrulous personality, much like his own. As the president's biographer and confidant, Taylor Branch, noted, Deutch was "the unusual wonk who could match Clinton's fountain of arguments."

There was just one problem. Deutch didn't want the CIA job; he was determined to become secretary of defense. So Clinton wore him down, according to Branch:

> *He reduced it to a test of personal will. "I told him, 'This is your country, and I need you over there,'" [the president] recalled. He told him the CIA was a mess. With the Soviet Union's demise [the CIA's purpose] had vanished. . . . Clinton bore in on Deutch being his indispensable choice to make major repairs. "I'll get you out of there as soon as I can," he promised, "but you don't want to turn your president down, and I know you won't."*

Clinton offered him cabinet rank, and Deutch finally relented. Clinton noted that it had taken his own version of Lyndon Johnson's relentless "presidential treatment" to bring him around.

On his first day as director, Deutch had a portrait removed from the gallery of former directors and hung prominently outside his seventh-floor office. It was of James Schlesinger, Deutch's close friend and former boss at the Department of Energy. Anointing Schlesinger as a role model struck agency veterans as odd at best— and a bad omen at worst. Jack Devine, former head of the Afghan Task Force, was a longtime operative who'd seen everything—from the Allende coup in Chile to the Iran-contra scandal. "Poor John," he said of Deutch. "If you asked, 'Who is the least popular director in the history of the agency,' it's probably Jim [Schlesinger]."

At Langley, few were neutral about Deutch. "To his supporters," wrote *The New York Times*, "the 58-year-old intelligence chief is brilliant, energetic and outspoken, a bull-in-a-china shop bureaucrat who is not afraid to air his agency's views regardless of policy and to make tough decisions in the hostile world of intelligence." To his detractors, the *Times* went on: "Mr. Deutch is full of himself, short-tempered and erratic, a political animal who . . . deserves the nickname he was given as a chemistry professor at M.I.T.: 'Shoot-ready-aim.'"

"He arrived in a sour mood and stayed that way for two years, as far I could tell," recalled Charlie Allen. Deutch seemed to consider the CIA a mere way station on his path to becoming secretary of defense. And many thought the new director looked down on CIA personnel compared to their military counterparts. (He had the odd habit of draping his arm around officers who came to brief him.) "We had officers in the Reserves at CIA," recalled Allen, "and he always said, 'It's good to see people in uniform'—i.e., 'these civilian chaps don't know what they're doing.' He was contemptuous of CIA and its culture."

Moreover, the new director brought in an abrasive outsider as his lieutenant: Nora Slatkin, who'd been an assistant secretary of the Navy and was a take-no-prisoners taskmaster who enjoyed cracking the whip on people she regarded as slackers. Deutch made her his executive director. "I liked Nora, but she could really put you in the dentist chair and drill on you," recalled a senior White House official. Agency wags, in a nod to Pearl Harbor, called her "Tora, Tora, Tora."

In the wake of Woolsey's directorship, the CIA was reeling. The Ames fiasco seemed to symbolize a broken and dysfunctional organization. One day Tenet told his friend Clarke he was leaving the White House to become Deutch's deputy. Clarke was incredulous. "I'm laughing myself silly and he's like, 'What's so funny about that?' And I said, 'You're the man who told me that the only thing we could do with CIA was to blow it up and start all over again. And now you're gonna go out there? You know how fucked up it is and now you're pretending like you don't know that?' He said, 'Yeah, I know—but we can make it better.'"

The CIA was also taking a battering in the court of public opinion. In August of 1996, the *San Jose Mercury News*, in a series titled "Dark Alliance," alleged that the agency had been complicit in creating the crack cocaine epidemic that was ravaging American cities. A Latin American guerrilla army run by the CIA had supposedly funneled tons of cocaine to a San Francisco Bay Area drug ring. On the internet, extreme versions of this ludicrous tale went viral: It was all supposedly part of a government conspiracy, orchestrated by the CIA, to keep black Americans in the throes of addiction. Frenzied media coverage led to investigations and then congressional hearings.

Deutch decided to tackle the explosive story head-on. Accepting an invitation by the House's Black Caucus, he flew to South Central Los Angeles to attend a televised town meeting, where he was met by a raucous and hostile crowd. "I took an hour of public abuse from the people there, who were convinced that the CIA was responsible," Deutch recalled. But he relished the challenge. "It was totally gratifying. First of all, at the end of the televised portion, many of the individuals who had been most vocal in the audience came up and said, 'You know, we see this now in a completely different light.' And second, the workforce back at Langley saw that the director was out there telling the American people what the CIA was trying to do." In the end there was no substantiation for the story, and the *San Jose Mercury News* retracted it.

The goodwill Deutch had earned didn't last. During his confirmation hearings, he'd pledged to change the culture of the clandestine service "down to the bare bones." And Deutch soon drew a bead on the Directorate of Operations' Latin America Division. Since the early days of the Cold War, the division had cultivated an unsavory cast of military officers, some of whom were murderers, torturers, and thieves. In Guatemala more than a hundred thousand civilians had perished at the hands of the military since the CIA-backed coup in 1954. Deutch's predecessor, Woolsey, had ordered a reassessment of the agency's relationships with these officials. The problem came to a head on Deutch's watch.

In late 1995 a Guatemalan colonel was implicated in the deaths of an American innkeeper, Michael Devine, and a Guatemalan guerrilla married to an American lawyer. The ensuing media uproar forced the U.S. to cut its military aid to the country. Compounding the problem, the CIA station chief didn't inform the U.S. ambassador that the colonel was on the CIA payroll. In September, Deutch summoned the agency's operatives to a meeting in "the Bubble," the amphitheater at the entrance to CIA headquarters. He announced that a review board had recommended the dismissal of the former Latin America Division chief and the station chief. Deutch said he intended to follow through: Heads would roll. From that moment forward, Deutch was persona non grata among the clandestine service. But Deutch insisted he'd had no choice. "Attention had to be given to changing the way the Directorate of Operations was maintaining its professional standards," he said. "There had to be a really significant change."

Deutch also took an axe to the agency's overseas stations. Early on, Charlie Allen recalled, "We were getting ready to brief him on various and sundry, and he walked in and said, 'Guess what? I just closed the fifteenth station in Africa.'" At a time when the CIA's focus had shifted from the Soviet Union to far-flung terrorist groups, Allen thought the boast was gratuitous—and shortsighted. "It didn't cost much to keep a station open in Africa. They're pretty damn small, just a communications officer and a couple of case officers and an administrative assistant. When 9/11 happened, George Tenet had to live with the legacy of those really bad decisions."

All this took a heavy toll on Deutch's standing at Langley. Bob Gates recalled attending a ceremony in the Bubble marking the CIA's fiftieth anniversary. A veteran operative sidled over to him and, pointing to Deutch on the stage, said: "You remember how you wrote that *Schlesinger* was the most unpopular director? Not anymore."

Yet Deutch still had Bill Clinton's ear. He was a fixture in the West Wing. "I had the opposite of Jim Woolsey's problem," Deutch said. "I couldn't get by without going to the White House two or three times a day. I was always going to policy meetings, endless policy meetings, about difficult issues." At NSC or principals meetings, some cabinet officials thought Deutch liked to hear himself talk, but Clinton welcomed his opinions. (A principals meeting, usually chaired by the vice president or national security adviser— and attended by top cabinet officials, intelligence community leaders, and the chairman of the joint chiefs of staff—is a forum for addressing national security and foreign policy issues.) While touring the CIA's overseas stations, Deutch sent the president memos on everything from policy ideas to covert operations, which he batted out on his portable Mac. Taking his work home was a habit that would come back to haunt him.

Deutch's championing of drones, begun under Woolsey, was about to pay off. After years of vacillation, Clinton had intervened forcefully in the Balkans. At first the CIA had been slow to detect the Serbian atrocities against Muslims, including the massacre of unarmed civilians—more than eight thousand boys and men—in Srebrenica. But drone coverage of the war zone improved, enabling an allied bombing campaign that drove the warring parties to the bargaining table. In November of 1995 the war ended in a landmark peace agreement, hammered out by American diplomat Richard Holbrooke, at an Air Force base in Dayton, Ohio.

In the fall of 1995, Deutch and his deputy Tenet turned their focus on terrorism. Khartoum, the capital of Sudan, had become a magnet for the world's most violent thugs, a "hootenanny of terrorism," in the words of legendary CIA case officer Cofer Black. A hard-charging operative and future head of the Counterterrorism Center, Black had collared the infamous Algerian terrorist known as Carlos the Jackal in Khartoum and handed him over to French intelligence. Now he was watching another terrorist who had taken up residence there, Osama bin Laden.

Expelled by Saudi Arabia, bin Laden had arrived in Khartoum five years earlier, in 1991. Deutch established a unit dedicated to pursuing him, a "virtual station" headquartered at Langley. It was called Alec Station, after the unit chief's son. At the time "there wasn't even an open Justice Department investigation against him," said Deutch. But the director, backed by Tenet and Clarke, was convinced that bin Laden and his followers were a gathering threat. Considered a backwater, Alec Station was at first staffed mostly by women. "They were chasing bin Laden before chasing bin Laden was cool," observed Michael Hayden, the National Security Agency head and future CIA director. "It was a sisterhood that would ultimately lead us to Abbottabad."

But bin Laden was still a shadowy menace; Saddam Hussein was considered a clear and present danger. Not only had Saddam tried to assassinate former president Bush, but he kept shooting at American planes enforcing the no-fly zone, and he was thought to be developing chemical and biological weapons. Clinton had had enough; he wanted to get rid of the Iraqi dictator by fair means or foul.

Deutch was determined to oblige him. "The Iraqi situation kept me up at night," he said. "We were having trouble dealing with Saddam and didn't know what to do next to make him go away— *really* go away."

Upon becoming director, Deutch had reached out to Richard Helms for advice. The retired spymaster, then eighty-two, met the new director for lunch. "He was skeptical of covert action and properly so," recalled Deutch. With Helms's guidance, Deutch developed a checklist of questions before launching a covert operation: "One, will the American people support you if it shows up on the front page of the paper? And second, do you have some confidence that you can do it effectively and competently?" For all that, the CIA's efforts to topple Saddam Hussein through covert action would end in disaster.

The first attempt was spearheaded by none other than Robert Baer, the Middle East hand who'd been obsessed with capturing or killing Imad Mughniyah, the Hezbollah mastermind. A twenty-one-year CIA veteran, Baer had been a classmate of George Tenet at Georgetown University, and a rakish troublemaker and prankster. One day during exams he roared into the university library on a motorcycle, his girlfriend on the back, and pulled a wheelie. Twenty years later, Baer recalled, he ran into Tenet in the White House. "He says, 'I remember you. I'll never forget you—Georgetown, Pierce Reading Room.' He'd been in the library, sitting there. And he didn't hold it against me. I like George Tenet."

Baer, undercover in Iraq, had lost none of his enthusiasm for troublemaking. And he had a plan to overthrow Saddam. "We had a so-called walk-in, an ex-general who proposed a coup d'état against Saddam," he recalled. "Which was basically his assassination. And I wrote six messages back to Washington and didn't get a single answer on any of these messages." Baer plowed ahead. "They were going to corner Saddam at his compound in a little town south of Tikrit. And if he didn't surrender they were going to blow him off the top of the mountain with T-72 tanks. Kill him. I said that sounded like a good plan. Let me see if I can get support in Washington." Once again, Baer got no response. "So I just told the Iraqis, 'Look, we can't live with this guy. So propose a time and a date.'"

Cooler heads recognized a doomed scheme when they saw one. "We called it the Bay of Kurds," recalled Riedel, "because we knew that if it went forward it would end up like the Bay of Pigs." The plot depended on cooperation not only from the Kurds but also their enemy, Turkey. "To support the Kurds we had to have the Turks' permission and the last thing the Turks are gonna do is help you with the Kurds."

Baer was undaunted. But then, he recalled, "As it got closer to the time and date, things started to go to hell." The Iranians went on full alert, sending tanks and planes to the border. The Iraqis replied in kind, and the Turks soon followed. Back in Washington, General John Shalikashvili, chairman of the Joint Chiefs of Staff, called Tony

Lake in the middle of the night. "What the hell is happening in Iraq?" he asked the bleary-eyed national security adviser.

Lake called Admiral William Studeman, who was acting CIA director at the time because Deutch was traveling. As Baer explained, "My division chief hadn't told him about any of these plans. And he told Lake, 'I don't know what's going on.' So Lake says, 'Goddammit, if the CIA director doesn't know what's going on, this has got to be a rogue coup.' So Lake called up Louis Freeh, the FBI director, and said, 'There's a rogue at the CIA and his name is Bob Baer.'"

Baer tried to call off the operation, but it was too late; the hoped-for uprising failed and more than a thousand Kurds were killed. Months later, when he returned to the U.S., Baer resigned from the CIA. Prosecutors wanted to bring him up on attempted murder charges. But the attorney general declined to prosecute.

The second coup attempt was based in Jordan. A CIA team met with a defector, a former commander of the Iraqi Special Forces, who belonged to a network of Saddam mutineers. The agency had spent millions of dollars cultivating members of Iraq's political and military elite, and the time seemed ripe for an uprising. But the plot was completely compromised by Iraqi spies. On June 26, 1996, Saddam's henchmen arrested more than two hundred of the plotters; eighty were executed. "The plot was totally penetrated and it all came crashing down," recalled Riedel.

At the White House, the failure of the Saddam coup plots accelerated Deutch's demise. "Deutch promised that he would get rid of Saddam Hussein within six months or something like that, a completely stupid thing to say," said Riedel. The coup de grâce came when Deutch testified before the Senate Intelligence Committee, confessing that the administration had failed to loosen Saddam's grip on power. "In the last six weeks, he has gotten stronger politically in the region," Deutch said. That was the last thing the president wanted to hear from his CIA director.

At Clinton's request, on December 15, 1996, Deutch sent a letter of resignation to the White House. Making a bitter pill even tougher to swallow, Clinton denied Deutch the job he'd wanted from the beginning: secretary of defense. That post, vacated by the outgoing William Perry, went to ex-Senator William Cohen.

But Deutch's troubles weren't over.

The day of his resignation, CIA technicians went to his Bethesda, Maryland, home to remove a classified computer and safe. What they found alarmed them. On Deutch's personal, unsecured computer were thirty-one files containing highly sensitive classified information, including memos to the president with material classified Top Secret. A CIA Inspector General report later found that Deutch had stored classified information on five unsecured computers, four of which had been connected to the internet. "High-risk internet sites had placed 'cookies' on the hard drives," the report said, "jeopardizing classified information." The investigation found that Deutch had "intentionally processed . . . large volumes of highly classified information, [including] Top Secret Codeword material."

Deutch faced possible prosecution for mishandling classified information, and a potential prison term of ten years. But on January 19, 2001, he agreed to plead guilty to a misdemeanor. The next day, his last as president, Bill Clinton pardoned him.

It fell to George Tenet, then the acting CIA director, to strip Deutch of his security clearances. He found the experience of disciplining his mentor painful. "I often wondered if I could have handled it differently," he told me twenty-five years later. "I just think the country has missed having a great brain on its side."

CHAPTER SEVEN

"They're coming here."

George Tenet, Bill Clinton, and George W. Bush

In January of 1997, at the start of his second term, Bill Clinton decided to make a clean sweep of his national security team. Warren Christopher, the buttoned-down, lawyerly secretary of state, would be replaced by Madeleine Albright, the first woman to hold the post; Tony Lake, the cerebral, mild-mannered national security adviser, would give up his position to his disheveled, workaholic deputy, Sandy Berger. But who would replace John Deutch as CIA director? Clinton's first choice was his old friend Lake.

Tony Lake was a formidable figure, respected for his acumen, integrity, and foreign policy gravitas; though he had the air of an absentminded professor, he was a skillful political infighter and knew how to navigate bureaucracies. With Capitol Hill mired in partisan gridlock, Lake expected a grueling confirmation battle. But he had no idea that he was walking into a free-for-all.

The hearings before the Senate Select Committee on Intelligence (SSCI) turned into a political brawl. Determined to block Clinton's agenda, Republicans accused Lake of politicizing the National Security Council; they impugned his managerial experience, integrity, and political beliefs. Richard Shelby, the Republican chair, launched an investigation into Lake's FBI files, and threatened to delay a confirmation vote indefinitely. After two months, Lake had had enough. Tired of being "a dancing bear in a political circus," he told Clinton he was withdrawing his nomination.

On Sunday, March 16, 1997, Lake called George Tenet and asked him to meet him by the C&O Canal in Georgetown. Tenet, who'd left the Clinton White House staff to become Deutch's deputy, was now acting CIA director. As they walked along the towpath, Lake told Tenet that he was recommending him as the next Director of Central Intelligence. "I am going to tell the president that he must nominate you to become DCI," Lake said. "Look, you know the place, you've got the skills, the president likes you, and the Senate will confirm you. Tell me anybody else that can be said about. You'd love the job."

Though he felt badly for his friend Lake, Tenet didn't need anyone to twist his arm. "I was like a Broadway understudy who'd just found out that his best pal, the star of the show, had been hit by a bus," Tenet wrote later. But the truth was Tenet had been studying for the role his entire career. Few people seemed better prepared to lead the CIA. Tenet had been staff director of the SSCI; presidential assistant on Clinton's NSC; deputy director to Deutch. But nothing could have prepared him for the tumultuous journey that lay ahead.

Tenet's seven-year tenure, the longest since Allen Dulles, would span a stunning succession of crises: the attacks of September 11, 2001; the brutal prisoner interrogation program known as "enhanced interrogation techniques" (EIT); the agency's botched estimate of Saddam Hussein's weapons of mass destruction (WMD). Any one of those ordeals would have consumed most directors; Tenet would endure them all. As CIA director, he was an almost Shakespearean character, leading the agency to victory over the Taliban; reviving its battered morale; bringing it back from fiscal and spiritual bankruptcy. But those achievements would be overshadowed by his ill-fated National Intelligence Estimate (NIE) on Iraq's WMDs, which gave Bush the pretext to launch an unnecessary war.

The son of a Greek diner owner in Queens, New York, Tenet was restless and ambitious from the moment he could walk; in contrast to his laconic fraternal twin, Bill, George wouldn't stop talking. Leslie Gelb, the veteran diplomat who taught Tenet at Georgetown's School of Foreign Service, was impressed by his loquacious student, but gave him a B-plus. "The reason I did not give him an A was because he always thought he could get by on bullshit," Gelb explained. "He's a character, a good storyteller, a good schmoozer—and usually people like that don't get jobs like CIA director."

Tenet's gregarious, extroverted personality bowled people over; his energy and enthusiasm were disarming. Yet he was disciplined and focused and famous for overpreparing; he spent hours mastering

CIA director Richard Helms meets with President Lyndon Johnson in the Oval Office in 1966. Helms regarded LBJ with fond admiration for his Great Society and complete exasperation over the Vietnam War. (Photo courtesy of Everett Collection)

At a White House state dinner for the Shah of Iran in 1975, Helms (at left) and his wife, Cynthia, dance alongside the *Shahbanou*, or empress (at center), and her American partner, the great dancer-entertainer Fred Astaire. (Photo courtesy of National Archives and Records Administration)

Director James R. Schlesinger was sent by Richard Nixon to shake up the CIA in 1973. "We're going to stop fucking Richard Nixon," he declared.
(Photo courtesy of Gerald R. Ford Presidential Library and Museum)

William Colby, who replaced Schlesinger as director, was denounced as a traitor—and celebrated as a reformer—when he released secret CIA abuses known as the Family Jewels.
(Photo courtesy of David Hume Kennerly)

During congressional hearings, Arizona senator Barry Goldwater waves a poisonous dart gun supposedly used by CIA operatives in covert operations.
(Photo by Bettman/Getty Images)

CIA director George H. W. Bush waits for a train at Philadelphia's 30th Street Station. Bush thought the directorship would end his political career. (Photo courtesy of Dick Swanson)

Bush conducts an intelligence briefing in the Cabinet Room with President Gerald Ford and advisers. (Photo courtesy of David Hume Kennerly)

Admiral Stansfield Turner, Jimmy Carter's CIA director, was blindsided by the 1979 Islamic revolution that toppled the Shah of Iran, a U.S. ally. "We were just plain asleep," Turner admitted. (Photo courtesy of David Hume Kennerly)

William Casey, Ronald Reagan's DCI, was the most powerful CIA director since Allen Dulles. But he was undone by a harebrained covert operation: the Iran-contra scandal. (Photo by Diana Walker/The LIFE Images Collection via Getty Images)

Director Casey, known as "Mumbles" for his unintelligible speech, confers with James Jesus Angleton (left), former head of CIA counterintelligence, known for his Byzantine theory of a diabolical Soviet "Master Plot." (Photo by Cynthia Johnson/The LIFE Images Collection via Getty Images)

Tapped by President Reagan to replace Bill Casey, "Judge" William Webster, a former FBI director, asked a CIA veteran: "Can I do the job as [CIA] director, being a man of the law?" (Photo courtesy of David Hume Kennerly)

A suffer-no-fools analyst, Robert Gates failed on his first attempt, in 1987, to be confirmed as Reagan's CIA director, but succeeded on his second try, under President George H. W. Bush, in 1991. (Photo courtesy of David Hume Kennerly)

CIA director James Woolsey, an eccentric technocrat with a "strange intelligence," had just one private meeting with President Bill Clinton. "They were like oil and water," said a White House aide. (Photo courtesy of David Hume Kennerly)

Aldrich "Rick" Ames, a longtime CIA officer, was exposed in 1994 as a Soviet spy. His betrayals led to the execution of dozens of CIA Soviet assets and cost Woolsey his job. (Photo by Luke Frazza/AFP via Getty Images)

A brilliant former MIT chemistry professor, Director John Deutch foresaw the age of drones. But he fell out of favor with Clinton after bungled CIA coup attempts against Iraq's Saddam Hussein. (Photo courtesy of David Hume Kennerly)

George Tenet watches President Bush on television after 9/11. The charismatic director warned of an imminent Al Qaeda attack and led the CIA's rout of the Taliban in Afghanistan. But Tenet would be tarnished by the agency's greatest debacle: the botched estimate of Iraq's WMDs. (Photo courtesy of Central Intelligence Agency)

Tenet's deputy director, John McLaughlin, a courtly intellectual, was sometimes called "George's brain." An amateur magician, McLaughlin could not make flawed intelligence estimates magically disappear. (Photo courtesy of David Hume Kennerly)

Left to right: Defense secretary Donald Rumsfeld, CIA director Tenet, and Vice President Dick Cheney confer in January 2002. Tenet disputed Cheney's claim that Iraq had links to the 9/11 hijackers. (Photo by David Hume Kennerly/ Getty Images)

On a visit to CIA headquarters in Langley, Va., President George W. Bush, flanked by CIA director Porter Goss, addresses the media. (Photo by Paul Morse, courtesy of the George W. Bush Presidential Library and Museum)

Director Goss, a former chair of the House Intelligence Committee, made enemies at Langley by bringing along a coterie of sycophants who came to be known as "the Gosslings." (Photo by Paul Morse, courtesy of the George W. Bush Presidential Library and Museum)

A former head of the National Security Agency (NSA), CIA director Michael Hayden, an Air Force general, wound down the controversial program known as "enhanced interrogation techniques." (Photo courtesy of David Hume Kennerly)

Imad Mughniyah, chief of operations of Hezbollah, was so elusive he was known as the "Scarlet Pimpernel of terrorism." For decades he was the number one target of the CIA and Israel's Mossad. (AP Photo/Hussein Malla)

Gregarious and outgoing, Director Leon Panetta, a former White House chief of staff, was beloved by the rank and file, and a masterful bureaucratic infighter. (Photo courtesy of Central Intelligence Agency)

Elizabeth Hanson, one of the agency's "targeters," was among seven CIA officers and contractors killed in a suicide bombing when a meeting with a supposed Al Qaeda infiltrator went tragically awry. (Photo courtesy of Colby College)

A razor-sharp analyst, Michael Morell was George W. Bush's CIA briefer on Air Force One during 9/11—and a two-time acting director under Panetta and General David Petraeus. (Photo courtesy of David Hume Kennerly)

David Petraeus, the celebrated former commander of U.S. forces in Iraq and Afghanistan, arrived at the CIA with a case of entitlement, or "four-star general disease." But he adapted to Langley's culture. (Photo courtesy of David Hume Kennerly)

Anwar al-Awlaki, a militant Islamic cleric—and an American citizen— waged jihad against the U.S. from Yemen. His killing there by a CIA drone in 2011 sparked debate among former CIA directors. (Photo by Tracy Woodward/The Washington Post via Getty Images)

Petraeus leaves a federal courthouse in Charlotte, N.C., in 2015. Charged with sharing classified information with Paula Broadwell, his biographer and lover, the ex-director pleaded guilty to a misdemeanor and admitted to lying to the FBI. (Photo by John W. Adkisson/Getty Images)

CIA director John Brennan is heckled by protesters at his Senate confirmation hearing in 2013. A dispassionate broker of intelligence, Brennan also had the moral streak of "an Irish cop." (AP Photo/J. Scott Applewhite)

Director Brennan, on a crutch after a hip operation, visits the agency's Memorial Wall with former president George H. W. Bush on January 29, 2016, the fortieth anniversary of Bush's swearing in as director of central intelligence. (Photo courtesy of Central Intelligence Agency)

Director Mike Pompeo at his Senate confirmation hearing on January 12, 2017. Pompeo catered to President Donald Trump's Twitter-size attention span. (Photo by Joe Raedle/Getty Images)

Visiting CIA headquarters the day after his inauguration, President Trump delivers a tone-deaf harangue, bragging about the size of his inaugural crowd in front of the agency's hallowed Memorial Wall. (Photo by Olivier Doulier – Pool/Getty Images)

Succeeding Pompeo, Gina Haspel was confirmed as CIA director in May 2018. "Gina's tough, she's strong . . . [and she] will never, ever back down," Trump said of his new director. But many wondered if Haspel was tough enough to stand up to the president. (Photo by Saul Loeb/AFP via Getty Images)

The architect of the CIA program known as rendition, detention, and interrogation (RDI), Jose Rodriguez became Gina Haspel's mentor, urging her to be more assertive and ambitious. (Photo courtesy of David Hume Kennerly)

President Trump meets with (from left to right): National Security Adviser John Bolton, CIA director Haspel, his daily CIA briefer, and Director of National Intelligence Dan Coats. (White House Photo by Shealah Craghead)

The brutal murder of *Washington Post* columnist Jamal Khashoggi (right), attributed by the CIA to a Saudi hit team sent by Crown Prince Mohammed bin Salman (MBS), became a flash point between the agency and the Trump administration. (Photo courtesy of The Asahi Shimbun/The Asahi Shimbun)

In June 2019, a Norwegian-owned tanker burns in the Gulf of Oman, part of a wave of attacks attributed by the CIA to Iran. The U.S.-Iran crisis would come to a boil in December 2019. (Photo by -/ISNA/AFP via Getty Images)

A lethal Predator drone. So-called targeted killings by the CIA increased dramatically under President Barack Obama—despite his pledge to shift authority for drone strikes to the military. (Super Nova Images/Alamy Stock Photo)

On January 3, 2020, on orders from President Trump, a lethal American drone obliterated Qassim Suleimani (above), a legendary Iranian general, near Baghdad's airport. The strike reignited an age-old CIA debate: Is assassinating a foreign leader ever justified? (Photo by Sipa via AP Images)

his briefs for NSC meetings, congressional appearances, and Oval Office sessions. Tenet was politically savvy and had cultivated allies on the Hill, in the West Wing, and in the intelligence community. On March 19, 1997, Clinton took Lake's advice and nominated Tenet as CIA director. He was confirmed by the Senate in a unanimous vote.

At Langley Tenet was always in motion, cradling a basketball in one hand, twirling an unlit Cohiba cigar in the other. He prowled the halls, worked the cafeteria, bragged about Georgetown sports, introduced himself. "He's gone walk-about," his secretary would complain when Tenet went roaming the building. He did a dead-on impersonation of PLO leader Yasser Arafat. Tenet littered his speech with "fuck it, godddamn it, screw it." "He had that sort of swagger where he could come into a room and talk very colloquially," recalled Steven Hall, an operative. "It was language that the vast majority of us were unused to hearing. That endeared him to a workforce that really likes that kind of straight talk; they thought this guy really isn't that different from the rest of us."

Tenet was popular not only at Langley but with overseas station chiefs. "It was always a big deal when the director of the CIA was going to come into town and talk to the foreign intelligence chiefs that you did business with on a daily basis," said a former operative. "He would have long dinners with these guys with innumerable toasts and did the required cultural shows. He would do it all. He would never say, 'Jeez, I really don't want to do that.'"

As director, Tenet embraced the CIA like a battered child. "They had gone through so many directors and had so many scandals that their morale was in the toilet," recalled his friend Dick Clarke, the White House counterterrorism adviser. "A lot of them had been laid off at the end of the Cold War. There was a downsizing and there were crises. George's philosophy was the way to solve this morale problem was to give the agency a big hug." Tenet hugged the workforce literally and figuratively; he fought for bigger agency budgets and created employee events like "Family Day" to boost morale.

He'd inherited an agency in free fall. "We were almost in Chapter 11, literally and figuratively," Tenet recalled. "We lost twenty-five percent of our people. We had lost billions of dollars in investment. Our infrastructure was crumbling. Our training facilities were in disarray. I was the fourth director in seven years. I want you to think about any multibillion-dollar enterprise operating in 120 countries turning over leadership that way."

Tenet continued: "Our training facilities were in absolute disrepair. We were hemorrhaging talent. Thirty people had just left the East Asian Division. We stopped recruiting. At one point there were twelve people being trained at the Farm [the secret CIA training facility]. The FBI had more special agents in New York City than we had in the entire world. We weren't keeping pace with technology. Morale was in the basement. Attrition was high but no one was measuring it, and nobody could tell you where the hemorrhage was occurring, whether it was in places you needed or places we didn't care about."

But in the gospel according to Tenet, crisis was opportunity. "I thought, this is a chance to put the place back together," he said. At one of his first meetings with the workforce in the Bubble, Tenet promised he'd have their backs, but they'd have to rise to the challenge of a new era. "It was necessary in order to resurrect the organization," he said. "We stood up and looked at our employees and said, 'We've just had our fiftieth anniversary. If we don't change, we won't get to our sixtieth anniversary.'"

Given the gathering threats, the CIA might be lucky to get to its fifty-fifth.

After becoming director, Tenet had lunch with Jack Devine, who had led the Afghan Task Force in support of the mujahideen, and had survived the debacles of Allende's overthrow and the Iran-contra scandal. Devine was worried about Iraq, where the CIA had deployed clandestine forces. Tenet was struck by Devine's premonition. "George, this isn't going to turn out well," he warned. "A bullet has been fired at you but I can't say where it it's going to hit."

That bullet—in the form of an ill-fated, misbegotten war—would strike Tenet between the eyes later in his tenure. But in the meantime other threats were jostling for attention. Al Qaeda and Hezbollah were gathering strength. And so was Hezbollah's chief of operations, Imad Mughniyah.

The official myth is that there is nothing personal about the way the CIA prioritizes its targets. But Mughniyah disproves that myth; for a generation of CIA officers, capturing or killing him was not only personal but visceral. It was Mughniyah who was thought to be behind the worst day in CIA history: the 1983 bombing of the Beirut embassy that left seven officers dead and blinded the agency in the Middle East. He was implicated in the devastating Marine barracks bombing, the hijacking of TWA Flight 847, and the capture of William Buckley, the Beirut CIA station chief. "Mughniyah was personal," said Bruce Riedel. "And it goes back to Bill Buckley. He was kidnapped, tortured, and then murdered, and Hezbollah sent us a video."

For some CIA officers, including Bob Baer, Mughniyah was an obsession. Baer believed that when it came to cunning and expertise no other terrorist could compare with him. "Bin Laden was a fraud compared to Mughniyah in terms of tactics and ability to strategize and to bring precise violence," he said. "Bin Laden slaughtered people. Mughniyah didn't slaughter people. He figured out who he had to take out."

As Hezbollah's weapons expert, Mughniyah pioneered a deadly explosive for use against Israeli troops in Lebanon. It was known as a shaped charge. The CIA had created the original weapon and shared it with the Afghan rebels. The mujahideen passed it along to the Iranians, Hezbollah's sponsors. Mughniyah had perfected the lethal device. This cemented his relationship with his Iranian patron, General Qassim Suleimani, who would be targeted by Donald Trump decades later. "Mughniyah led a group of people who could manipulate explosives and build these devices like we'd never seen before," said Baer. "And they basically could kill any head of state they wanted. Because of the penetrating power and the accuracy of these shaped charges they could cut through an armored vehicle like a knife through butter."

Mughniyah used them to almost singlehandedly drive the Israelis out of Lebanon. In February of 1999, Brigadier General Erez Gerstein, the senior Israeli military official in Lebanon, was in an armored car, racing down a highway, when an explosion ripped through the vehicle, killing him and three others. It was a shaped charge, remotely detonated by an infrared sensor hidden in a roadside rock. The killing shocked Israel; labor leader Ehud Barak vowed that if elected he'd pull Israeli troops out of Lebanon—a promise he kept. "So one of these charges caused Israel to withdraw under fire, the first time in its history," said Baer. "And the best we can determine it was Mughniyah."

And yet unlike his high-profile mentor, General Suleimani, Mughniyah was shrouded in secrecy; no one at the CIA would talk about him. In separate interviews for a Showtime documentary, I asked the directors about him, in these exchanges that never aired:

> Chris Whipple: *What can you tell us about a person named Imad Mughniyah?*
> Michael Morell: *Nothing.*

> Whipple: *What can you tell us . . . ?*
> Bob Gates: *Nothing.*

> Whipple: *Is there anything you can tell us . . . ?*
> Leon Panetta: *No, there isn't.*

> Whipple: *And why is it that nobody can tell us about [Mughniyah]?*
> Michael Hayden: *Don't have anything to offer on that.*

> Whipple: *Why won't anybody talk about him?*
> Michael Morell: *I'm not going to talk about him.*

Finally, Bob Gates offered this: "Mughniyah, from my standpoint, was the personification of evil."

In the summer of 2019, Charlie Allen, the CIA's former NIO for Warning, was more forthcoming about the terrorist they dubbed "Maurice." "God, the days and nights I worried over how we could get rid of him," he told me. "We tried to get him many times. I tried. He was our highest priority. Not only to find him but to ensure that he didn't live any longer."

The CIA had come tantalizingly close to capturing Mughniyah. In 1995, the agency learned that he was on a plane bound from Khartoum to Beirut. The flight had a stopover in Jedda, Saudi Arabia, and the CIA seized its chance: U.S. officials persuaded Saudi authorities to hold the plane until the FBI could board it and grab him. Cofer Black, the veteran operative, was in Khartoum. "The plane landed," he recalled. "They were going to hold it, and the bureau [FBI] was going to come board the plane. Read him his rights. Put him on a plane. Take him home. Sweet. No muss, no fuss."

But the plan unraveled. "The FBI plane was coming in to land—and as it was approaching its entrance into the kingdom, Saudi airspace was denied," said Black. The Saudis had evidently developed cold feet. Allen was devastated. "We missed him by a matter of minutes," he said. "It was very, very close."

Since then there had been no trace of him.

Then, on George Tenet's watch, came a breakthrough. Through painstaking intelligence work, Black, now head of the CIA's Counterterrorism Center (CTC), had drawn a bead on Mughniyah, and had a chance to grab him. It's a story that hasn't been reported before.

Mughniyah was known to be in Lebanon, but he moved constantly; neither the CIA nor Mossad could pinpoint his whereabouts long enough to take action. But then came a tip from Lebanese sources. Maurice, they said, liked to make sporadic nighttime visits to the home of a girlfriend. During these visits he'd have sex with her—and then beat her. "When he did that," said the sources, "he would drop his protective detail and tell them to go home for the night."

CIA operatives approached the girlfriend, according to a source with knowledge of the operation. "They said, 'Let's do a deal, we'll get a lookout post in a nearby apartment. You do something to indicate when he's there and we'll have a standby team.'" Mughniyah's lover agreed to lure him into the trap. But could she be trusted? Charlie Allen thought so. "Oh, she wanted to *kill* him," he said. "She was willing to do it because she hated him so much."

The operation was risky but the possible upside of capturing the elusive Hezbollah terrorist was immense. "He killed hundreds of Marines and foreign service officers," said a former official. "I would've done anything to get him. And risking a team of CIA officers to get him? Fuck it, risk them." The plan was to grab Mughniyah, bundle him into a speedboat, and make a dash for the open Mediterranean. The CIA team told the girlfriend: "We'll come in, break down the door, grab him—and you, if you want—run downstairs, get in a couple of Suburbans, and go to the harbor. We'll have a fast boat and get the fuck out of Dodge and we'll have a ship offshore."

If capturing Mughniyah went awry, the CIA team would kill him. But that raised the old conundrum: When was the agency, and the

U.S., authorized to kill? Executive Order 12333 proscribed assassinations. But the prohibition wasn't ironclad. There were always ways around it. "What Clinton and Sandy Berger did, dragging Attorney General Janet Reno along," said the former official, "was to say, 'What we're talking about is killing the command and control element of a nonstate military force.'"

But the operation fell apart at the last moment. "Cofer thought it was a great idea," said the former official. "George Tenet never approved it. Too risky." But Allen disputed this version; he insisted that Tenet wouldn't have scuttled a chance to collar—or kill—the CIA's most important target. "Tenet wouldn't call that off," he said. Allen suggested that something went wrong on the ground, but wouldn't elaborate: "There's a lot of other things I could say, but they'd be extremely classified."

Tenet wouldn't comment on the mission. "I'm not going to talk about what happened on my watch with regard to Mughniyah," he told me flatly.

Whatever the reason for his narrow escape, Imad Mughniyah would continue to terrorize the U.S. and Israel for another ten years.

By 1997 Tenet was focused on another target: Al Qaeda. A year earlier Osama bin Laden and his inner circle had left Sudan for Afghanistan. Ensconced in the tribal regions, the well-funded Saudi began plotting attacks on American interests. Sandy Berger, the new national security adviser, asked Tenet to draw up a plan to destroy Al Qaeda. "He said, 'I want you to imagine that you had all the authorities you needed and all the resources you needed,'" recalled Tenet. "'What would you do?' We knew exactly what to do: Get into the Afghan sanctuary, launch a paramilitary operation. We were ready to do it." Tenet called this plan "the Blue Sky paper."

Cofer Black, head of the CTC, couldn't believe the volume of threats he was seeing from Al Qaeda. "The first week that I was there, they stick you in a conference room and all the people start coming in and briefing you on their areas of activity," Black recalled. "I don't shock easy. But I was shocked. This was a wave of threats coming at the United States. There was no doubt in my mind that the United States was going to be struck and struck hard. Lots of Americans were going to die."

But the Blue Sky paper languished; there was little appetite in the Clinton administration for a wholescale assault on Al Qaeda's Afghan sanctuary.

As president, Bill Clinton had been reluctant to use lethal force. Lake recalled that after Saddam's attempted assassination of George H. W. Bush, Clinton almost called off the cruise missile strike on Iraq's Intelligence Ministry for fear of civilian casualties. "I said, 'Yes, you'll kill some people now, but you'll save a lot more people later,'" said Lake. "'You've got to do it.'"

When it came to killing bin Laden, the legal bureaucracy reinforced Clinton's skittishness. As Clarke explained: "Janet Reno, the attorney general, had a problem with saying, 'Just go kill him.' So we'd say, 'Try to apprehend him.' We already had bin Laden under sealed indictment, so we could arrest him. But only if that failed could you kill him." The legal contortions drove Cofer Black up the wall. "I mean, I *love* this," he said sarcastically. "This is such a *Washington* thing: Our instructions were to capture him. And that's what we attempted to do. And the difference between capturing—and the alternative—is significant."

Tenet was equally reluctant to kill bin Laden. His reasons weren't just legalistic. "The CIA always used that as their excuse for not killing him," said Clarke, "but in fact they just didn't want to get in the killing business." In Tenet's view, the issue went to the heart of his role as CIA director.

Tenet recalled an eerie moment when he and his lieutenants were watching footage from a drone flying over Afghanistan. "We saw a very tall man in white robes who we assumed at the time was bin Laden," Tenet said. "Of course, we couldn't do anything about it because these drones weren't armed at the time." But Tenet envisioned a day when drones would carry missiles—and someone would decide who lived or died. Should that person be the CIA director? "I had a question: Do you want the civilian head of an intelligence organization firing a weapon outside of the chain of military command? It's a big question." Tenet raised the issue at NSC meetings. "We never got the answer," he said. It was a question that would arise repeatedly in the era of drone warfare yet to come.

The rules of engagement for bin Laden led to some convoluted covert schemes: One involved sending warriors from the Northern

Alliance into Bin Laden's compound, a place called Tarnak Farms, then kidnapping him, rolling him up in a blanket, taking him to a hideout, and awaiting evacuation by a CIA plane. Tenet thought the plan was crazy and called it off.

But on August 7, 1998, everything changed. Suicide truck bombers struck the American embassies in Dar es Salaam, Tanzania, and Nairobi, Kenya, in East Africa. The nearly simultaneous explosions were devastating, killing 224 people, including two CIA officers. It was immediately clear that Al Qaeda was responsible. Clinton was now resolved: He wanted bin Laden dead.

But retaliating posed a political risk. At the time Clinton was embroiled in the Monica Lewinsky affair; and a movie had been released, *Wag the Dog*, based on a fictional president who starts a war to distract from a scandal. Nevertheless, Clinton authorized cruise missile attacks on two targets: a pharmaceutical plant in Sudan (where the CIA claimed it had detected traces of chemical agents) and an encampment in Afghanistan where bin Laden was thought to be spending the night. But by the time the missiles struck, the Al Qaeda leader was gone.

The embassy bombings were a wake-up call for Tenet. "After the East Africa bombings, I sat at home and furiously drafted a memo," he said. "It was called 'We're at War.' Enough swatting at flies. We need to put a worldwide plan in place where we can start demonstrating that we can penetrate this adversary through human sources, technical collection, the use of foreign liaison partners, to not only disrupt and stop this organization, but hopefully take action against it." But once again, the plan had no takers at the White House.

In the waning months of the Clinton administration, a month before the 2000 presidential election, Al Qaeda struck again. On October 12, in the port of Aden in Yemen, a small skiff, riding low in the water, pulled alongside the USS *Cole*, a guided missile destroyer. The skiff's cargo of TNT exploded, blowing a hole in the side of the American warship. The blast killed seventeen sailors and injured thirty-nine.

There was no doubt about who was responsible. "We went to the president and said, 'This is obviously an Al Qaeda attack,'" recalled Clarke, who was continuing to act as counterterrorism adviser to the NSC. But persuading him to retaliate was a tough sell; Clinton, his national security team, and Tenet were all preoccupied with the second Palestinian intifada that followed the failure of Clinton's Arab-Israeli summit at Camp David in 2000. And there was another problem. Neither the CIA nor the FBI would officially link the bombing of the ship to Al Qaeda.

According to one senior intelligence official, the agency deliberately repressed the intelligence. "We were told we could not assign the blame for the USS *Cole* attack to bin Laden because if we did that then the Clinton administration would have been forced to take action," he said. "The message was 'you cannot write about it, do not assign blame.'" A definitive finding, this official said, might have affected the upcoming presidential election. "The political commissars all thought that Gore would win, but it would have been a bad thing—Democrats would have been seen as weak—if we assigned blame to bin Laden and didn't do anything. And so nothing was ever done about the USS *Cole*."

If true, this would have been a flagrant case of skewing intelligence for partisan political reasons. But Tenet emphatically denied that it happened. No such message, he insisted, was sent to his analysts. According to Tenet, only the FBI, in charge of the USS *Cole* investigation, could have given a green light to retaliate. Clarke begged to differ: "We never needed an FBI conclusion in order to retaliate. All we needed was an intelligence conclusion. George would never give it to us."

Another opportunity to strike Al Qaeda had passed on Bill Clinton's watch. Later *The 9/11 Commission Report* would conclude: "Bin Laden's inference may well have been that attacks, at least on the level of the *Cole*, were risk free."

With the election of George W. Bush in 2000, George Tenet's directorship appeared to be over. Bush's first choice to run the CIA was Donald Rumsfeld, Gerald Ford's acerbic former chief of staff and defense secretary. In fact, even before the Supreme Court decided the closest presidential election in American history, Rumsfeld's aides were in Tenet's seventh-floor office, literally measuring the drapes. But Bush's plan was scuttled when his first and second choices for defense secretary declined his offer; he'd need Rumsfeld to run the Pentagon. Never mind the bad blood over Rummy supposedly sending his father into political exile at the CIA back in the 1970s. "W" considered that ancient history.

Tenet hoped Bush might keep him on as CIA director. After all, George H. W. Bush believed the job should be above politics, and had urged his son to let Tenet stay. (As CIA director, the elder Bush had failed in his bid to persuade Jimmy Carter to keep him.) It wouldn't hurt Tenet's chances that he'd presided over the ceremony renaming CIA headquarters "the George Bush Center for Intelligence" in April of 1999. "When that happened," said Dick Clarke, "we all said: This is George's insurance policy."

During his stint as acting director, the extroverted Greek and the backslapping Texan immediately hit it off. Tenet shared Bush's off-color sense of humor; the president called Tenet "Jorge." Like his father, Bush was an eager consumer of intelligence; unlike Clinton, he preferred in-person sessions where he could joust with the briefer. Bush wanted Tenet to attend these sessions. The president asked his daily briefer from the CIA, Michael Morell: "Does George know that I want him to be here?" Morell replied: "He will as soon as I get back to the office." From then on, Tenet attended almost every morning briefing, providing the "color" commentary to Morell's "play-by-play."

"The president was just easy to be around," said Tenet. "He was very direct, very focused, very clear. The thing I liked about him was, when he said something he meant it and he was going to ask you the next day, 'Did it get done?' And that appealed to me because there was a back-and-forth. I liked him and he liked me." Tenet had Bush's ear and the CIA had its raison d'être: a seat at the presidential table. But he still had no idea if Bush wanted him to stay on. One morning the president said to his acting director: "Why don't we try this out?" Tenet recalled. "Then we just kept going."

The millennium had brought a flurry of Al Qaeda threats; Dick Clarke, Cofer Black, and the Counterterrorism Center had gone into overdrive and had thwarted multiple plots, including attacks on LAX Airport and a major tourist hotel in Jordan. Now, in the spring of 2001, the warning lights were flashing again. Tenet presented to the Bush national security team an updated version of the Blue Sky paper, an aggressive paramilitary assault on the Afghan sanctuary. Bush's NSC team not only rejected it, they deep-sixed it. "The word back was, 'We're not quite ready to consider this,' " said Tenet. " 'We don't want the clock to start ticking.' " What did *that* mean? Tenet would not say. But the message seemed clear: In the event of a major Al Qaeda attack, the Bush administration did not want anyone to know that they'd been warned.

To Bush's advisers, the enemies were nations, not terrorists. This group included Vice President Dick Cheney, Rumsfeld, Paul Wolfowitz, the deputy secretary of defense, and Douglas Feith, the undersecretary of defense for policy. "Rumsfeld, Wolfowitz, Feith, and others were worried over Saddam Hussein, Iran, and missile defense, getting radar in Czechoslovakia, ballistic missiles in Poland," said Charlie Allen. "That's what was driving them. They were in another world, a time machine."

Dick Clarke pressed Condoleezza Rice, Bush's national security adviser, to convene a principals meeting to address the Al Qaeda threat. But there was no getting through to her. "They were mentally stuck back eight years ago, the last time they were in power," said Black. "They were used to terrorists being euro-leftics: you know, drink champagne by night, blow things up during the day. So it was very difficult to communicate the urgency to this."

In truth, the administration was obsessed with one country: Iraq. "It was transparently clear to me and to George Tenet very early in the administration," said Clarke, "that the Bush inner circle had come into office with the intention of going to war with Iraq." The very first National Security Council meeting was devoted to Iraq. There'd be seventeen NSC meetings devoted to Saddam in the first year alone. "George knew what they wanted from day one," said Clarke. "We all did."

But Al Qaeda demanded attention. At the Counterterrorism Center, Black and his team were monitoring a constant stream of threats. "For us the system was blinking red in the sense that we thought what we were uncovering was a top-down plot," said Tenet. "Something was being ordered from Afghanistan out. But it was very difficult for us to figure out what it was."

The chatter grew louder throughout the spring and early summer of 2001. Then, on July 10, it became deafening. Richard Blee, head of the Bin Laden Unit, was tracking a cascade of threats. The intelligence, while not specific about targets, left no doubt that major attacks were imminent. "You saw fifty different signs of impending attack," he recalled. "They'd never say, 'on 5 July we're going to go attack the World Trade Center.' Instead, they'd say, 'something really big is going to happen,' or 'there's going to be a really big football match,' all sorts of signs like that where you just said, 'Oh, fuck, it's coming.'"

Blee barged into Black's office. "He goes, 'Okay, the roof's fallen in,'" recalled Black. "I said, 'Whatcha got?' The information that we'd now compiled was absolutely compelling. It was multiple-sourced. It was sort of the last straw. So I picked up the phone, called Tenet's secretary and said, 'I have to see the director, I'm coming up with Rich.' She says, 'Well, I'm sorry, he's in with the head of some foreign intelligence service.' I said, 'Kick the guy out, we're coming up now. Tell him to get ready.'"

Black and his deputy briefed Tenet. "I wish I had a film of it," Black recalled. "Chewing on his cigar, going back and forth, jumping up and down, his eyes flashing." Tenet got the message. "It wasn't just red lights and chatter," the director recalled. "There were real plots being manifested. The world was on the edge of eruption. There were pronouncements by Al Qaeda that there would be eight major celebrations coming. The world was going to be stunned by what would soon happen. Terrorists were disappearing. Camps were closing. Threat reporting was on the rise. And this started building to a crescendo."

Tenet picked up the white phone that connected his office to the White House. George W. Bush was traveling that day in Boston, but Tenet got through to Rice. "I said, 'Condi, I have to come see you.' It was one of the rare times in my seven years as director where I said, 'I have to come see you. We're comin' right now.'"

When they got to the White House, Tenet, Black, and Blee met in the national security adviser's office with Rice and Clarke. To underline the urgency, the CIA team sat not on the couch but at the table. Then Blee began his briefing with a PowerPoint presentation. "I always did PowerPoint," he said, "and I personally wrote, 'this is what I am going to tell Condi Rice, this is what I am going to tell the DCI,' because I knew after the fact everybody would say, 'Yeah, Rich never told me that.'"

Blee got straight to the point. "There will be significant terrorist attacks against the United States in the coming weeks or months," he said. "The attacks will be spectacular. They may be multiple. Al-Qaeda's intention is the destruction of the United States." He continued: "This is an attack that is intended to cause thousands of American casualties somewhere. We cannot say it will be New York City or the United States, but it is geared toward U.S. citizens."

When Blee finished, Rice spoke up: "What should we do now?"

Cofer Black slammed his fist on the table. "This country's got to go on a war footing now!" he snapped. Tenet was silent. He left the talking to his deputies.

Afterward, on their way across the West Wing parking lot, Black and Blee high-fived each other, convinced their message had been heard. "Cofer and I came out and said, 'Boom. We hit a home run. She got it,'" said Blee. "I mean, Condi said all the right things: 'We've got to do something, policy papers need to move forward, we've got to be more aggressive.'" Even Black, the eternal cynic, was sanguine: "We congratulated each other: We thought we'd finally gotten through to these people. We had executed our responsibilities."

The trouble was, their warning had not been heard. One might expect the nation's top national security official to do something when alerted to an imminent, catastrophic attack. But Rice took no action. Alert levels were raised for U.S. personnel abroad, but there was no White House follow-up; no principals meeting was convened to discuss how to respond to the threat. "What happened?" I asked Black, almost fifteen years later. He paused. "Yeah, what *did* happen? Nothing happened." To Blee, Rice's inaction was incomprehensible. "We're going to her and saying, 'We need help.' There should have been some order that said, 'INS do more, FBI do more, NSA do more, DOD get ready.' She didn't do any of that. From July to September, nothing happened."

Rice would later write that that her memory of the meeting was "not very crisp because we were discussing the threat every day." It makes you wonder what it would have taken to get her attention. As one senior intelligence official put it: "When the director of Central Intelligence, the chief of counterterrorism, and the head of the Bin Laden Unit are saying, 'Fuck me. They're coming. Thousands of people are going to die. Get it on,' the correct response is not to do nothing. The correct response is to call a principals meeting."

A principals meeting might have untangled the hidden threads of the 9/11 plot. "The big failure in all of this," said Bruce Riedel, "was the failure of the national security adviser to summon the various parts of the intelligence community. What that often produced was that if the FBI didn't want to tell you something, the CIA ratted on them and said, 'we know this.' And it forced information to the surface and people to talk to each other. To make it happen, you have to have the heads of agencies directly at the table being cross-examined."

Clues to the attack were everywhere. A process was needed to bring those clues to the attention of senior officials. Some CIA officers knew that two Al Qaeda operatives, Khalid al-Midhar and Nawaf al-Hazmi, had entered the United States, arriving in Los Angeles from Malaysia. Riedel believed that these men—two of the 9/11 hijackers—could have been flagged and the plot uncovered: "If Condi Rice had been convening NSC meetings, principals meetings, in August or September, you would have found this out. You would have been able to chase them down."

The national security team might also have learned about another potential hijacker, Zacarias Moussaoui, an Al Qaeda operative who was taking flying lessons in Minnesota. The FBI knew that he was learning to fly—but not land—commercial airliners.

At the end of the month, George Tenet and his counterterrorism team met in the conference room outside his office. "We were just thinking about all of this and trying to figure out how this attack might occur," Tenet recalled. Until now, the intelligence had pointed to an attack on American interests overseas. Suddenly Blee spoke up. "They're coming here," he said.

In the silence that followed, Tenet said, "You could feel the oxygen come out of the room."

CHAPTER EIGHT

"It's a slam dunk."

George Tenet and George W. Bush

At 8:46 a.m. on September 11, 2001, George Tenet was having breakfast at Washington's St. Regis Hotel with former Oklahoma senator David Boren. "The head of my security detail came over to me and said a plane had hit one of the towers of the World Trade Center," he recalled. "My instinctual reaction was, 'This is Al Qaeda. I've gotta go.'"

The drive to Langley took twelve minutes, an eternity to Tenet, who had no secure phone reception. Upon his arrival at CIA headquarters, the director went to the seventh floor and huddled with Cofer Black, head of the Counterterrorism Center, and his senior staff. Both of the World Trade towers were ablaze; Tenet, remembering an Al Qaeda plot to crash a plane into Langley headquarters, ordered nonessential CIA personnel to go home, and the rest to move to another building. But Black was having none of it; he refused to evacuate his staff. "People could die," Tenet told his notoriously gruff lieutenant. Black replied: "Well, sir, then they're just going to have to die." The Counterterrorism Center was staying put.

George W. Bush had been speaking to an elementary school class in Florida that morning. Later, aboard Air Force One, he summoned his CIA briefer, Michael Morell, to his cabin. "Michael, who did this?" the president demanded. Morell replied that he'd bet his children's future that it was Al Qaeda. For hours, Tenet tried to reach Bush but couldn't get a clear connection. Finally, a little after 3 p.m., in a video conference with Tenet from Offutt Air Force Base in Nebraska, the president learned the truth: On the passenger manifests of the hijacked planes were the names of known Al Qaeda terrorists Khalid al-Midhar and Nawaf al-Hazmi.

The 9/11 Commission would famously call the nation's inability to prevent the attacks a "failure of imagination." But that wasn't really true: Not only had the CIA been warning all summer about an imminent attack but it had previously warned of an Al Qaeda attempt to hijack commercial airliners. In 1995, in the so-called Bojinka plot, Al Qaeda operatives had planned to commandeer as many as ten commercial flights out of Manila in the Philippines and blow up the planes over the Pacific; the plot was foiled when the terrorists' safe house caught fire. The CIA had warned that its failure wouldn't deter Al Qaeda from deploying airliners as weapons again. "So dismissing something because it didn't occur," said Tenet, "turns out to be a terrible, terrible mistake."

In retrospect, Tenet thought the real failure was the administration's refusal, in the face of the CIA's warnings, to take defensive precautions on a national scale. Only an effort involving the CIA, FBI, Federal Aviation Administration (FAA), and other agencies could have thwarted the attacks. "An entire government failed to recognize all the things that needed to be done," he said. "When you don't have a system of protection and defense built in place, when you don't understand what's going on inside the United States, when you don't button up your airports, button up your buildings, harden your cockpits, change your visa policies, create a mechanism where there's a quick swivel between foreign and domestic intelligence, you're going to get hurt."

But no one wanted to hear that prior to 9/11, and afterward the CIA bore the brunt of the blame; after all, in Washington there are only policy successes and intelligence failures. *The 9/11 Commission Report* never mentioned the July 10 meeting at which Tenet and his team warned Condi Rice. That was odd, because Tenet testified about the meeting in a closed session. Rich Blee, head of the Bin Laden Unit, who led the July 10 briefing, believed that both the commission and Congress were determined to deflect blame. "A deliberate effort was made by both the Democratic and Republican leadership to give Bill Clinton a pass and George Bush a pass—and I think Condi Rice got a pass."

Still, in the walk-up to 9/11 the CIA had failed. To its credit, it had sounded the alarm about an Al Qaeda attack. But the agency knew that Midhar and Hazmi were on U.S. soil, and it hadn't made sure that they were run to ground. Midlevel CIA officers had learned in January of 2000 that the future hijackers had obtained visas to the U.S.; a year later, they knew that the two men had arrived in Los Angeles. Although the FBI denied it, Blee insisted that the CIA had shared this information with the bureau's agents: "They said, 'Well, we don't have the names of al-Midhar and al-Hazmi.' Well, they *did* have the names. I had six FBI officers assigned to the Counterterrorism Center, there were seventy-two cables on al-Hazmi and al-Midhar. All of 'em were read by the FBI."

Senior CIA officials, including Cofer Black and Charlie Allen, the longtime National Intelligence Officer (NIO) for Warning, learned that Hazmi and Midhar were in the U.S. in August; Black said he ordered his staff to alert the FBI. "The agency did all it could," said Blee, "but the INS never did anything, the Bureau did very little, NSA was like pulling teeth, DOD did absolutely nothing whatsoever. The White House did very little. So it was kind of like us against the world."

The future hijackers not only weren't apprehended, they were never put on a "no-fly" list. And Tenet insisted he didn't learn about Midhar and Hazmi until the morning of September 11, 2001.

At best, this was incompetence on a colossal scale: a tragic communications failure. At worst it was something more sinister: Dick Clarke, the White House counterterrorism adviser, suggested that the CIA might have kept the future hijackers' whereabouts a secret because they were trying to recruit them as spies. But there was no evidence for this; it would have required a byzantine deep state conspiracy involving the CIA director, Cofer Black, and innumerable other agency officials. When Clarke first broached this suspicion more than a decade after the attacks, Tenet seriously considered filing a defamation suit against his former friend.

Still, Tenet couldn't explain the agency's bungled handling of the Al Qaeda operatives on U.S. soil. "Nobody did much to go find them," he said. "If someone had run some software, you might have found them using common credit cards to buy airline tickets."

Speaking with me about the attacks, Tenet was alternately defensive and prideful, apologetic and defiant. "If we'd been asleep at the switch, not warning, not acting, not preventing people from being killed, and not living this . . ." His voice trailed off. "So we failed. We didn't stop the plot. When I think of what we did, how hard we worked against this, it was no failure of creativity or effort on our part."

"Was there ever a moment in all of this time," I asked him, "when you blamed yourself?" Tenet pivoted in his chair, fidgeted, and twirled an imaginary cigar. (Tenet's wife had made him give up tobacco after a heart attack.) "Well, look," he said finally. "I still look at the ceiling at night about a lot of things—and I'll keep them to myself forever. But we're all human beings."

Afterward people would ask Cofer Black: "How does it feel to be responsible for the biggest intelligence failure since Pearl Harbor?" Black would ignore them. But he was furious inside. "You know what really does piss me off?" he said. "When people call this an intelligence failure. We knew this was coming. American interests were going to be attacked. Could very well be in the United States. It's serious. It's coming. Sometimes when I drive my car I think about it, and to me it remains incomprehensible still. I mean, you just want to pinch yourself. How is it that you could warn senior people so many times and nothing actually happened? It's kind of like the Twilight Zone."

But in the days following 9/11 there was no time for introspection. The CIA was going to war.

On September 15, Tenet and Black were summoned to Camp David. They gathered around a table in the president's cabin with President Bush and his war cabinet: Donald Rumsfeld; Paul Wolfowitz, his deputy; Condoleezza Rice, the national security adviser; Colin Powell, the secretary of state; Andrew Card, White House chief of staff. Black presented an updated version of the Blue Sky paper, requested but never acted upon by Clinton's national security adviser Sandy Berger: the CIA paramilitary assault on the Al Qaeda sanctuary in Afghanistan. "We outlined our plan to seal the borders of Afghanistan, go after their leadership, shut off their money, destroy Al Qaeda, and operate against ninety-two countries in the rest of the world," said Tenet. When he was finished, Cofer Black looked at Bush. "Mr. President," he said dramatically, "when we get through with these guys, they're going to have flies walking across their eyeballs." It took Bush a moment to grasp what Black was talking about.

A few weeks later, on October 7, CIA paramilitary teams, supported by the U.S. military, swept into Afghanistan. Linking with the warrior tribes of the Northern Alliance, they proceeded to rout the Taliban; within five weeks they controlled Kabul and had uprooted Al Qaeda and its infrastructure. The last Taliban-held city was captured by the end of November. One hundred CIA officers had taken part; a handful were casualties. It was a rare case of an intelligence agency successfully leading a nation into war. Although U.S. troops would remain mired in the country for almost two decades to come, the invasion had been one of the CIA's finest hours.

But one of the agency's darkest and most controversial periods was about to begin.

In the days and weeks following September 11, Tenet believed that Al Qaeda wasn't finished targeting the U.S.; extraordinary measures were needed to prevent a second-wave attack. "The quality of threat reporting would make the hair on the back of your neck stand up," Tenet recalled. "We received reporting that Al Qaeda had placed a nuclear weapon in New York City. We never found a weapon. But we were learning about plots against infrastructure, apartment buildings, suspension bridges: If you put all of this together, everything that we hold dear was at risk. What we were seeing made it feel as if we were living a ticking time bomb every single day."

From his office in the Old Executive Office Building, across from the West Wing, Tenet, accompanied by the president's briefer, Michael Morell, would make his daily trek to the Oval Office. "Every morning we used to walk across to brief the president and we'd wonder whether today was the day we were going to be hit again," said Tenet. "We needed to get real-time information as fast as we possibly could to protect the country and ensure there wasn't another attack on the homeland."

The CIA wasn't in the business of detaining prisoners. But that was about to change; capturing and interrogating members of Al Qaeda was the only way to find out if new attacks were imminent. In March of 2002, in pursuit of a terrorist named Abu Zubaydah, joint CIA-FBI teams launched simultaneous raids on sixteen locations in Pakistan. After a firefight, they captured Zubaydah; he was so severely wounded that the CIA flew in a top American surgeon to treat him. Zubaydah was thought to be a high-ranking Al Qaeda operative with knowledge of future plots. The question was where to put him until interrogators could go to work.

Detaining Al Qaeda suspects posed a quandary for Tenet and the CIA. As Porter Goss, the future director, explained: "We needed a place to talk to them. Where's that going to be? If you're going to do it in a jailhouse in Pakistan, you're going to get a hugely bad outcome because (a) nothing's going to be secret, and (b) probably nobody is going to survive the session. Plus there will be a riot on the main street in about fifteen minutes." John Deutch, the former director, posed a rhetorical question: "Should we bring 'em back to the United States? Give them the full protection of the U.S. Constitution? Allow them to have lawyers present to protect their rights as if they were American citizens? What are you going to tell the director of Central Intelligence to do?"

Jose Rodriguez, soon to replace Cofer Black as head of the Counterterrorism Center, thought he knew the answer. In the past, suspected terrorists had been sent to allied countries for interrogation, a process known as "rendition." (This practice began during the Clinton administration, and the questioning wasn't always friendly.) But those countries, Rodriguez thought, couldn't be counted on to interrogate detainees about attacks on the U.S. homeland. So Rodriguez set up a network of so-called black sites, secret prisons that would eventually hold at least 119 suspected Al Qaeda terrorists.

Rodriguez, born in Puerto Rico and educated at the University of Florida, where he got a law degree, was a wily, aggressive operative. He'd served as chief of station in Panama, Mexico City, and the Dominican Republic. Rising to head of the CIA's Latin America Division, he'd been fired from that post, accused of intervening to help a friend beat a drug-dealing charge in the Dominican Republic. Rodriguez denied the accusation. Now he was in charge of the most controversial program in the CIA's war on Al Qaeda.

With Zubaydah in custody, there was no time to waste. Promised lots of cash and total secrecy, Thailand agreed to host the CIA's first post-9/11 black site. To run the facility, Rodriguez assembled a trusted staff, including two female veterans of the clandestine service. Jennifer Matthews was a driven analyst, in the mold of Carrie Mathison from the television show *Homeland*, who got so excited when she received a terrorist tip she literally would start shaking.

Another woman, tough as nails but with a calm, unflappable demeanor, was Rodriguez's favorite, destined to rise to the top of the agency. Rodriguez was so high on her that he put her in charge of the site. Her name was Gina Haspel.

Haspel had come to the CIA from the University of Louisville in Kentucky. She'd become one of the first women to crack the overwhelmingly male ranks of the clandestine service. "She was very unusual," said Rodriguez. "No ego. None of that testosterone shit." Haspel was quiet, almost shy—a striking contrast to the "knuckle draggers" who populated the Directorate of Operations (DO). Yet she was grounded and focused, traits that would serve her well. Women operatives had to deal not only with the sexist culture of the DO but with often hostile environs overseas. "Women served in places where they were running up against men who are *machistas*, or the equivalent in the Middle East," said Rodriguez. Female officers' efforts to recruit agents, most of them male, were often subject to misinterpretation. "If our females became too friendly," said Rodriguez, "immediately the signal is maybe she wants to sleep with me."

But Haspel thrived. Charlie Allen called her "a natural at clandestine operations." Dispatched to Africa, she quickly learned the ropes as a case officer, recruiting agents in dangerous circumstances. "She proved her mettle when she had her first assignment, paying money to this military officer, and doing it in the middle of the night," recalled Allen. "For a young girl out of Kentucky who liked Johnny Cash, that's pretty good."

Rodriguez met Haspel when he was head of the Counterterrorism Center and she was a deputy chief of a CIA office nearby. "I was instantly impressed by her demeanor, her knowledge, her experience," he said. She was fluent in Russian and Turkish, and had served as a case officer in Ankara, Turkey, and Azerbaijan. Rodriguez needed someone with savvy and a cool head to navigate the uncharted territory of the CIA's rendition, detention, and interrogation (RDI) program.

By this time, Zubayda had been interrogated by a CIA team and an FBI agent named Ali Soufan. Just how to interrogate him triggered an ugly dispute between the FBI and CIA teams; Soufan wanted to create personal rapport (designed to build a prosecution case); the CIA insisted on using their "enhanced" techniques (designed to get information in a hurry about imminent attacks). Rodriguez thought Soufan was an egomaniac. "He was the world's biggest dick," he said. Apparently, Zubaydah didn't like Soufan either. A Muslim, Soufan antagonized the Al Qaeda operative by arguing with him about the meaning of Islam. By contrast, Zubaydah would consider Gina Haspel a breath of fresh air.

Zubaydah's CIA interrogators were convinced he knew more than he was telling: "Zubaydah had provided some early useful information and then he stopped talking," said Rodriguez. Matthews and her team decided to try unconventional methods: isolation, sleep deprivation, and bombarding his cell with noise. (These went beyond the normal techniques but weren't prohibited.) But they had no effect. "George Tenet was going to the White House every day and the president was asking him, 'What is Abu Zubaydah saying about the second wave of attacks and about all these other programs?'" said Rodriguez. "Well, he was not saying anything. We knew we had to do something different. So we put together what became the enhanced interrogation program."

The president signed off on the program. "People are throwing the word 'torture' around—as if we were torturers," Tenet said. "I'm not ever going to accept the use of that word for what happened here." At least twelve so-called enhanced techniques were presented to Bush for approval. "The president read the memo," said Tenet, "looked at the techniques, and decided he was going to take two techniques off the table himself." (Tenet said he couldn't recall which two, but Rodriguez believed one was "mock executions.") "These techniques and the proposal to use them on any human being were sent to the Department of Justice immediately," Tenet said. "Because we wanted to know that it was legal under U.S. law and did not in any way compromise our adherence to international torture statutes. And the attorney general of the United States told us that it did not."

That was debatable, of course. Critics, including Bush's successor, Barack Obama, would later label the techniques torture. What was clear was that the program went well beyond FBI protocol and the Army Field Manual. "A lot of people thought: Just have tea with the guy and establish some sort of rapport," said Michael Hayden, a future CIA director. "I get that if you've got time—but we didn't have time. We needed to accelerate the process. What we were trying to do was to move individuals from a zone of defiance into a zone of cooperation—and then the intelligence-gathering began." Vice President Dick Cheney, who'd declared that America must fight terrorists on "the dark side," was an enthusiastic defender of the techniques.

As consultants for the program, Rodriguez recruited two psychologists, James Mitchell and Bruce Jessen, from a Seattle–based program called SERE (Survival, Evasion, Resistance, Escape). It was a course designed to train U.S. airmen to resist enemy torture. Under the CIA program, detainees would be slapped and grabbed; deprived of sleep; forced onto liquid diets; confined in a coffinlike box with live insects. There was nudity, cramped confinement, stress positions. Finally, there was a technique known as waterboarding, which made the subject think he was drowning.

Haspel arrived at the Thailand black site in the fall of 2002. Mitchell and Jessen were already there. Years later, at the CIA's insistence, ProPublica retracted a story that Haspel, as chief of base, had supervised Zubaydah being waterboarded. Exactly when CIA interrogators stopped waterboarding the Al Qaeda terrorist is unclear. But Haspel was intimately involved in Zubaydah's interrogation. And she evidently impressed him. "She had a good rapport, a *very* good rapport with Zubaydah," said Rodriguez. He called her the "Emira"—Arabic for "princess" or "leader."

Something else took place at the Thailand black site that would trigger future controversy. CIA videographers taped the sessions. According to Rodriguez, there were several reasons for taping: Zubaydah was gravely injured; if he died, the video would show that the techniques weren't to blame; the tapes would supplement the written interrogation record; and they could be studied for "nonverbal cues." But there'd also be an unintended consequence: Cameras would record not only the brutality of the techniques but also the faces of the CIA officers who were inflicting them.

Rodriguez insisted that the actual CIA interrogations bore no resemblance to the Hollywood versions. "The opening scene of *Zero Dark Thirty*, where you see all these prisoners being abused by CIA officers, spontaneous waterboarding with a pail—it's total bullshit," he said. The CIA techniques, Rodriguez insisted, were carefully designed not to cause lasting harm. "Waterboarding as practiced by the Chinese, the Nazis, the Spanish Inquisition was torture. But the waterboarding that was applied here was different. It didn't use as much water. We didn't drown anybody. We had doctors there to make sure that no harm came to the individual." Rodriguez added: "Only three detainees were ever waterboarded, by the way. Three killers that had American blood on their hands were waterboarded by us. Give me a break."

Some at the CIA said they were troubled by the interrogations. John Brennan, a future director, was Tenet's executive assistant. "There were a number of those techniques that I personally felt were inappropriate, not necessary, beyond the pale," he said. "I was not in the chain of command, but I was a senior CIA officer at the time. And I expressed my discomfort and my concerns about these techniques, believing that they were going to come back to haunt the CIA. I did that with individuals, colleagues at the agency."

But Tenet couldn't remember Brennan ever complaining. "He never came to you and said, 'Hey, you know what, George? I think this is wrong'?" I asked him. "Nope," replied Tenet. Brennan explained: "It's not as though I went up and down the halls of CIA and said, 'We shouldn't be doing this.' Looking back on it now, should I have spoken out more loudly about it? Maybe. I think about that a lot."

There was a lot to think about, including cases where prisoners died. In 2002, one detainee, severely injured during his capture, died after he was left untreated during a CIA interrogation at an Iraqi prison. Another was shackled half-naked on a cold floor at a CIA black site in Afghanistan. He was found dead of hypothermia. No charges were ever brought against the officers involved. "At the beginning of 2002, when we started to take prisoners, we just did not know what we were doing," said Rodriguez. "We are not jailers. We don't have those skills. And abuses were made. And we fessed up to those."

On March 1, 2003, in Rawalpindi, Pakistan, a CIA-Pakistani team captured Khalid Sheikh Mohammed. KSM, as he was known, had masterminded the foiled Bojinka plot and was thought to have planned the 9/11 attacks. He was taken to the same Thailand black site. "He was smart, scary smart," said Rodriguez. "Hannibal Lecter. Pure evil. The type of individual that is able to dream up different ways of killing us. We asked him, 'What do you know about plots against the U.S.?' And his answer was, 'Soon you will know.' "

At first harsh techniques had little effect on KSM; he was able to outwit his waterboarders. "He knew that in all likelihood we would stop at ten seconds," said Rodriguez. "And he would count with his fingers. He would then look at us like, 'You know, hey, it's time to stop.' " But it was sleep deprivation that finally wore KSM down. He eventually confessed to the killing of Daniel Pearl, the *Wall Street Journal* reporter, who'd been beheaded on videotape by Al Qaeda in February of 2002.

Critics would later argue that the brutal techniques yielded no valuable intelligence. But Rodriguez insisted that KSM, deprived of sleep, provided a tip that helped lead to bin Laden. The name of a possible courier to the Al Qaeda leader, Ahmed al-Kuwaiti, had been gleaned from other detainees. "We then raised the name al-Kuwaiti to Khalid Sheikh Mohammed," said Tenet. "And because we had the place wired for sound, we heard KSM tell other detainees, 'Don't talk about the courier.' After that our folks in the bin Laden unit went after Abu Ahmed one grain of sand at a time and followed him eventually to Abbottabad."

Years later, in December of 2014, after an investigation of more than six million pages of CIA documents, the Democratic majority of the Senate Select Committee on Intelligence would issue a scathing report. It would claim that no evidence was produced from the techniques that disrupted plots or saved lives. Senator Dianne Feinstein said they'd examined twenty cases in depth. But Tenet and his allies were adamant that the techniques had been effective. They pointed out that none of the directors had been interviewed by the committee.

Michael Morell, the future acting director, defended the program—up to a point. "If I were captured by an adversary and somebody slapped me in the face would I come back and say I was tortured? No. But if somebody waterboarded me, would I say I was tortured? Yes." Despite his unease about waterboarding, Morell insisted, "enhanced interrogation techniques without any doubt in my mind produced unique intelligence that stopped plots, saved lives, and took additional senior Al Qaeda officers off the battlefield." Moreover, he said, Feinstein's committee was wrong about the twenty cases it cited. "One of the twenty cases is a senior Al Qaeda operative telling us that Al Qaeda had moved to a particular city in Pakistan. That's what he told us *before* enhanced interrogation techniques. *After* the enhanced interrogation techniques, he actually sat down with satellite photography and pointed out the actual buildings where senior Al Qaeda operatives were, which allowed us to go and deal with them."

"Without this program, Heathrow Airport would have been bombed," said Tenet. "Other facilities in Great Britain would have been bombed. Buildings in New York would've exploded. Suspension bridges would have been taken down." One of Tenet's successors, Michael Hayden, believed the stakes were too high to pass up the techniques. "Let's have a CIA director being interviewed here after a second wave attack has struck and you get to ask him the question: 'Now, the Department of Justice said it was legal but you refused to do it. How do you feel about your decision now?' So let's not pretend that this is the forces of light versus the forces of darkness. These are two damn ugly decisions."

Of course, there were no second wave attacks. That was either because the techniques disrupted plots—or because the threat was exaggerated. It is impossible to know which.

But another key question involved values. "Should the United States of America, which stands for human rights in the world, which stands for human dignity, use those techniques on another human being?" asked Morell. "That's a really reasonable question." John McLaughlin, Tenet's deputy director, believed there was an ethical case to be made for using the techniques. "We didn't do this in a moral vacuum. We understood the criticism we would get when this eventually came to light. But we also thought it would be even less moral if we didn't get this information and Americans died as a result of it."

Tenet maintained that the "context of the times" left him no choice; innocent lives were at stake. And he adamantly insisted that everyone was on board. "You can debate whether they're right or wrong, but the lawyers told us unequivocally, 'You did not torture. You did not shock the conscience. You did not violate the Constitution, the Fifth, the Eighth, and the Fourteenth Amendments. And you did not impugn any of the national treaties or conventions.' We briefed the Congress with their full knowledge. We briefed the president, the vice president, the national security adviser, the secretary of defense."

Since December 30, 2005, the techniques have been prohibited by the Detainee Treatment Act, passed by the Senate and signed by President Bush. But during his presidential campaign Donald Trump famously suggested reviving the brutal methods. "I'd bring back waterboarding, . . . and a hell of a lot worse," he proclaimed. To that, Hayden replied: "If a president wants to bring back waterboarding, he'd better bring his own bucket—because the agency isn't going down that road again."

Another scandal loomed, one that would cast a cloud over the CIA for a generation. George W. Bush needed a pretext to invade Iraq. George Tenet ended up providing it.

A few days after 9/11, walking into the West Wing early one morning, Tenet bumped into Richard Perle, the hawkish, neoconservative Bush adviser. "Iraq has to pay a price for this," Perle told him. "They bear responsibility." Tenet wondered what he was talking about—since there was no meaningful connection between Al Qaeda and Iraq. Tom Twetten, the retired head of the Near East Division, tried to warn the boss. "I said, 'Be sure the agency gets out of the way, because this is not going to end well. Anybody who reads tea leaves could see that the neocons had made up their minds.'"

Brent Scowcroft, the former national security adviser to George H. W. Bush, summed up the philosophy of the younger Bush and his inner circle: "After 9/11, I think they said, 'Look, this is a nasty world, we're the only superpower and while we've got that unprecedented power, we ought to use it to remake the world. Why don't we take this little jerk of a dictator, kick him out, and make Iraq a democracy, it'll spread to the region, and we will have done something for the world.'"

It was an article of faith in the Bush White House that Saddam and Osama bin Laden were allies. Never mind that all the evidence showed they were rivals. "Right after 9/11, we were getting this, 'Could this have been Iraq?'" recalled John McLaughlin, Tenet's deputy director. "And we kept saying, 'No. This bears none of the hallmarks of Iraq. This is all Al Qaeda.'"

The day after 9/11, the president corralled Dick Clarke, the NSC counterterrorism czar, who was a holdover from the Clinton administration. "Bush really cornered me physically and urged me to get a report that said Iraq did it," Clarke said. "And so I went both to the FBI and the CIA and said, 'This is a presidential request: don't tell me what you already know. Go back and write a new report and look in places you haven't looked. Look for connections you haven't found.' And it didn't take them long, but they both came back with reports that said, 'No, we've got nothing.'"

But the neocons were undaunted. At one point ex-director Woolsey, now a private citizen, was dispatched to the United Kingdom by Paul Wolfowitz; he was to dig up evidence linking one of the Iraqi hijackers to Iraqi intelligence. Nothing came of it. "You can't have a fool's errand without a fool," quipped one CIA wag. "They were making a case that just couldn't be made," said Scowcroft. "Saddam was a radical, not a conservative. In fact, he wasn't religious at all."

Still, publicly and repeatedly, Scowcroft's old friend Cheney touted a connection between the hijackers and Iraq. "There was a sharp difference of view between the CIA and the Office of the Vice President about this connection," said Tenet. "This connection did not exist. We intervened on numerous occasions to say so. I remember going to the president and saying, 'Look this has gotta stop. We just can't support this language.'"

Cheney told me it was Tenet who showed him a photograph, taken in Prague, of Mohamed Atta, a 9/11 hijacker, with an Iraqi intelligence official. "Afterward, it was alleged that I'd dug something up," Cheney said. "The fact of the matter was George gave it to me and told me that the source was the Czech Intelligence Service." Tenet replied: "The vice president knows that we came to the conclusion that Mohamed Atta was not in Prague, that there was no such meeting." According to Tom Twetten, the tug-of-war with the vice president took a toll on Tenet. "George spent a lot of capital," he said. "He worked really hard at that and he successfully threw that argument out the window despite Wolfowitz and Cheney not being happy with him."

But Tenet didn't always challenge the administration's lies. In October 2002, Bush declared that Iraq "possesses and produces chemical and biological weapons" and was a threat to the U.S. McLaughlin had just told a Senate committee the opposite. "When I was asked in closed testimony, 'Do you have any intelligence that indicates Saddam is going to use his weapons of mass destruction on the United States?,' my answer was, 'no,' " he recalled. "I was then asked, 'Would his propensity to use them on us increase if we attacked him?' And I said, 'probably.' " Yet Tenet issued a statement saying there was no inconsistency between the CIA's view and the president's.

When it came to Iraq, George W. Bush didn't want to hear nay-sayers. Rand Beers, an NSC official, vividly remembered an NSC meeting in the fall of 2002, months before the invasion. The subject was possible repercussions in Muslim countries of a U.S. invasion of Iraq. Two officials had spoken about the potential for adverse reactions in the Islamic world. Then it was Rice's turn. "Condi was starting to agree with the prior two comments," recalled Beers. Then, suddenly, the president cut her off. "No," he said crisply. "*Victory* will take care of that." Bush was in no mood for any second-guessing of his war plans.

As the connection between Saddam and Al Qaeda seemed less persuasive as a casus belli, the administration turned to Saddam's alleged possession of weapons of mass destruction. In trying to make the case for WMDs, Cheney and his allies would not be deterred. I. Lewis "Scooter" Libby, his chief of staff, scoured other intelligence agencies for evidence of Iraq's biological, chemical, and nuclear programs. And the vice president made frequent visits to Langley for meetings with CIA analysts.

It's widely assumed that the CIA, under pressure from Cheney, politicized intelligence about WMDs, telling the administration what it wanted to hear. Tenet and his deputies vehemently denied that charge. And four official investigations failed to find evidence that intelligence was slanted to make the case for war. In his study of two CIA debacles, the Iran revolution and the Iraq War, *The Failure of Intelligence*, Robert Jervis agreed. In a chapter titled: "What Everyone Knows Is Wrong," Jervis concluded: "Political pressures cannot explain the intelligence failure."

"I have not seen people purposely shade intelligence so that policy conclusions will be drawn," said Steven Hall, a thirty-year veteran CIA operative. "I never saw anybody at CIA say, 'Okay, we need to say this so that he comes to this conclusion.' " But politicization of intelligence is a difficult thing to pin down. As an analyst at the confirmation hearings for Bob Gates put it: "Politicization is like fog. Though you cannot hold it in your hands, or nail it to a wall, it does exist, it is real, and it does affect people." Pressure can succeed or fail: What one analyst regards as a probing question another might see as coercion.

Richard Kerr, the former deputy director, who performed a CIA postmortem on the WMDs debacle, put it this way: "You have an intelligence organization that's being asked again and again, 'Do they have weapons of mass destruction?' You're asked to come to a conclusion. It was kind of a classic analytic problem: too little information, a lot of pressure to come to conclusions. I think there was outside pressure, but it was also internal." During an interview with the staff of the Senate Select Committee on Intelligence, Kerr engaged in the following exchange:

> Kerr: There's always people who are going to feel pressure in these situations and feel they were pushed upon.
> Interviewer: That's what we've heard. We can't find any of them, though.
> Kerr: Maybe they are wiser than to come talk to you.

The CIA's National Intelligence Estimate (NIE) on Iraq's weapons of mass destruction was completed in October 2002. It concluded: "Iraq has chemical and biological weapons." And it added: "If Baghdad acquires sufficient fissile material from abroad, it could make a nuclear weapon within several months." The estimate was riddled with nuances and caveats. But few members of Congress read the entire report before approving, in early October 2002, a resolution authorizing the Iraq War. The vote was 296–133 in the House, and 77–23 in the Senate.

Bruce Riedel said the footnotes were a dead giveaway. "For every judgment, the people who actually knew the most about it—nuclear, chemical, biological—are clearly saying this doesn't add up," he said. "When he received that kind of NIE, the director should have thrown it back and said, 'This is ass backwards. We should be writing an NIE that says there is very little evidence of a WMD program, here are the few bits and pieces, rather than there *is* a WMD program, and these crappy pieces of information support the case.'"

Tenet's friend Dick Clarke summed up the problem: "Suppose there are reports that say the moon is made of green cheese. What they didn't do was say, 'Okay, but we haven't been there to take a sample.' That's what you're supposed to do. What they're now teaching CIA to do is say, '*This* is what we'd want for high confidence. And *this* is what we've got. We probably shouldn't be making a judgment at all based on *this*.' That was the mistake."

Charlie Allen, the CIA's veteran analyst, thought Tenet's belief in the estimate was sincere. "I think he believed Iraq had WMDs," he said. "He was convinced that Saddam had retained certain capabilities, particularly on the chemical side. There were a lot of caveats in the estimate. But they were brushed over. People wanted to believe."

Tenet, prickly and prideful as always, insisted the CIA's estimate was honestly arrived at. "So nobody cooked the books?" I asked him. He practically jumped out of his chair. "No," he said. "Look, if we wanted to cook the books all we needed to do was say that Iraq was directly involved in 9/11. Game, set, match, over. We never did that. There were no political agendas here.

"Everything that could go wrong did go wrong," he conceded. "We have to live with the fact that on a high-consequence issue our analysis was used to enable war. We were wrong. Now the French were wrong. The British were wrong. The Germans were wrong. Everybody else was wrong. Everybody believed this. Saddam's deception was mind-boggling in terms of how Machiavellian it was."

Indeed, the CIA had totally misunderstood Saddam and his intentions; one mistake was to interpret his behavior as proof that he possessed WMDs rather than a ploy to make his enemies *think* he had them. Once again, as in Vietnam in 1963, the agency was ignorant about the regime, and the region's culture. As Leslie Gelb, the acerbic Defense and State Department veteran, observed: "These are wars that depend on knowledge of who the people are, what the culture is like. And we just jump into them without knowing anything." Andy Card, Bush's chief of staff, lamented: "There were factions and tribes and I guess we in America didn't really understand the nature of the tribal community in Iraq to the extent that we should have. I wish that Lawrence Wright had written his book, *The Looming Tower*, before we went to war in Iraq."

"You can dress this up any way you want," said Tenet, "but I don't think it helps for the Director of Central Intelligence to make excuses." He went on: "I have to live with this and reflect on it for eternity in terms of how a community that had performed so well on so many different issues on my watch got something this wrong. I have to reflect on that and accept the responsibility."

A pivotal moment in the march toward war was still to come. On Saturday, December 21, 2002, Tenet and McLaughlin, accompanied by a young analyst, went to the Oval Office. The president, Cheney, Rice, and Card were there. As Bush looked on, McLaughlin presented the case for Saddam's WMDs. But the briefing was lackluster. When McLaughlin finished, Bush was underwhelmed.

As Bob Woodward described the scene, in *Plan of Attack*:

> *Bush turned to Tenet: "I've been told all this intelligence about having WMD and this is the best we've got?"*
>
> *From the end of one of the couches of the Oval Office, Tenet rose up, threw his arms in the air. "It's a slam dunk case!" the DCI said.*
>
> *Bush pressed. "George, how confident are you?"*
>
> *Tenet, a basketball fan who attended as many games of his alma mater Georgetown as possible, leaned forward and threw his arms up again. "Don't worry, it's a slam dunk!"*

Tenet insisted that the "slam dunk" meeting had no bearing on Bush's decision to go to war. Its purpose was to decide what could be said in public. "The way it was portrayed was this was the seminal moment in terms of deciding whether to go to war or not," he said. "And that's not what happened at all. What I wanted to convey is there was probably a better way for us to make a public case. We might be able to declassify sources, methods, some other data that would make this a better public case. The decision to go to war had already been made."

Still, it was a missed chance for Tenet to confront Bush with the truth about WMDs: The case was weak, the evidence circumstantial, the risks grave. "George is a friend of mine and I have to acknowledge that right up front," said a former close associate. "But he couldn't stand not to be liked." Hence, according to this friend, Tenet's tendency to pull his punches with the president. "He's got no political standing of his own, the only thing he's got is a special relationship with W."

Another CIA veteran thought Tenet was worn out: "There's nothing left in the tank for George. He's fought the fight on Saddam and Al Qaeda and he can't do this one, too." Corny as it might sound, Riedel thought Tenet had failed to live up to the inscription at the entrance to Langley headquarters: *"And ye shall know the truth, and the truth shall make ye free."* "It's telling truth to power," he said. "it's the thing on the wall when you come in."

Tenet did not dispute that he used the now infamous phrase "slam dunk." It was "probably the dumbest thing I've ever said," he admitted. But his allies suspected that the president told Woodward the anecdote to throw Tenet under the bus. According to this theory, Bush's aides prodded him to plant the story. "I think Tenet got fucked in the 'slam dunk' comment," said a friend. "They were trying to distance the president from the decision to go to war." McLaughlin lamented: "It's just a shame that George ends up with that as his marquee."

But the public case for war had yet to be made; a few months after the "slam dunk" meeting, on February 5, 2003, Colin Powell, the secretary of state, made the argument for Saddam's WMDs before the U.N. Security Council. "The president had decided in January that military action was going to be needed," Powell told me. "And he said, 'We now have to make our case to the world. And therefore I need you to go to the U.N.'"

To prepare for his speech, Powell spent four days and nights at Langley with Tenet, poring over the intelligence. The result was a fiasco, which would permanently tarnish Powell's storied career.

Powell was given a draft prepared not by Tenet but by Cheney's chief of staff and confidant I. Lewis "Scooter" Libby. "I was expecting a product that I could fix up or finish and go forward with," Powell recalled. "We got the first draft and we couldn't track it with anything. It was a statement with no sourcing. It was not an intelligence document." Powell's deputy Richard Armitage recalled: "He was under enormous pressure from the vice president to put Scooter's bullshit in there. I mean, it was total bullshit." Powell tried to stall. "I called Dr. Rice and said, 'Hey, I need more time.' And she said, 'Sorry, too late. The president's already announced that you're going to do it next Tuesday.' So I said, 'Okay, we'll put the product aside and write a new one.'"

Powell regarded his speech as "an Adlai Stevenson moment," recalling the U.N. ambassador's dramatic 1962 appearance, when he unveiled aerial photos of Soviet missiles in Cuba. "We told the agency, 'Don't put anything in the speech that you don't have multiple sourcing on,'" Powell said. "'No single sourcing. Multiple sourcing. It's got to be solid.'" Powell did not trust a CIA assessment that Saddam was using aluminum tubes to make nuclear centrifuges. (The Department of Energy thought they might be used for rocket bodies.) He decided to couch the claim in caveats, and nixed the idea of holding up an aluminum tube for the TV cameras.

"There was not a word in there that was not approved by the Director of Central Intelligence," said Powell. "So I felt pretty comfortable." Powell was taking no chances on the optics. During a phone call the night before the speech, Tenet told Powell he would meet him at the U.N. "No, I'll pick you up," the secretary replied, offering him a ride. Powell wanted to be sure the CIA director sat directly behind him, on camera. A worldwide audience watched as the secretary of state methodically laid out his case, vetted by George Tenet, that Saddam's WMDs were a mortal danger to the United States and the world.

The centerpiece of the speech was a dramatic claim about Iraq's biological warfare capability. "The most famous item was the so-called bacteriological vans," Powell said, "where we had four sources who had experienced and seen these things. That was pretty good stuff and I made that a central part of the presentation." Powell proclaimed: "We have firsthand descriptions of biological weapons factories on wheels and rails. [Saddam] has the ability to dispense these lethal poisons and diseases in ways that can cause massive death and destruction." As it turned out, the only source for this was someone known by the code name "Curveball."

"Curveball" was an Iraqi defector in the custody of German intelligence; he'd failed polygraphs and was considered a drunk. The Germans hadn't allowed the CIA to interview him. All of this was known to some officers at the CIA, yet Tenet insisted that he was never told. The fictitious biological weapons trailers stayed in Powell's presentation.

In the words of Robert Jervis, who wrote the postmortem on the Iraq War, Powell's speech was "almost entirely fallacious."

It wasn't until weeks later that Powell was told that "Curveball" was a fraud. "And when I said, 'What about the other sources, the four sources?' it all fell apart," he said. "And I literally slumped in my chair. How could this have happened?"

"It's probably equally painful for both of us," said Tenet. "We were dealing with a horrible White House draft that we had to unpack and repack. What they sent over to us was unrecognizable and for days we fought to try to figure out how to be as credible as we could be for the secretary. It was a perfect storm." Perhaps. But it was a storm on Tenet's watch. Powell did not say so in public, but he blamed Tenet. I asked Tenet if he'd spoken to Powell about the speech. "It's too hard," he said. "It's just too hard. I have a great deal of respect for him."

Powell told me he has never discussed the speech with George W. Bush either. "By then, the invasion was over," he said. "We'd done what we were going to do militarily and we had to look to the future. I think I'm probably the one who gets questioned about it continually as opposed to the others. It's just a burden I bear. I get asked about it almost every day."

"The secretary was really unhappy with Tenet," one of Powell's confidants told me. "I called George one day and said, 'You gotta make it right with the secretary. He'll take his lump. His reputation's going to take the hit eternally, but you ought to correct the record a little bit.' Tenet said, 'Don't worry, I'm gonna take care of it.' " Tenet promised he'd say something about Powell in an upcoming speech at Georgetown University. But the speech came and went. There was nothing in it about Powell.

On December 14, 2004, George Bush awarded his CIA director the Presidential Medal of Freedom, the nation's highest civilian honor, in a solemn White House ceremony. Two other key players in the Iraq War—Paul Bremer, head of the Coalition Provisional Authority, and General Tommy Franks—were also given the award. Tenet, Bush proclaimed, was "one of the first to recognize and address the growing threat to America from radical terrorist threats."

That was undoubtedly true. And Tenet's tenure at the CIA had been transformative. He and his team had warned of the Al Qaeda threat before 9/11. On his watch the CIA had disrupted terrorist plots that targeted Americans, and disarmed Muammar Gaddafi. He'd routed the Taliban, brought the agency back from bankruptcy, and revitalized the clandestine division. He'd built up the agency's fleet of armed drones with missiles, creating a new and lethal weapon against terrorists. Tenet and the CIA had warned the Bush White House about the dangers of a post-invasion insurgency in Iraq— another warning the administration didn't want to hear. And with his outgoing personality Tenet had become the most popular director in recent history.

But even Tenet's friends wondered if the Medal of Freedom should go to a director who provided the pretext for an unnecessary war. And his critics were appalled. The WMD fiasco had profoundly damaged not just the CIA but the country. As one former acting director put it: "It used to be generally accepted that the U.S. was a force for good in the world. That is not the case anymore. The Iraq War was the defining moment." One of Powell's close friends directly challenged Tenet. "The *Medal of Freedom*?" he said. "For a war that should not have been fought? You need to give it back."

The question lingers: Would an accurate intelligence estimate have prevented the Iraq war? It is naive to think that good intelligence always drives good decisions. Robert Jervis, who studied both the debacles of Iran in 1979 and Iraq in 2003, concluded: "Better intelligence would not have led to an effective policy." People assume, Jervis wrote, that "fixing the intelligence machinery will solve the problems. Politically this makes a good deal of sense; intellectually it does not." He concluded that Bush would have invaded Iraq in any event. "It is unlikely that any intelligence that was true to the information available would have produced a different decision."

"Countries don't go to war just because of National Intelligence Estimates," Tenet told me. "Countries go to war because of geopolitical reasons, policy considerations, and their own view of the world at the time—in this instance, perhaps, how to remake the Middle East." Indeed, the evidence is overwhelming that with or without the CIA's flawed NIE, Bush and Cheney would have gone to war.

"Our analysis was wrong and we have to take responsibility for it," said Tenet. "But policymakers need to be more forthcoming about what their own motivations were." On this point, Tenet's old

Georgetown professor, the late Leslie Gelb, eighty-two at the time of our last interview, believed the eager-to-please director had made the war possible: "They would not have been able to go to war without his estimates. Period. They couldn't have done it without his 'slam dunk.'"

The WMDs debacle was the agency's lowest moment since the Bay of Pigs, and its most significant intelligence failure. "If the CIA had come out and said, 'We don't have a clue whether there are weapons of mass destruction there,' it would've been a very different story," said Bob Gates, the former director. "An intelligence failure like that changes history."

CHAPTER NINE

"He died quickly."

Porter Goss, Michael Hayden, and George W. Bush

By the spring of 2004, George Tenet was nearing the end of his rope. He'd been director for seven years, longer than anyone except Allen Dulles. The Iraq War, launched with Tenet's assurance that Saddam possessed weapons of mass destruction, had turned into a fiasco; not only had no WMDs been found but a vicious insurgency had turned the American occupation into a bloody quagmire. Within the beleaguered Bush White House, the prospects for reelection looked bleak.

Tenet was incensed when, on April 17, *The Washington Post* published a piece based on Bob Woodward's book *Plan of Attack*; the story described the Oval Office meeting at which Tenet called the case for WMDs a "slam dunk." Tenet felt like "the guy being burned at the stake." He called up Andy Card, Bush's White House chief of staff, and read him the riot act. "What you guys have gone and done is make me look stupid and I just want to tell you how furious I am about it," he snapped. "For someone in the administration to now hang this around my neck is about the most despicable thing I have ever seen in my life."

"There were just so many things going wrong," recalled John McLaughlin, Tenet's friend and longtime deputy director. "And there's always a blame game under way when things go wrong. And everyone was stressed and angry and tense and pissed off." Charlie Allen saw the toll the unrelenting stress had taken on his boss. "He sacrificed so much," said Allen. "Worked so hard. He was not in shape in those days. He was overweight and alarmingly so." Tenet was exhausted. "I felt that in the interest of the organization it was time for somebody new to move in," the director told me fifteen years later. "So I called Andy Card and said I needed to see the president that afternoon and I told him why." Later that day Tenet gave Bush his resignation letter. The president didn't try to change his mind.

The next day Tenet went to the Bubble to give his farewell speech. His deputy McLaughlin, introducing him, cited terrorism, 9/11, and a host of other crises—and remarked that compared to Tenet "most previous DCIs presided over a kind of formal dance party." When it came his turn, Tenet gave a stem-winding speech lauding the courage and sacrifice of the CIA workforce; he ended by quoting Theodore Roosevelt, the same passage Richard Nixon cited in his bitter, maudlin White House farewell a quarter century earlier:

> *It is not the critic who counts; not the man who points out how the strong man stumbles, or where the doer of deeds could have done them better. The credit belongs to the man who is actually in the arena, whose face is marred by dust and sweat and blood.*

But Tenet delivered it without any of Nixon's self-pity; to his credit he even alluded to the elephant in the room, WMDs: "These have been eventful years. Filled with exhilaration and triumph. With pain and sorrow. And, yes, with questions about our performance." Donald Rumsfeld, the secretary of defense, and Robert Mueller, the FBI director, praised Tenet in brief remarks. But not a single senior White House official attended. "I didn't really care," Tenet insisted. "I thought this was a family thing, an in-house thing." But his friend Charlie Allen was offended. "I felt very pained that the White House turned its back on George," he said.

It would be hard to imagine anyone less like Tenet than the new acting director, John McLaughlin. Calm, silver-tongued, and professorial, McLaughlin was a career CIA analyst and a dapper, bespectacled intellectual who wore tweed suits with pocket squares and never raised his voice. As Tenet's deputy, he was sometimes referred to as "George's brain." Like many of his colleagues, McLaughlin was a workaholic, but he always told young CIA officers to cultivate a hobby so as not to go insane.

McLaughlin was an amateur magician (his nickname was Merlin)—and he'd often perform tricks on business trips. Once, on a visit to Moscow with Tenet, over dinner with members of the SVR

(Sluzhba Vneshney Razvedki), a successor to the KGB, he was asked how the CIA kept its budget out of the red. Borrowing a 10,000 ruble note, McLaughlin folded it repeatedly and then unwrapped it, revealing a 100,000 note. Another time, at Blair House, to the delight of Argentine president Carlos Menem, McLaughlin turned a $1 bill into $100. About a week later Menem cabled McLaughlin, offering him a job as his finance minister.

But McLaughlin couldn't make the CIA's problems vanish. "We look back at that period and think mainly of Iraq and 9/11 and terrorism," he recalled, "but we also had issues in the Balkans and Russia and China and South Asia and Pakistan." The press had revealed the existence of the rendition, detention, and interrogation program (RDI)—with its black sites and infamous enhanced interrogation techniques. At one meeting, John Ashcroft, the attorney general, expressed doubts about the program. "It was a hesitation about whether we were on solid legal ground," recalled McLaughlin. "At that point, I said, 'Well, then we're not doing it. Period. End of story.'" McLaughlin ordered a temporary halt to the program. He wouldn't let his operatives get hauled into the dock and prosecuted for things they'd been assured were legal.

A public relations nightmare was looming. The Senate Select Committee on Intelligence was about to report its conclusions about the WMD fiasco. Then, on July 22, 2004, the National Commission on Terrorist Attacks Upon the United States, better known as the 9/11 Commission, released its long-awaited report. Based on 2.5 million documents and 1,200 interviews in ten countries, the commission concluded that the 9/11 attacks were the result of "four kinds of failures: in imagination, policy, capabilities, and management." The CIA came in for scathing criticism. "We just took an absolute beating in the press and on the Hill," said McLaughlin. "And I remember at some point saying to the leadership team, 'Guys, we have to get up off the mat. We're like baby seals on the beach here with people clubbing us.'"

McLaughlin called a press conference and promised to come clean. "Let me say up front that we get it," he began. "We're not in denial. Let me walk you through what we think went wrong and what we're doing about it." McLaughlin gamely took questions for more than an hour. "I wanted people to see that the acting director was doing this to defend the agency, but also not to deny error."

McLaughlin vividly remembered the moment he learned that he wouldn't succeed Tenet as CIA director. He was getting ready to go to work one morning in August when he got a call from Andy Card. "The president is going to nominate Porter Goss," Bush's chief of staff told him. Goss, an eight-term congressman from Florida, was the Republican chair of the House Permanent Select Committee on Intelligence (HPSCI), and a friend of McLaughlin. "I had no choice but to say thanks, I'll do everything I can to assist Porter and make his entry smooth and ensure his success," said McLaughlin. "I don't think it had anything to do with me personally. It wasn't, 'I'm getting rid of that guy who screwed everything up.'" But the news stung. McLaughlin had hoped to land the top job in the agency he had served for thirty years.

The traumas of 9/11, the enhanced interrogation program, and the debacle over WMDs had stacked the deck against McLaughlin. "The agency was under fire and politically the president needed to make a change," he said. "I was disappointed because I was really ready to do this. But as John Kennedy said, 'Life is not fair.'"

On paper, Porter Goss seemed well qualified to steer the agency through the political minefields of the post-9/11 era. Garrulous and amiable, he was knowledgeable about intelligence; he'd served as a CIA case officer for almost a decade right out of college. "Few people came to be director as well prepared as Porter," said McLaughlin. "He'd been chairman of the committee that oversees the agency. He'd been a case officer. And he was a damn nice guy." Nominated by Bush, he was sworn in as CIA director on September 4, 2004. Alas, the CIA under Goss was headed into treacherous waters, with a crew of bumblers who were in way over their heads.

As it turned out, Goss would be the last Director of Central Intelligence, or DCI. Under a new law, the Intelligence Reform and Terrorism Prevention Act, all fifteen spy services, including the CIA, would soon report to a director of national intelligence, or DNI. So Goss's successors, no longer DCIs, would now be DCIAs, or directors of the CIA. The idea, recommended by the 9/11 Commission, was to coordinate the nation's unwieldy intelligence apparatus. But in truth the new office of the DNI was a political fix that muddied lines of authority, touched off turf battles, and confused everyone.

• • •

Porter Goss had stumbled into the CIA almost by accident. As a junior at Yale in 1959, looking for the job placement office, "I went into the wrong room and literally ended up talking to a CIA recruiter," he recalled. After a two-year stint in the Army, Goss signed up with the agency and was sent to Florida, where he was a case officer during the Cuban Missile Crisis. In 1970, stationed in London, Goss caught a bacterial infection that nearly killed him. He resigned in order to regain his health, and didn't return to the agency.

With a family inheritance, Goss didn't need to work; he owned houses on Sanibel Island, Florida, and Fishers Island in Long Island Sound, and a farm in Virginia. But he bought a Florida newspaper and later went into business. Elected to the House in 1989, he specialized in intelligence issues and worked his way up to chair the HPSCI. Now, as CIA director, he was coming full circle. But he was about to commit a cardinal sin from which he'd never recover.

Tom Twetten, the former head of the Near East Division, tried to warn the new director. "Porter, don't bring your staff with you," he told him. "You need to have people on the inside who understand what's going on here as your aides." But Goss was on a mission. He believed he was empowered, by both the White House and Capitol Hill, to "crack the whip" on the agency. The new director arrived at Langley with a Praetorian Guard of deputies from his congressional office. Ignorant of intelligence matters and inept as managers, they were dubbed "the Gosslings."

The Gosslings immediately launched a purge. "These guys started settling scores with officers who talked back to them," said one operative. Anyone thought to be disloyal to Bush or who questioned the Gosslings' authority was a target. The more valuable the CIA officer, it seemed, the more expendable. Making matters worse, Goss declared that the CIA should support the president and his policies. *Support policies?* Tailoring intelligence to a political agenda was not what anyone at Langley signed on for. It was all too reminiscent of James Schlesinger decreeing that the CIA "was going to stop fucking Richard Nixon."

Goss's deputies were right out of a Carl Hiaasen novel. One of his first picks for executive director, or ExDir, the CIA's number three job, had to step aside after a *Washington Post* story revealed he'd shoplifted a pound of bacon from a Safeway store. To replace him, Goss chose a picturesque character with the unforgettable name of Kyle "Dusty" Foggo. Foggo's chief qualification was that he'd wined and dined the Gosslings during overseas trips; he'd also served in the Directorate of Administration, the CIA's logistical division. Foggo also had a history of alcohol abuse, physical violence, philandering, and corruption. The ExDir was a regular at poker games thrown by a shady GOP fundraiser. Foggo was often accompanied by a retired CIA pal who went by the name "Nine Fingers."

The Gosslings didn't enhance their reputation on their first overseas trip. Over dinner the night before a meeting in Brussels, Belgium, several drank heavily and caroused like a bunch of frat boys. The next morning they were so hungover they were late to a scheduled meeting; one was in such dire condition he had to be treated by a doctor. A senior CIA official who attended the meeting said it was the ugliest scene he'd witnessed in thirty years.

Meanwhile, Goss floated above the fray in his seventh-floor aerie. "Porter Goss was a genuinely good person, a decent man," said Charlie Allen. "But you can't let the staff do everything. You have to make some hard decisions. And Goss said, 'I don't do personnel decisions.'" Left to their own devices, the Gosslings turned the clandestine service against them. Few officers were more respected at Langley than Steve Kappes, the Assistant Deputy of the Directorate of Operations (ADDO). Kappes had led the CIA team that disrupted the black-market network of the rogue Pakistani nuclear scientist A. Q. Khan; he'd also gone toe-to-toe with Libya's Muammar Gaddafi, persuading him to surrender his nuclear, chemical, and biological weapons. But Goss did not get along with Kappes or his deputy, Mike Sulick. There were shouting matches in the halls. Kappes and Sulick resigned.

Jose Rodriguez, head of the Counterterrorism Center, was incensed: "The Gosslings were running amok," he said. "We're not used to having our boss fired and his deputy fired and being left adrift." By November, McLaughlin, who'd tried and failed to give the Gosslings his advice, had seen enough: "When you're trying to keep them from going over the cliff and they say, 'No, we're going over the cliff,' it's time to say, 'Nope, I'm out of here now.'" McLaughlin announced his retirement.

Rodriguez, architect of the agency's controversial enhanced interrogation techniques, steered clear of the "heavy thuds from the seventh floor where the elephants wrestled with each other." But he reluctantly agreed when Foggo, the ExDir, asked him to become head of the agency's National Clandestine Service (renamed from the Directorate of Operations). Rodriguez had one person in mind as his chief of staff: his protégé and future CIA director, Gina Haspel. "It took two seconds for me to say, 'Gina, come with me,'" he recalled.

Haspel had returned from the black site in Thailand where she'd been chief of base. She was now working at Langley as deputy to a senior CIA official. But she immediately accepted Rodriguez's offer. Haspel and Rodriguez were about to be embroiled in one of the most controversial scandals of the CIA's post-9/11 era.

The story had begun in March of 2002. That was when CIA officers had begun videotaping detainees at the Thailand site; the tapes showed prisoners being subjected to EITs, including waterboarding. In August 2002, CIA officers in Thailand asked Rodriguez: "Why are we still taping?" The tapes provided no useful intelligence and were taking up a lot of space, they said. They wanted permission to stop recording—and destroy the existing tapes.

A senior CIA officer flew out to the site and catalogued all the tapes; there were ninety-two, twelve of which captured the brutal techniques. The CIA's Inspector General, its legal counsel, and the chairs of the congressional intelligence committees had all been informed of the tapes' existence. But Rodriguez couldn't get approval to get rid of them. "Despite firm legal opinions from within the agency that we had the right to destroy the tapes and either support or lukewarm opposition from the Hill," he later wrote, "the agency's top leaders still wouldn't pull the trigger on the destruction of the tapes."

In late April 2004, *60 Minutes II*, an offshoot of the CBS News magazine, aired a sensational story about an Iraqi prison called Abu Ghraib. Photographs revealed horrific abuse by U.S. soldiers of detainees: They were threatened by snarling dogs, attached to electrodes, forced to pose naked attached to a leash. The images were nauseating, and galvanized sentiment against the war.

Rodriguez thought the abuses at Abu Ghraib, run by the Defense

Department, were far worse than the CIA's enhanced interrogation techniques. But the techniques weren't pretty; Rodriguez knew that if the videos became public—showing waterboarded prisoners gasping for breath—it would be a distinction without a difference. "I was concerned about the survival of the clandestine service," he said. "I knew the tapes would play as if we were psychopaths." Moreover the tapes would reveal the identities of CIA personnel. "I was concerned about the people who work for me whose faces were shown on those tapes."

Rodriguez told the senior leadership of the congressional oversight committees that "the early interrogations had been videotaped, but that we intended to stop that practice and destroy the tapes." Jane Harman, congresswoman from California, warned him against that. "Watch it," she said. "You know, the perception will be that you are hiding something. So you shouldn't do it." Rodriguez also made sure his boss, Porter Goss, was briefed. The CIA director assumed the tapes had been destroyed; when he learned they still existed he recalls saying, "I don't think you ought to destroy them."

"I asked if they were being properly safeguarded," Goss remembered. "And the answer was yes."

By the fall of 2005, Rodriguez had lost all patience. He turned to Gina Haspel for help. "I had many deputies but Gina was my closest confidant," he said. "She was the person that everything filtered through, and everybody that needed anything, they all went to her." Rodriguez told Haspel to meet with the lawyers and ask two questions: (1) Would destroying the tapes be legal? And (2) Did Rodriguez have the authority to make that decision on his own? The answer she got to both questions was yes.

"Gina was a big reason for whatever successes I had," said Rodriguez. "She was my conscience." Haspel was firmly in favor of destroying the tapes, concerned for the safety of CIA officers at the Thailand base. "She reminded me about people who were there. I spent a weekend thinking about it and came back on Monday and I said, 'I'm gonna do this.'"

Haspel drafted a cable to the black site. "The cable left nothing to chance," said Rodriguez. "It even told them *how* to get rid of the tapes. They were to use an industrial-strength shredder to do the deed." On Wednesday, November 9, 2005, Rodriguez sat at his computer reviewing the message that Haspel had drafted. "I was not depriving anyone of information about what was done or what was said, I was just getting rid of some ugly visuals that could put the lives of my people at risk. I took a deep breath and hit *Send.*"

A few days later Porter Goss was having his morning briefing. As the director recalled: "Somebody said, 'Oh by the way, the tapes were destroyed.' And I rose out of my chair and said, '*What?*' It was a huge surprise to me and a very unhappy one." Goss was furious. He understood Rodriquez's reasoning; releasing the tapes "would inflame riots around the globe." But he saw nothing but trouble ahead. "This is really bad, what you've done," Goss told Rodriguez. "There's another dimension here—and it's the politics of ensuring the well-being and safety and the future activity of this agency. And this is going to cause us a political problem that you cannot believe. It's my purview to say 'Yes' or 'No'—and I wasn't consulted. You didn't give me my vote, which would have been: 'No, you can't destroy them.'"

I asked Rodriguez why he'd destroyed the tapes on his own authority. "So you had the director of the CIA and a member of Congress saying, 'We don't want these tapes destroyed,' and you did it?" He replied: "I made an executive decision. I was not stupid, I didn't one day decide to get out of bed and destroy the tapes. I got approval to do this. I consulted with our lawyers. I would do it all over again."

I asked if he and Haspel had discussed informing Goss before they sent the cable. "Did she ever say, 'We'd better tell Goss? Don't you think we should tell the director?'" Rodriguez replied: "Porter Goss is a sweetheart and I love the guy. He didn't have the balls to do this."

The "torture tapes" would ignite a scandal a few years later, when the story of their destruction broke in *The New York Times*. By then, Porter Goss would be gone.

Goss's troubles were mounting. He'd never developed a close relationship with President Bush. After one briefing at the Oval Office, the new White House chief of staff, Joshua Bolten, asked the president: "Are you happy with this guy? Do you ever call him up?" Bush said no, he didn't.

Goss was also fighting a rearguard battle with his nominal superior, the new Director of National Intelligence.

On April 22, 2005, John Negroponte began his first day as DNI. A former ambassador to Honduras under Reagan and, most recently, U.S. ambassador to Iraq, Negroponte knew that he'd taken a thankless job. Former CIA director Bob Gates, Bush's first choice for DNI, had opposed the creation of the office and turned down the offer. While Negroponte was now technically the intelligence community's top dog, in practice the DNI had limited power and an amorphous mandate.

Although Goss and Negroponte got along, the CIA welcomed the new DNI like a Visigoth at the gates. "Once this thing went into force, there were parts of the CIA that just fought it tooth and nail," said Negroponte regarding the DNI's office. "They thought it was wrong, they didn't believe in it. They still don't believe in it." The CIA was supposed to provide the DNI with support and personnel. But Negroponte and his deputy, Air Force General Michael Hayden, ran into opposition at every turn.

A seasoned and savvy diplomat, Negroponte was philosophical about these skirmishes. "I was in Baghdad, minding my own business, when the president asked me to take this job," he said. Negroponte took a realist's view of the job: First, the DNI was the president's principal intelligence adviser (the DNI supervised the President's Daily Brief, or PDB—though the CIA still produced it and supplied the briefers); second, he managed the intelligence community, coordinating the agencies and budgets; and third, he took the lead in dealing with Congress. Negroponte had enough to do; he wasn't interested in encroaching on the CIA director's turf.

But Goss had been fatally weakened by the drama over the Gosslings and the destruction of the EIT tapes. Goss also believed that the White House wanted him out because he was balking at restarting the EIT program—suspended by John McLaughlin. And finally there was a scandal involving ExDir Dusty Foggo. For months Foggo had been under investigation by the CIA Inspector General for his dealings with a corrupt GOP fundraiser and defense contractor. Negroponte had tried to warn Goss about his ExDir; but by the time Goss got the message it was too late. "Porter called me up and said, 'You know, John, not only were you right but it's worse than I thought.'"

The coup de grâce for Goss came in a turf battle with Negroponte. The DNI had asked Goss to lend some analysts to the newly created National Counterterrorism Center (NCTC). Not to be confused with the CIA's Counterterrorism Center (CTC), the NCTC was an extra layer of bureaucracy created after 9/11, charged with looking more broadly at national and international threats. Goss turned him down. As Negroponte recalled it, "Porter ultimately wrote me a letter saying, 'We're very sorry but because of this, that, and the other thing, we cannot give you the people you are requesting.'" Negroponte reported this to Bush and his national security adviser, Stephen Hadley.

Shortly thereafter, Joshua Bolten, the chief of staff, asked Goss to come to his White House office. When he arrived, they made small talk about Bolten's father, who'd worked at the CIA when Goss arrived as a young case officer. Then Bolten broke the news: The president had decided "it was time for a change." As a White House official recalled, "the next thing you know, Goss was in the Oval and they're photographing him with the president, big handshake and all: 'Thanks, I had a wonderful time, and good career, and sayonara.' So it happened very quickly." Porter Goss's tenure as DCI was over— an ending that came as a relief. "My blood pressure was so high that it was very unhealthy," Goss told me. "It's been a lot better ever since."

It would take a little longer to dispose of Goss's notorious executive director. On May 12, 2006, investigators from five federal agencies, acting under search warrants, raided Foggo's home in Vienna, Virginia. They also took over his CIA office, turning his corner of the seventh floor into a crime scene. Foggo would be indicted for fraud, conspiracy, and money-laundering, and plead guilty to one count of steering a CIA contract to his friend, the contractor. Foggo ended up serving a thirty-seven-month sentence in a federal prison at Pine Knot, Kentucky.

On May 30, 2006, Foggo's office at Langley was still sealed off with yellow police tape when General Michael Hayden reported for duty as CIA director.

Michael V. Hayden was the first man in uniform to run the CIA since Admiral Stansfield Turner under Jimmy Carter. A four-star Air Force general, Hayden had gotten to know George W. Bush during his six-year stint as head of the National Security Agency; in 2005 he became DNI Negroponte's deputy. He'd grown up in Pittsburgh and served in the Air Force's Air Intelligence Agency. At the NSA, Hayden earned his stripes in Bush's eyes by launching a surveillance program known as Stellar Wind; it enabled the intelligence community to scoop up metadata—records but not content—of phone calls, emails, and texts in the U.S. that were connected to suspected terrorists. Post-9/11, Hayden believed that protecting the country required walking right up to the edge of illegality—or, as he put it, "playing to the edge."

At Langley, Hayden was greeted with some skepticism. Many wondered if a former NSA director could appreciate the importance of human spies, or HUMINT. "He's another one of these engineers, has done all this tech stuff and has every reason to fail," recalled Charlie Allen. Some CIA officers questioned whether a military officer should run a civilian agency. (Hayden would discard the uniform two years and one month into his tenure as director, retiring from the Air Force on July 1, 2008.) With a covert war against Al Qaeda heating up, and the enhanced interrogation program still up and running, Hayden would need to win over the CIA workforce to have any chance of success.

The new director got off to a good start by making a clean break with the Gosslings. Hayden offered them platinum parachutes and pushed them out the door. He also brought Steve Kappes out of retirement and made him his deputy director; Mike Sulick also returned. Immediately after being sworn in as CIA director at the White House, on May 30, 2006, Hayden drove to Langley for his first "all-hands" address to the workforce in the Bubble. "Number one, nobody sent me up here to blow anything up," he said. "You people are the best in the world at what you do. . . . I got the stuff beyond the fence line. That's *my* job." Hayden meant that he'd defend them against Congress, the White House, and the press.

It was a tough crowd. "We'd had George Tenet, who everybody called George and felt was your locker room buddy," recalled Stephanie O' Sullivan, head of the Directorate of Science and Technology. A hand went up in the back of the crowd. "What do we call you?" the general was asked. Hayden, famously glib, was momentarily at a loss for words. "It was the only time I ever saw him not sure what to say," said O'Sullivan, "Because the natural response would have been, 'General'—but he didn't want to go there." Wearing his dress uniform with four stars on each shoulder, Hayden finally answered: "Whatever makes you comfortable." He'd later observe that it was the most important thing he said that day.

Hayden faced an immediate question: what to do about the enhanced interrogation program? McLaughlin, as acting director, had put a temporary hold on the techniques and Goss had extended the hiatus after the passage of the Detainee Treatment Act, which banned "torture." But Dick Cheney and the White House wanted the interrogations to continue.

Hayden was walking a tightrope. "Nobody had thought through the endgame," said Michael Morell, the veteran analyst. "Mike was defending his people, but he also knew that the agency couldn't do this anymore." For the time being, Hayden decided to eliminate half of the techniques—waterboarding, cramped confinement, and stress positions. As he later wrote, he'd preserve "a grasp of the lapels and of the chin, two slaps (a backhanded belly slap and an insult slap to the face), and the authority to manipulate diet and sleep. Enforced nudity was sometimes on and sometimes off our amended list."

In December of 2007, *The New York Times* was poised to break a huge story. Its reporter, Mark Mazzetti, was calling around, asking his sources about rumors that tapes of CIA interrogations had been destroyed. "Our network began to light up," Hayden recalled, "as CIA alumni called in with reports that Mazzetti was chasing after the destruction of the videotapes." As CIA legal counsel John Rizzo put it, "It was the ultimate nightmare scenario . . . a huge, holy shit, sensational story about the CIA and our congressional overseers would be finding out about it for the first time. Congress would go berserk." The "torture tapes" scandal was about to break.

On December 6, Hayden beat the *Times* to the punch by coming clean in an open letter to the CIA workforce. He wrote that the agency had told the intelligence committees' leadership about the tapes and its intention to destroy them. "What matters here is that it was done in line with the law," he wrote. The tapes posed a "serious security risk" and if made public "they would have exposed CIA officials and their families to retaliation from Al Qaeda and its sympathizers."

But the *Times* story caused a sensation. Watergate and obstruction of justice were in the air. "We haven't seen anything like this since the eighteen-and-a-half-minute gap in the tapes of Richard Nixon," thundered Massachusetts senator Edward "Ted" Kennedy from the Senate floor. Hearings were convened by the two intelligence committees. Members inveighed against the CIA and its perfidy. Commentators declared that evidence of heinous crimes had been destroyed. The attorney general appointed John Durham, a federal prosecutor, to investigate.

At the height of the uproar, before an open session of the Senate Intelligence Committee, Hayden tried to put the story in perspective. "CIA had waterboarded three people: Zubaydah, Nashiri, and Khalid Sheikh Mohammed," he said. The last waterboarding had taken place in March of 2003. The CIA wasn't asking to revive the practice and hadn't used it in almost five years.

Undoubtedly, there were some at the CIA who believed that destroying potential evidence was wrong. But many were relieved that Rodriguez had deep-sixed the tapes and spared the agency its own Abu Ghraib. "He'll forever be remembered as a hero for it," Hayden wrote.

Still, the uproar raised the question: Could CIA officers be punished or prosecuted for things they were assured were legal? Many believed that if anyone should be prosecuted, it was Bush, Cheney, and Tenet. After all, everyone else was following orders. "This is a problem that goes back to the contras and afterwards," said Negroponte. "It's the idea of criminalizing this stuff, which is very demoralizing." Jose Rodriguez worried about ending up in prison. "You get the feeling that your government has abandoned you," he said. "You worry that some overzealous prosecutor is going to indict you." Rodriguez feared he could be hauled into some international court if he set foot outside the country. Ex-Director Bob Gates believed that the folks on the ground, not the politicians, always ended up suffering the consequences. "It's this repeated willingness to put intelligence officers in the dock, either of public opinion or in court, that is troubling when these operations are authorized by the president."

On November 8, 2010, Durham, the special counsel, announced that he wouldn't bring criminal charges against anyone for destroying the CIA's interrogation tapes. But Hayden could see that the era of enhanced interrogations was at an end. "We had finally succeeded in making it so legally difficult and politically dangerous to grab and hold someone," he said, "that we would simply default to the kill switch to take terrorists off the battlefield."

The war against Al Qaeda was accelerating. And so was the CIA's use of a game-changing weapon: drones. It was on George Tenet's watch in 2001 that drones, once just eyes in the sky, had become lethal birds of prey. But Tenet and others at the agency had resisted having authority over drone strikes outside the chain of military command. That reticence vanished after 9/11.

Hayden valued the precision of drones in the war against terrorism. "When you can stare at a target unblinkingly for hours, if not days, and then use a fourteen-pound warhead against that target with an accuracy measured in inches," he said, "this actually makes warfare more precise and that should be a good thing. They give you the ability to minimize civilian casualties."

But Hayden also saw another side to killing people with devices remotely triggered from the other side of the world. "The dark side," he said, "is the ease with which a political decision-maker can make the decision to do this." As Bob Gates put it, "You can be sitting in Nevada, in front of what looks for all the world like a big video game, push a button, and a pickup truck explodes in Afghanistan." Charlie Allen, the crusty NIO who'd seen everything, watched Hayden wrestle with the quandaries of drone warfare. "He had some hard decisions to make. Decisions that don't come naturally to a person who lived his life as an Air Force officer, working always within the law." The CIA was no longer just a gatherer of intelligence; it was becoming a killing machine.

Some directors blamed George Tenet for turning the CIA into a paramilitary army; in the aftermath of 9/11, they believed he'd been seduced by covert operations at the expense of the agency's core mission, intelligence-gathering. "There's a tendency to get so caught up in the scintillating covert world," said one ex-director, "that we forget that it's on the analytical side that CIA actually earns its money."

Yet Tenet was blunt about the perils of the so-called pointy end of the spear. "Sometimes I think we get ourselves into a frenzy, believing that killing is the only answer to a problem," he said. "And the truth is, it's not. People need to be careful about being so happy with the use of the term 'kill.' Intelligence officers in particular have to worry about the use of that term. That's not what our reason for existence is."

Tenet's longtime deputy McLaughlin sometimes dressed down CIA officers who reacted giddily to a successful drone strike. "There are many times when people are talking loosely about it or enthusing to me about it," he told me. "And I will say to them . . ." McLaughlin paused. " 'Have you ever killed someone?' " He arched an eyebrow for emphasis.

Before Hayden arrived at Langley, drone strikes were rarely conducted outside war zones. The trouble was, that was where Al Qaeda militants were regrouping in 2008, in Pakistan's tribal areas. "We made the case," Hayden recalled, "that we had to begin targeted killings outside of internationally agreed theaters of conflict. 'Get this guy off the battlefield because he's going to come kill you and your children' was an absolutely compelling argument." George W. Bush gave the go-ahead to an escalation of drone strikes in Pakistan.

In January 2008, Jose Rodriguez decided it was time to retire. But what about his protégé, Gina Haspel? Rodriguez wanted to know about her career plans. She told him she wanted to be a station chief. Where? Rodriguez asked. "Well, I'm thinking about Geneva," she said. Rodriguez recoiled. "That's *too small* for you," he told her. Like too many women at the CIA, Rodriguez thought, she was aiming too low, selling herself short. "It's a common thing," he said. "At the agency the men always think they can do the job no matter what. The women *never* think they're good enough to do it. And many times the women are the ones that are better at it!"

Rodriguez gave Haspel a pep talk. Forget about Geneva, he said, she should ask for London. It was the most important station, and the way to advance her career. "Everybody goes to London. The Congress goes to London, the intelligence committees go to London, and they all want to get a briefing, and they all come to the embassy." Rodriguez pointed out that the British had their first female MI6 chief in Washington, but "we never had a female chief in London." Haspel replied: "Well, I don't know if that's possible. What do you think?" Rodriguez was exasperated by Haspel's timidity. "I said,

'Gina. You do the day-to-day in this office. You are a participant in all the major decisions. I come to you to tell me what I should do about this stuff. *Of course* you can!'"

Soon thereafter, Haspel became chief of the CIA station in London. It was, as Rodriguez promised, the most prestigious overseas station, a magnet for important American visitors. One of them was a conservative congressman from Kansas named Mike Pompeo, the future CIA director, who'd eventually make Haspel his deputy at Langley. By design or not, the reserved operative from Louisville had begun her ascent toward the directorship of the CIA.

In 2008 nothing alarmed the Bush White House more than the prospect of a nuclear-armed Iran. One day in the Oval Office, after a briefing on the subject, George W. Bush grabbed Hayden and said, "Mike, I don't want to be left with only two choices here." As Hayden later wrote, "the two choices were bombing or the bomb." Bush wanted options other than a full-scale invasion to prevent Iran from developing a nuclear weapon.

There was someone else who was determined to stop Iran with methods short of war: Israel's spymaster Meir Dagan. The legendary head of Mossad, Dagan was a rotund man with a sly smile who wielded a cane rumored to conceal a sharp blade. On the verge of retirement, the old spy was determined to deprive Iran of a nuclear weapon. A few years later, when he became CIA director, Leon Panetta would pay Dagan an unforgettable visit. "Meir was one of these guys who came right out of central casting," Panetta told me. "The first time I met him we were having dinner and I said, 'how would you handle going after Al Qaeda? What would you do?' And he looked at me, and he said, 'You *kill* them.'" Panetta let out a booming laugh. "So, okay, you *kill* them. I never forgot that."

The CIA had worked closely with Mossad to sabotage Iran's nuclear program, but there was a line it wouldn't cross: Assassination was off the table because Executive Order 12333 prohibited it. So it fell to Mossad to target Iranian nuclear scientists. One by one, they kept dying, six out of fourteen, usually blown up by bombs attached to their cars by motorcyclists who pulled alongside.

But when it came to assassination there was still one person who was considered fair game: Imad Mughniyah.

Since the devastating bombings of the 1980s—of the American embassy and Marine barracks in Lebanon—the Hezbollah operations chief had been responsible for the killings of scores of Americans and Israelis. He'd been behind the 1992 car bombing of the Israeli embassy in Buenos Aires, which had killed twenty-nine people, including four Israelis, five Argentinian Jews, and twenty children at a nearby school. (Two hundred forty-two people were injured.) And he'd killed dozens of Israeli soldiers in southern Lebanon with his signature weapon, the shaped charge.

The shaped charge was a terrorist's silver bullet. "He'd hide these things in rocks, trees, trash, whatever," said Bob Baer, the CIA Middle East operative who chased him for years. "One of these shaped charges—with enough copper in the right shape and the right speed—will cut right through an Abrams tank. The Israelis could never detect them. These devices defeated the Israelis in a major way, drove them off the roads. We set up a whole agency in Washington to try to defeat this stuff developed by Mughniyah. Millions of dollars were spent on it. And not a penny made a difference."

It had been ten years since the CIA's failed operation to abduct Mughniyah in South Beirut, when his girlfriend had agreed to set a trap for him. That miss had been costly: In the decade since, Mughniyah had perfected his shaped charges in camps in Lebanon. "And then they turned around with this expertise, took it to Iraq, and essentially disabled our Abrams tanks," said Baer. "That speeded our departure from Iraq, no doubt." CIA director Hayden was determined to get Mughniyah off the battlefield. "He was very active supporting Shiite militias in Iraq to kill American and other coalition soldiers," Hayden said. "A very bad guy." Mughniyah was also thought to be involved in a brazen 2007 attack on Iraq's Karbala provincial headquarters, which killed five U.S. military personnel.

Many at the CIA believed that the notorious Hezbollah fugitive was more dangerous than his Al Qaeda counterpart. As one former operative later put it: "Bin Laden was locked up in a compound in Abbottabad. Imad Mughniyah was the real thing. He could project violence against the United States anywhere he wanted to, including Asia and South America. Bin Laden always talked about what he was going to do next. You didn't know what Mughniyah was going do until he did it. Bringing precise violence against an enemy was his specialty. Bin Laden was just a mass murderer. This guy was a tactician."

But Maurice, as he was known, was still a phantom, captured in just one grainy photograph—and he seemed to taunt his American and Israeli pursuers. "On the battlefield he would travel around on a little motor scooter, pretending to be a butcher or a tailor, completely evading the Israelis," said a former intelligence official. "He moved his troops under cover of darkness, out of satellite range, out of drone sight."

In 2007, on a visit to Tel Aviv, Israel, Bruce Riedel, the retired CIA Middle East analyst, called on the country's head of military intelligence, the Military Intelligence Directorate, to discuss Iranian-backed terrorism in the region. "I asked him, 'Who are the key people in this?' And he said, 'Well, there's this Syrian general, Mohammed Suleiman. There's Qassim Suleimani, head of Iran's Revolutionary Guard Quds Force. And there's Imad Mughniyah, who is the most important of all.'"

Within eight months, two of the three would be dead. The lone survivor, Qassim Suleimani, would continue to direct Iranian-backed terrorism against the U.S. and Israel until his assassination by an American military drone in January 2020.

In 2008, Imad Mughniyah moved from Beirut to Damascus. He had business there with Syria's intelligence services and counted on their protection. As always he was cautious about his movements and fastidious about his security detail. "He never established a routine or hired anybody around him whose loyalty he couldn't count on one hundred percent," said Baer. But Syria posed new challenges for him. "Moving to Syria is a different story. Intelligence sources are easier to come by. A lot of rumors go around. It's a very modern city in a lot of ways."

After years of frustration, Mossad had finally picked up Mughniyah's trail. But the Israelis had difficulty operating in Damascus; Syrian intelligence kept a close eye on their comings and goings. The Americans, by contrast, could operate more freely and had a functioning embassy. The stage was set for a joint Mossad-CIA operation to take down their common adversary.

Dagan, the head of Mossad, had an ironclad rule never to involve other countries, not even the United States, in assassinations. This time he decided to break the rule. He approached his CIA counterpart Hayden and asked for help. Executive Order 12333 was a problem—but the CIA's lawyers argued that Mughniyah was a legitimate target under the doctrine of self-defense: He'd sent men to help the Shiite militias carry out attacks against Americans in Iraq. (This argument would be dusted off and used again to justify the targeting of Mughniyah's friend General Suleimani in January 2020.) Hayden agreed in principle to a joint CIA-Israeli covert operation to kill Mughniyah. But of course one other person's approval was needed.

In his book *Rise and Kill First*, Ronen Bergman, an Israeli journalist, wrote:

> *President Bush then granted Dagan's request for assistance, but only on the condition that it be kept secret, that Mughniyah alone would be killed, and that Americans would not be the ones to do the actual killing. Prime Minister [Ehud] Olmert himself guaranteed this to the president.*

But how to carry out the joint operation?

Shooting Mughniyah on the street was ruled out; it would be almost impossible to extricate a team of snipers from a bustling city crawling with spies. Blasting him with a lethal drone was also problematic. "It's one thing dropping a drone in the tribal areas of Pakistan," explained Baer, "but in a so-called friendly city, like Damascus, you can't do that. You might blow up a school. In the CIA we used to say, 'Oh, we're gonna end up blowing up a school bus full of kids.' It's precisely what they did not want to do."

Planting a cell phone with an embedded explosive on Mughniyah was considered too risky: The Hezbollah mastermind discarded his phones frequently. But there was one possession Mughniyah was almost never without: his luxurious Mitsubishi Pajero SUV. If CIA operatives could get access to it, they could plant a bomb in or on the vehicle. It would have to be a remotely triggered device so accurate that it would kill Mughniyah, and Mughniyah alone.

The irony was not lost on the operation's planners. The device they needed was a shaped charge.

The bomb was constructed under CIA auspices at a facility in North Carolina. "It had to be encrypted," said a former CIA officer. "What you don't want is a cell phone or something else driving by which reproduces the signal and sets it off early because you could end up killing kids, or whatever. So the circuitry, the encryption, had to be perfect. The direction of the device had to be perfect."

The plan was to embed the device in the spare tire on the rear door. (Surveillance showed that the terrorist's bodyguards never looked there.) But that posed a delicate and painstaking engineering challenge. "We had to replace the entire door on his car and it had to match perfectly," said a former senior government official. "The paint had to be faded the same way as the paint on the door. And that was the beauty of the American contribution—to be able to perfectly match the door so it didn't look like it was a new door and swap it out, without anybody seeing that."

The blast would be lethal only if Mughniyah was standing outside the vehicle. "You've got one chance at this," said Baer. "You can't have an incomplete explosion, a partial explosion, because you might just wound the guy or miss him altogether. And then you're done. You don't get another chance. He goes back underground. So they had to be a hundred percent certain this would work."

It helped that Mughniyah had picked up a bad habit. On visits to girlfriends, reportedly supplied by Syrian intelligence, he'd drop his security detail. (Mughniyah had done the same thing visiting his lover in South Beirut ten years earlier.) During one of these assignations, a Mossad operative swooped in and swapped out the SUV's rear door, replacing it with the identical new one, smuggled in by the CIA from North Carolina.

Now the Mossad team watched—and waited for the right moment to pull the trigger. The wait was excruciating. That's because the presidential finding for the operation was exacting. "The finding was very specific—he had to be alone, so there couldn't be anybody else killed," said a former senior government official. The team watched Mughniyah driving around Damascus. One day in February 2008 they saw him conferring with another man, leaning on the side of the SUV, who looked familiar. Suddenly, they realized who it was: Qassim Suleimani, the Iranian Revolutionary Guard commander. "And they thought, 'Fabulous, we want him too. It's a twofer!'" Suleimani was of course one of Mossad's—and the CIA's—top three targets. But there were problems: Suleimani was a leader not of a terrorist organization but of a sovereign government, Iran. And George W. Bush hadn't authorized his killing. They let the chance pass.

That same evening the stars finally aligned. At a safe house in the affluent Kafr Sousa neighborhood of Damascus, Mughniyah attended a meeting with aides to the Syrian general Mohammed Suleiman, the third man on Mossad's most-wanted list. Mughniyah parked outside, just a few hundred yards from the headquarters of Syrian Intelligence, and walked to the house. At 10:45 p.m., just before the meeting ended, he left the house. He returned, alone, to the Pajero.

As he reached the driver's door, the vehicle exploded; a fireball lit up the sky and the ground shuddered. Windows shattered at the intelligence headquarters down the block. The world's most elusive and deadly terrorist was incinerated.

Mughniyah had been killed by a device like the one he'd used against so many Israelis and Americans. Bob Baer remarked, "It's a little bit of divine justice, don't you think?"

On a Friday afternoon, August 1, 2008, just a few months after Mughniyah's demise, Mohammed Suleiman, the Syrian general, set out from Damascus in a convoy of vehicles for the port city of Tartus. An hour later he arrived at his weekend residence, a spacious villa with a large stone patio overlooking the Mediterranean. He invited guests to join him and his wife for dinner on the outdoor terrace.

After the plates were cleared, the general and his party sat around a table, smoking Cuban cigars. Suddenly, Suleiman lurched forward, his head slamming on the table. Blood and brain matter splattered his wife and guests. He'd been shot six times—in the forehead, chest, and throat, and three times in the back. The general died instantly.

From two locations on the beach, Israeli military snipers clambered back to the water's edge. Within moments they'd slipped onto their rubber dinghies and were paddling back to their ship.

General Suleiman's death went almost unnoticed; the Syrians preferred to keep the incident quiet. But Mughniyah's demise was a different story. At his funeral, held in a large hangar in South Beirut, thousands of mourners paid their respects to "the great martyred hero." The walls were festooned with posters bearing his photograph, only now revealed. In the bitter, bloody struggle against Israel and the U.S., Imad Mughniyah was irreplaceable.

But Suleiman and Mughniyah had something in common. When I pressed John Brennan, then the CIA director, to tell me what had happened to Mughniyah, he repeatedly refused to comment. Finally he answered.

"He died quickly," Brennan said.

CHAPTER TEN

"You just have to hope that ultimately God agrees with you."

Leon Panetta and Barack Obama

Michael Hayden was in a secure room in the Kluczynski Federal Building in Chicago, waiting for Barack Obama and his entourage to arrive. It was December 9, 2008, and George W. Bush's CIA director had flown in from Washington, D.C., to give the Democratic president-elect his first briefing on the agency's covert operations. A month earlier, Obama had been briefed on global threats by Mike McConnell, the Director of National Intelligence. During this session, Hayden hoped to talk Obama into preserving the CIA's scaled-back enhanced interrogation techniques (EITs). On the retired general's watch, waterboarding and five other techniques had been abolished; only six were still authorized. And Hayden had another, more personal goal: He hoped the incoming president might keep him on as CIA director.

Hayden knew the chances were slim: He'd served under Obama's bête noire, George W. Bush, and had defended the infamous interrogation techniques. But Hayden thought he might impress the president-elect with a bold gambit: He'd take the bull by the horns — and give him a rudimentary "demonstration." The brutality of the interrogation methods had been exaggerated, Hayden believed. What better way to show that than by acting them out?

Hayden didn't have to wait long for Obama and his national security team to arrive. After reviewing the CIA's ongoing covert operations, Hayden briefed them on renditions — the practice of moving prisoners to other countries for interrogation. The director told Obama that the CIA insisted on "guarantees of humane treatment" before sending prisoners anywhere. Suddenly, Joe Biden interrupted: "Oh, come on, General. You shipped them to these places so that you could rough them up, so you could get information." Hayden recoiled. "Mr. Vice President–elect, that's simply not true," he protested.

When it came time to demonstrate the interrogation techniques, Hayden turned to a CIA colleague. "Stand up, David," he ordered. Hayden grabbed him by the lapels and yanked him close. Then he slapped him twice in the face. These "grabs" and "slaps," he explained, caused no lasting harm. "Mr. President," Hayden said, "we also manipulated diet and sleep." With that, he sat down. Obama stared at the CIA director. "What were the other techniques?" he asked, skeptically. Hayden began to explain, but the president cut him off. "Greg will get back to you," he said, referring to Greg Craig, his White House counsel designate. Obama thought Hayden's show-and-tell was both awkward and underwhelming. He'd blown any chance of being retained as director.

There were plenty of other contenders to head Obama's CIA. The clear favorite was John Brennan. The twenty-year veteran CIA analyst, who left the agency to run the new Terrorist Threat Integration Center (later to become the National Counterterrorism Center, or NCTC), would soon become Obama's friend and intelligence adviser, so close to the president that they were said to enjoy a "mind-meld." But Brennan had a strike against him: He'd been George Tenet's deputy executive director at the CIA during the enhanced interrogation program, though he insisted he wasn't in the chain of command. "The left thought he was this guy who was involved in the EITs, part of the Bush CIA, and they weren't having any of it," recalled Nick Shapiro, who would later become Brennan's chief of staff at Langley. "They made it clear they weren't going to stand for him being nominated."

Still, Obama wanted to keep Brennan close by. As Denis McDonough, the future White House chief of staff, put it: "The president always said, 'I *love* that guy.' And he just wanted him closer." Brennan would stay in the White House as assistant to the president for homeland security and counterterrorism.

So it was that another name rose to the top of the list for CIA director: Leon E. Panetta.

On Sunday, January 4, 2009, Panetta, who'd been visiting his son

Carmelo in Minneapolis, was leaving a Minnesota Vikings football game when his son's cell phone started ringing. It was Panetta's wife, Sylvia, who couldn't get through on Leon's phone, with an urgent message: The president-elect was trying to reach him.

Panetta, the former California congressman and Bill Clinton's OMB director and White House chief of staff, knew why Obama was calling. His friend John Podesta, Obama's transition director, had been pushing his nomination as CIA director and had called him the day before. "Whoa, I don't know about that," Panetta had said, doubtfully. "You know my background is in budgets and oceans and stuff like that." Podesta replied: "Well, the president really feels that the CIA has to restore some trust with the American people and that you'd be good at doing that." Panetta said he'd think about it.

After getting Sylvia's message, Panetta drove to his hotel and called Obama. The president-elect got straight to the point. "I'd like you to take this job," he said. "Mr. President," Panetta said, "obviously, I haven't been deeply involved with the CIA but I know what it's about and I know the most important responsibility is to tell you the truth."

Panetta reminded Obama that he'd once paid a price for speaking hard truths. In 1970, as the thirty-two-year-old head of the Office for Civil Rights in Richard Nixon's HEW (Health, Education and Welfare department), Panetta had opposed the president's backpedaling on desegregation; he resigned before Nixon could fire him. "You know my background," he told Obama. "I had a responsibility to enforce the law and that's what I did—and I lost my job as a result of that. What I'm saying is: I will tell you the truth, whether you like to hear it or not." The president-elect replied: "That's why I want you to take the job." Good answer, Panetta thought. He told Obama he'd need direct access to him, and frequent trips home to California. With that, Panetta agreed to become his CIA director.

Born in Monterey, California, to Italian immigrant parents, Panetta wasn't a total neophyte at spycraft; he'd served in Army Intelligence at Fort Gordon, Georgia. After his clash with Nixon he became a Democrat and served nine terms in Congress before joining the Clinton White House. Panetta was gregarious and good-natured and proudly Italian; when he was amused, his eyes twinkled and his entire body erupted into a booming laugh that registered on the Richter scale. He was an unabashed people person, an extrovert—and a hugger. But Panetta's avuncular manner concealed a no-nonsense resolve. He was a skilled and disciplined political infighter, known for wielding an "iron fist inside a velvet glove."

No one was better connected in the White House and on Capitol Hill, where so many of the CIA's battles were waged. "A lot of my colleagues were saying, 'we should get an intelligence professional to be director,'" said Mike Sulick, who became one of Panetta's deputies. But Sulick thought directors should be able to manage Capitol Hill: "We can overthrow foreign governments, but we have a more difficult time dealing with our own." Panetta, along with Reagan's James A. Baker III, was considered the gold standard among White House chiefs. He was a master at the thrust-and-parry of governing, and he possessed the gravitas and authority that come with being comfortable around power.

Still, skeptics at Langley braced themselves for a political partisan. Rich Blee, who'd run the Bin Laden Unit, or "Alec Station," on the eve of the September 11, 2001, attacks, sensed angst among the Republican-leaning operatives. "A lot of people I know thought he'd be a left-wing Democratic hack," Blee said. During his confirmation hearings, Panetta referred to waterboarding as "torture"—a word that rankled at Langley, even among those who objected to the technique. "Even I was sort of skittish about this person who'd been very vocal in opposing CIA practices and excesses during the post-9/11 days," said Ned Price, an analyst with liberal views. "There was a pervasive sense of fear that he'd handcuff the agency entirely when it came to the counterterrorism mission."

But from the moment Panetta stepped off the elevator on the seventh floor, even the CIA's hard-core conservatives found it hard to dislike him. And Panetta liked them back.

The new director dropped F-bombs, and remembered everyone's names. He told lousy jokes: "So a priest and a rabbi go to a prizefight. And the boxer is in the ring and he crosses himself. And the rabbi says, 'What's he doing?' And the priest says, 'It doesn't mean anything if he can't fight.'" This was always followed by a Panetta howl. The new director had no pretensions. On his first morning, an attendant tried to serve him coffee in a fancy bone china cup. No thanks, he said; Panetta poured his own coffee into a mug marked "CIA."

At counterterrorism meetings around the big table in his office, Panetta unleashed his dog Bravo, a sloppily affectionate golden retriever. "We're out of ideas. Whaddya think, Bravo?" the director would quip. "You'd see someone's hand go down and scratch Bravo's head," recalled Stephanie O'Sullivan, head of the Directorate of Science and Technology, "and then Bravo would go to the next person and he just went around the table. He was like a therapy dog. It was a welcome touch of normalcy amid truly sobering things."

"Leon just likes people," said O'Sullivan. "He had an extraordinary ability to connect with folks at a very personal level. It was like having the Italian grandfather I never had." Panetta asked questions without pretending to know the answers. O'Sullivan went on: "He told the staff, 'I'm not going to micromanage you, but I expect you to deliver.' He showed trust but put us on our toes. That's something that the agency appreciates." And Panetta wasn't looking to get promoted to some big cabinet job. "With Leon, it was about the mission and public service," said a senior intelligence officer. "He had no other mountains to climb."

Panetta took a page from George Tenet; they'd both grown up washing dishes in their fathers' greasy spoons. "I'd worked with George in the Clinton White House," Panetta said. "He's Greek and his father worked in a restaurant so we had something in common. He made clear to me the human side of the CIA. You can oftentimes forget that these people aren't Democrats or Republicans; they're good Americans who are dedicated to the job. It made me understand that this is not just a bunch of yahoos doing their own thing, James Bond types. These are real people doing very serious work."

Panetta wisely avoided Porter Goss's mistake of bringing in outsiders. As his chief of staff, he chose a savvy intelligence officer named Jeremy Bash—who advised him to keep Steve Kappes on as his deputy director. (Kappes, the revered operative who talked Muammar Qaddafi into giving up his WMDs, had been forced out by the Gosslings but brought back by Mike Hayden.) Michael Morell, the razor-sharp analyst who'd been George W. Bush's briefer on 9/11, became head of the Directorate of Intelligence; Sulick was made head of the clandestine service. In basketball terms, they'd play the inside game at Langley while Panetta patrolled Capitol Hill and the White

House. "It was like the '92 Olympic basketball team," said Bill Danvers, the congressional liaison. "It was a dream team."

But a showdown was coming that would be a test of Panetta's leadership. It had been four years since Congress had created the Office of the Director of National Intelligence (ODNI), and there had been two DNIs—John Negroponte and Michael McConnell, a former head of the National Security Agency who'd served from 2007 to 2009. Now a third, retired Navy Admiral Dennis Blair, had been sworn in—and he was nominally Panetta's boss. But the new position, meant to coordinate intelligence, was undefined; the DNI's responsibilities overlapped the DCIA's. "The day-to-day job of doing the intelligence of the nation puts the CIA at the center of the chessboard," explained Morell. "And the new legislation put the DNI at the center of the chessboard. So you've got this fundamental problem." While the CIA director might report to the DNI, he still ran the world's most powerful intelligence agency. As Panetta put it: "You walk in as DNI and look around and try to figure out, 'Well, what the hell do I do here?' And to find out that you don't have any operational authority is a shock."

If that lack of authority was a shock to his predecessors, it would prove humiliating for Admiral Blair. He was about to receive a master class in bureaucratic infighting from Leon Panetta.

Blair, a former Rhodes Scholar and commander of U.S. forces in the Pacific, got off to a bad start with Panetta by barging into his office while he was huddling with his deputies. "Party's over, Leon and I have a meeting," Blair announced brusquely. Since then there'd been petty squabbles over office space and turf. "Every meeting would begin with somebody saying, 'What has he done now? What do they want *now*?'" recalled one of Panetta's deputies. Then, in what had been a slow-simmering feud, Blair suddenly turned up the heat. "Blair wanted to pick a fight and flex his muscles," said a senior intelligence official.

In the spring of 2009, Blair decided to make an issue of the CIA's overseas station chiefs. The new DNI proposed that *he* should appoint those officers. Panetta countered that while the station chiefs could serve both offices, they worked for the CIA, were paid by the CIA, and should be appointed by the CIA director. What Blair didn't know was that the CIA's control of the station chiefs was considered sacrosanct. "For CIA to give up that right is to cross the red line that you don't cross," said Charlie Allen. "Denny should have known better, but he didn't." In an embattled agency that often felt like a band of brothers, the station chiefs were sure to rebel against any outsider's attempt to mess with their chain of command.

"Leon tried to reason this out with Blair over a long period of time," recalled his deputy Sulick. "Finally, we hit a stone wall." Blair now made a critical blunder. The DNI sent out a cable to CIA stations worldwide. It decreed that the DNI would appoint all station chiefs.

Panetta was blindsided. But not for long. "You know, I'd just turned seventy," Panetta told me. "I'd been around for a while and that was really helpful because few people gave me a lot of shit. People gave me room. The president gave me room. And I've always thought: 'If you don't like what I'm doing, Carmel Valley is not a bad place to go home to.'" Panetta let out his thundering laugh.

He continued: "So I did something that only a guy who had been around the block for a long time would have done." Panetta called in Kappes, his deputy director, and told him to draft a WWSB ("World Wide Stations and Bases"): an email to all overseas stations. The message read: "Ignore the previous instruction." Panetta hit the "send" button.

Blair had picked the wrong fight, and the wrong opponent. Allen had never seen an operator as well connected as Panetta. "You don't take on Leon," he said. "He had direct access to someone named Obama." Panetta also had access to Vice President Joe Biden, who in this case was the mediator. It didn't take a genius to guess whose side the vice president would come down on. "When Panetta and Blair walked in to see the vice president," recalled one official, "Panetta said to Biden: 'Hey, Joe, before we get going, our tee time is still at 9:30 tomorrow, right?' They were playing golf the next day—and Blair knew he was dead." Biden upheld Panetta's position: The chiefs of station would be named by the CIA director.

His wings thoroughly clipped, Blair would never recover his authority as DNI. He resigned a year later.

Back at Langley, Panetta's smackdown of the DNI made him a hero with the rank and file; in a showdown with a bureaucratic interloper, Panetta had shown that he had their backs. "When you have that kind of relationship with your workforce," said his deputy, Morell, "there isn't anything that they won't do for you." From that moment forward, said a former senior intelligence official, "Leon Panetta was a *god* at CIA."

Yet nothing in his experience had prepared Panetta to *play* God. As CIA director, he was about to command a covert paramilitary army; when approving drone strikes, he would decide who lived or died. Before his confirmation hearing, outgoing director Mike Hayden warned him: "You're about to become a combatant commander."

Indeed, Panetta was about to preside over a dramatic escalation of drone warfare. It was no small irony that this happened during the presidency of a constitutional law professor and Nobel Peace Prize laureate, Barack Obama.

The awarding of the Nobel Prize to the forty-fourth president on December 10, 2009, came as an embarrassment to Obama; the honor was so premature that it suggested he was all glitz and no substance. But the Oslo ceremony triggered one of the best speeches of Obama's presidency, a meditation on the use of power. "I am living testimony to the moral force of non-violence," he declared, citing Mahatma Gandhi and Dr. Martin Luther King. "I know there is nothing weak—nothing passive, nothing naïve—in the creed and lives of Gandhi and King. But as a head of state sworn to protect and defend my nation, I cannot be guided by their examples alone. I face the world as it is."

The world as it was in 2009 was growing more dangerous: Al Qaeda, once in retreat, had regrouped in the tribal areas of Pakistan, where it was plotting new attacks on the U.S. homeland. "Negotiations," the new president said in his Nobel speech, "cannot convince Al Qaeda's leaders to lay down their arms." Panetta wondered if Obama was prepared to make the hard decisions to take up arms himself.

"That's something that you have to go through with every president," Panetta explained. "I remember doing that with Clinton and then doing it with Obama. Can they make that turn where they suddenly understand in a very pragmatic way the shit they've got to do in order to protect this country? If you can make that turn, where suddenly you understand that you have to make that decision—and why you have to make that decision—that is when you become president of the United States."

Drone warfare posed a moral challenge for Panetta as well. "I was raised a Catholic, I believe in my faith and I relied a great deal on my faith throughout my life," he said. "I've always carried a rosary and always said a hell of a lot of Hail Marys in tough situations. And suddenly I found that I was making decisions on life and death as director. And those decisions are never easy, and frankly they shouldn't be easy."

But like Obama, Panetta had made his own pragmatic turn. "When you're confronting an enemy that's prepared to blow up innocent men, women, and children," he said, "you have to go at them using the capabilities that we have. For me that's the basic rule: Do we protect our people or do we not protect them?" He wouldn't permit a catastrophic terrorist attack on his watch. "If we fail to do this and God forbid this country faced another 9/11, you know what the first question would be: Why the hell did you let this happen?"

With Panetta as his combatant commander, Obama would take the battle to Al Qaeda.

The agency's go-to weapon, the Predator, was the CIA's worst-kept secret; hovering over a target for days at a time, it could fire missiles with extraordinary precision at enemy combatants. The CIA was uniquely suited to fly the Predator outside war zones, where the hand of the U.S. had to be concealed. In 2008, it was George W. Bush who gave the agency authority to strike Al Qaeda terrorists in the tribal regions of Pakistan—with or without the host country's permission. Since then there'd been a steady increase in drone attacks—but on Obama's watch they spiked dramatically. There were as many strikes during Obama's first nine and a half months as in Bush's last three years.

The decision to pull the trigger was often Panetta's alone. "I think there was one case where he decided to go to the White House," recalled Sulick, the head of Operations. "Other than that, he made all the decisions himself." The calls from the CIA's Operations Center often came to Panetta's home late in the evening. "This became almost an every-other-night affair," he said. "I go into the job and the first thing I'm doing is getting calls in the middle of the night to try to decide on targets—and making decisions on those targets. You're making life-and-death decisions. You're sending people into harm's way and you're not sure what the hell is going to happen."

Drones weren't much help in the hunt for the CIA's number one target. At one of their first White House meetings, Obama took Panetta aside. "He called me into his office and said, 'You know, it's important that you focus on going after bin Laden. He is Enemy Number One. And I want to do everything possible to make sure that we try to get him.'"

At the CIA, the frustration over bin Laden's disappearance was palpable. It had been eight years since the Al Qaeda leader had vanished at a mountainous cave complex known as Tora Bora. Panetta told his senior staff he wanted out-of-the-box ideas, no matter how outlandish. Panetta turned every assumption upside down. "Everybody thought he was in a cave attached to a dialysis machine," said Jeremy Bash, his chief of staff. Panetta was saying, "What if he's in a suburb attached to cable TV?"

"Almost every lead went nowhere," Panetta recalled. "I kept saying, 'Look, it's not acceptable. You've got to come in and give me ten or twelve ideas. I don't give a damn what they are, just give me some ideas to work with.'"

Suddenly, in August 2009, there was an apparent break: a tip from Jordan's General Intelligence Directorate (GID). A jihadist claimed he could get close to Al Qaeda's second-in command, Egyptian doctor Ayman al-Zawahiri. He had video of Zawahiri to prove it and offered to act as a double agent and lead them to his lair in Pakistan. "It was the first break we'd had in a hell of a long time," said Panetta. "Everybody was excited about the idea that we might finally have somebody who could get us not only to Zawahiri but possibly to bin Laden." But before proceeding, the CIA needed to meet this would-be double agent face-to-face. His name was Human Khalil al-Balawi. A rendezvous was arranged in Afghanistan, at Camp Chapman, a concrete fortress in a desolate place called Khost.

The newly arrived chief of the CIA base at Khost was Jennifer Matthews, a forty-five-year-old agency veteran. "She was one of these outstanding officers who was bright, capable, and really devoted to the job," recalled Panetta. Matthews had entered the CIA as a case officer in 1989. Before the September 11 attacks, she'd joined the

Bin Laden Unit known as Alec Station; it was a mostly female staff so obsessed with finding the Al Qaeda leader that they called themselves the Manson Family. Later, she'd been posted to the CIA's first post-9/11 black site, in Thailand—along with Gina Haspel, the base chief. One of the agency's top Al Qaeda experts, Matthews had helped provide questions for Abu Zubaydah's interrogation.

For Matthews, this was a career-making—or breaking—assignment; even President Obama had been briefed about it. She'd tried for months to arrange a meeting with their new undercover jihadist in Pakistan but couldn't find a safe location. "We decided the better thing to do was try to bring him across the border to Khost," recalled Panetta. "We'd bring him there and be able to have our officers sit down, talk with him, and try to determine what level of comfort they had. To make sure that this guy was bona fide." After months of wrangling, Balawi had agreed to the location.

Matthews led a team of fourteen CIA officers and security guards. It was an impressive and diverse group. Elizabeth Hanson, a thirty-year-old operative with blond hair and bright blue eyes from Rockford, Illinois, was on her first overseas assignment. Adventurous and extroverted—voted "most talkative" in her high school class—she'd graduated from Colby College in Maine and joined the CIA after 9/11. Hanson had become one of the agency's star "targeters," tracking suspected terrorists and feeding their locations to drone operators. Darren LaBonte, an ex-Army Ranger, was a CIA officer on loan from the agency's station in Amman, Jordan. Dane Paresi, an ex–Green Beret, was an Afghan War veteran with a Bronze Star. Jeremy Wise, thirty-five, an Iraq veteran, was a former Navy SEAL. Both he and Paresi were working for the security company Xe, better known as Blackwater. The security team leader, Harold Brown, thirty-seven, was an ex–Army intelligence officer who led a Cub Scout troop in Virginia. A Jordanian intelligence captain, Ali bin Zeid, the only person who'd laid eyes on Balawi, had also flown in from Amman. This was the reception committee for the CIA asset who, if all went well, would lead them to bin Laden's inner circle.

The CIA team waited for Balawi for ten days. Finally, on December 30, the word came in coded messages: The "Wolf," as they called him, was headed their way through the jagged mountains. Matthews had picked out a spot inside the fortified base, a gray concrete enclosure surrounded by high walls where the team would await his arrival. Everyone agreed that Balawi was to be treated respectfully, as an honored guest. There'd be no intrusive vehicle or body searches at the outside gates; that could wait until he arrived at the inner sanctum.

Just before 5:00 p.m., a plume of dust could be seen in the distance; a red Outback was approaching, traveling fast to elude Taliban snipers. When the vehicle reached the base's outside gate, the Afghan guards, by prearrangement, rolled back the barriers to let it pass. Once inside, the vehicle turned left and followed an airfield to a second gate, where it was waved through again.

While Matthews and the others kept their distance, bin Zeid and LaBonte stepped toward the approaching vehicle, which rolled to a stop. Scott Roberson, the thirty-nine-year-old security chief, and two guards fingered the triggers of their rifles. Roberson opened the rear door farthest from the CIA team. The man inside hesitated, then slid toward the opposite door and stepped out. He was small and wiry, wearing tribal dress and sunglasses, with a long gray shawl over his shoulders. The man was clutching a metal crutch in one hand; the other hand was hidden under his shawl. He limped forward.

Paresi and Wise began shouting: "Hands up! Get your hand out of your clothing!" The man mumbled softly. Then he said loudly, in Arabic: "*La ilaha illa Allah!*" There is no god but God.

The explosion was instantaneous and blinding: A blast wave lifted the car in the air; humans were thrown like ragdolls against walls and a nearby truck. Steel ball bearings flew in every direction, cutting down anyone standing, and lodging in the concrete walls. Five officers nearest the suicide bomber were killed instantly. They were the lucky ones. Jennifer Matthews, with gaping wounds on her neck and legs, lay on the ground, still conscious and moaning. Elizabeth Hanson ran a short distance and then collapsed, bleeding from a chest wound. A CIA medical officer, knocked briefly unconscious, crawled among the wounded and tried to save them.

Eight lay dead, seven of them CIA officers—and six others were gravely wounded. It was the second worst day in the CIA's history, next to the 1983 bombing of the American embassy in Beirut, which killed sixty-three people, including seventeen Americans, eight of them CIA officers. Dead, too, was the prospect of penetrating bin

Laden's inner circle: Balawi had turned out to be not a double but a triple agent—still working for Al Qaeda.

Panetta was at home in Monterey for Christmas when he got a phone call from Jeremy Bash, his chief of staff. "It's hard to find the words when suddenly you're told that seven of your officers have been killed and others seriously wounded," Panetta said. "What went through my mind was the families who within a few hours were going to be informed that someone they loved had been killed."

Panetta went on: "It was very personal. Personal for me, personal for the other officers at the CIA. I kept asking myself, 'How could you let that happen? What do we do to make sure it doesn't happen again?' Probably the biggest consequence was the gut feeling in every officer's inner being that their goal was to go after the leadership of Al Qaeda."

On February 5, 2010, Obama went to Langley to honor the CIA officers killed at Khost. The ceremony, in front of the Memorial Wall, was closed to the press but attended by more than a thousand CIA officers, and families of the fallen. "They served in secrecy," the president said, "but the record of their service—and of this generation of intelligence professionals—is written all around us. It's written in the extremists who no longer threaten our country—because you eliminated them."

Two days later, Panetta and his deputies gathered at Arlington Cemetery for a memorial service for Elizabeth Hanson. The weeks following the Khost disaster had been a blur of funerals, memorials, burials, and meetings with the victims' families. But this service was different; at their families' request, Panetta had gone to Bob Gates, the secretary of defense, to get special dispensation for Hanson and a few others to be buried at Arlington. It was an honor normally reserved for fallen soldiers, not spies.

"That memory of going to Arlington to bury Elizabeth Hanson is one that will be with me for a long time," Panetta told me. "They put their lives on the line to serve this country, and that's what Elizabeth Hanson did." Her simple gravestone, at Section 60, Site 8978, was marked "ELIZABETH CURRY MARIE HANSON, CIVILIAN, AFGHANISTAN." Panetta felt a pang of Catholic guilt. "I knew that the CIA officers were there because I ordered them to be there. I had to bear some of the responsibility for having taken this risk."

There was another reason why Panetta would not soon forget Hanson's burial. While standing by her grave, he received a call from the CIA Operations Center. The news he got posed an excruciating ethical dilemma.

Immediately after the catastrophe at Khost, the agency had gone into overdrive trying to find out who was behind the bombing. Balawi had blown himself up, but who'd put him up to it? "We spent a lot of time trying to figure out who were the ones who pushed that button," Panetta said. "We have a lot of sources—spies—and we immediately asked them, 'Who the hell was involved in this tragic suicide bombing?' We were able to get pretty good intelligence and found out who the individual was. This was a bad guy. And he was clearly a leader. He'd been involved not only in going after our officers but in killing members of our forces in Afghanistan."

Now, according to the Operations Center, a Predator drone had this terrorist in its crosshairs over Pakistan. But there was a catch. "Unfortunately, he had family and wife and children around him," said Panetta. "And so the tough question was: 'What should we do?' If there were women and children in the shot, we normally would not take the shot."

Panetta called the White House. He spoke first to John Brennan, Obama's counterterrorism adviser, and then Jim Jones, the national security adviser. "They were aware of how tough a decision this was. And they basically said, 'Look, you're going to have to make a judgment here.' So I knew at that point that it was a decision that I was going to have to make. *I'm* the one who's going to have to say Hail Marys here."

Panetta went on: "I felt it was really important to do what I could to protect this country. So I passed the word. I said, 'If you can isolate the individual and take the shot without impacting women or children, then do it. But if you have no alternative and it looks like he might get away, then, well, take the shot.'"

A half a world away, a Hellfire missile, fired by the Predator, slammed into the target. The drone's cameras captured the aftermath: Among the smoke and debris, it was clear that in addition to the terrorist, innocents had been killed. "It did involve collateral damage," Panetta told me. "But we got him." He turned somber. "These are tough decisions—you're damned right these are tough decisions.

But you know, this is a war. On 9/11, these people didn't hesitate for a moment to kill three thousand people and take down the Trade Centers and hit the Pentagon. These are individuals that would not hesitate to attack us again."

He paused. "In the end, what you do has to be based on what your gut tells you is right. That's really what it's all about. You have to be true to yourself—and just hope that ultimately God agrees with you."

As CIA director, Panetta had yet to deliver on the promise he made Obama: telling the president what he did not want to hear. As White House chief of staff, Panetta had seen CIA directors fail the test. "I think that almost all of the CIA directors I associated with were a little hesitant to really lay it on the line if there was something happening that wouldn't please the president of the United States," he said. "So I thought it was important to be honest whether the president wanted to hear it or not." Panetta would get his chance soon enough.

On his first day in office, Barack Obama had announced that he was ending George W. Bush's notorious enhanced interrogation program. But now Obama, Panetta, and the CIA faced another question: How much of the controversial program should be made public?

The American Civil Liberties Union had filed a lawsuit demanding the release of the so-called torture memos. These were legal documents used to justify the techniques—analyzing them in terms of American law, international norms, and American obligations under its membership in the United Nations. When Panetta was asked by Greg Craig, the White House counsel, if he objected to having the CIA memos made public, he said no, without giving the issue much thought.

A few days later acting CIA general counsel John Rizzo learned that the White House was preparing to release the memos. Alarmed and unable to reach Panetta, who was traveling overseas, Rizzo alerted former CIA directors George Tenet, Porter Goss, and Michael Hayden. They immediately started rallying supporters in a campaign to lobby the White House to keep the memos secret.

White House chief of staff Rahm Emanuel tracked down Panetta. "Why were the former directors ganging up on the administration?" he demanded. Panetta told Emanuel to put a hold on the release until he could get back and assess the situation.

After consulting with Rizzo and the directors, Panetta came to believe that releasing the memos would be a mistake. Their exposure would damage agency morale, break promises to allies that the program would remain secret, perhaps even heighten the clamor to prosecute CIA officers. Those officers had been asked to take risks for their country and had been assured that the techniques were legal. "After hearing Rizzo out, I became convinced that he was right and I was wrong," Panetta later wrote.

Panetta took his case to the president. A vigorous debate ensued—with Emanuel supporting Panetta, and Dennis Blair, the DNI, opposing him. Obama agreed to receive a delegation of seven top CIA officials, who buttressed Panetta's argument. But on April 15, 2009, with a court order pending, the president overruled Panetta and the CIA: The "torture memos" were made public.

For Panetta it was a rare defeat in the bureaucratic wars that were his specialty. But the fact that he'd fought the battle only enhanced his standing among the workforce at Langley; once again the new director had had their backs.

Panetta would solidify his popularity at the agency in a showdown with House speaker Nancy Pelosi. The flap over the torture memos revived the controversy over enhanced interrogation techniques. In May, the California congresswoman declared that the CIA hadn't informed her that waterboarding had taken place; in effect, she accused the agency of lying. Panetta knew that wasn't true; the CIA had fully briefed her. He immediately issued a statement contradicting her, in an email to CIA employees that was made public:

> There is a long tradition in Washington of making political hay out of our business . . . but the political debates about interrogation reached a new decibel level yesterday when the CIA was accused of lying to Congress.
>
> Let me be clear: It is not our policy or practice to lie to Congress. That is against our laws and our values. . . .
>
> My advice—indeed, my direction—to you is straightforward: ignore the noise and stay focused on your mission. . . . Our task is to tell it like it is—even if that's not always what people want to hear. Keep it up. Our national security depends on it.

A few weeks later, Panetta called up his old friend Pelosi, the San Francisco Democrat. They buried the hatchet, agreeing to let the matter go.

Despite his run-in with Pelosi, Panetta was a staunch believer in congressional oversight. He'd lived through the CIA scandals of the 1970s, when the exposure of the Family Jewels triggered headlines and investigations. The reforms that followed, he was convinced, had saved the agency. Panetta believed that only oversight could prevent future abuses by rogue CIA operatives and presidents alike. While the CIA reported to the president, he believed it *answered* to Congress.

The Obama national security team, by contrast, took a dim view of congressional meddling. So a showdown between the White House and Panetta was inevitable. It came when Dianne Feinstein, chair of the Senate Select Committee on Intelligence, launched an investigation into Bush-era interrogation techniques. Panetta told her the CIA would cooperate, but that her staffers would have to read classified documents and cables in a secure reading room in Virginia. It wasn't long before the White House got wind of Panetta's offer to cooperate with Feinstein. He was summoned to a meeting by Emanuel.

Panetta was greeted by Emanuel, John Brennan, Admiral Blair, and Denis McDonough, the deputy national security adviser. The chief of staff threw a profanity-laced fit. "The president wants to know who the fuck authorized this release to the committee," he shouted. Panetta shot back: "This fucking White House decided to reveal all of this information [the "torture memos"], and now *you're* bitching because *we're* working with the committee? They have oversight responsibility. I can't tell them to go to hell!" Emanuel slammed his fist on the table. "I have a president with his hair on fire and I want to know what the fuck you did to fuck this up so bad!"

Even Blair got into the act, shouting: "I want to know who the fuck set his hair on fire!" But Panetta was unfazed. He'd known Emanuel for thirty years and could read him like a book: Rahm was just throwing a tantrum to appease Brennan and McDonough.

Panetta kept his cool. He let everyone vent—until they realized there was nothing anyone could do; Panetta's deal with Feinstein was a fait accompli. The meeting was over in fifteen minutes. But it wouldn't be the last time Panetta locked horns with the White House.

Much has been written about the covert operation that made Panetta famous — the raid that killed Osama bin Laden. Operation NEPTUNE SPEAR, perhaps the CIA's most daring and successful covert operation, has been rightly portrayed as a model of interagency teamwork. But behind the scenes, there was plenty of drama. At one point the White House accused Panetta of jeopardizing the mission.

In early 2011, the trail to the world's most wanted terrorist, stone-cold for a decade, was warming up. In Pakistan the CIA had been tracking two of bin Laden's couriers to a house on a dead-end street. On January 13, the President's Daily Brief described a compound outside Abbottabad, Pakistan, that was being closely watched in the hope that it could be bin Laden's hiding place. But even the agency's best analysts couldn't be sure. "You have a house with no internet connection, higher walls than normal, and they burn their trash," recalled Rahm Emanuel. "Do you think a judge in the United States would give you a search warrant based on that data?"

As Obama and his national security team weighed its options, Defense Secretary Bob Gates, the ex–CIA director, issued a warning. "I remember when I was a young member of the National Security Council staff," he said, "sitting in the Situation Room back in 1980 when everything went wrong." Operation EAGLE CLAW, Jimmy Carter's ill-fated mission to rescue the American hostages in Tehran, was still a vivid memory. That operation had ended in disaster, with the wreckage of helicopters and the charred bodies of eight U.S. soldiers lying in the Iranian desert.

The case for the bin Laden mission was entirely circumstantial. Satellite pictures showed a tall man pacing inside the compound. He looked like bin Laden, but Panetta and his team had to guard against believing it just because they wanted it to be true. At one meeting with the president, Morell cautioned against repeating the CIA's blunder with Iraq's WMDs: not being honest about how little they knew. Panetta repeatedly grilled his experts. "I sat all of my key analysts down in my office and I had them sit around the table," said Panetta. "And I said, 'Give me your best judgment.' And I had one woman who said, 'I am ninety percent certain he's there.' And then I had somebody who was very experienced who said, 'I think it's about thirty percent.' "

Operation NEPTUNE SPEAR was a CIA-led mission. But whose paramilitary personnel would carry it out: the military's or the agency's? As other options were discarded—bombing the compound into rubble or destroying it with cruise missiles—the CIA's paramilitary operatives showed eagerness to conduct a helicopter raid. "There were people who believed we could do this. We could do this, boss—we don't need anyone else," recalled Panetta's deputy Stephanie O'Sullivan. Instead, Panetta decided to tap the military's Joint Special Operations Command (JSOC), led by Vice Admiral Bill McRaven. "The biggest problem was that it would be very difficult to deploy them as a unit," said Panetta of the CIA's operatives. "Each of them would have to sneak into Pakistan under a different guise and somehow put the logistics together. It was asking too much." Panetta's decision bruised some egos in the Clandestine Service. Hearing this, Michael Morell fell on his sword by telling people it had been his decision, not Panetta's.

Panetta never regretted choosing McRaven. "I sat down with him and watched the twinkle in his eye when I told him what we had," Panetta said. "This was something he was doing ten times a night in Afghanistan. Shit, these guys go out and they get the target and they get the hell out!"

McRaven's original plan called for two stealth helicopters and twenty-four Navy SEALs. But Obama worried that it wasn't enough: What if Pakistan's military detected them and responded in force? The president sent his three-star vice admiral back to the drawing board. When McRaven returned, he'd added two more helicopters to the raiding party—and a backup force that would wait just across the Afghan border in case they had to fight their way out.

But as the clock ticked down, Obama received unexpected, and unwelcome, news. He and his new White House chief of staff, Bill Daley, learned that Panetta had briefed the congressional leadership about the impending mission. "We were flabbergasted," recalled Daley. "I was livid and the president was livid." Obama and his chief were sure that news of the raid would leak, scuttling the mission. As Daley put it: "I figured any morning I'd get up and there would be *The Washington Post* on the doorstep with the headline, 'BIN LADEN IN PAKISTAN, U.S. PLANNING AN ATTACK.' "

Daley called the CIA director and gave him a tongue-lashing. "I remember Daley saying, 'what are you doing informing the Congress?'" recalled Panetta. "And I said, 'A, we had to because we were reprogramming funding for it. And B, if we go in and for some reason bin Laden's not there, I think we are in a much better position with the Congress if they know about it than if we keep it a secret.'" The president was unconvinced. But once again Panetta had gone ahead and done his duty as he saw it.

"There are very few one hundred percent decisions when you're president of the United States," said Panetta. "Most of the decisions are between fifty and sixty percent as to what you're doing. The rest is sheer risk, sheer chance." On Thursday, April 28, Obama convened a final National Security Council principals meeting to discuss whether to go forward with the raid. Going around the room, he asked for everyone's best judgment: How confident were they that Osama bin Laden was in the compound? Gates noted that the evidence was circumstantial and worried about a helicopter raid; if the decision was to go, he favored using a bunker-busting bomb. Hillary Clinton, the secretary of state, conceded that more time might bring better intelligence, but thought Obama should seize the opportunity to go. Vice President Biden argued that there was too much uncertainty; the mission should wait.

Then it was Panetta's turn. This was the best intelligence they'd ever had, their best chance to get bin Laden, he argued. Any delay risked a leak. "There's a formula I've used since I was in Congress and faced a tough decision," he said, "which is to think about asking the average citizen, 'If you knew what I knew what would you do?' In this case I think the answer is clear. This is the best intelligence we've had since Tora Bora. I have tremendous confidence in our assault team. If we don't do it, we'll regret it."

Fairly or unfairly, these are the decisions that seal a CIA director's place in history. As a senior intelligence official put it: "Joe Biden said don't do it. Bob Gates said don't do it. Panetta took a risk."

Obama kept his own counsel; he would sleep on the decision.

The next day, Tom Donilon, the national security adviser, called Panetta. "It's a go," he said.

"Then I called up Bill McRaven," recalled Panetta. "And I told him, 'Look, Bill, I want you to go in there and I want you to get bin Laden. And then I want you to get the hell out of there.' "

"He was rolling the dice on the presidency," said Daley of Obama. "He knew that. As a matter of fact, I wore a coat and tie that Sunday because I figured it was going to be a big day one way or the other: Either this presidency is over today or it's going to be a historic day for our country." Panetta kept his usual routine. "I did what I always do on a Sunday morning, which was go to mass to pray like hell that it would be a good day. And after that I went to CIA headquarters." A few hours later, Panetta relayed to the Situation Room the words Obama's team had been waiting for: "Geronimo EKIA"—enemy killed in action. That evening, at the White House, the CIA director basked in the sound of cheering from Pennsylvania Avenue. "Hearing people outside the gates of the White House chanting, 'USA. USA. CIA.' It is a memory that I'll have for the rest of my life."

Even as the CIA celebrated bin Laden's demise, a rumor was swirling at Langley: Panetta was leaving the agency.

The idea had been broached by Bob Gates, who after more than five years of running the Department of Defense, wanted out. After a meeting one day in his cavernous Pentagon office, Gates asked Panetta to stay behind. "Leon," he said, "I'm about ready to go and I just want you to know that I'm going to recommend you to succeed me." Panetta balked. "Bob, at some point I gotta go home," he said. Panetta had promised his wife, Sylvia, that he wouldn't stay in Washington beyond four years.

Panetta thought he'd nixed the idea of going to the Pentagon. He told his friends he wasn't budging from Langley. "People would ask me in the hall, 'Is Panetta leaving?,' " recalled his deputy Morell. "And I'd say, 'Guaranteed no! He could not be clearer about his desire to stay here.' But they kept ratcheting up the pressure on him."

In a meeting with the vice president at the White House in the spring of 2011, Biden pushed Panetta again to replace Gates at DOD.

Panetta asked whom they had in mind as the next CIA director. Biden said they were thinking of David Petraeus. Panetta took a deep breath. "Are you *sure* you want to do that?" he said.

General David Howell Petraeus, the former head of CENTCOM

and commander of the International Security Assistance Force (ISAF) in Afghanistan, was perhaps the most celebrated U.S. general since Colin Powell. He was the renowned architect of the "surge" that had changed the course of the Iraq War.

"He'd attained this kind of godlike charisma," said Panetta. The CIA director paused. "But everybody also knew what the hell he was like."

Without a doubt, Petraeus possessed one of his generation's best military intellects. His critics thought he also possessed one of its gargantuan egos. On his first visit to Petraeus's office, Panetta noted: "It was a shrine . . . to him."

Panetta thought this might not bode well for his old friends at Langley.

CHAPTER ELEVEN

"Everyone thinks this stuff is easy.

None of this stuff is easy."

David Petraeus, John Brennan, and Barack Obama

Robert Gates, Barack Obama's secretary of defense, was waiting out-side the office of the commander of the International Security Assistance Force (ISAF) in Kabul, Afghanistan. It was March of 2011, and Gates had flown all the way from Washington, D.C., for a private meeting with General David Petraeus. He'd come bearing bad news, which he wanted to deliver in person.

Obama and his national security team thought highly of Petraeus. The president was grateful to the renowned four-star general for taking over as U.S. commander in Afghanistan from his embattled predecessor, General Stanley McChrystal. (McChrystal had been forced to resign after making disparaging remarks about key Obama administration figures in a *Rolling Stone* interview.) Petraeus had given up his powerful post as CENTCOM commander and, in effect, taken one for the team. But Obama's gratitude had its limits. The president had decided to deny his top general the job he truly wanted: chairman of the Joint Chiefs of Staff.

No one questioned his credentials. Petraeus was a proven leader, with a Princeton degree in international relations and economics, and he was a bold strategist. "He's an unrivaled thinker in that space," said Denis McDonough, the deputy national security adviser who'd become Obama's White House chief of staff. But Petraeus also had a towering ego; his rivals found him insufferable. His outstanding résumé notwithstanding, it was always about Petraeus.

Finally, Gates was escorted into the general's office. Seated across a table from him, the defense secretary got straight to the point. "David, you're not going to become chairman of the Joint Chiefs," he said. "It's just not going to happen under Obama. I just feel obligated to be honest with you. I tried three times to persuade him to choose you and I could not convince him. But what other job would you like?" The general didn't bat an eyelash. Petraeus looked Gates in the eye. "How about your old job, Mr. Secretary?" he said finally. "Which one?" Gates replied. "Director of the CIA," Petraeus said.

Gates perked up at this idea. After almost six years running the Pentagon, he was dying to retire to his house on a rustic lake in Washington State. But making that happen was like sinking a complicated billiard shot: Leon Panetta, the CIA director, had reluctantly agreed to replace Gates at DOD, but who would take over at the CIA for Panetta? The job called for someone with stature and familiarity with intelligence. Petraeus seemed like the perfect solution.

Sending Petraeus to the CIA would be attractive to Obama and his team for another reason: The storied general was a rock star among Republicans for leading the Iraq War "surge"; there was even talk that he could become their 2012 presidential nominee, or number two on the ticket. "I think Obama recognized his military prowess, and he also recognized his political power and influence," said John Brennan, the future director. For Obama, making Petraeus CIA director could be a twofer: It would fill the agency's top job and eliminate a potential political rival.

Upon his return to the U.S., Gates went to see the president at the White House. When he arrived, Obama was waiting for him in the Oval Office. (Obama and his team put such stock in Gates's sage advice that they nicknamed him "Yoda.") "I have a potential replacement," Gates told the president. "David Petraeus has told me he would like to be the director of CIA." Obama looked up. "You know, that's very intriguing," he said. "It's a great carom shot," Gates replied. "Panetta takes my place. Petraeus takes his place. Petraeus is going to be easy to confirm because he's so popular on the Hill."

Indeed, on June 30, 2011, the most decorated general of his generation would be confirmed as CIA director in the Senate by a vote of 94–0. But little more than a year later, he'd undergo a dizzying fall.

• • •

Petraeus would be the eighth director who'd come from the military (if you counted all those generals who served briefly back in the 1940s). And he was the second after Michael Hayden to serve out of uniform; on August 31, 2011, in a ceremony at Fort Myers, he retired from the U.S. Army.

As CIA director, Petraeus would have to adjust to a much smaller organization. At CENTCOM, he'd commanded 250,000 soldiers and had almost unlimited resources. By contrast the CIA was a much tighter ship; it's been estimated that the military spends more in a day than the agency does in a year, though the amounts are classified. In Afghanistan, preparing for his confirmation hearing by secure video conference, the four-star general asked his CIA briefer, "Okay, that's great. But what's the black budget? How much else is there? Where's the covert action money?" His briefer replied, "No, General, that's it."

A clash of cultures was looming. On a visit to Petraeus's 1,400-man military headquarters in Kabul, a senior intelligence official had been astounded by the sheer number of aides, handlers, and hangers-on who swarmed around Petraeus, catering to him; his personal staff, the official guessed, numbered at least fifty. One soldier appeared to do nothing but empty his out-box.

Petraeus was famously attentive to his publicity, ardently courting the press; reporters returned the favor with flattering coverage. Some biographers were positively fawning. Regarding Petraeus's imminent arrival at the CIA, one of his chroniclers wrote:

> *After six straight military commands leading up to the end of his career, the prospect of taking off his uniform had initially left him pensive. But he was grateful to have a demanding new job on the horizon, another opportunity to serve the nation. He hadn't lost his will to win by leaving the military. He hadn't forsaken his competitive nature. David Petraeus was still "all-in."*

The writer was a young Army reserve soldier and PhD student named Paula Broadwell.

Petraeus had been forewarned about the CIA's aversion to outsiders. "He was told, make sure you don't show up to work in military uniform, because that's going to get antibodies going," recalled Steven

Hall, a veteran case officer. Petraeus was also warned not to repeat Porter Goss's blunder: "If you come in and completely replace your support staff with your own political insiders, that's going to raise eyebrows—and not in a good way."

So far so good: Petraeus had shed his uniform and had no plans to install his own staff. But the habits of this four-star general would be harder to shake.

The trouble began on Petraeus's first day. All over Langley, a rumor had spread: Arriving at his suite on the seventh floor after a brisk morning run, the director was served a plate of bananas. But there was a problem. The bananas were sliced improperly. Petraeus wasn't happy. Henceforth, he let everyone know, his bananas should be sliced . . . *just so.*

There may be no workplace in the world where gossip travels faster than at CIA headquarters at Langley. That's because the work force handles top secret material that can't be discussed with anyone else. Within hours, Petraeus's rumored commandment about bananas was the talk of the CIA.

The bananas episode was followed by other stories of entitled behavior. Petraeus complained that his apples were too small. One aide was chewed out for failing to properly hand off a water bottle during a morning run. Before leaving a room, the new director supposedly would wait for someone to put his coat on for him. "Sir, we don't do that here," someone finally said.

"Petraeus was just a fish out of water," said Ned Price, a former analyst. "He came from a culture that is just about the opposite of Langley's culture. The military is hierarchical. It's large. It's bureaucratic. The agency is relatively small. It prides itself on its ability to be nimble. And he brought a formality and hierarchy to the building that I think rubbed a lot of people the wrong way."

Eyebrows were also raised by Petraeus's exacting and specific travel demands. "If you ever really want to get the unvarnished view of what a director is like, talk to the people who support him," said one officer. "Holy Christ, the eye rolls, I mean, the faces people made." The pièce de résistance for Langley gossips was an instruction sent to CIA stations before Petraeus's visits. "There was this cable that was circulated around that was guidance to station chiefs," recalled a former senior intelligence official. It reminded him of a story about the 1980s rock group Van Halen; the band had a rider in its contract demanding that all the brown M&Ms be removed from its candy bowls. "Petraeus had his own rider—with everything he wanted in his hotel room," said this official. "It wasn't a thousand brown M&Ms—but it was a bathtub of ice, thirty-one bananas . . . stuff like that."

According to one other official, there was something else in Petraeus's rider that was unusual. Station chiefs were advised: "Don't ask him tough questions."

Petraeus told me that accounts of his entitled behavior are untrue. The story about sliced bananas, he insisted, is "absolute nonsense—I eat my bananas whole." After years of being deployed in Iraq and Afghanistan," he said, "my needs were pretty simple—just don't keep me from doing my morning run!" Yet multiple CIA officers said that Petraeus suffered from "four-star general disease." The perception damaged the new director's leadership right out of the gate. "The slicing of the bananas and the prep, all of that stuff, the support guys were just completely repulsed by all that," said one officer. "It was a real contrast with directors who came up through the agency and treated all of those people almost deferentially. That was not Petraeus's style."

Petraeus's management style also took getting used to. "He's not a warm and fuzzy guy," said a former top intelligence official. "He's not Leon Panetta or George Tenet. He's not a hug-you kind of guy. He's a give-an-order kind of guy—and his attitude was, 'I expect it to get done and I'm going to ask for the next five days whether it's done yet.'"

Petraeus was better at managing up; Obama respected his knowledge and experience. But some of Obama's inner circle said he was slow to grasp the CIA director's role as honest broker. "What the president needs when he's making a decision is the best available intel," said McDonough. "He doesn't need another policy voice from his intel guy. I think that was a really hard transition for General Petraeus to make."

Obama was a stickler about separating intelligence from policy; he expected his CIA director to deliver his brief and depart. "He was meticulous about that," said James Clapper, the Director of National Intelligence. "Whenever I'd go in the Oval to brief him, he wouldn't start a conversation with his team until I was out of the room." But Petraeus opined on policy. "A lot of times Dave would come straight with a policy brief," said McDonough.

Obama and his CIA director locked horns over Middle East policy. Petraeus had strong views on the unfolding disaster in Syria; he argued for arming rebel groups to take the fight to the regime of Bashar al-Assad. After all, Obama had declared publicly that the Syrian dictator would have to step down. When Petraeus made his argument, the usually professorial Obama got right in his CIA director's face. "The president was *sparky*," said McDonough. "He'd push back. Notwithstanding his respect for David, they went at it." Petraeus's advocacy for the rebels stemmed from deeply held conviction about the stakes. Petraeus, according to a former senior government official, believed that Obama's indecision—and his refusal to establish a no fly/no drive zone—had led to more than half of Syria's population being displaced, the death of over 500,000 Syrians, and the establishment of the ISIS caliphate.

Before his confirmation hearing, Petraeus had consulted former directors for advice. As he was leaving the home of Michael Hayden, the ex-director pulled him aside. "Dave," he said, "the CIA has never looked more like OSS than it does right now. But it's not the OSS. It's the nation's global espionage service. And you're going to have to work every day to impose that reality upon yourself and on the agency."

Petraeus knew what Hayden meant. Since 9/11, many believed the CIA had become focused on lethal covert operations at the expense of its original mission: intelligence gathering. Petraeus's deputy, Morell, shared that view. "There's no doubt that the CIA today has a much larger paramilitary mission than it ever has," he said. "That's not a healthy thing, because the primary job of the Central Intelligence Agency is to collect secrets: to find out what our adversaries are doing and planning to do and to tell the president of the United States."

The Memorial Wall in the CIA's entrance hall was a solemn reminder of the agency's darker side. One of Petraeus's first acts was to move the swearing-in ceremony for new officers from the auditorium known as the Bubble to the entrance hall. "They sat facing the wall of stars—each representing an officer who has fallen in service,"

Petraeus said. "That was a big deal in my mind. And every one of these lives lost is very difficult, very tough. The symbolism of that front hallway is extraordinary. There's an intimacy in the agency that is greater than in a vast military organization. And so a loss in that organization is very deeply felt and shared."

The CIA's lethal drones posed a quandary for Obama. Even as he expanded the use of CIA drones to kill Al Qaeda terrorists in Pakistan, the president was uneasy about it. He wanted to gradually shift responsibility for drone warfare away from the agency to the military.

Petraeus was less reluctant to flex the CIA's paramilitary muscle. "I think I'm uniquely qualified to assess what is available in the military and what is available in the CIA," he told me. In Petraeus's view, covert operations, conducted under Title 50 of the U.S. military code (military operations come under Title 10), gave the U.S. a vital option against terrorists—the ability to strike without the knowledge or consent of the country involved. "The unique aspect of Title 50 operations, covert action is that you don't acknowledge them," he explained. "It's not that you deny them. You just don't talk about them."

Indeed, though Petraeus didn't want to talk about them, on his watch the CIA would step up its paramilitary operations in the wild, ungoverned spaces of Yemen. And one terrorist in particular posed an ethical and legal challenge for Obama, Petraeus, and their national security team.

Anwar al-Awlaki was a sworn enemy of the United States—and an American citizen. He was the most controversial target in the history of drone warfare—at least up to that point. In January 2020, an equally contentious debate would erupt over the targeting of Iran's General Qassim Suleimani by Donald Trump.

Born in San Diego, Awlaki moved with his family to Yemen at the age of seven and returned to the U.S. eleven years later. Awlaki became a charismatic Muslim cleric and was based first in San Diego and later in Falls Church, Virginia, where he was imam of a mosque. Investigators would later learn that, prior to 9/11, Awlaki had been in contact with Khalid al-Midhar and Nawaf al-Hazmi, the notorious Al Qaeda hijackers whom the CIA and FBI had failed to track down before the attacks.

In 2002 Awlaki moved to the United Kingdom and then returned to Yemen, where he preached a message of violent jihad against the U.S., amplified by social media and a jihadist magazine called *Inspire*. "Anwar al-Awlaki was a very, very significant individual in the world of jihadism," said Petraeus. "He was a colloquial American English speaker, he had religious credentials. He was attractive and he was inspirational, especially online."

Awlaki had conspired with the so-called underwear bomber in a failed plot to blow up an airliner over Detroit on Christmas Day 2009. And his violent exhortations on the internet inspired the jihadist militant who killed thirteen and injured more than thirty in a shooting spree at Fort Hood, Texas. William Webster, the ex–CIA director, was asked to study the Fort Hood case. "I was asking, 'Why are we interested in al-Awlaki?' And someone said, 'Well, he's a bad guy. He's on the president's list.' So I said, 'What list is *that*?' And they said the 'goodbye list.' "

The "goodbye list"—also known as the "kill list"—was the grim roster of terrorists targeted for execution by the U.S. government. Panetta explained: "We went through the process to make a case for why al-Awlaki was dangerous, and the Justice Department along with our general counsel felt that a good case had been made to put him on that list." The kill list was an open secret—so open that Awlaki's father went to a U.S. court in a desperate effort to have his son's life spared. On August 30, 2010, Nasser al-Awlaki, represented by lawyers from the American Civil Liberties Union and the Center for Constitutional Rights, filed a lawsuit against President Barack Obama, CIA director Leon Panetta, and Defense Secretary Robert Gates. But the suit was later dismissed.

Petraeus had been CIA director for barely two weeks when, on September 30, CIA drone pilots in Nevada drew a bead on Awlaki in Yemen. They'd been watching him for days. He was sitting outside a large tent in the village of Al Jawf, in Bedouin country, south of the Saudi border. Awlaki was accompanied by one of his protégés, Samir Khan, twenty-five, and two tribesmen. Hovering overhead, two Predator drones fed high-resolution video to CIA operators at Creech Air Force Base in Nevada, 8,500 miles away. Also hovering nearby was another drone, a much larger Reaper, with multiple Hellfire missiles under each wing.

A split second before the missiles struck, the men tried to run for their vehicles; one of them must have heard the buzz of the drones. But although Awlaki had eluded an attempted strike once before, this time there was no escape for the jihadist cleric and his companions. All four men were vaporized by the exploding missiles, which left deep craters at the site.

Petraeus wouldn't talk about how the order to kill Awlaki was executed. In fact, to this day the CIA doesn't publicly acknowledge that it operates lethal drones. But Petraeus did talk to me about the personal calculus involved in pulling the trigger. "I think you always do soul-searching when you're putting individuals in harm's way," he said. "You turn these over in your mind and there are occasions where you say, 'Let me mull this one. Let me think on it.' But if you ensure that you're within the rules of engagement, then you press forward and make a decision."

Awlaki's killing touched off an intense debate among the former CIA directors. Not since the Civil War had the U.S. government executed one of its citizens without an indictment, trial, or sentencing. Bob Gates was troubled by the process. "The precedent of an American president being able to kill an American citizen under any circumstances, on just his signature, is dangerous," he told me. Gates believed that such strikes should be reviewed by an independent board of judges. "I would prefer that the president present the evidence to some kind of external body to say, 'I think this is conclusive. Do you think this is conclusive?'"

Leon Panetta argued that a terrorist's citizenship was irrelevant. "There were Nazis who were U.S. citizens," he said. "Does that make them less of an enemy? There are terrorists who are U.S. citizens. Does that somehow make them less of an enemy? I don't think so. In my book, a terrorist is a terrorist." Petraeus maintained that lethal strikes are thoroughly vetted. "When the president makes a decision," he said, "he has heard from his own legal team; he's heard his national security team, the NSC members, the vice president, the secretaries of state and defense, the director of the CIA, the DNI, the chairman of the Joint Chiefs, and all the other individuals at the Situation Room table." John Brennan agreed: "I never saw the president alone make a decision on something like this. There are a lot of people involved in that discussion, debate, and decision-making."

Gates remained unconvinced: "There's a process and a discussion—

but at the end of the day, they are all the president's appointees. And then it's the president's signature. There is no outside review. There is no external evaluation of the evidence." In the summer of 2014, I asked Judge William Webster, then ninety, what he thought of the decision to kill Awlaki. "We do harm to the country and damage to the president," he said, "by just leaving it up to unprocessed whim to use these instruments of destruction." The Judge had lost none of his passion for due process and the rule of law. "This was an American citizen and he was ultimately taken out. But it's not something that should be left to one person—no matter who that person is."

On May 23, 2013, Obama addressed drone warfare in a speech at the National Defense University in Washington. "This technology raises profound questions," he said, "about who is targeted and why; about civilian casualties, and the risk of creating new enemies; about the legality of such strikes under US and international law; about accountability and morality." He conceded that civilian casualties occurred: "Those deaths will haunt us as long as we live." But as president, he said, "I must weigh these heartbreaking tragedies against the alternatives. Of Awlaki, Obama said "his citizenship should no more serve as a shield than a sniper shooting down an innocent crowd should be protected from a SWAT team. I would have been derelict in my duty had I not authorized the strike that took him out."

Targeting American citizens was contentious enough; even more controversial were so-called signature strikes. These were drone strikes targeting suspected terrorists whose names were unknown, but they were thought to be plotting attacks against Americans. CIA officials rarely talk about signature strikes. When I broached the subject with Petraeus, he practically leapt out of his chair. "I can't talk about signature strikes!" he snapped, before adding: "*If* they are even taken, I don't know what they are." Michael Morell, the two-time acting director, also bristled when I asked. "I'm not talking about those," he said. "I don't *believe* these directors are talking about this stuff! *I'm* not talking about them."

But other directors considered the subject fair game. Michael Hayden defended the practice. "In a signature strike you have every reason to believe that there are bad guys there at the moment," he said. "You don't quite know the name of the bad guy but you know the van, you know the weaponry, you know the size of the group, you know what kind of meetings have been held there before, you know the other vehicle that pulled up. And you make a decision." But Hayden conceded that drone strikes may create more enemies than they kill. "We feed the jihadi recruitment video that these Americans are heartless killers."

Gates warned that, just as enhanced interrogation techniques became indefensible, the CIA's reliance on lethal drones could come back to haunt the agency. "Ten years from now," he said, "will people be asking the same questions about the use of these drones? When it comes to the blame game, we've seen this movie before and it's never the politicians who suffer the consequences; it's the folks on the ground who are trying to make sense of the rules they're given by Washington."

A year into his directorship, Petraeus had recovered from his "four-star general" jitters; Morell thought he'd found his footing and had become an effective director. "There's no doubt in my mind that he learned over time what the culture was," said Morell.

On the evening of September 11, 2012, eleven years after the attacks of 9/11, the State Department facility in Benghazi, Libya, came under assault by Islamic extremists. Security guards from the CIA base, or "the Annex," at the site responded. The attacks on the TMF, or temporary mission facility, came in three waves during the night; when it was over, four Americans were dead, including Ambassador Chris Stevens, known for his fearless diplomacy in the region; Sean Smith, a State Department communications officer; and Glen Doherty and Tyrone Woods, two security officers.

A controversy would soon erupt over the nature of the attack, fanned by sloppy "talking points" delivered by National Security Adviser Susan Rice on the Sunday TV shows: Was it a spontaneous demonstration that turned violent? Or was it a preplanned and premeditated Al Qaeda assault that the State Department and CIA should have anticipated—and therefore prevented?

Tea Party Republicans, led by Congressman Trey Gowdy and future CIA director Mike Pompeo, pounced. They accused Obama's State Department of underestimating the danger, failing to respond to the attacks, and covering up the disaster. It was true that security at the compound had been inadequate, but the Benghazi affair was a bogus scandal—there was no evidence of negligence or a cover-up. That didn't prevent the incident from becoming a cynical Republican cudgel against Hillary Clinton. Yet before the affair could gain critical mass, David Petraeus would be sidelined by a scandal of his own making.

Bruce Riedel, the former Middle East analyst, had left the agency for a job at the Brookings Institution. One day he got a phone call from a woman who was working on a book about Petraeus. She was attending a Brookings dinner event that night; could she stop by his office beforehand for an interview? Her name was Paula Broadwell.

"At about 5:00 p.m. in the evening she shows up," Riedel recalled. "And she is dressed in this tight little black cocktail dress with platform heels six inches high. I was sitting there saying to myself, 'Who comes to a Brookings dinner in a cocktail dress? That's not our thing.' And it never occurred to me. Thirty years in the intelligence business! It was right in front of my face and I couldn't put it together!"

Broadwell was researching *All-In: The Education of General David Petraeus*. Since November 2011, she'd also been having an affair with the celebrated general, whom she'd met during his tour in Afghanistan. Broadwell had sent harassing emails to a Florida socialite named Jill Kelley, a family friend of the Petraeuses. After Kelley reported the emails to the FBI, the Bureau traced them to Broadwell—and discovered intimate messages to the CIA director in an email account they shared. The director and Broadwell had tried to conceal their email correspondence by accessing them in a draft folder. But with the FBI's discovery, their secret emerged.

On October 26, 2012, agents from the bureau's Tampa, Florida, office came to Langley, where they questioned the CIA director about his secret email account. Petraeus admitted to the affair with Broadwell, saying he'd lost his "moral compass." When asked if he'd shared classified information with his lover, Petraeus denied it.

But that wasn't true. Executing a search warrant at Broadwell's home, investigators found more than one hundred photographs of highly classified information from eight bound notebooks belonging to Petraeus. They included code words for secret intelligence programs, the identities of covert officers, and confidential discussions with the NSC. Disclosure of these secrets could have caused "exceptionally grave damage," according to the government.

DNI James Clapper called Petraeus and urged him to resign. A week later, the embattled CIA director gave President Obama his resignation letter. On November 9, announcing Petraeus's departure in a ceremony at the White House, Obama said he hoped the circumstances "would be just a footnote to a brilliant career."

Petraeus faced possible felony charges of lying to the FBI and violating the Espionage Act; he could have served prison time and lost his pension. But in the end, on April 23, 2015, in Charlotte, North Carolina, Petraeus would avoid prison by pleading guilty to a misdemeanor and admitting to making false statements to the FBI. The judge would raise his fine from $40,000 to $100,000.

Afterward, Petraeus reflected on his fifteen-month tenure as CIA director. "This is the most unbelievable, extraordinary job in the world," he told me. "It's the kind of job you'd love to do for many, many years. And so, obviously, it was with enormous regret that I went to see the president and said, 'I feel that I should resign.'" I pointed out that he'd been confirmed by a vote of 94 to 0—"a precipitous fall. How tough was that?" Petraeus stared straight ahead. "Precipitous falls are very tough," he said. "You know, there's a saying in the military: 'The higher you go up the flagpole the more chance you have to show your backside.' I was well up the flagpole and did just that."

Did Petraeus believe, as Obama suggested, that the scandal would be just a footnote to a brilliant career? "I'll leave that to history," he said.

On November 9, 2012, Michael Morell became acting CIA director for the second time; his first stint had come after Panetta departed for DOD and before the arrival of Petraeus. As both deputy and acting director, Morell had essentially run the agency and had earned high marks. On his first tour as deputy, with no expectation of succeeding Panetta, "there was no wondering about the job, there was no anxiety or anything," Morell said. "It was very natural for me to just keep going in the same direction that he was going."

But this time Morell had set his sights on becoming director. He was respected but not beloved by his fellow analysts. "I think he had a tendency to kiss up and to kick down," said one. "I think the power went to his head a little bit. It wasn't all that long ago that he was writing PDBs and briefing them. Now he would pepper us: How do you know this? And why do we think that? And who is the source of that? When was it collected? And he would follow up with twelve taskings a day. And whether he wanted to make his authority known, or whether he really needed the information, I never quite understood."

Morell had cultivated the agency's operatives, and he had powerful political allies; he'd impressed both George W. Bush and Barack Obama as a crisp, no-drama broker of intelligence. Panetta and Hillary Clinton called Obama to recommend him, as did several members of Congress. But Morell faced a daunting obstacle: John Brennan was also in the running to become director, and no one was closer to Obama.

There was one other problem. Controversy over the rendition, detention, and interrogation (RDI) program had contributed to Obama's decision to pass over Brennan as his first CIA director; now Morell's defense of the same program hurt his chances of succeeding Petraeus. His comments had been enough to push Dianne Feinstein, chair of the Senate Select Committee on Intelligence, into Brennan's camp. "Dianne had a preference for John over Michael," said Clapper, "mainly because of the RDI business."

Ultimately, Obama chose Brennan. "More than anything else," said Nick Rasmussen, head of the National Counterterrorism Center, "I think it was an alignment of worldview between the president and John—they thought of America and the role that we play in the world, and the application of U.S. power, in the same way. That was attractive to President Obama even before he was president."

Like George Tenet's deputy John McLaughlin, Morell had come within a hairsbreadth of achieving his career ambition. And, as it had for McLaughlin, the disappointment stung.

For John Brennan, returning to the CIA as director was the fulfillment of a lifelong goal. During thirty years at the agency, he'd lived and breathed CIA; the place was in his DNA. He was proud that he shared a birthday with Nathan Hale, whose statue, erected by William Colby, stood outside the CIA entrance.

Not that Brennan ever looked happy. "He looks like he's mad," said Morell. "He looks like he's pissed off, right? But Brennan's just the opposite of that. He's a sweetheart. He cares deeply about people." Brennan's deputies cared back. "He seems a little gruff, but that is so in contrast to who he is," said Avril Haines, who replaced Morell as deputy director. "He's like this teddy bear. He's this really warm, generous, lovely human being."

Brennan had been Obama's Middle East tutor and his guide through the intelligence world. Obama found him fascinating, a little exotic, and a kindred adventurous spirit. "The president referred to him as a modern-day Lawrence of Arabia," said Nick Shapiro, Brennan's chief of staff. "He'd lived in Egypt. He'd traveled through Indonesia. He had these tales of riding a motorcycle across Indonesia and playing basketball in Cairo. There's this great picture of him and some of his agency buddies in ridiculous basketball attire that anyone would laugh at today. But the rumor was that he could dunk." Obama ate it up.

Panetta was a master at cutting to the heart of an issue—but Brennan commanded all the particulars and nuance. At NSC meetings, "John knew the details in a way that thrilled the backbenchers," said Haines. "Panetta doesn't have that. Other people don't have it. It's a fascinating quality." It was the result of relentless preparation. "He was the hardest working person in that government," said Shapiro. "There was not a meeting that guy didn't prepare for—and I mean lock himself in his office, go days without eating." Brennan had an almost ascetic work ethic. After a hip operation, he was back in the office, on crutches, the same day.

Brennan's new role as honest broker was an adjustment, since he'd been up to his eyeballs in policy as Obama's White House counterterrorism adviser. "There were times when I could see John holding his tongue during policy discussions," said Shapiro. "He would offer a view of the consequences of this or that policy choice—because that's part of the CIA director's role, forecasting what X or Y might lead to. But there was a clear sense that he was now someone who was an intelligence officer again." Still, Obama would often tease out his policy views. "Maybe I'm not a good poker player," said Brennan. "A lot of times I would be at the table and I'd be furrowing my brow or something, and I'd steal a look at the president and he'd see me. I'd look away—and he'd say, 'John, what do you think?'"

Brennan was raised with his sister and brother in North Bergen, New Jersey, the son of a blacksmith who immigrated from Ireland in the late 1940s. He was educated by Franciscan nuns and read about all the popes. "His dream was to be the first American pope," said Shapiro. After traveling in Africa and Indonesia, he enrolled at Fordham, where he answered a newspaper ad and interviewed for the CIA. He was asked, while strapped to a polygraph machine, whether he had ever belonged to an organization that advocated the overthrow of the U.S. government. Nervous about seeming deceptive, Brennan confessed that in 1976 he'd voted for Gus Hall, the Communist Party candidate for president. It was a youthful protest against the corruption of Watergate.

David Axelrod, Obama's political adviser, called him "the cop from Queens." Indeed, Brennan had the slightly jaded air of the sergeant on the TV show *Hill Street Blues*, who admonished his cops on the morning roll call, "let's be careful out there." The truth was, Brennan had a stubborn moral streak. "You can tell when he feels that something's not right," said Shapiro. "When something doesn't comport with either our interests or our values. And it's almost like it bubbles up inside him. It's the Jesuit thing, I guess." There were some things that just got Brennan's Irish up.

People who knew Brennan believed that if Obama had proposed something unethical, the CIA director would have hammered him. "You couldn't stop John Brennan from saying what he believes if you tried," said McDonough, Obama's White House chief of staff. "That's what made him an excellent DCIA. He'd come in there with an analysis that directly contradicted what you hoped to hear and he'd deliver it. He wasn't gonna swallow anything. He wasn't gonna hide anything. He was gonna give it to you straight." James Clapper, the director of national intelligence, agreed. "Well, John's Irish shows," he said.

Clapper had become the fourth DNI in August 2010. An experienced intelligence professional, he'd been a three-star Air Force lieutenant general and director of both the Defense Intelligence Agency (DIA) and the National Imagery and Mapping Agency. "Clapper is what you want in that job," said McDonough. "You want somebody who understands all seventeen agencies, understands what their mission is, understands where they're lagging, or where they're not sharing."

Wry, amiable, and world-weary, with an uncanny resemblance to Ernst Blofeld, the Bond villain in *You Only Live Twice*, Clapper also understood how to make the DNI role work. Unlike some of his turf-conscious predecessors, he floated above the fray at thirty thousand feet, avoiding unnecessary battles. Clapper and Brennan had worked out a modus vivendi. "We likened ourselves to foxhole buddies in the Situation Room," Clapper explained. "And John and I worked at this, there was always a little Kabuki dance about who says what in meetings."

Brennan believed that effective policy required *process*: dotting the i's and crossing the t's. Every week, on "Terror Tuesdays," Brennan briefed Obama on global terrorist threats. This didn't always run like clockwork; one NSC holdover quipped: "At least with Bush the fake meetings started on time." But nothing got Brennan's Irish up more than someone doubting his commitment to fair process. One official recalled the time when Sean Joyce, deputy FBI director, complained about a "policy merry-go-round. Here we are," he said, after a couple of hours, "back where we started again." The back of Brennan's neck turned red "because John's the conductor of this policy, it's *his* meeting," said this official, "and he's pissed: 'Wait a minute. Them's *fighting* words. Policy *merry-go-round*?'"

As CIA director, Brennan inherited a Middle East in turmoil. The once promising Arab Spring had devolved into chaos and bloodshed. It had begun on December 17, 2010, when a Tunisian street vendor, humiliated after the police confiscated his vegetable cart, doused himself with gasoline and set himself on fire. The self-immolation touched off a wave of protest that raised hopes among the downtrodden and struck fear in the autocracies of the region. But the Arab Spring quickly turned to winter—and grew worse on Brennan's watch as CIA director.

The uprisings caught the CIA flat-footed (the rest of the world's intelligence services were equally slow to grasp what was happening). A succession of crises followed for which the Obama administration had no good answers. The most serious flashpoint was Syria, where protests against the regime of dictator Bashar al-Assad were met by bloody repression in March 2011. While Obama resisted the exhortations of Petraeus and others to act, a bloody civil war ensued.

In contrast to Petraeus, Brennan was wary of arming Syria's rebel militias, many of which were allied with Al Qaeda. He shared Obama's reluctance to get involved in another Middle Eastern conflict.

Years later, at a restaurant near the White House, Brennan sat down with me to talk about his directorship. (At one point an admirer came over and shook the former director's hand. "I hope that wasn't a Russian agent passing me some type of bio-agent," Brennan quipped.) He seemed weary just thinking about the multitude of crises on his watch. "On a lot of these things, whether it be Libya or Syria or Iraq or Afghanistan, it was frequently the least worst choice," he said.

"President Obama, to his credit—but also sometimes it was paralyzing—was somebody who had the ability to see second- and third- and fourth-order effects," Brennan said. "He was playing multidimensional chess. A lot of others were just on the checkerboard." But when it came to the Middle East, Obama saw so many effects that he often made no move at all—or refusing to arm the rebels or initially enforce a red line over Assad's use of chemical weapons.

Charlie Allen judged the CIA's performance on the Middle East harshly. "Not warning of the Arab Spring, I would argue is a failure," he said. "So was the birth of ISIS in 2012. Extreme failures."

"I most regret not being able to turn the situation in Syria around," Brennan told me. Did he think there was a missed opportunity to make a difference? "Maybe, sure," he replied. "But, again, these are all hypotheticals. ISIS wasn't a phenomenon back then. It was Al Qaeda in Iraq—it had like eight hundred people or something. But things happened—and all of a sudden you had ISIS, which overwhelmed, or took up a significant portion of, the opposition in Syria. And so one of the real concerns that Obama had, and I shared, was that if you bombed Damascus, that might have led to Assad's toppling. Would a military cabal have taken over? And then run the government smoothly and gone on a better track? Or would it have evolved into chaos? The last thing you want is for Damascus to implode."

He continued: "Libya was another situation that was unfortunate. I felt deeply, personally about the Arab Spring because I spent so much time in the Middle East." Brennan had done two tours in Saudi Arabia, as an analyst in the 1980s and chief of station in the mid-1990s. "And it happened at a very early stage in the Obama presidency. I was counseling some of these younger, very energetic, evangelistic members of the Obama administration that the Middle East is a complicated place. Just because you sweep aside an authoritarian leader doesn't mean democracy is going to flourish."

In March 2014, the scandal over the CIA's Bush-era enhanced interrogation program (EIT) erupted all over again. On the floor of the Senate, Dianne Feinstein of California, chair of the Senate Select Committee on Intelligence, delivered an extraordinary, forty-five-minute speech lambasting Brennan: In the course of her committee's five-year, $40 million investigation into EITs (described in chapter 8), she charged, the CIA unlawfully hacked into her staffers' computers; it was a "potential effort to intimidate" the investigation. In July, the CIA's Inspector General confirmed that the agency had improperly searched the committee's computer network and read the staff's email. Meanwhile, Brennan was fighting a rearguard action against Obama's chief of staff Denis McDonough over how much of the SSCI report should be declassified and made public. (Ultimately, only a 525-page summary was released.) "It got really tense," said McDonough. But Obama was usually in Brennan's corner. "Sometimes the president would just say to me, 'Back off, man. Don't forget that you're working with John Brennan.'"

The CIA-SSCI showdown would be dramatized in a scathing 2019 film, *The Report*, starring Adam Driver. But the film, like the SSCI majority report, was riddled with inaccuracies—suggesting, among other things, that neither Congress nor the president had been briefed about the brutal interrogations or the existence of the "torture tapes." The truth was, Feinstein, House majority leader Nancy Pelosi—and George W. Bush—were all informed.

Conscious of his place in history, Brennan was determined to leave his own stamp on the CIA. (He saw himself in the mold of Robert Gates, who rose up through the agency and left his mark on it.) Brennan wanted to do something about the insularity of the place. "If you're in the Langley ivy tower, you have this myopic view that doesn't take into account the real world," he said. His experience as head of the NCTC reinforced that conviction. "I had more exposure to capabilities, to data, to expertise." The answer to the CIA's myopia, Brennan thought, was to integrate the once separate worlds of the analysts and operatives. Toward that end, he launched a major "reorganization" of the CIA.

But the world's troubles wouldn't wait for Brennan to tinker with the agency's gears. A major test was looming, one that would define his tenure. It began in the tiny republic of Estonia.

The Russian assault on the U.S. presidential election of 2016 was foreshadowed almost ten years earlier. In 2007, the Estonian government decided to move a World War II–era monument, known as the Bronze Soldier, from its capital, Tallinn, to a military cemetery outside the city. The decision was contentious because the monument was a divisive symbol—to the Russians, of the Red Army's victory over the Nazis; to the Estonians, of Russian domination. Moscow responded to the statue's removal with a cyberattack that paralyzed the country, disabling the online services of banks, media outlets, and government bodies. Russia unleashed a similar cyber assault before its invasion of Georgia in 2008.

These were dress rehearsals for the sophisticated assault Russia would carry out against the U.S. presidential election in 2016. "Ever since the fall of the Soviet Union, the United States has thought of itself as impregnable in a lot of ways," said Steven Hall, who headed the CIA's Russia operations until 2015. "We saw the Russians get into servers in the Ukrainian Parliament. We saw them attack German servers in the German Bundestag. But the idea that this would evolve into hybrid warfare—both cyberwarfare and social media disinformation—was a failure of our imagination mixed with a bit of hubris."

The architect of Russia's hybrid warfare was a former armor officer, a veteran of the Second Chechen War named Valery Gerasimov. Vladimir Putin had appointed Gerasimov chief of the general staff in late 2012. The following year, the general enunciated a new doctrine of Russian warfare. "A perfectly thriving state," he wrote, "can, in a matter of months or even days, be transformed into an arena of fierce armed conflict . . . and sink into a web of chaos."

Gerasimov saw conventional war between armies as "a thing of the past." Instead, he called for "long-distance, countless actions against the enemy . . . informational actions, devices and means. . . .

The informational space opens wide asymmetrical possibilities for reducing the fighting potential of the enemy." New "models of operations and military conduct," he wrote, were needed.

Gerasimov's doctrine was weaponized in 2014 when Russia annexed Crimea and occupied parts of the Donbass region in eastern Ukraine. This was "hybrid war," Michael Hayden would later write, combining "surprise, ambiguity, and plausible deniability in a way that seemed to freeze any opposition." Russian hackers attacked the country's power grid, compromising three energy distribution companies and causing chaos. As Hayden put it: "Gerasimov's notorious 'little green men'—special operations forces with modern Russian weaponry but no insignia and wearing balaclava masks—effected a bloodless takeover of the Crimean peninsula."

The Russians were simultaneously becoming bolder in American cyberspace. "You could see the Russians get much more aggressive than they'd been in the past," said Michael Daniel, cybersecurity coordinator in the Obama White House, and now president of the Cyber Threat Alliance. In the past, after a cyberattack, "they'd vanish like smoke. But starting in 2014, you'd see the Russians hanging around. It was almost like they were saying, 'I dare you to try to kick us out of this network.'" But the Russian cyber trolls weren't just hanging around. "When the information began to be leaked to things like Guccifer 2.0 and to DCLeaks and to WikiLeaks," said Daniel, "we were like, 'Oh, wait a minute, we're playing a different game here.'"

By August of 2016, with the presidential election campaign in full swing, Daniel said, "we started to put the full power of the U.S. intelligence community into looking at this. And we started going through every bit of intelligence that we had: HUMINT, SIGINT, anything we could scrape up. And when you start putting all of that analytic horsepower in there, your picture starts to clarify: This wasn't just some random one-off Russian operation; this was a serious campaign that was being directed from the highest levels of the Kremlin. It's not a Eureka moment. But you suddenly realize that the cumulative weight of all the intelligence paints this picture."

These were the "storm clouds" that Brennan saw from his seventh-floor office in early August 2016, as he immersed himself in the raw intelligence on Russia. "There were several days and nights that I basically sequestered myself," recalled Brennan, "and pored through material, assessments, and other things so that I would have as good and complete a picture as possible." There was only one possible conclusion. The Russians were poised to launch a major cyberattack on the presidential election; their goal was to hurt Hillary Clinton and elect Donald Trump.

Brennan picked up his secure phone to the White House. "I said, 'I need to see the president' [tomorrow]," he recalled. "And they said, 'Well, can you at least give us a subject?' But I didn't feel comfortable talking about it." Instead Brennan composed an "eyes only" memorandum. "What I did was send down a very cryptic note. Maybe it was three or four sentences dealing with the Russian election activities, and that I needed to talk to the president personally about this." The note was hand-delivered by a courier to the White House.

The next day, in the Oval Office, Brennan met with the president and his team: McDonough, National Security Adviser Susan Rice, and her deputy Avril Haines. "I think we all were really seized with the gravity of that assessment," said Homeland Secuirty Adviser Lisa Monaco. "You have a foreign adversary who is conducting an active major assault, targeting our democratic processes." Brennan was struck by how different Obama was from the untested commander in chief of the first year. "By now he was president for almost eight years. He'd gone through the whole illegals episode (the swap of a sleeper cell of ten Russian spies for four Americans held by Moscow); he'd gone through meetings with Putin and he was very worldly by now. He was thinking about it from a national security standpoint, from a counterintelligence standpoint, from a law enforcement standpoint, as well as from a political standpoint."

DNI Clapper, who'd been out of town, was briefed on the Russian threat the next day. "It really affected me viscerally," the veteran intelligence chief recalled. "I've seen a lot of bad stuff over fifty years of intelligence, and I understood the magnitude of it—but the fact that Putin was orchestrating it was really disturbing to me. And the objective was to fundamentally undermine our system."

It was decided that Brennan should fire a shot across the Kremlin's bow. On August 4, the CIA director called his counterpart Alexander Bortnikov, the head of Russian intelligence agency FSB

(Federal Security Service). "I told him in no uncertain terms that we knew what they were up to, and if they continued to do it, all Americans would be outraged and they would pay a significant price," Brennan said. But Bortnikov blew off the CIA director's warning, denying Russian involvement.

The most immediate threat was to the electoral machinery of the 2016 U.S. election. "The president said, 'Look, most important is that we protect the integrity of the elections,'" recalled Haines. "So Lisa [Monaco] got tasked to do everything she could to figure out the vulnerabilities in the electoral infrastructure and how do we do something to defend them."

The assault on the election infrastructure had been far-reaching; the Russians had penetrated the electoral machinery in thirty-nine states (it would later turn out that all fifty states had been compromised). "My worst-case scenario was not that vote counts would be changed, but that voter registration databases would be tampered with," said Monaco. "So if John Williams shows up to vote, and says, 'I'm John Williams who lives at Green Street,' they say, 'Well, we don't have you here. We have John Williams at Smith Street.' And if that happens on a large scale, it's chaos."

Monaco and Homeland Security chief Jeh Johnson began reaching out to state electoral boards to warn them—and to offer federal help to fend off the expected attacks. But to their astonishment and frustration, this offer was about as warmly received by the secretaries of state as Brennan's phone call to Bortnikov.

"The then secretary of state from Georgia was really pushing back," said Monaco. "And that got the Republicans on the Hill really fired up." One option involved designating state electoral systems as "critical infrastructure," which would streamline federal assistance. Republicans on the Hill portrayed this as a diabolical Democratic takeover. "It would have helped the states, but there was a narrative here that it was a federal power grab," said Monaco. In the end, Republican secretaries of state preferred to disarm unilaterally against a Russian election threat rather than appear to cooperate with the Obama administration.

Obama had ruled out making a public statement about the crisis; he feared that would lend credence to Trump's claim that the election was rigged. A better option was to persuade the congressional leadership to issue a joint statement. Brennan agreed: "I thought it was critically important for us to let the Congress know. And I proposed reaching out to the Gang of Eight," the group of eight U.S. senators, four from each party, who are briefed on classified intelligence. But once again, when it came to sounding the alarm against the Russians, Obama's pleas would fall on deaf, partisan ears.

McDonough, Monaco, Haines, Johnson, and Clapper pressed their case on Capitol Hill. "We were trying to get [out] a bipartisan message of unity about helping the states to shore up their systems and to push back against Russians," said Monaco. "But that briefing almost immediately descended into a partisan scrum." Majority Leader Mitch McConnell accused them of pushing a pro-Obama plot. "There was questioning by McConnell about our motives. And questioning about the underlying intelligence. He said, 'You intelligence people shouldn't let yourselves get used.'" Haines found the experience deeply depressing. "It was really extraordinary because there was no earthly reason why we shouldn't have been able to come out with a bipartisan response, and a statement about what the Russians were doing."

Clapper was disgusted by the Republicans' apathy in the face of the Russian threat. And he concluded that their obstruction was driven by something uglier than mere partisanship. "It was resentment against Obama personally," he said. "And unfortunately, I think it was because he's black. No one ever overtly said that. But I think there was a lot of resentment among Republicans about that."

In early September, at a G20 summit in Hangzhou, China, Obama took Vladimir Putin aside. "We know what you're doing and if you go further, this is a serious crime," he warned him. "There will be consequences." Like Bortnikov, Putin denied everything.

What would those consequences be? Obama had warned the Russians publicly about the prospect of a U.S. cyber strike: "We've got more capacity than anybody, both offensively and defensively." Privately, Obama and his team knew that a U.S. cyber offensive could bring the Russian economy to its knees. "We had a whole series of meetings where we said, 'What are the options?'" said Haines. "'We're not sending the bombs in. What are we gonna do?'" James Clapper favored action. "You could do a lot of damage to the Russian economy if you essentially cut them off from the world financial system," he said. "We talked about it." I asked Clapper if he'd advocated such a cyberattack. "Yeah, oh, yeah," he replied. "And I wasn't alone."

"We had some very high-end options," said Michael Daniel, Obama's cybersecurity coordinator. "You could certainly do a tremendous amount of damage to the Russian economy. But one of the things that we don't fully understand is: What are the unintended consequences that come with that?" Brennan shared Daniel's concern: "In the physical world, there are established doctrines about how you escalate or de-escalate, but in the cyberwar realm very little of that. And so, yes, we could have rattled the cyber cages of the Russians. Would that have provoked a Russian response of some sort?"

As Michael Morell put it: "Everyone thinks this stuff is easy. *None* of this stuff is easy. President Obama was reluctant, because we're the ones who live in a glass house. We're the ones most vulnerable to cyberattacks. So number one, do you want to set a precedent that it's okay to do this? And number two, the servers that you're attacking and destroying aren't in Russia. The Russians are hopping from server to server around the world—trying to hide who they are. And so the server you're attacking might be in Switzerland. That would be an act of war against Switzerland."

Unwilling to risk the unknown consequences of a cyberattack, and unable to sway the congressional leadership, Obama and his team decided to make a public announcement: a clarion call to the nation about the imminent Russian threat.

At 3:30 p.m. on October 7, 2016, Johnson and Clapper released a public statement: "The U.S. Intelligence Community (USIC) is confident that the Russian Government directed the recent compromises of emails from US persons and institutions, including US political organizations. The recent disclosures . . . are intended to interfere with the US election process. . . . We believe, based on the scope and sensitivity of these efforts, that only Russia's senior-most officials could have authorized these activities."

On any ordinary day, such an announcement would have dominated the news. But October 7 was far from ordinary. Barely a half hour later, *The Washington Post* broke a different story: Donald Trump, the Republican nominee, had been captured on videotape bragging about sexually assaulting women. The tape was from a program called *Access Hollywood*. And just a few minutes later, as if to ensure that the intelligence community's warning would be buried, WikiLeaks released a tranche of emails that Russian hackers had stolen from the account of John Podesta, the Clinton campaign chairman. As Glenn Simpson and Peter Fritsch would later write in their book, *Crime in Progress*, it was as though "outside forces were doing what they could to trample on a story doing damage to Trump. The Russians were riding to Trump's rescue."

On election day, Clapper was traveling in Oman. Over lunch, at 11:31 a.m. his time—2:31 a.m. EST—he learned that the Associated Press had declared that Donald Trump would be the next president of the United States.

The Russians were euphoric. Applause broke out in the Duma, the state assembly, when the election result was announced. But Obama wasn't done with the Russians. He ordered new sanctions; expelled thirty-five known Russian spies; and closed two Russian-owned facilities in Maryland and New York. (Trump's incoming national security adviser, Michael Flynn, assured the Russian ambassador, Sergey Kislyak, that sanctions would soon be lifted.) Obama also ordered a thorough review of all the data the intelligence community could gather about the Russian election assault.

The results of the review, completed in early January 2017, were alarming. While the Russians hadn't tampered with the electoral machinery or altered the actual vote count, they'd been much more aggressive—and effective—than anyone had realized. It was right out of General Gerasimov's playbook: a multifaceted and ingenious digital disinformation campaign, using social media and other internet platforms to spread falsehoods and divide Americans from one another. The breadth and sophistication of the attack was something the intelligence community had never seen before.

Morell, who'd left the CIA a few months after Petraeus's departure, called the attacks "the political equivalent of 9/11." "At least in my time, there was no strategic warning that a nation might do this," he said. "No warning that they might use our social media as a weapon. If you go back and read all of the worldwide threat testimonies of directors and DNIs, there's always a section on cyber that talks about taking down electrical grids and financial systems. But you would never, ever see anything about what the Russians did this time. There was no strategic warning on that."

Did this amount to a major intelligence failure comparable to missing the Iranian revolution or the Arab Spring? Michael Daniel, the White House cybersecurity expert, thought so. "I think it was certainly a failure of imagination to actually think through all that could be done," he said. For his part, James Clapper was "disturbed and a little sickened to think the Russian efforts could have changed the outcome of the election." Clapper would later conclude that the Russian social media campaign *had* elected Trump (though he couldn't prove it); the ex-DNI believed that the campaign had swayed more than enough votes—eighty thousand in three states— to change the result. Brennan was less certain that the Russians had actually tipped the scales.

Alarmed as he was by the outcome, Brennan insisted it was too easy to blame the intelligence community: "As Jim Clapper likes to say, there are only two things in Washington: policy successes and intelligence failures." But it was hard to believe that the Jesuit-trained "cop from Queens" didn't partly blame himself. Brennan couldn't stomach the idea of Trump as president, and he wouldn't be quiet about it. "I don't think he is on the payroll of the Russians," he said. "But is he an asset to the Russians? Absolutely."

CHAPTER TWELVE

"I would like you to do us a favor though."

Mike Pompeo, Gina Haspel, and Donald Trump

Donald Trump was seething. It was Saturday, January 21, 2017, and Trump was riding in "the Beast," the presidential limousine, winding his way on Route 123 toward Langley, Virginia. Earlier that morning, the president, sworn in less than twenty-four hours before, had called Reince Priebus, his White House chief of staff, at home. *The Washington Post* had published photos showing Trump's inaugural crowd dwarfed by that of his predecessor, Barack Obama. Trump was livid. "This story is *bullshit!*" he screamed. Priebus had tried to talk the president off the ledge, but there was no way to tamp down his fury; the press was his mortal enemy and would do anything to deny his legitimacy. Now Trump was headed toward CIA headquarters, an institution he despised even more than the mainstream media.

Richard Nixon thought the CIA was populated by elite liberals who opposed his agenda. But Nixon's contempt for the "clowns out at Langley" paled in comparison to Trump's. The forty-fifth president had attacked the intelligence community as a hostile "deep state" that was out to get him. His hatred of the intelligence services was stoked by their conclusion that the Russians had intervened in the election on Trump's behalf. "These are the same people that said Saddam Hussein had weapons of mass destruction," he said. Never mind that Trump was for the Iraq War before claiming to be against it. The presidential candidate rejected the unanimous finding of the U.S. intelligence agencies, declaring during his first debate with Hillary Clinton: "It could be Russia, but it could also be China. It could also be lots of other people. It also could be somebody sitting on their bed that weighs 400 pounds, okay?"

The simmering feud between Trump and the intelligence community had come to a full boil on January 6, 2017. That afternoon, CIA director John Brennan, Director of National Intelligence James Clapper, and FBI director James Comey paid a visit to the president-elect at Trump Tower in New York City. While Trump's aides listened, Clapper briefed him on the intelligence community's comprehensive review of the Russian assault on the election. When he was finished, Clapper said there was one other matter—something for the FBI director and president to discuss. "Do you want us to stay or to do this alone?" asked Priebus. "I was thinking the two of us," said Comey.

When the others departed, Comey briefed Trump on the contents of a document known as the Steele dossier. The salacious findings, compiled by a former intelligence officer of Britain's MI6, had been widely shared, though not yet published, in the press; Comey was presenting them to the president-elect not because they were corroborated but as a heads-up. The upshot was that Vladimir Putin allegedly possessed compromising information, or *kompromat*, on Trump—involving not only business dealings with the Russians but tawdry escapades with prostitutes at a Moscow hotel. Without losing his composure, Trump denied everything: "Do I look like someone who needs hookers?" he asked Comey. But alone with Priebus and his aides afterward, Trump exploded. "It was a shakedown!" he snapped. Things went downhill from there. On January 11, Trump compared the leaking of the dossier, which he falsely blamed on the intelligence community, to the propagandizing of Hitler's henchmen. "I think it's a disgrace . . . that's something that Nazi Germany would have done and did do."

But that was ten days ago; no one knew what would happen today when Trump set foot on the CIA campus. After all, a visit to Langley on the first full day of his presidency could be seen as a sign of respect; maybe Trump would rise to the occasion and extend an olive branch to the men and women who would be his eyes and ears for the next four years. (At least, Priebus hoped so.) The backdrop fit that type of gesture: Trump would be speaking to the workforce on hallowed ground, in front of the Memorial Wall.

Arriving at Langley, Trump climbed out of the Beast and was greeted by the CIA's acting director, Meroe Park. (Director John Brennan and DNI Jim Clapper had resigned the day before.) Moments later, standing in front of 117 stars etched in marble, each representing an officer killed in the line of duty, the president addressed a throng of CIA employees:

I want to thank everybody. Very, very special people. And it is true: This is my first stop. Officially. We're not talking about the [inaugural] balls, and we're not talking about even the speeches. Although, they did treat me nicely on that speech yesterday.

A smattering of nervous laughter came from the crowd.

The wall behind me is very, very special. We've been touring for quite a while, and I'll tell you what . . . we really appreciate what you've done in terms of showing us something very special. . . .

That was Trump's only mention of the Memorial Wall. Now he took a veiled shot at Barack Obama, Hillary Clinton, and John Brennan, the former director.

I know maybe sometimes you haven't gotten the backing that you've wanted, and you're going to get so much backing. Maybe you're going to say, "Please don't give us so much backing, Mr. President, please, we don't need that much backing." But you're going to have that . . . probably, almost everybody in this room voted for me, but I will not ask you to raise your hands if you did.

There was some clapping from the front rows, where a gaggle of White House aides was seated. The senior CIA leadership sat in silence.

. . . as you know, I have a running war with the media. They are among the most dishonest human beings on earth. And they sort of made it sound like I had a feud with the intelligence community. And I just want to let you know, the reason you're the number one stop is exactly the opposite—exactly.

Next Trump talked about numbers—not of CIA officers killed in the line of duty but of people who attended his inaugural.

> ... we had a massive field of people. You saw them. Packed. I get up this morning, I turn on one of the networks, and they show an empty field. I say, wait a minute, I made a speech. I looked out, the field was—it looked like a million, million and a half people.

Finally, Trump denounced a *Time* reporter for writing a story, later retracted, that he'd removed a bust of Martin Luther King from the Oval Office. Trump also claimed to have been on the cover of *Time* more than anyone else in history. (This was false even if you counted the phony *Time* covers hanging at Trump resorts.)

> So I only like to say that because I love honesty. I like honest report-ing. I will tell you the final time: Although I will say it, when you let in your thousands of other people that had been trying to come in, because I am coming back. We may have to get you a larger room.

More light applause and nervous laughter.

> We may have to get you a larger room.

It was a bizarre performance: maudlin, egocentric, mendacious, tone-deaf—delivered on the CIA's most sacred ground. A veteran agency analyst summed it up: "What should have been a celebration turned into a desecration."

To be sure, there were Trump supporters among the CIA crowd that morning; after all, they'd volunteered to come in on a Satur-day to see him. But much of the workforce was, in the words of one officer, "angered, disgusted, and troubled." John Brennan, who didn't attend but watched on cable television, called it "a despicable display of self-aggrandizement."

At least Trump had someone in mind to replace Brennan as CIA director.

Michael Richard Pompeo, a fifty-three-year old former Tea Party congressman from Kansas, was an unlikely choice to head Trump's

CIA. A backer of Florida senator Marco Rubio during the campaign, Pompeo had opposed the New York real estate tycoon, calling him an "authoritarian"—and vowing, in a speech delivered in Wichita on March 5, 2016: "Marco Rubio will never demean our soldiers by ordering them to do things that are inconsistent with our Constitution." This was a reference to Trump's boast that he could order soldiers to commit war crimes and they'd obey.

But when Trump clinched the Republican nomination, Pompeo abruptly changed his tune, endorsing the insurgent nominee. And after his election victory, Pompeo beat a path to Trump Tower, joining aspirants for a big job in the new administration. He'd once been a conservative internationalist, opposed to the new president's "America First" approach to the world. Now, even among the most obsequious Trump flatterers, Pompeo stood out. As a former American ambassador put it to *New Yorker* writer Susan Glasser: "He's like a heat-seeking missile for Trump's ass."

The affection was mutual. "I met Mike Pompeo, and it was the only guy I met," Trump gushed about his selection process for CIA director. "I didn't want to meet anybody else. I met him and I said, 'He is so good. Number one in his class at West Point.'" Pompeo's CV *was* impressive. After West Point he'd joined the Army and served five years as a tank commander in West Germany before enrolling at Harvard Law School. Upon graduation, Pompeo moved to Washington, D.C., and joined a prestigious law firm. In the 1990s he divorced his wife and moved to Kansas, where he started a company called Thayer Aerospace, an aviation manufacturer.

In Kansas, Pompeo met a local bank vice president named Susan Mostrous; he married her in 2000 and adopted her son from a previous marriage. He cultivated wealthy patrons, including the Koch brothers, and joined Wichita's Presbyterian Eastminster Church. (Pompeo kept an open Bible on his desk.) In 2010, he ran for Congress in a heavily Republican district and won. He was overweight and wore ill-fitting, boxy suits. "Beauty and the Beast," Trump shouted out when Pompeo was onstage with his daughter Ivanka. But he was charming, self-confident, and brash. As Pompeo's defeated congressional opponent told writer Glasser, "I give him massive respect, the way he mapped Wichita power, the way he mapped D.C. power, the way he mapped Trump."

But would Pompeo serve as an honest broker of intelligence? In Congress he'd been a partisan zealot; his relentless pursuit of a baseless Benghazi conspiracy had raised eyebrows at Langley. And even by Washington standards his ambition was off the charts. Would he serve the CIA or Trump?

As the new presidency began, it was an open question: Would Trump even bother to sit for CIA briefings? Given his hostility toward the agency, and his Twitter-sized attention span, it was anyone's guess. During the presidential transition, Trump had disdained regular agency briefings, ducking them whenever possible. His low regard for the CIA's presentations was reinforced by his mercurial, conspiratorial political strategist Steve Bannon. On the morning of Trump's Langley visit, Bannon sat in on Trump's President's Daily Briefing. "I was underwhelmed," he told me. "If you read the *Financial Times* of London, *The Economist*, three or four defense blogs, and *Aerospace Week & Space Technology*, you have essentially ninety percent of it." Of course, Trump read none of those things. Bannon went on: "It's five percent gossip on how fucked up guys are and how kinky they are and five percent great aerial photos—missile canisters pulling out. Other than that, you've got it. I mean it! We're paying a trillion dollars for this shit?"

Trump would be a unique challenge for any briefer. To be sure, every president consumes intelligence in his own way: Barack Obama received his PDB on his iPad and read it thoroughly, making detailed notes and queries. Ronald Reagan preferred watching movies to reading the PDB—so the CIA created short videos for him on world leaders. But there'd never been a president like Trump. He didn't listen. He didn't read. He was uninformed. During the campaign it was clear that he'd never heard of the nuclear triad. And he was incurious. He thought he knew everything worth knowing.

A senior intelligence official described one of Trump's counterterrorism briefings, which hasn't been reported before. "We were talking about surveilling domestic terrorism suspects, and at some point he just said, 'Why wouldn't we just deport them?' And we had to say, 'Well, we're talking about people who are U.S. citizens, sir. So no, deporting them isn't really an option.'" Trump seemed confused, so the official explained: "We have a criminal justice system, we can charge them with material support. FBI and Justice Department can put 'em away for a long time. But no, they're not just foreigners that can all be thrown out of the country."

"That was kind of an 'Oh' moment," this official told me. "It was just discovering: 'Okay, he just didn't know.' Something I wouldn't have thought had to be explained. But I should make no assumptions, apparently."

Trump's regular briefer was Ted Gistaro, a career CIA officer on loan to the Office of the Director of National Intelligence, where he oversaw the PDB. He was, by all accounts, a straight shooter. "He's the quintessential career intelligence professional—in all the best senses of the word," said Nick Rasmussen, head of the National Counterterrorism Center, a holdover from the Obama administration. "I couldn't have told you a personal view he had. I couldn't have told you if he thought the Redskins sucked." John McLaughlin, the former deputy director under George Tenet, also knew Gistaro, and thought if anyone could deal with Trump, it was he. "He's a pleasant person," he said. "He's not a showboat in any way. He's very matter-of-fact. He has a sense of humor. But I wouldn't want to be Trump's briefer."

A bungled briefing could be calamitous. Trump was so impulsive that he might demand action on anything. "First, you expect him to erupt now and then," said McLaughlin. "And you don't want to put him in a situation where you're giving him something half-baked that could stimulate an action. This is true of all presidents in some degree. You're there to help them understand something, and to not put them in a position where they're going to go off half-cocked. And that must be true ten times over with Trump."

The slightest misstep could also end the CIA's access. Trump could cancel the briefings—and the agency's influence on decision-making—on the slightest provocation. "He had to be very careful, and he was," said a senior intelligence official of Trump's briefer, "because he held within his hands the intelligence community's reputation with the president."

The biggest challenge was telling Trump anything that contradicted his beliefs. "I think it's dangerous when the intelligence community is afraid of sending bad news to the guy who needs to hear it most," said Steven Hall, former head of the CIA's Russia operations. "I believe it's actually dangerous when the PDB briefers are either told ahead of time or when they arrive, 'let's not say this because he's just going to get pissed off or he's going to blow up or it's not going to go well.'" How would a briefer tell Trump when he's wrong? "I think you just tell him," said McLaughlin. "But you have to have built a personal relationship with him. You have to have somehow established that you're not trying to subvert his presidency, which is how I think he feels about almost everyone."

From the beginning it was clear that Trump wanted Pompeo around. Partly it was chemistry. The president was bored by his national security adviser, H. R. McMaster, who gave long Power-Point presentations and dressed, Trump said, like "a beer salesman." And partly it was familiarity. Trump didn't know his CIA briefer—so why listen to him? Chief of staff Priebus called Pompeo. "The boss is much more likely to do it if you're there," he said. But Pompeo at first resisted attending the daily briefing. Finally, Bannon got into the act. "I called Pompeo and I said, 'I know it's going to be a pain in the ass, and this is going to fuck your life up, but every day you're in town, you have to be here and give the brief.'"

Pompeo got the message. "He realized that the only way the agency was going to get information to the president was if he delivered it personally," said Bruce Riedel, the former CIA Middle East analyst. "The president's not going to listen to a briefer. He'll listen to a fellow politician." The second week, Pompeo showed up—and from that day on he became a kind of Trump whisperer, attuned to the president's volatile mood swings and limited attention span.

But few thought Pompeo was an honest broker. "He paid a price for his closeness to Trump," said John Walcott, a writer for *Time* and veteran CIA observer. "What did Pompeo *not* tell Trump? I think you'll find a pretty significant level of disappointment among the analysts about whether their views were fully and forcefully presented." Indeed, Pompeo often lapsed into his "heat-seeking missile" mode, telling Trump what he wanted to hear, as when he repeatedly and falsely declared in public that Iran was in violation of Obama's nuclear deal. Pompeo often brought someone else along to the presidential briefings: Gina Haspel, the deputy director. When Pompeo was out of town, Haspel took his place. "That's how Gina came to be known to the president," said a White House official. "She was down there often when Pompeo was away traveling." Luckily, on her first encounter with Trump, Haspel avoided Fiona Hill's fate; not realizing Dr. Hill was the NSC's top Russia expert, Trump told her to fetch him a cup of coffee.

Pompeo and his team tried to keep things simple. Riedel, then a senior fellow at the Brookings Institution, spoke often with the CIA director. "Trump would not read things, did not like to be read to, did not like to be talked to," Riedel said. "But he *would* look at pictures—and if you showed him the right pictures, you could move him to do things." The briefers gave Trump a kind of show-and-tell with photographs. "The art of the brief was pictures," said Riedel. "Pictures, pictures, and pictures." Trump understood the pictures better when they showed familiar things, preferably iconic New York City or Florida landmarks. So in an effort to help him grasp the scale of North Korea's nuclear arms program, they built a model of the kingdom's underground nuclear facility and put a miniature Statue of Liberty inside it.

Pictures were a decisive factor in the administration's first international crisis: the chemical weapons attack in Syria. On April 4, 2017, three months into Trump's presidency, Syrian dictator Bashar al-Assad's forces launched a deadly sarin gas attack on civilians in the town of Khan Sheikhoun. The assault was horrific, killing dozens— including women, children, and babies. Trump was shown photographs and video of gruesome scenes: children choking, their mouths foaming, and the despair of grief-stricken parents.

The president was galvanized. "Let's fucking kill them!" he said. "Let's go in. Let's kill the fucking lot of them!" At one point he asked Pompeo to prepare a covert operation to eliminate Assad and his government. Meanwhile, Defense Secretary James Mattis slow-walked the president's order to kill everyone; instead of an all-out attack aimed at toppling the regime, a more practical strike was ordered: fifty-nine Tomahawk cruise missiles aimed at Syrian military bases.

Trump believed the CIA had been emasculated under Obama. Director Brennan had imposed strict rules on the Directorate of Operations. ("Some of the country's greatest heroes were there," Brennan told me, "but there were also people who thought the end justifies the means.") Now Pompeo declared that the gloves were coming off; operatives would be left alone to do their jobs. A retired senior intelligence official spoke to a friend in the DO: "I asked, 'So how are things going?' He said, 'It's great. We can do what we want to do. We don't have a lot of handwringing. We don't have to go down to the White House, or if we do, they all kind of approve it.' "

"One of my colleagues was a longtime CIA guy," recalled Rasmussen, the NCTC head. "And when Trump won and Pompeo was named director, he said, 'It's not Make America Great Again, it's Make CIA Great Again.' " That meant "more willingness to put more people closer to harm's way, to work with the Syrian rebels, or to spot for Iraqi forces in Mosul as they're doing bombing campaigns. Or being closer to the fight. It wasn't as if they went from zero to sixty, it was that they went from sixty to eighty."

Whether this made the CIA great or not depended on your point of view. During the campaign Trump had said that the U.S. should kill terrorists *and take out their families*. Early on, Trump was shown video of a lethal drone strike on a terrorist's lair; the drone operator waited before pulling the trigger until innocents cleared the area. Trump seemed baffled by this. "Why did you wait?" he asked. "Because killing noncombatants is a crime!" one CIA officer said to me privately. While some at the agency welcomed Trump's anything-goes ethos, others were appalled by his complete lack of empathy.

And there was something else that troubled many at the CIA: Trump's love affair with the Russians.

You didn't have to be a spy to know that Putin and Trump were on the same page. There'd been more than a hundred contacts between the campaign and Russian officials. There was nothing normal about this coziness with Russia—from the candidate's televised plea to hack Hillary Clinton's emails; to attempting to create a secret back channel to Moscow; to meeting at Trump Tower with a Russian attorney promising dirt on Clinton; to National Security Adviser Michael Flynn's secret talks about lifting sanctions with Ambassador Sergey Kislyak.

Three months into his presidency, on May 9, 2017, Trump abruptly fired FBI director James Comey. The Justice Department initially said it was because of his handling of Hillary Clinton's emails. But then, in an interview with NBC News's Lester Holt, the president came clean: He wanted to be rid of "this Russia thing."

The very next day, Trump invited Russian foreign minister Sergey Lavrov and Ambassador Kislyak to the Oval Office. Trump greeted them like old fraternity pals, backslapping and joking, and said of Comey: "I just fired the head of the FBI. He was crazy, a real nut job." During the visit, the president revealed to the Russians details of an ISIS plot involving laptop computers on aircraft. The intelligence, from an allied spy service, was considered so sensitive it was classified as "code word" intelligence. Its disclosure could have compromised sources and methods. (Indeed, Trump's cavalier sharing of these secrets may have been a factor in the CIA's decision to exfiltrate a valuable Russian asset in the Kremlin, a story to be told later in this chapter.) Bizarrely, Trump's powwow with Lavrov and Kislyak was captured not by American media outlets, which had been barred from the meeting, but by the Russian news service, TASS. Just to make the whole episode more outrageous, it was later learned that as his Russian guests departed, Trump assured them that he didn't care if they interfered in the 2020 election.

But it was Trump's meetings with Vladimir Putin that truly raised eyebrows at Langley. The first encounter between the two leaders was on July 7, 2017, during a G20 economic summit meeting in Hamburg, Germany. The two men met for more than two hours; afterward Trump confiscated the interpreter's notes and told her not to brief anyone on the discussion. That evening, at a dinner, Trump pulled up a chair beside Putin and had a private chat shared only with an interpreter. Their next meeting took place on November 11, 2017, during a "pull-aside" at a meeting of the Asia-Pacific Economic Cooperation forum in Da Nang, Vietnam. The two men chatted, and afterward Trump declared that Putin had denied any election interference: "I really believe that when he tells me that, he means it."

All of this was just a warm-up for a diplomatic disaster still to come, when Trump and Putin would hold a summit meeting in Helsinki, Finland.

Trump was a human wrecking ball, shattering norms. In previous administrations, an interagency process ensured that decisions were made with the best available intelligence, and careful deliberation. In the Obama White House, the president attended a weekly counterterrorism meeting on "Terror Tuesdays." As one participant put it: "John Brennan would say: 'Mr. President, here's the whole range of things that we're worried about from a terrorism perspective on threats.' Then he would guide the principals around the table in the discussion of who's doing what. 'So, Janet Napolitano, what is Homeland Security doing to lock down the harbor in New York City on New Year's Eve? Bob Mueller, what is the FBI doing? We've got this many more agents working overtime and more dogs than you can shake a stick at.'" These principals meetings were the most effective way to get agencies to coordinate and prepare for the worst.

Under Trump, the meetings stopped.

The breakdown of process could be seen in Trump's ardent courtship of Saudi Arabia and its crown prince, Mohammad bin Salman, or MBS. On May 20, 2017, Trump touched down in Riyadh on his first overseas trip as president; it was a lavish, over-the-top production—with gigantic Trump portraits plastered on the side of buildings, capped off by a surreal scene in which Trump and his Saudi hosts laid hands on a glowing orb. It was a romance fueled by Trump's hatred of Iran, his love of arms sales, his Saudi business ties, and his indifference to human rights (on this score the Saudis were a big problem). The trip was the brainchild not of Trump's secretary of state, Rex Tillerson, but of his son-in-law, Jared Kushner. "Promoting Mohammad Bin Salman as this great reformer who was going to change not just Saudi Arabia but the entire region, this all came from Jared," said a senior intelligence official.

Like Bannon, Kushner was critical of the CIA; he thought the President's Daily Brief was too focused on terrorists, and not enough on trade and economics. But Kushner and his wife, Ivanka, were big fans of Mike Pompeo. And the feeling was mutual; with his keen antennae for power, the CIA director had carefully cultivated Trump's daughter and son-in-law. When it came to cozying up to Saudi Arabia, Pompeo was all-in. On his first overseas trip as CIA director, he went to Riyadh and awarded Saudi intelligence chief Muhammad bin Nayef the George Tenet Medal, for counterterrorism. "There was no George Tenet Medal," said a former senior intelligence official. "It's an idea they came up with on the plane."

"It was an enticing story, that this young man, MBS, was going to change the kingdom, the ripple effects would be so beneficial," said Bruce Riedel. "But you needed to take a closer look at the crown prince before you bought into it." MBS was young and cosmopolitan and promised reforms; but he was also immature and ruthless in stamping out his opponents; his thuggish security force rivaled the Shah of Iran's notorious SAVAK of the late 1970s. Before long, MBS would drag the CIA into an international scandal: the vicious murder and dismemberment of a *Washington Post* columnist, and U.S. permanent resident, named Jamal Khashoggi.

Charlie Allen, the veteran analyst who often made comparisons across decades, thought Donald Trump's embrace of MBS was reminiscent of Jimmy Carter's blind loyalty to the Shah just before the Iranian revolution. "I understand the need for Saudi support against the Iranians, but we had better not repeat what we did in the late 1970s, because that turned out to be disastrous," said Allen. "We did not do the collection of intelligence on the Shah that we should have. MBS is sort of childish too. Don't we learn from history?"

But MBS was a slow-simmering scandal; the more immediate threat—for Trump and his CIA director—was North Korea's Kim Jong Un.

In his two-hour Oval Office meeting with Trump after the election, Barack Obama tried to forewarn the president-elect: North Korea would be his most difficult challenge. Kim Jong Un had made alarming strides in the development of both missiles and nuclear weapons; he'd soon have a ballistic missile with a nuclear warhead that could reach the U.S. mainland.

On July 3, 2017, Pyongyang tested its first intercontinental ballistic missile (ICBM); it flew only 578 miles but U.S. intelligence officials believed that with a flatter trajectory it might be capable of reaching the United States. Trump was briefed that night, but he dismissed the report. The test was a hoax, he said; the North Koreans weren't capable of launching such a weapon. How did he *know* that? the president was asked. Because Putin told me, Trump replied.

Denuclearizing North Korea was an exceedingly complex challenge; almost all the options were bad, the CIA briefers told Trump. A preemptive strike could trigger a retaliation that would kill tens of millions of South Koreans and thousands of American troops. Negotiating with North Korea was difficult; the agency assessed that the hermit kingdom's national identity was inextricably linked to nuclear weapons. Kim Jong Un was unlikely to give them up. The young leader was also volatile and unpredictable. Provoking him could be dangerous.

A month after North Korea's missile test, at his golf club in Bed-minster, New Jersey, Trump lashed out. "North Korea best not make any more threats to the United States," he told reporters. "They will be met with fire and fury like the world has never seen." This attempt to intimidate Kim Jong Un immediately failed. Hours later, North Korea warned that it would create "an enveloping fire" around Guam, home to a U.S. military base.

Trump's summits with the North Korean dictator were equally half-baked, and ultimately unsuccessful. In June 2018, Trump met with Kim Jong Un in Singapore in an elaborately choreographed photo-op that produced no concrete agreements. A year and half later—despite a follow-up summit in Hanoi; an exchange of "love letters"; and Trump's boast that "there is No Longer a Nuclear Threat"—the North Koreans hadn't only failed to denuclearize; they'd bolstered their arsenal of missiles and bomb-ready nuclear material. By January 2020, North Korea was preparing for another test of an intercontinental ballistic missile with the potential of reaching the United States.

In March 2017, Dan Coats had become the nation's fifth Director of National Intelligence. A former ambassador to Germany and sixteen-year senator from Indiana, Coats had been a member of the Senate Select Committee on Intelligence and was a friend of his fellow Hoosier, Vice President Mike Pence. Knowledgeable and even-keeled, Coats was a smooth operator who avoided ruffling feathers. He often attended the president's daily briefing, where he was careful to avoid subjects that aroused Trump's ire. But Coats would eventually earn Trump's wrath by contradicting him in public on Russia, Iran, North Korea, and global warming. Like almost everyone else who dared to tell the truth, he'd eventually head for the door.

By early 2018, Rex Tillerson's time was up. Trump had never met the ExxonMobil chairman before he hired him as secretary of state in a meeting at Trump Tower during the transition. Tillerson had been unable to strike that balance of arrogance and obsequiousness that was Pompeo's specialty; in exasperation, Tillerson had called Trump a "moron" in front of White House staffers. Most damaging, he'd made enemies of Jared and Ivanka by ignoring them; they couldn't even get him on the phone. (It was hard to say whom Jared and Ivanka disliked more: Tillerson or John Kelly, Trump's second chief of staff, who tried to restrict their access to the Oval Office.) On March 13, Trump announced that Tillerson had been fired, and that Mike Pompeo would be his new secretary of state. Pompeo's replacement as CIA director would be Gina Haspel.

Gina Cheri Haspel, sixty-two, had spent most of her career trying to be invisible. Born in Ashland, Kentucky, she grew up an Air Force brat, one of five children, and went to high school in the United Kingdom. Back in the States, she graduated from the University of Kentucky at Louisville and then studied to become a paralegal at Northeastern University in Massachusetts. In 1977 she married an Army officer named Jeff Haspel; they divorced just before she joined the CIA in 1985.

Stationed first in Ethiopia—and later in Turkey, Central Asia, and Azerbaijan—Haspel thrived as a covert operative. "She knew what the hell she was talking about," said Steve Hall, former head of the CIA's Russia operations. "She was very, very, very deep in all the different disciplines, but also . . . reserved is probably too strong of a word. She just had this quiet projection of capacity and competence." That quiet competence served her well in two tours as chief of station in London, where she worked closely with her counterparts at MI6. It was the high-profile post Haspel's mentor Jose Rodriguez had dared her to set her sights on.

None of this would matter if Haspel couldn't get along with Trump. Fortunately, from her frequent visits with Pompeo and Coats, Trump seemed comfortable with her low-key, no-nonsense demeanor. The question was, would Haspel be too eager to please the president?

If confirmed, Haspel would be only the third director—after Richard Helms and William Colby—to rise from the ranks of the Directorate of Operations. (Robert Gates and John Brennan had come up as analysts.) More significant, of course, she'd be the first woman to head the world's most powerful intelligence agency.

But Haspel's confirmation was far from certain. Donald McGahn, the White House counsel, was worried. The hearings were sure to revive the controversy over the CIA's enhanced interrogation techniques; after all, Haspel had been chief of the Thailand black site where EITs had first been used. A former ACLU official called her "quite literally a war criminal." The executive director of the Center for Constitutional Rights said in a statement, "Gina Haspel should be prosecuted, not promoted."

Haspel downplayed her participation in EITs at the Thailand site; she insisted she hadn't been present when Abu Zubaydah was waterboarded. But she'd been there when another Al Qaeda terrorist, Abd al-Rahim Nasiri, was waterboarded three times. And she'd been a key player in the destruction of the infamous "torture tapes."

To Trump, all this was a plus. During his campaign he'd famously pledged to "bring back waterboarding, . . . and a hell of a lot worse." In February of 2016 he declared: "Torture works. Okay, folks? Believe me, it works." The truth was, Trump *loved* the idea of nominating someone who supported "torture." In fact, according to the news website Axios, the president asked Haspel point-blank about waterboarding. In Trump's telling, Haspel said she was one hundred percent certain that the brutal technique worked. "He seemed impressed with how sure she was about something so controversial," said the Axios source, "that she did not bat an eye, did not sugarcoat it."

If true, Haspel was telling Trump what he wanted to hear, not what the evidence showed. The fact was that waterboarding worked only rarely. After all, it was sleep deprivation, not waterboarding, that had loosened Abu Zubaydah's tongue. (Defenders of the technique insisted that waterboarding *had* caused Khalid Sheikh Mohammed to signal fellow detainees not to speak about Osama bin Laden's courier; this confirmed to his CIA captors the significance of the courier.) If Haspel was being truthful, she might also have told Trump that the very idea of waterboarding was now moot—because it was illegal; and the agency was no longer in the business of detaining prisoners.

Haspel's confirmation hearings before the Senate Select Committee on Intelligence began harmlessly enough. The nominee insisted she was a "typical, middle-class American" who stumbled into the exciting world of spying. She had a knack for the "nuts and bolts" of her profession, acquiring secrets "in brush passes, dead drops, or in meetings in dusty alleys of Third World capitals." (A brush pass is a way of secretly exchanging information when walking near someone.) But then the session turned contentious. A protester had to be hauled out of the chamber, chanting "Waterboarding is torture! Bloody Gina!" The questioning turned to Haspel's activities at the Thailand black site.

Senator Kamala Harris, Democrat of California, asked: "The president has asserted that torture works. Do you agree with that statement?" Haspel replied: "Senator, I don't believe that torture works." But there was a "but" coming. Haspel added: "Valuable information" *was* obtained from Al Qaeda operatives who were subjected to the techniques. "Is that a yes?" the senator asked. "No, it's not a yes," Haspel replied. "We got valuable information from debriefing Al Qaeda detainees, and I don't think it's knowable whether interrogation techniques played a role in that." It was the same dodgy answer that John Brennan had given when asked about the effectiveness of EITs: It was unknowable what information detainees *might* have given up if subjected to conventional techniques alone.

Haspel concluded with a promise. "Having served in that tumultuous time, I can offer you my personal commitment, clearly and without reservation, that under my leadership, on my watch, CIA will not restart a detention and interrogation program." Virginia senator Mark Warner asked Haspel what she'd do if Donald Trump asked her to do something "morally questionable." She replied:

Senator, my father's watching today. He served thirty-three years in the Air Force. My parents gave me a very strong moral compass. I support the higher moral standard that this country has decided to hold itself to. . . . I'll tell you this, I would not put CIA officers at risk by asking them to undertake risky, controversial activity again.

On May 17, 2018, Gina Haspel was confirmed by the Senate as CIA director by a vote of 54–45.

For her swearing-in as CIA director, on May 21, Donald Trump returned to Langley for the first time since his disastrous tirade at the Memorial Wall. This time he was on his best behavior, reading from a script. When introduced, Haspel received a loud ovation from her CIA colleagues. "Our enemies will take note," Trump declared. "Gina's tough, she's strong, and when it comes to defending America, Gina will never, ever back down. I know her. I've spent a lot of time with her."

Haspel's first day as director was one for the history books. Not only was she the first woman to run the agency but most of her principal deputies were female: Cynthia "Didi" Rapp, deputy director for analysis; Elizabeth Kimber, deputy director for operations; and Dawn Meyerriecks, the deputy director for science and technology. In the months ahead, Haspel would keep a low profile. While Dan Coats and the DNI's briefer trekked to the White House for daily briefings, Haspel would stay at Langley. She'd make few public appearances and avoid reporters at all costs. Interviews, she told colleagues, always turned out one of two ways: bad or disastrous.

"I wouldn't have made her CIA director," said Bruce Riedel. "I think someone so deeply involved in the torture business and the cover-up of the torture business should never have been nominated." John McLaughlin was more sanguine. "I think she's probably just the right person to be doing that job right now," he said. "This is not a self-promoter; she is all about business. All about professionalism. All about mission. And that's just the right person to have there now because I think she can speak the truth—and do it in a flat, matter-of-fact way that makes it hard for people to get their hand around her. And she's unflappable."

But there was one thing that would test Haspel's unflappability: Trump's suspicious fondness for Vladimir Putin.

Since his meeting with the Russian leader at Hamburg, Trump had been agitating for a summit with Putin. It finally took place on July 16, 2018, in Helsinki, Finland. Once again, the president wanted no witnesses. While his advisers sat outside, Trump and Putin disappeared into a private room at the Presidential Palace. Scheduled for ninety minutes, the talk lasted two hours. No notetakers were permitted and no communiqué was issued afterward. That was strange enough; even more bizarre was the news conference, televised worldwide, that followed.

The two leaders stood side by side at separate lecterns on a flag-draped stage. Putin, smirking and confident, was in command, crisply fielding questions. Though he was a head taller, Trump, by contrast, seemed almost cowed. Then came a question from Jonathan Lemire of the Associated Press:

> *President Trump, just now President Putin denied having anything to do with election interference in 2016. Every U.S. intelligence agency has concluded that Russia did. My first question for you, sir, is who do you believe? My second question is, would you now, with the whole world watching, tell President Putin—would you denounce what happened in 2016 and would you warn him never to do it again?*

Trump launched into a tangled monologue about the missing server from the Democratic National Headquarters. Why hadn't the FBI seized it? Trump demanded. Where is the server? Finally, he circled back to the question of who'd interfered in the 2016 U.S. election: "My people came to me, they came to me, Dan Coats came to me and some others, they think it's Russia. I have President Putin, he just said it's not Russia. I will say this, I don't see any reason why it *would* be. . . . President Putin was extremely strong and powerful in his denial today."

Current and former CIA officials were dumbfounded. "This was alarming on so many levels it was hard to keep track," said Steven Hall. Head of the CIA's Russia operations for three decades until he retired in 2015, Hall had been invited to attend the Helsinki conference. "Then my wife reminded me that Finland has a long land border with Russia and that the Russians knew who I was—and about my attempting to do as much damage to their national security as possible—and God forbid I get hustled into the back of a van or something."

Hall wasn't kidding. Making matters worse, in his private meeting with Trump—and the subsequent news conference—Putin had suggested that former Obama administration officials such as former Russian ambassador Michael McFaul be sent to Russia to help "investigate" what happened in 2016. Trump thought this was "an incredible offer." In truth, the proposal was absurd. The Americans might be arrested or disappear. "Vladimir Putin said, 'Yeah, maybe you could provide some of your senior officers who have [been in charge of Russia policy], and we'll send them back to Moscow for questioning by the FSB,'" Hall said sarcastically. That a U.S. president would entertain this idea disgusted him.

What *had* Trump and Putin talked about? No one knew. To make matters even more surreal, the two leaders had reached "agreements," the Kremlin later said. But U.S. officials knew only what they could glean from electronic SIGINT interceptions of Russian officials.

"Helsinki, for me, was a real watershed moment," said Hall. "I remember distinctly watching that press conference and just feeling sick about it and thinking they actually *do* have something on him. What better explains his approach to this? I couldn't think of anything."

Other CIA veterans, active and retired, were thinking the same thing. "His actions with Russia are incredible," said one. "Most intelligence professionals think that Putin has some sort of compromising information on him."

A few weeks after the Helsinki summit, I called Leon Panetta, the former director. He was still baffled by Trump's behavior. How was it possible that no one in the U.S. government knew what Trump and Putin had discussed? "I'll tell you what," he told me, "if I had been CIA director, I would have made damn sure we got an audio recording of what was said in that meeting." Did Gina Haspel have a recording? Does the National Security Agency? That is unknown.

The Helsinki fiasco raised another troubling question. "The CIA is supposed to recruit spies inside of Russia, preferably as high as possible, to steal secrets and to find out what's going on," said Hall. "So what if this president comes to the head of the CIA and says, 'I want you to give me your top five Russian spies? I want their true names. I want their addresses, and I want their telephone numbers.' What do you do when the president himself asks you something that he's legally entitled to ask but you know he shouldn't be asking, and you know you probably shouldn't tell him? How do you deal with that?"

This was far from academic. After Trump's Oval Office meeting with Foreign Minister Lavrov and Ambassador Kislyak in May 2017—in which the president inappropriately shared top secret "code word" intelligence—anything was possible, even this worst-case scenario: What if Trump were to betray the identity of one of the CIA's most treasured assets—the CIA mole inside Putin's Kremlin?

Of all the CIA's "hard targets," the Kremlin was among the hardest. Vladimir Putin, the former KGB officer, knew how to frustrate American surveillance; he rarely used cell phones or electronic communications. That made HUMINT, or human spies, essential in any effort to penetrate his inner sanctum. But recruiting and grooming a Soviet asset could take decades and amounted to a crap shoot: You could never be sure the spy would stay loyal, much less gain access to valuable secrets. But in the late summer and fall of 2016, after decades of cultivation, the CIA had just such an asset inside the Kremlin, with access to Putin. While he wasn't part of the Russian leader's inner circle, he was a regular visitor. He'd photographed documents on Putin's desk. And he was a key source for the CIA's conclusion, in the fall of 2016, that the Russian assault on the U.S. presidential election had been ordered by Putin himself.

In May 2017, American intelligence officials were alarmed: News reports had referred to this source; it might be only a matter of time before Putin or Russian intelligence figured out who he was. Moreover, Trump's infamous Oval Office session with Lavrov and Kislyak suggested that Trump himself might tip off the Russians, inadvertently or otherwise. (Trump knew of the Kremlin source's existence, though presumably not his name.) CIA officials decided it was time to take an extraordinary step: to conduct an exfiltration of their Kremlin asset, removing him and his family from Russia and resettling them in the U.S.

Was the exfiltration triggered by media reports, or Trump's Oval Office meeting with the Russians, or both? Within the intelligence community there was disagreement on this. The CIA had first proposed extracting its Kremlin mole in the fall of 2016, before Trump had taken office, but the mole refused. (This set off alarm bells at Langley: Could he be a double agent?) Finally, in May 2017, he agreed to uproot his family and relocate in the U.S. By September 2019, the Russian expatriate was living—inexplicably, under his own name—in the Washington, D.C., area. But whatever the cause of his exfiltration, a rare window into the Kremlin's inner sanctum had suddenly been shut. The CIA had lost an irreplaceable source.

By tradition, retired CIA directors stay above the political fray, rarely criticizing current presidents. But Trump's visceral attacks on the intelligence community, his kowtowing to Putin, and his disregard for democratic norms were hard for some to stomach. Trump drew fire from a few retired intelligence officials, including James Clapper, the former DNI, and Michael Hayden, the ex–CIA director. (Hayden had suffered a stroke in November 2018 but was recovering and wouldn't be silenced.) But the most vitriolic critic of Trump was John Brennan, Obama's last director. Brennan appeared frequently on MSNBC, denouncing the forty-fifth president. He'd labeled Trump's behavior at Helsinki "treasonous."

In August 2018 Trump struck back. He called Brennan "a political hack" and lashed out on Twitter: "John Brennan is panicking. He has disgraced himself, he has disgraced the Country, he has disgraced the entire Intelligence Community." Then he revoked Brennan's top secret security clearance, accusing the ex-director of "erratic" behavior.

The truth was, many fellow directors disapproved of Brennan's outspoken criticism of a sitting U.S. president. But this time Trump had gone too far. On August 16, many of them joined in an open letter to the president:

> *Insinuations and allegations of wrongdoing on the part of Brennan while in office are baseless. . . . We have never before seen the approval or removal of security clearances used as a political tool, as was done in this case. Beyond that, this action is quite clearly a signal to other former and current officials. As individuals who have cherished and helped preserve the right of Americans to free speech . . . that signal is inappropriate and deeply regrettable. Decisions on security clearances should be based on national security concerns and not political views.*

The letter was signed by William Webster, Porter Goss, Michael Hayden, John McLaughlin, Leon Panetta, David Petraeus, George Tenet, ex-DNI James Clapper, and ex-deputies Michael Morell, Avril Haines, David Cohen, and Steve Kappes.

But Trump wasn't finished with Brennan. In the summer of 2019, he'd order his attorney general, William Barr, to investigate Brennan's actions in the CIA's assessment of Russian interference in the 2016 election.

• • •

In the fall of 2018, relations between Trump and the intelligence community were about to take another ugly turn. The dispute was over the murder of journalist Jamal Khashoggi.

Khashoggi, a fifty-nine-year-old columnist for *The Washington Post*, was born in Saudi Arabia and had been close to the royal family before a falling out that drove him into exile in the U.S. In September 2017, Khashoggi was living in Virginia and writing critical opinion pieces about MBS, who'd become the kingdom's de facto ruler. He was engaged to be married to a Turkish woman named Hatice Cengiz.

On September 28, Khashoggi, who was divorced, visited the Saudi Arabian consulate in Istanbul to inquire about papers he needed for his wedding. A Saudi official told him to return in five days to obtain the documents.

At 1:14 p.m. on October 2, accompanied by his fiancée, Khashoggi returned to the Saudi consulate. He gave her his two cell phones, said "Wish me luck," and strode up to the consulate entrance. The last images of Khashoggi alive were captured by a surveillance camera on the roof of a guard's hut. What happened next caused worldwide outrage.

Khashoggi was escorted to the second floor of the building to the office of the general counsel; suddenly, two men came into the room and dragged him away. He was taken to another room—where, for the next seven minutes, he was tortured, mutilated, injected with a sedative, and then killed. His fingers were cut off while he was held down. Then he was carried into another room, lifted onto to a table—and dismembered. One of the killers brought a special bone saw for the occasion. He put on headphones and said, "When I do this job, I listen to music. You should do that too." Unbeknown to the Saudis, audio of the entire grisly encounter was recorded by intelligence officials from Turkey's national spy agency, MIT. "It was like *Pulp Fiction*," a Turkish official told *The New York Times*.

The Saudis at first denied everything. Khashoggi had departed the consulate through a back entrance, they said, and gone missing in Turkey. But that cover story soon crumbled. Three days after Khashoggi vanished, Turkey's leader, Recep Tayyip Erdoğan, was told in Ankara that his spies had incontrovertible proof that Khashoggi had been butchered by a Saudi security team linked to

MBS. Fifteen men had flown in on two chartered jets and carried out the premeditated operation.

Days later, forced to concede that Khashoggi had been killed in the consulate, the Saudis first blamed the death on a fistfight gone awry, and then a chokehold. Finally, they said it had been the result of a "rogue operation." The crown prince had known nothing about it.

Khashoggi's murder spurred congressional opposition to a Saudi-led war in Yemen that had killed tens of thousands of civilians. A majority in Congress voted to suspend weapons sales and curtail U.S. military assistance. But for Trump, the grisly murder of a U.S. national was just the price of doing business with the Saudis. "We don't like it even a little bit," the president said on October 11. "But whether or not we should stop $110 billion from being spent in this country. . . . That would not be acceptable to me." What if Saudi Arabia's leaders were implicated in the assassination? "I don't like stopping massive amounts of money that's being poured into our country," Trump said.

As the crisis escalated, on October 22, Gina Haspel traveled to Turkey. It was a familiar place; as a young operative she'd lived in Ankara and had become fluent in Turkish. But this time she'd come on a grim mission: to visit the headquarters of Turkish intelligence and listen to the audiotape of Khashoggi's killers. The recording captured the chilling banality of the assassins as they prepared for Khashoggi's arrival. Would it "be possible to put the trunk [of his body] in a bag?" one asked. "Joints will be separated. It is not a problem," another replied. "If we take plastic bags and cut it into pieces, it will be finished." Haspel was horrified by the tape.

In November the CIA concluded with "high confidence" that the Saudi crown prince, Mohammad bin Salman, was involved in Khashoggi's murder. But Trump quickly rejected the assessment. He issued a written White House statement under the headline "America First!":

> The world is a very dangerous place! . . .
>
> After my heavily negotiated trip to Saudi Arabia last year, the Kingdom agreed to spend and invest $450 billion in the United States. This is a record amount of money. . . .
>
> Our intelligence agencies continue to assess all information, but

*it could very well be that the Crown Prince had knowledge of this
tragic event—maybe he did and maybe he didn't!*

This was a direct contradiction of the CIA's "high confidence"
that MBS was involved. Would Gina Haspel defend that assessment? The evidence implicating the crown prince was overwhelming; eleven messages had been exchanged between the killers and the
Saudi palace; intercepts of phone conversations caught the leader of
the assassination team talking to the crown prince's office. In a 101-
page report, a U.N. special rapporteur, Agnès Callamard, would later
find "credible evidence" linking the murder to MBS. "On the more
grizzly side," one former senior intelligence official told me, "I've
been told that at least some body parts went back to Riyadh, to the
crown prince."

On November 28, 2018, before a vote on aid to the Saudis for the
war in Yemen, Congress asked the administration for a briefing on
Khashoggi's killing. Secretary of State Mike Pompeo and Defense
Secretary James Mattis appeared as scheduled for a closed hearing.
But Gina Haspel was a no-show.

The senators were furious. "The most persuasive presence at
today's security briefing on the murder of Jamal Khashoggi was the
empty chair meant for CIA Director Gina Haspel," snapped Illinois
senator Dick Durbin. Afterward Pompeo, protecting the president,
minimized the CIA's findings. There was "no direct reporting" connecting the crown prince to the journalist's death, he told reporters.
It was Pompeo who reportedly told Haspel to stay away from Capitol Hill.

Haspel had failed a major test: Asked to testify to Congress about
a matter of national importance and international interest, she'd
caved to White House pressure and stayed away.

Two weeks later Haspel returned to the Hill for a closed-door
hearing with a small group of senators. This time, by all accounts, she
delivered an unvarnished assessment of the crown prince's complicity in Khashoggi's killing. Afterward Tennessee senator Bob Corker
commented: "I have zero question in my mind that the crown prince
directed the murder and was kept apprised of the situation all the
way through it."

Haspel, belatedly, had fulfilled her responsibility. The CIA director reports to the president, but he or she answers to Congress and the American people. Haspel didn't need Trump's—or Pompeo's—permission to testify.

On December 23, 2019, Saudi authorities would announce the verdicts of a secret trial: Five of eleven men accused in Khashoggi's murder were condemned to death and three others sentenced to twenty-four years in prison. But neither MBS nor his principal deputy, Saud al-Qahtani, was found culpable. Agnès Callamard, the U.N. rapporteur, denounced the verdicts as "the antithesis of justice" and "a mockery."

While Trump cozied up to Saudi Arabia, he was lurching toward another crisis involving his conduct toward Ukraine; it would soon lead to his impeachment in the House of Representatives.

The United States has previously had presidents who were delusional. Richard Nixon was convinced that the Kennedys were involved in something nefarious connected to the Bay of Pigs; surely Richard Helms and the CIA must be hiding it. Nixon also believed that there was dirt on his opponents in documents tucked away in a safe at the Brookings Institution. "Break into the place, rifle the files, and bring them in!" he ordered his White House chief of staff, H. R. Haldeman. (Haldeman wisely ignored this command.) These were figments of Nixon's imagination. But they were nothing compared to Donald Trump's obsession with reimagining the 2016 presidential election.

What happened was clear: The Russians interfered to help Trump win. Everyone agreed on this, including all the U.S. intelligence agencies. Except Trump. That's because he couldn't accept the idea that his election might be tainted and his presidency illegitimate. Trump would believe *any* alternative to that version of events. So what if it turned out it was the Ukrainians, not the Russians, who interfered in the election—and that they were helping not him but Hillary Clinton? This was a fictional narrative, pure Russian propaganda, invented by Vladimir Putin and spread by an ex–New York mayor and a gaggle of hangers-on—but Trump believed it. Tom Bossert, his former Homeland Security chief, called it the president's white whale.

On July 25, nursing this obsession, Trump had placed a phone call to the president of Ukraine, Volodymyr Zelensky. (Three days later, Trump announced that Dan Coats, his Director of National Intelligence, was stepping down.) The fateful call remained a secret for nearly six weeks. Then, on September 13, California congressman Adam Schiff announced that he'd learned of a complaint by a government whistleblower involving an "urgent concern." But the acting director of national intelligence, Schiff complained, was unlawfully withholding it; the complaint should have been sent to Congress ten days earlier. Schiff demanded that it be turned over.

The matter involved the president's call to Zelensky, a former comedian and talk show host. Russia and Ukraine had been at war since 2014, when Moscow forcibly annexed the Crimea; fighting still raged along the countries' border in the Donbass region. Congress had appropriated nearly $391 million in U.S. military aid to bolster its beleaguered ally—but the aid had been mysteriously withheld.

As Trump was patched though to Zelensky, several officials were listening in, including National Security Council officials who were taking notes.

The subject quickly turned to Ukraine's need for antitank missiles.

> *President Zelensky: We are ready to continue to cooperate for the next steps, specifically we are almost ready to buy more Javelins from the United States for defense purposes.*
> *President Trump: I would like you to do us a favor though because our country has been through a lot and Ukraine knows a lot about it. I would like you to find out what happened with this whole situation with Ukraine, they say CrowdStrike . . .*

CrowdStrike was the U.S.-based internet security company that investigated the hack of the Democratic National Committee's servers. Trump went on to ask Zelensky to do "whatever you can do" to investigate Joe Biden, who'd just emerged as the front-runner among Trump's rivals in the next election. He also wanted Ukraine to announce a probe of Biden's son Hunter, who'd served on the board of a Ukrainian company—and told him to contact Rudy Giuliani and "the attorney general." The phone call lasted thirty minutes. Afterward, Trump's apparent shakedown of a foreign leader—withholding aid in return for a personal, partisan favor—was the talk of the NSC. Troubled by what they'd heard, several NSC officials shared their concerns with a colleague, a CIA officer who was assigned to the NSC.

That Friday, Courtney Elwood, the CIA general counsel, was told that one of her staff lawyers wanted to speak with her. A colleague who wished to remain anonymous, the lawyer told her, wanted to file a whistleblower complaint.

The complaint began:

> In the course of my official duties, I have received information from multiple U.S. Government officials that the President of the United States is using the power of his office to solicit interference from a foreign country in the 2020 U.S. election. This interference includes, among other things, pressuring a foreign country to investigate one of the President's main domestic political rivals. The President's personal lawyer, Mr. Rudolph Giuliani, is a central figure in this effort. Attorney General Barr appears to be involved as well.

The seven-page letter was carefully written, and thoroughly footnoted. But Elwood didn't forward the complaint to Congress. Instead, she sent it to NSC legal counsel John Eisenberg, at the White House, and to the Department of Justice. A week went by and the whistleblower worried: Would the complaint be swept under the rug? For advice, he reached out to a staffer he knew on the House Permanent Select Committee on Intelligence, headed by Adam Schiff. "Get a lawyer and go to the Inspector General," the staffer said.

The Inspector General of the Intelligence Community, Michael Atkinson, received the complaint on August 12. Finding it "urgent and credible," he forwarded it to the acting DNI, Joseph Maguire, who, under the whistleblower statute, was required to send the complaint to Congress within seven days. Instead, Maguire sat on it. Later, in his testimony to Congress, he argued that such complaints had to be "intelligence-related." And besides, he maintained, the statute didn't apply to the misconduct of presidents. The situation, he said, was "unprecedented."

The possible impeachment of Donald Trump might have ended there, with the report buried. But after sending the complaint to DNI

Maguire, Atkinson informed Schiff that it was in the pipeline. When Schiff learned that Maguire was withholding evidence of alleged presidential wrongdoing, he went public.

The fuse to a political crisis had been lit. Soon the whistleblower's complaint became public. On September 25, the White House released a transcript, or memo, of the phone call between Trump and Zelensky. Trump said it was "perfect," but his words—"I would like you to do us a favor though"—looked a lot like a "quid pro quo," demanding a bogus investigation of his political opponent in return for military aid. Commentators likened it to the "smoking gun" that drove Nixon from office: the recording of the president ordering the CIA to call off the FBI investigation into Watergate.

Then, on October 17, Mick Mulvaney, the acting White House chief of staff, made a stunning appearance in the Press Briefing Room: Asked about Trump's demand for an investigation into Ukraine and the Bidens, he said: "That's why we held up the money. We do that all the time with foreign policy. . . . And I have news for everybody. Get over it. There's going to be political influence in foreign policy."

In the House of Representatives, impeachment hearings were begun. Despite being ordered by the White House *not* to testify, a parade of witnesses appeared before the House Permanent Select Committee on Intelligence. NSC Russian expert Fiona Hill quoted John Bolton, the national security adviser, saying he wanted no part in "whatever drug deal Giuliani and Mulvaney are cooking up." And Trump's handpicked European Union ambassador, Gordon Sondland, declared not only that there was a quid pro quo but that "everyone was in the loop."

As the scandal grew, Trump repeatedly demanded to know the identity of the whistleblower. Who was he? Since the infamous July 25 phone call, the whistleblower had left the NSC and returned to the CIA. Given what was known publicly—he was a CIA Russia expert on rotation at the NSC—it wouldn't be hard to identify him; indeed, Breitbart and other hard-right news outlets had bandied a name about for weeks. Republicans joined the clamor to "unmask" him.

On September 26, at a meeting at the U.N., Donald Trump made a bald-faced threat. "I want to know who's the person that gave the whistleblower the information," he said, "because that's close to a spy. You know what we used to do in the old days when we were smart? Right? With spies and treason, right? We used to handle them a little differently than we do now." Cell phones for the whistleblower's attorneys immediately lit up. "Really threatening phone calls; cursing; horrific, anti-Semitic statements; sexual statements," said one of them. "It was a direct threat not only to our client's safety and security but also to ours. The FBI got involved. And we had to take specific security precautions."

On December 18, 2019, after twelve weeks of hearings, the House approved, on a party-line vote, two articles of impeachment against President Donald J. Trump—for abuse of power and obstruction of Congress.

Was the whistleblower's anonymity in jeopardy? Whose job was it to protect him? Ultimately, that responsibility fell to Gina Haspel. According to his attorney, the CIA had been "very protective" of his client. But in a showdown between the whistleblower and his superiors there were no guarantees. "Courtney, the CIA general counsel, could have compelled her lawyer to tell her his identity," the attorney said. "As far as I know, she respected the process and never asked."

But what if Donald Trump ordered the CIA to tell him who the whistleblower was?

More than four decades earlier, in 1973, Richard Helms had protected the CIA by standing up to Richard Nixon, defying H. R. Haldeman's order to participate in the Watergate cover-up. A veteran former officer wondered if Haspel was up to the challenge. "Her test is coming," he said. "What's she going to do? Dick Helms was given an order by Nixon and said, 'hell no.' What will Gina Haspel do when the president calls up and says, 'This is what we want you to do.' Now, she can say, 'No, I can't do that' and risk getting fired. I don't know. She might. She might not."

As his trial loomed in the Senate, Trump, in a precipitous act, brought the U.S. to the brink of war in the Middle East.

A crisis with Iran had been building. In January 2019, Dan Coats and Gina Haspel had gone to Capitol Hill to deliver the intelligence community's annual assessment of worldwide threats. Sitting side by side before television cameras, they surveyed the globe: North Korea was "unlikely to give up all of its nuclear weapons and production capabilities"; ISIS remained a serious threat; global warming was intensifying. Finally, they said, Iran was in compliance with the 2015 nuclear arms agreement, known as the Joint Comprehensive Plan of Action (JCPOA).

Every one of these assertions was anathema to Donald Trump. But it was what Coats and Haspel said about Iran that infuriated him. The president lashed out in a tweet:

The Intelligence people seem to be extremely passive and naive when it comes to the dangers of Iran. They are wrong! When I became President Iran was making trouble all over the Middle East, and beyond. Since ending the terrible Iran Nuclear Deal, they are MUCH different. . . . Perhaps Intelligence should go back to school!

Trump telling the experts to go to school was, of course, absurd; this was the same president who, before taking office, didn't know the difference between the Quds Force, elite members of Iran's Revolutionary Guard, and the Kurds. (He repeatedly confused the two in a 2015 interview with conservative radio host Hugh Hewitt.) In late 2019 Trump was faced with a fateful decision: Should he order a lethal strike on one of the leaders of a sovereign state? It would become a critical test for both Donald Trump and Gina Haspel.

The truth was that until Trump took office in 2017, Iran had been relatively restrained in its military adventurism. All of that changed when the president tore up the nuclear deal and slapped Tehran with crippling economic sanctions. Trump was warned about what might follow: exactly the kind of Iranian misbehavior that the U.S. was trying to prevent. That was just what happened.

In May of 2019 the CIA attributed a wave of attacks on tankers in the Strait of Hormuz to Iran. Days later, Iranian-backed Houthi rebels in Yemen launched an attack on a Saudi oil pipeline. On May 19, after a rocket landed near the U.S. embassy in Baghdad, Trump tweeted: "If Iran wants to fight, that will be the official end of Iran. Never threaten the United States again!"

Iran's leaders ignored this bluster; on June 12 they launched attacks on two oil tankers in the Gulf of Oman. Eight days later, Tehran shot down a U.S. military drone over the Strait of Hormuz. (In response, Trump planned but then canceled a retaliatory missile strike with ten minutes to spare.) In August Iran's president announced a new long-range surface-to-air missile defense system.

The crisis came to a head in late December 2019.

Iranian-backed Kataib Hezbollah militias launched a series of rocket attacks; an American civilian contractor was killed at an Iraqi military base outside Kirkuk. The U.S. retaliated with air strikes against three locations in Iraq and two in Syria, killing twenty-four militia fighters. The American embassy in Baghdad's Green Zone was soon besieged by protesters setting fires.

The prospect of his own Benghazi crisis enraged the president. Perhaps he feared a replay of the 1979 debacle, and the seizure of American hostages. On the evening of January 2, 2020, Trump was presented with a choice of retaliatory options. The most radical was to target the head of Iran's Revolutionary Guard Quds Force, the legendary Major General Qassim Suleimani.

It was the same General Suleimani who'd been spotted by a CIA drone over Damascus a decade earlier, standing next to his good friend Imad Mughniyah. Mughniyah would soon be dead, oblite-rated by a CIA-built bomb concealed in his SUV. But George W. Bush hadn't authorized the killing of Suleimani, and so the Iranian general walked away unharmed.

Both Bush and Obama had rejected many opportunities to kill Suleimani. To be sure, the Quds commander had been responsible for the deaths of hundreds of Americans, on the battlefield in Iraq and elsewhere. But unlike Osama bin Laden or Mughniyah, Suleimani wasn't a terrorist. Killing him would draw a target on the back of every senior U.S. government official. It also risked retaliation by Iran and its proxy militias against U.S. targets. That could lead to dead Americans, and to war.

It was a moment of crisis—for the Trump presidency and the CIA. Neither had much credibility: Trump had squandered his by lying about almost everything during three years in office; the agency was still recovering from its disastrous estimate of Iraq's WMDs.

At 5:00 p.m. on January 2, 2020, Trump gave the order to elimi-nate Suleimani. The next day, on the outskirts of Baghdad's Interna-tional Airport, the Iranian general was riding in a car. The leader of Kataib Hezbollah's militia, Abu Mahdi al-Muhandis, was in another vehicle nearby. An American drone, an MQ-9 Reaper, took aim and fired four missiles, two at each vehicle. They exploded in a fireball; eight other members of the entourage also died.

From Mar-a-Lago, Trump claimed that the general posed "imminent and sinister threats" to Americans. But he cited no evidence, and in the days that followed the intelligence looked dubious at best. The president finally admitted his real motive: Suleimani should have been killed a long time ago.

No one could say for sure what the long-term consequences would be. For Trump the stakes were huge: war and peace, and possibly his presidency.

But it was also a defining moment for Gina Haspel. She reportedly told Trump that *not* striking Suleimani might be more dangerous than killing him. Was she being an honest broker? Or telling the president what he wanted to hear? Many of her colleagues at Langley wondered. Few were reassured when she was spotted at the president's State of the Union address a month later. Traditionally, in public, CIA directors strive to appear nonpartisan. Haspel applauded Trump's speech like a cheerleader. "Gina's never had a battlefield command, she was never in Islamabad, Kabul, or Baghdad," said a former senior CIA official. "She would make a great prison camp commandant. She'd get everything done and say, 'I was following orders. The president gave me an order.'"

Epilogue

The CIA director is the person Americans depend on to prevent another Pearl Harbor or 9/11. He or she is also the person who all too often must tell the president what he doesn't want to hear. In 1967, Lyndon Johnson was enraged when Richard Helms insisted that the strategic basis for the Vietnam War, the domino theory, was flawed. Imagine how many American and Vietnamese lives might have been saved if LBJ had listened. Similarly, given his hostility toward Iran, President Donald Trump was furious when, in January 2019, his director of national intelligence (DNI) Dan Coats testified that Tehran was in compliance with the nuclear agreement. Almost unnoticed in that year's Worldwide Threat Assessment (WWTA), on page 21, was even worse news for Trump: the threat of a deadly global pandemic.

The finding, made a year before anyone had heard of COVID-19, was chilling and prescient: "We assess that the United States and the world will remain vulnerable to the next flu pandemic or large-scale outbreak of a contagious disease that could lead to massive rates of death and disability, severely affect the world economy, strain international resources. . . . [Preparations] may be inadequate to address the challenge of what we anticipate will be more frequent outbreaks of infectious diseases . . ."

It was a warning that Donald Trump didn't want to hear. Not then—and not a year later, when this theoretical threat had turned into an all-too-deadly pandemic. Trump's oblivious response to the looming threat was reminiscent of George W. Bush's refusal to heed warnings of an Al Qaeda attack before September 11. But Trump's failure was far more egregious. After all, in less than four months after its first appearance in the U.S., the coronavirus would kill more than a hundred thousand Americans and bring the U.S. economy to its knees. Moreover, compared with 9/11—which was telegraphed by blinking red lights—the COVID-19 pandemic arrived with sirens blaring, horns honking, and a virtual parade down Main Street. Tens of thousands of American lives depended on immediate action. Trump looked the other way.

The primary responsibility for pandemic warning belongs to health agencies such as the Centers for Disease Control and Prevention (CDC). But the intelligence community plays a supporting role, and it tried to alert Trump. In January and February of 2020, as the virus was already spreading on U.S. soil, warnings appeared frequently in the President's Daily Brief (PDB). Unfortunately, as we have seen, Trump doesn't read the PDB. Making matters worse, the president's oral briefings by the DNI's office had almost completely broken down. Trump's original CIA briefer, Ted Gistaro, who had become exhausted by the president's constant harangues, retreated to a desk job; his replacement was Beth Sanner, a highly regarded veteran CIA analyst. But the president was barely speaking to Sanner's boss, Joseph Maguire; the acting DNI had enraged Trump by briefing Congress on the Russian threat to the 2020 elections. As a result, throughout January, Trump was briefed not two or three times a week, as had become usual for him, but *once a week*. The president's indifference to timely intelligence no longer surprised anyone in the White House or the CIA. But in the face of a swift-moving pandemic, it would prove disastrous.

Still, Trump blamed the intelligence community for downplaying the threat. Speaking to Fox News in a virtual town hall at the Lincoln Memorial on May 3, he said that the first time he'd heard of the virus was during a CIA briefing on January 23. (By now, Sanner's name had been revealed in the press.) Trump claimed he was told the virus "was not a big deal," effectively throwing his CIA briefer under the bus. "I was told that there could be a virus coming in but it was of no real import." On CBS's *Face the Nation*, Trump's National Security Adviser Robert O'Brien joined the blame game: When the president cut off travel from China at the end of January, he claimed, "the IC (Intelligence Community) and others did not believe that this was a serious health risk or even a global pandemic."

This version of events was false on many levels. First, health officials and advisers had been sounding the alarm since January 3, when

Robert Redfield, head of the CDC, learned of the COVID-19 outbreak from his counterparts in China. Two weeks later, Trump's Secretary of Health and Human Services (HHS) Alex Azar called Trump directly at Mar-a-Lago to warn him. (Azar was treated to a presidential diatribe on e-cigarettes.) Second, by definition, everything in the PDB is a big deal, and only the *biggest* deals are briefed to the president orally—as the January 23 warning was. "I find it difficult to believe that you would put something in the PDB that actually downplayed the threat and said, 'This is not a big deal,' " said a former senior intelligence official. "That's not what the PDB is for. The PDB is for reporting threats." Bob Gates concurred. "On its face it doesn't make sense," the former director told me of Trump's story. "They wouldn't have briefed the president if they didn't think it was important."

Moreover, in January, the CIA was briefing Congress about the pandemic. "The American people would have been absolutely astonished and appalled" by the seriousness of the threat, said Richard Blumenthal, a Democratic senator from Connecticut. While the specifics were still classified, "this disease was more deadly than the commonly transmitted flu," he told me. "It was more efficiently transmitted than H1N1 and some of the other viruses. It was a bigger deal, it was more serious, it was more threatening." Blumenthal was briefed on January 25, just two days after Trump claimed the CIA had minimized the threat. "It's inconceivable to me that [they] didn't tell the president that something serious was happening in China at that point."

While Trump tried to wish it away, the virus overwhelmed the country's feeble pandemic defenses. It was no accident that they were enfeebled. In 2018, John Bolton, Trump's third national security adviser, had famously abolished the National Security Council's pandemic unit, officially called the Directorate for Global Health Security and Biodefense, which made it more difficult to get high-level attention for an emerging health crisis. But the problem went deeper than that—to Trump's aversion to science and facts, his belief that nothing from the "deep state" could be trusted, and his rejection of governance generally. After all, Trump hadn't just run against the federal government; he'd run against the whole *idea* of governing. His presidency was an attempt to prove that competence was for losers. In his book *The Fifth Risk*, Michael Lewis described the problem with that:

> The United States government might be the most complicated organization on the face of the earth. Its two million federal employees take orders from four thousand political appointees. . . . Still, many of the problems our government grapples with aren't particularly ideological, and the Obama people tried to keep ideology out of the briefings. . . . How to stop a virus, how to take a census, how to determine if some foreign country is seeking to obtain a nuclear weapon or if North Korean missiles can reach Kansas City: these are enduring technical problems.

Barack Obama ordered the most thorough presidential transition in history—complete with a pandemic crisis exercise and a sixty-nine-page playbook. But almost no one in the incoming Trump administration took the exercise seriously. Voluminous briefing books went, unread, into the trash. Trump and his team weren't interested.

The game was given away on the first day of the Trump presidency. When the clock struck noon on January 20, 2017, marking the official transfer of power, Obama's White House chief of staff, Denis McDonough, was at his West Wing desk, waiting for Reince Priebus, the incoming chief of staff, and his team to arrive. An hour went by but no one showed. McDonough finally turned off the lights and left. By January of 2020, three years had gone by and the lights were now on in the West Wing. But when it came to qualified people in top jobs, almost no one was home.

Many believed that Trump had gutted, and then politicized, the Office of the Director of National Intelligence. He had removed the IC inspector general (and four other IGs), his acting DNI Joseph Maguire, his deputy Sue Gordon, and principal executive Andrew Hallman. And Trump had succeeded in getting an unqualified partisan confirmed by the Senate as Maguire's successor, former Texas congressman John Ratcliffe. This was largely because Ratcliffe's predecessor, acting DNI Richard Grenell, was considered even worse. "It was absolutely the worst time to decapitate the leadership of the intelligence community," said Jeremy Bash, former chief of staff to CIA director Leon Panetta. "Not only did they need the intelligence community firing on all cylinders to present information to the president about the coronavirus, but also to keep their eye on all the other national security challenges and threats around the world, from North Korea to Iran to Russia to China."

Meanwhile, the administration's health officials were overmatched by the crisis. Luciana Borio became the director for Medical and Biodefense Preparedness in Trump's NSC after the pandemic unit was abolished. Born in Brazil, she had come to the U.S. in the 1990s, earned her MD at George Washington University, and done fellowships in infectious diseases and critical care medicine. She had worked on the Ebola and Zika outbreaks. In the Trump administration, she was shocked by what she called "the tremendous deficit of expertise in critical positions." Dr. Borio had no political axe to grind and was reluctant to talk with me. (A mutual acquaintance, a former NSC staffer, introduced us.) While she stressed that many of her colleagues were talented and dedicated, top political appointees were in way over their heads. "They just didn't have the experience to really manage something like this," Borio told me. "Or to even ask the right questions." It wasn't just the bungled tests and the shortages of personal protective equipment (PPE) and ventilators and the depleted national stockpile; it was the unwillingness of HHS Secretary Alex Azar, a former pharmaceutical industry lobbyist, to tell Trump and his inner circle hard truths. After being brushed off by the president on January 15, it was two weeks before the HHS secretary again managed to brief Trump about the crisis. "He said the president wouldn't understand, wouldn't listen and all that," she said. "To me it was like, well, that's your *job.*"

Only an empowered pandemic czar—in the mold of Obama's Ebola czar Ron Klain—could have galvanized an effective response. But no one was in charge. "There was nobody who had the expertise and the understanding," said Borio, who left the NSC in March 2019. "It would have been very difficult to manage the rapidity of the response without bringing somebody in at a very senior level— with access to the Oval Office—early on." And Borio feared another potential crisis: a shortage of needles, syringes, and vials to administer a vaccine. There was no antidote to Trump's hands-off response— and no Wizard of Oz. "There's nobody behind the curtain," she said. "There's nobody that's going to come and save the day."

As we have seen in earlier chapters, this country has previously been led by presidents who were delusional, but no other president has dealt with a major national crisis by denying that it existed. When he could no longer pretend that the pandemic was not real, Trump pinned the blame for it on everyone else: the CIA's failure to warn, the World Health Organization's perfidy (too "soft" on China), Barack Obama's incompetence, etc. The pandemic must have been cooked up by Trump's enemies—perhaps even concocted by the communist Chinese. Mike Pompeo, Trump's former CIA director and current secretary of state, parroted the unfounded claim that COVID-19 had been created in a Wuhan laboratory. Would Trump order DNI Ratcliffe to produce intelligence implicating the Chinese?

In the wake of the widespread protests triggered by the horrific May 2020 killing in Minneapolis of George Floyd, a black man who died with a knee pressed to his throat by an arresting police officer, would Trump pressure the intelligence community to blame the unrest on his political enemies? At the height of the Vietnam War, with protesters surrounding the White House, President Lyndon Johnson had ordered Richard Helms to find evidence that they were being directed by foreign Communist powers. A half century later, was it so farfetched to imagine that Trump might order Ratcliffe—or Gina Haspel—to gin up evidence that the protesters were being directed by Trump's favorite scapegoat, Antifa (militant anti-fascists)?

This wasn't an idle question. Trump had goaded his attorney general into launching a spurious probe of the DOJ's Russia investigation. He'd charged Barack Obama with unspecified crimes, and, with no basis in fact, he had accused Joe Scarborough, the MSNBC anchor and a former Republican congressman, of murder.

In the case of Ukraine president Volodymyr Zelensky, the CIA had helped put the brakes on Trump's abuse of power; an anonymous, midlevel analyst had blown the whistle on the president's Mafia-style shakedown of an ally. (It's often forgotten that Mike Pompeo, the former CIA director, listened to every word of the call and then tried to hide the fact.) But would Pompeo's successor, Gina Haspel, resist an illegal order from Trump? What if the president demanded dirt on his presidential rival Joe Biden?

In the eyes of many at the CIA, Haspel had been seduced by her proximity to presidential power. "There's been an evolution among all the intelligence community leaders—maybe most striking with Gina," said a former agency official. "And that evolution has been from holding the line on objectivity and integrity to, eventually, Trump's breaking down that wall—and the loss of objectivity and integrity. She started out in the right place, and now she's in a really bad place."

When a former federal prosecutor, on conservative radio, referred to the CIA whistleblower as "John Wilkes Booth," Haspel said nothing publicly. This infuriated a former senior intelligence official. "This horrible, horrible thing that this person says about one of her employees—and she does absolutely nothing?" he exclaimed. "If I'd been Gina Haspel, I would have publicly defended my whistle-blower." This same official was also incensed when Haspel failed to support the CIA briefer, Beth Sanner, whom Trump accused of downplaying the pandemic. "I would have done two things," he said. "I would have said to the national security adviser, 'If it happens again, I'm quitting. With a lot of fireworks.' And then, two, I would have told my office of public affairs to defend the hell out of her on background."

CIA directors must be prepared to deal with presidents who trample the rule of law. As we've seen, Richard Helms went along with illegal domestic surveillance at home (LBJ's Operation MHCHAOS) and skullduggery in Chile (Nixon's Project FUBELT). "They were all asked to do things they shouldn't do," lamented Helms's wife, Cynthia. But when Nixon tried to enlist him in the Watergate cover-up, Helms drew the line, defying chief of staff H. R. Haldeman's order to do Nixon's criminal bidding. More than forty years later, Jeremy Bash said the CIA director must be above suspicion: "Never do the president's political bidding, or the bidding of one party. Provide equal briefings on Capitol Hill to Democrats and Republicans. Don't look at party labels, ever."

Not least, the CIA director must tell the truth—in private and in public. As the world learned in 2020, the danger comes not only from terrorists and hostile armies. A year after the 2019 Worldwide Threat Assessment warned of a potential pandemic, another threat session was scheduled—for February 12, 2020. But the briefing, given annually, was abruptly canceled. "I don't recall any worldwide threat briefing ever being canceled before," said Bob Gates. I asked

Senator Blumenthal what happened. "I've asked and I've received no satisfactory answer," he said. But the reason seemed clear. "The leaders of the intelligence community didn't want to do it," said Michael Morell, the former acting CIA director, "because they knew if they answered questions truthfully the president would get mad at them. They'd be undercutting his view of the world." Nothing would have undercut Trump's view of the world more than an urgent warning about the COVID-19 pandemic.

Morell was troubled by the directors' silence. "I find it dangerous that Trump has so intimidated the leadership of his intelligence community that they don't want to speak publicly," he said. "This worldwide threat briefing is a key part of oversight of intelligence activities in a democratic society." Having the CIA director testify in public, he stressed, makes it harder for policymakers to politicize intelligence in private.

In the epilogue to my book about the White House chiefs of staff, *The Gatekeepers*, completed right after the 2016 election, I wrote: "President Trump may try to run the White House himself—his gut instincts unchecked, his decisions uninformed, his Twitter account unfiltered. Or he may empower his chief of staff to implement his agenda, advise honestly on difficult choices, and tell him what he doesn't want to hear."

Trump chose the former, and the country paid a heavy price. The stakes are just as high, if not higher, when the CIA director fails to tell the president hard truths.

Chris Whipple
June 15, 2020
New York City

Acknowledgments

Like my previous work, *The Gatekeepers*, this book began as a collaboration with close friends. The springboard for *The Spymasters* was a documentary that debuted on Showtime in 2015. My partners on that film, *The Spymasters: CIA in the Crosshairs*, were the brilliant filmmakers Jules and Gedeon Naudet and Susan Zirinsky. The Naudet brothers are best known for their landmark documentary *9/11*. Susan is the pioneering broadcast news producer and the first female president of CBS News. Working with them is as good as it gets—in filmmaking or any other profession. While I was holed up for almost a year writing this book, I missed them like hell.

I am grateful to the entire *Spymasters* documentary team: My friend David Hume Kennerly, the Pulitzer Prize–winning photographer, was our co-executive producer. He also provided many of his superb photos for this book. David Martin and Mary Walsh of CBS News screened a rough cut of the film and kept us honest. *Showtime*'s David Nevins and Joan Boorstein gave us brilliant notes. And then–CBS News president David Rhodes was supportive and enthusiastic.

Our talented and creative film crew, led by the great Ron Hill, included R.J. Hill, Alex Klymko, Sam Painter, Mark Falk, Thomas Hildreth, John Taylor, Edmond W. Anderson, David Mitlyng, Oliver Lumpe, Armando Allen, Michael Cucuzzo, Anthony Di Leo, Kevin Fox, Justin Hill, Sean Monesson, John Thaler, and Matt Witgenstein.

At CBS News, our amazing production team, led by Al Briganti, consisted of Mead Stone, Jamie Stolz, Jason Schmidt, Gary Winter, Pat Milton, Elizabeth Elizalde, Kelly Kern, Shoshanah Wolfson, Dena Goldstein, Catherine Harrington, Michelle Harris, Bruce Spiegel, Emily Wichick, Laura Chang, Rob Klug, Matt Devoe,

Jeremiah Turits, Nick Stevenson, Kat Teurfs, Nour Idriss, and Walter Cronkite III.

And then there was our narrator. On Halloween, 2014, we flew to Berlin for a taping session with the actor Mandy Patinkin. (His Showtime series *Homeland* was shooting a season there.) Mandy is a tortured soul who agonizes over every line he utters. But under Zirinsky's effortless direction, that brilliant actor (and big-hearted mensch) got every word just right. Then Susan got us all pizza.

Writing this book was a lonelier enterprise—but equally dependent on collaborators. Two people stood out. The first was Caroline Borge Keenan. This is our second book, and it's hard to imagine writing one without her. Caroline mined the CIA archives and directors' papers; chased down elusive sources; conducted extra interviews; almost single-handedly tracked down every photograph (Randa Cardwell also helped); painstakingly checked facts, many of which, given the subject matter, no one would confirm or deny; and rarely complained about my stubborn inability to keep track of published sources while I was writing. She was practically a coauthor, and is a wonderful friend.

The other indispensable person was my sister Ann (Whipple) Marr, to whom this book is dedicated. Ann might have missed her calling as a professional book editor, but generations of students at Manhattan's Rodeph Sholom and Convent of the Sacred Heart in Greenwich, Connecticut, are lucky that she decided to be an educator. Her constant encouragement and sharp editorial eye kept me going.

The CIA's overseers are known as the Gang of Eight; I had my own brilliant Gang of Eleven. The following friends, writers, and shrewd political observers read portions of the manuscript in progress and gave me their editorial notes: Peter Baker, chief White House correspondent of *The New York Times* and political analyst extraordinaire; Thomas Powers, author of the classic Richard Helms biography, *The Man Who Kept the Secrets* (whose course on nonfiction writing inspired me as an undergraduate at Yale); Jonathan Larsen, former editor in chief of *The Village Voice* and *New Times* (and my ex-boss at *Life* magazine); Josh Getlin, former New York bureau chief of the *Los Angeles Times*; Jack Watson, Jimmy Carter's superb chief of staff and my close friend; and Kenneth Duberstein, Ronald Reagan's equally superb chief. "It's too bad Bill Casey isn't alive," Ken remarked when I first told him about this book. "At least, I don't *think* he is." Lynn

Langway, an editor at *Newsweek* in its glory days, also weighed in. Jeremy Bash, Leon Panetta's consummate CIA chief of staff, read my epilogue and contributed excellent suggestions.

I am especially indebted to three people who read and dissected the book in its entirety: David Martin, the incomparable Pentagon correspondent for CBS News and author of the excellent CIA book, *The Wilderness of Mirrors;* Bruce Riedel, the legendary CIA Middle East analyst who is now a senior fellow at the Brookings Institution; and Greg Zorthian, former president of the *Financial Times* in America and Worldwide General Manager of *Time* (and my freshman college roommate).

At Scribner, I was fortunate to have a superb editor, Rick Horgan; he also commissioned my first book, *The Gatekeepers*, and signed me up for two more when he arrived at Scribner. Rick is a kind of literary gardener, weeding out unclear antecedents and bollixed chronologies and sometimes dubious arguments. Nan Graham, Scribner's publisher, was supportive and enthusiastic from the outset, as was Colin Harrison, the editor in chief. Brian Belfiglio, Scribner's publicist, threw all of his considerable energy and skill into spreading the word about *The Spymasters*. My friend Judy Twersky, another terrific publicist, kicked in her excellent ideas and contacts. Chatwalee Phoungbut applied her keen designer's eye to my website, chriswhipple.net. Scribner's Mark LaFlaur and Beckett Rueda kept us all on schedule. Two of my best friends happen to be among the world's best entertainment lawyers and literary agents: David Chidekel and Lisa Queen, respectively. Lisa wore three hats—as my agent, early chapter reader, and reality therapist.

The heart of this book, of course, is the interviews I conducted with the CIA directors themselves. Almost every living director agreed to my (sometimes multiple) requests for interviews; a highlight was interviewing Admiral Stansfield Turner, who, despite suffering from dementia at the age of eighty-nine, came alive during his interview, recalling his tenure with a twinkle in his eye. I am indebted to his delightful widow, Marion Turner. Another unforgettable experience was interviewing George H.W. Bush. Though he was battling a form of Parkinson's disease that made speaking a struggle, the revered former CIA director insisted on participating—even after his chief of staff, Jean Becker, had politely declined my original request.

I am grateful to George Tenet, who sat with me for hours during our first session and generously agreed to multiple follow-ups for this book. There is no better guide through the CIA's wilderness of mirrors than Bill Harlow, Tenet's longtime friend and collaborator—and coauthor of several top CIA officials' memoirs. Bob Gates, the legendary analyst-turned-director, welcomed me at his rustic lakeside cabin outside Seattle, and gave me a CIA master class. At the Panetta Institute in beautiful Seaside, California, Leon Panetta generously shared his recollections and entertained me with lousy jokes, punctuated by his booming laugh. John Brennan reflected thoughtfully on his own tenure as director, and walked me through the history of the agency.

John Deutch, Bill Clinton's brilliant, acerbic director, interrupted his busy schedule to speak with me in his office at MIT. Generals David Petraeus and Michael Hayden generously sat for several insightful, in-depth interviews; General Hayden continues to make remarkable progress in his recovery from a recent stroke. James Woolsey was candid about his rocky relationship with President Clinton. Porter Goss was charming, engaging, and reflective about the challenges he faced as director. "Judge" William Webster shared his contagious enthusiasm for the rule of law; at the age of ninety-six, he continues to inspire his legion of admirers, including me. And John McLaughlin and Michael Morell, superb deputy and acting directors, shared their unmatched intelligence expertise over breakfasts and lunches in Manhattan and Washington, D.C. Only two of the living CIA directors declined to talk with me: Mike Pompeo and Gina Haspel.

One of the rewards of researching this book was getting to know some of the directors' relatives. Cynthia Helms, charming and irrepressible at the age ninety-five, regaled me with marvelous, untold stories about her late husband. I was saddened to learn of Cynthia's death in the summer of 2019. Dennis Helms was generous with his recollections of his father—as were Paul and Carl Colby with memories of William Colby. Colby's widow, Sally, shared her insights, as did his grandson Elbridge. Cora Schlesinger talked about her brilliant father, James Schlesinger, with my colleague Caroline Keenan.

I relied heavily on the directors' colleagues and deputies. Many chose to remain anonymous. Some who did not include Charles Allen, the CIA's legendary "Cassandra"; James Clapper, former director of national intelligence, the model of an effective DNI; John

Negroponte, his whip-smart predecessor; Cofer Black, who ran the CIA's Counterterrorism Center on 9/11; Richard Blee, who headed the Bin Laden Unit and led the infamous July 10, 2001, White House briefing; Jose Rodriguez, who supervised the EIT program and mentored Gina Haspel; David Priess, author of *The President's Book of Secrets*; Thomas Twetten, former head of the CIA's Near East bureau; Burton Gerber, veteran operative and Helms contemporary; Nick Rasmussen, head of the National Counterterrorism Center; Michael Daniel, White House cybersecurity coordinator; Bob Baer, veteran Middle East operative; Jack Devine, head of the Afghan Task Force; Bobby Ray Inman, Bill Casey's deputy director; Richard Kerr, a deputy director; Steven Hall, head of Russia operations; Nick Shapiro, John Brennan's chief of staff; Mel Goodman; Lisa Monaco; Dan Meyer; Meroe Park; Ned Price; Rand Beers; Stephanie O'Sullivan; Mike Sulick; Gina Bennett; Adam Ciralsky; Charles Battaglia; Greg Craig; Avril Haines; Bill Danvers; Fred Hitz; Mark Lippert; Laurence Silberman; Stephanie Smith; Al White; and Mark Zaid.

Sara Lichterman, the CIA's public affairs officer, was unfailingly helpful, as was Brian Hale of the Office of the Director of National Intelligence; David Robarge, the CIA's distinguished historian, shared his deep knowledge of the directors.

John Podesta and Denis McDonough, two of history's best White House chiefs of staff, gave me their insiders' perspective on the intelligence community during the Clinton and Obama administrations. Thomas F. "Mack" McLarty, one of this country's great public servants, was a constant source of wisdom and support. I also owe special thanks to Richard Armitage, Frank Wisner Jr., son of the CIA legend Frank Wisner Sr., and General Anthony Zinni.

Every chronicler of the CIA depends on the journalists who have gone before. Max Holland helped steer me and Caroline Keenan through the labyrinth of the agency's archives. (Thanks to the Booth Family Center for Special Collections at Georgetown University Library, home of the Richard Helms Papers; the National Security Archive at George Washington University; and to Muckrock.com.) Jeff Stein, James Rosen, John Walcott, and Mark Mazzetti shared their intelligence world expertise. *The Washington Post*'s great CIA observer, David Ignatius, generously gave me advice in the early stages of this book. And Bob Woodward, the definitive chronicler of Washington's powerful, went out of his way to educate me about Bill Casey, the subject of his magisterial biography *Veil*. I owe Bob a great debt.

Three wise men deserve special mention. Stuart Eizenstat, Jimmy Carter's domestic policy expert; Anthony "Tony" Lake, Bill Clinton's national security adviser; and the late Leslie Gelb, former Defense Department official, editor of *The Pentagon Papers*, and Pulitzer Prize-winning columnist for *The New York Times*. When I met him while researching *The Spymasters*, Les had lost his eyesight and could no longer read, but he was full of humor, wisdom, and hilarious stories about Washington's power brokers. He died in August 2019. How I wish that he and our mutual friend, the famously combative Richard Holbrooke, were still around to argue about this book.

Finally, I will single out just a few good friends. *Life* photographer Dick Swanson contributed his amazing picture of CIA Director George H.W. Bush, alone at a train station. Olive Talley, a first-rate investigative filmmaker, unearthed nuggets of intelligence for me in the archives at Texas A&M. My pals, the great Harry Benson and his wife, Gigi, kept me on my toes, critiquing my appearances on MSNBC and CNN. Ward and Susan Pennebaker took great care of me on my visits to Houston. My Deerfield friends Jeff VanNest, John Hutchins, and Kc Ramsay entertained me in Zoom sessions during the great pandemic of 2020. Heidi Evans, Nancy Collins, and David Friend, brilliant journalists and friends, never tired of listening to my stories. Finally, I don't know how I could have written *The Spymasters* without my dear friend Trip McCrossin, who kindly made his beautiful house on Shelter Island available when we needed a refuge from the madding crowds of Manhattan.

Has anyone ever had better mentors than Joe Hartman, Joe Duffey, Elizabeth Holtzman, Dick Holbrooke, Paul Trachtman, and Diane Sawyer? I doubt it.

Finally, there was nothing in her wedding vows about it, but my wife, Cary, transcribed endless hours of interviews with mostly elderly white men; tracked down obscure footnotes; and performed countless other thankless tasks that made this book possible. Most important, she made me feel loved. As always, Sam Whipple made me feel both loved and proud.

Author's Note on Sources

Quotations of CIA directors and other major sources, except where otherwise noted, are drawn from interviews conducted by the author on the following dates:

CIA Directors, Acting Directors, and Directors of National Intelligence

Brennan, John: May 16, 2015; July 10, 2018
Bush, George H. W.: October 24, 2011; January 30, 2014
Clapper, James: January 15, 2019
Deutch, John: February 3, 2015; March 5, 2019
Gates, Robert: December 15, 2014; April 21, 2015; August, 17, 2018
Goss, Porter: March 7, 2015; May 19, 2015; February 22, 2020
Hayden, General Michael: December 17, 2014; April 28, 2015; October 1, 2019
McLaughlin, John: May 18, 2015; November 13, 2018; September 6, 2019
Morell, Michael: April 11, 2015; April 25, 2018; August 8, 2018; August 2, 2019;
     October 10, 2019
Negroponte, John: October 4, 2018
Panetta, Leon: November 9, 2012; May 20, 2014; February 23, 2015; September 21,
     2018; September 9, 2019
Petraeus, General David: March 17, 2015; July 22, 2015; February 21, 2020
Tenet, George: June 29, 2015; August 18, 2015; November 12, 2018; August 5, 2019;
     September 5, 2019
Turner, Admiral Stansfield: April 7, 2015
Webster, William: December 18, 2014; April 7, 2015; September 28, 2018
Woolsey, James: February 5, 2015

Other Sources

Allen, Charles: November 29, 2018; December 14, 2018; August 5, 2019
Armitage, Richard: January 17, 2019
Baer, Bob: June 17, 2015; January 14, 2020
Baker, Howard H. Jr.: August 16, 2011
Baker, James A. III: November 20, 2013; May 24, 2016
Bannon, Steve: November 6, 2017
Battaglia, Charles: January 17, 2019
Beers, Rand: January 14, 2019
Bennett, Gina: June 16, 2015
Black, Cofer: April 17, 2015; May 15, 2015; May 18, 2018; March 18, 2019

335

Blee, Richard: July 20, 2018; January 12, 2020
Bolten, Joshua: September 26, 2011
Bush, Barbara: October 24, 2011
Card, Andrew: October 12, 2011; February 28, 2015
Carter, Jimmy: September 14, 2011
Cheney, Dick: July 15, 2011; April 30, 2015
Ciralsky, Adam: July 26, 2018
Clarke, Richard: February 6, 2019; July 11 2019
Colby, Carl: September 6, 2019
Colby, Paul: February 25, 2019
Colby, Sally: March 22, 2019
Craig, Greg: May 9, 2019
Daley, Bill: May 3, 2012
Daniel, Michael: February 1, 2019
Danvers, Bill: September 13, 2018
Dean, John: April 3, 2016
Devine, Jack: March 8, 2019
Duberstein, Ken: August 10, 2011; September 23, 2014
Eizenstat, Stuart: May 15, 2015; January 17, 2019
Gelb, Leslie: July 6, 2018
Gerber, Burton: February 6, 2019
Goodman, Mel: March 5, 2019 (Caroline Keenan)
Hall, Steven: February 8, 2019
Haines, Avril: February 23, 2019
Helms, Cynthia: September 17, 2018
Helms, Dennis: August 22, 2018
Inman, Bobby Ray: March 14, 2019 (Caroline Keenan)
Kerr, Richard: February 14, 2018
Lake, Anthony: August 2, 2019
Lippert, Mark: September 13, 2018
Martin, David: December 14, 2018
Mazzetti, Mark: December 12, 2019
McDonough, Denis: October 5, 2016; January 18, 2019
McLarty, Thomas F. "Mack": September 22, 2011; September 18, 2018
Meese, Edwin: September 24, 2016
Meyer, Dan: December 9, 2019
Monaco, Lisa: February 4, 2019
O'Sullivan, Stephanie: September 18, 2018
Podesta, John: November 9, 2012; August 17, 2016
Park, Meroe: April 9, 2019
Powell, Colin: June 27, 2014; August 25, 2016
Powers, Tom: May 3, 2018
Price, Ned: July 11, 2018
Rasmussen, Nick: February 7, 2019; February 21, 2019
Reich, Robert: May 8, 2014
Riedel, Bruce: December 6, 2018; February 6, 2019; July 10, 2019; July 18, 2019;
    August 29, 2019; January 10, 2020
Robarge David: August 8, 2018; March 19, 2019

Rodriguez, Jose: April 24, 2015; February 27, 2019
Rumsfeld, Donald: June 14, 2011; May 17, 2012; May 6, 2014
Schlesinger, Cora: January 31, 2019 (Caroline Keenan)
Scowcroft, Brent: May 7, 2014
Shapiro, Nick: February 26, 2019; April 9, 2019
Silberman, Laurence: March 12, 2019 (Caroline Keenan)
Smith, Stephanie: February 21, 2019; February 27, 2019 (Caroline Keenan)
Spencer, Stuart: March 21, 2016; March 2, 2018
Sulick, Mike: September 19, 2018
Twetten, Thomas: March 8, 2019
Walcott, John: August 29, 2019
Watson, Jack: August 11, 2011; February 17, 2015; February 12, 2019
White, Al: August 1, 2018
Wisner, Frank Jr.: October 2, 2018
Woodward, Bob: June 19, 2019
Zaid, Mark: December 13, 2019
Zinni, Anthony: March 18, 2019

Notes

Introduction

2 *"Russia, if you're listening":* Ashley Parker and David Sanger, "Donald Trump Calls on Russia to Find Hillary Clinton's Missing Emails," *New York Times,* July 27, 2016.

8 *"It's not enough to ring the bell":* Tim Weiner, *Legacy of Ashes: The History of the CIA* (New York: Doubleday, 2007), p. 479.

8 *if you know what the president wants:* Thomas Powers, email to the author, June 21, 2019.

9 *John Brennan has publicly questioned the loyalty of Donald Trump:* Emily Goodin, "Ex-CIA chief John Brennan calls Trump 'nothing short of treasonous' after fawning press conference with Putin and says performance goes beyond 'high crimes and misdemeanors,'" *Daily Mail* (UK), July 16, 2018.

9 *"Nazi Germany":* Donald Trump, Twitter post, January 11, 2017, 7:48 a.m. EST.

11 *"When I was growing up in Texas":* Robert Gates, *From the Shadows: The Ultimate Insider's Story of Five Presidents and How They Won the Cold War* (New York: Simon & Schuster, 1994), p. 566.

11 *"Victory has a thousand fathers, but defeat is an orphan":* Arthur M. Schlesinger Jr., *A Thousand Days: John F. Kennedy in the White House* (Boston: Houghton Mifflin, 1965), p. 289.

11 *"clowns out at Langley":* Jeet Heer, "Trump's War on the Intelligence Is All About Ego," *New Republic,* January 4, 2017.

15 *"They are hanging out there in words that never go away":* John McLaughlin, email to the author, April 5, 2018.

16 *"Now you won't have to do those things":* Ted Sorensen, *Counselor: A Life at the Edge of History* (New York: HarperCollins, 2008), p. 499.

16 *"Could I, as a lawyer":* Ibid., p. 486.

17 *"I would bring back waterboarding, . . . and a hell of a lot worse":* "Trump Says He'd Bring Back Waterboarding and 'a Hell of a Lot Worse' to Torture Terrorists," *Express* (UK), February 7, 2016, www.express.co.uk/news/world/641795/Donald-Trump.

Chapter One: Richard Helms, Lyndon Johnson, and Richard Nixon

19 *"enemies, obstructionists and saboteurs":* Thomas Powers, *The Man Who Kept the Secrets: Richard Helms and the CIA* (New York: Alfred A. Knopf, 1979), pp. 228–29.

20 *"I commend him to you":* Richard Helms with William Hood, *A Look over*

My Shoulder: A Life in the Central Intelligence Agency (New York: Ballantine, 2003), p. 376.

20 *"We protected Helms from one hell of a lot of things"*: OVAL 741–002, June 23, 1972, White House Tapes, Richard Nixon Presidential Library and Museum, Yorba Linda, California.

21 *"bright blue eyes, coarse skin, with a pinkish tinge"*: Helms with Hood, *A Look over My Shoulder*, p. 24.

22 *"anything but benign postwar world seemed obvious"*: Ibid., p. 67.

22 *"Dear Dennis"*: Richard Helms, Letter to his son, Dennis, May 8, 1945, CIA Museum, McLean, Virginia.

25 *"Run it by Dick"*: Seymour Hersh, *Reporter: A Memoir* (New York: Alfred A. Knopf, 2018), p. 173.

26 *"They tell me you're the closest thing"*: David C. Martin, *Wilderness of Mirrors* (New York: Ballantine, 1980), p. 129.

26 *"were eventually to catch up to him"*: Helms with Hood, *A Look over My Shoulder*, p. 152.

27 *"who agreed entirely—to close it down"*: Ibid., p. 202.

27 *"the assassination of troublesome persons is morally and operationally indefensible"*: Ibid., p. 170.

28 *"with discretion lest the blade lose its edge"*: Ibid., p. 183.

28 *"exactly the right man"*: Ibid., p. 191.

29 *"and that there were no co-conspirators"*: Ibid., p. 229.

29 *"Oswald was put up to it by the Russians"*: Interview with Richard Helms by Mary McAuliffe, Office of the Historian, Central Intelligence Agency, June 19, 1989.

30 *"perpetually bending toward someone's ear to whisper a secret"*: Martin, *Wilderness of Mirrors*, p. 204.

32 *"can for very long be any better than its counterintelligence component"*: Helms with Hood, *A Look over My Shoulder*, p. 34.

33 *"You know the agency. Red doesn't"*: Ibid., p. 246.

34 *"a paper general in a paper war"*: Powers, *The Man Who Kept the Secrets*, p. 203.

34 *"it seemed I would never be free of it"*: Helms with Hood, *A Look over My Shoulder*, p. 308.

34 *"It simply is not true that the agency had anything to do with [it]"*: Ralph W. Weber, *Spymasters: 10 CIA Directors in Their Own Words* (New York: Scholarly Resources, 1999), p. 243.

34 *"My role was to keep the game honest"*: Helms with Hood, *A Look over My Shoulder*, p. 306.

35 *"the intelligence bingo of my time"*: Interview with Richard Helms by R. Jack Smith, Office of the Historian, Central Intelligence Agency, June 3, 1982.

35 *"So I've got to rely on you to get this stuff"*: Telephone conversation with Richard Helms and President Lyndon Johnson, September 6, 1967, Richard M. Helms Papers, Collection 1, Box 10, Folder 73, Georgetown University Library Booth Family Center for Special Collections, Washington, D.C.

36 *"no positive step toward a negotiated settlement"*: Memorandum: "The Effectiveness of the Rolling Thunder Program in North Vietnam, November

1966," Johnson Library, National Security File, Country File, Vietnam, 3 H (1), Appraisal of Bombing of NVN.

36 *"bad enough to make them stop fighting"*: Memorandum: "The Vietnamese Communists Will to Persist," August 26, 1966, Directorate of Intelligence, CIA, https://www.cia.gov/library/readingroom/docs/DOC_0001169545.pdf.

36 *"going its own way"*: Helms with Hood, *A Look over My Shoulder*, p. 310.

37 *"to engage in serious or meaningful discussion of evidence"*: Carver Memorandum for the DCI, "1967 Order of Battle Cables," 28 November 1975. (S). "GAC Files (SAVA-NIO)," Folder 9, CIA Archives.

37 *"I didn't take a lot of backtalk from him"*: Interview with Richard Helms by J. Kenneth McDonald, Office of the Historian, Central Intelligence Agency, September 29, 1982, p. 9.

37 *"Our national honor is at stake"*: Clark Clifford and Richard Holbrooke, "Serving the President 1—The Vietnam Years," *New Yorker*, April 28, 1991.

38 *"Would abandonment of the effort really generate other serious dangers?"*: Memorandum: "Implications of an Unfavorable Outcome in Vietnam," September 11, 1967, https://www.cia.gov/library/readingroom/docs/DOC _0001166443.pdf.

39 *"President Johnson never mentioned the document to me"*: Helms with Hood, *A Look over My Shoulder*, p. 315.

39 *"is certainly no way to run a government"*: Robert McNamara, *In Retrospect: The Tragedy and Lessons of Vietnam* (New York: Vintage, 1995), p. 294.

40 *"and then they go back to the way they wanted to do it before"*: Interview with Richard Helms by R. Jack Smith, Office of the Historian, Central Intelligence Agency, June 3, 1982.

40 *"Don't ask me to explain the workings of a president's mind!"*: Jack R. Smith, *The Unknown CIA: My Three Decades with the Agency* (Washington, D.C.: Potomac Books, 1989), p. 187.

40 *"and to do what is necessary"*: Helms with Hood, *A Look over My Shoulder*, p. 280.

41 *"So MHCHAOS was an effort to put in real life terms the solution to his problem:* Interview with Richard Helms by R. Jack Smith, Office of the Historian, Central Intelligence Agency, April 4, 1983.

41 *"other operational activity and firmly under my control"*: Helms with Hood, *A Look over My Shoulder*, p. 280.

41 *"had thought to be indefatigable"*: Ibid., p. 333.

41 *"Nixon just didn't like to deal"*: Interview with Richard Helms by J. Kenneth McDonald, p. 46.

42 *"There are forty thousand people out there, reading newspapers"*: Christopher Andrew, *For the President's Eyes Only* (New York: HarperCollins, 1995), p. 350.

43 *"we're going to want to run with it"*: OVAL 587–007a, October 8, 1971, White House Tapes, Richard Nixon Presidential Library and Museum, Yorba Linda, California.

43 *"I said, 'Now do you want these papers?'"*: Interview with Richard Helms by J. Kenneth McDonald, p. 46.

43 *"I'd appreciate knowing it"*: Ibid.

44 *"Chile is like a dagger pointing to the heart of Antarctica":* Alistair Horn, *Kissinger: 1973, the Crucial Year* (New York: Simon & Schuster, 2010), p. 197.

44 *"Truman had lost China":* Helms, *A Look Over My Shoulder*, p. 404.

45 *"48 hours for a plan of action":* Central Intelligence Agency, Job 80B01285A, DCI Helms Files, DCI Miscellaneous Papers on Chile, January 1, 1970-December 31, 1972.

45 *"President Nixon had ordered me":* Helms with Hood, *A Look over My Shoulder*, p. 405.

45 *"and then decide that the President did not mean what he said?":* Ibid.

46 *"Howard Hunt also seems to be involved in some way":* Ibid., p. 3.

46 *"None whatsoever," the chief replied:* Ibid.

47 *"the exposure of certain agency assets and channels for handling money":* Ibid., p. 9.

47 *"like a scalded cat":* John Ehrlichman, *Witness to Power: The Nixon Years* (New York: Simon and Schuster, 1982), p. 350.

48 *"cannot even remember having shouted in my own office":* Ibid.

48 *"which Helms desperately wanted to hide":* H. R. Haldeman with Joseph Di Mona, *The Ends of Power* (New York: Times Books, 1978), p. 40.

48 *"the agency's credibility would have been ruined forever":* Interview with Richard Helms by Stanley I. Kutler, July 14, 1988, Wisconsin Historical Archives, Box 15, Folder 16.

48 *"Don't you agree?":* OVAL 916–007, May 11, 1973, White House Tapes, Richard Nixon Presidential Library and Museum, Yorba Linda, California.

49 *"Maybe the lesson":* OVAL 587–007a, White House Tapes, Richard Nixon Presidential Library and Museum, Yorba Linda, California.

49 *"What about Moscow?":* Helms with Hood, *A Look over My Shoulder*, p. 411.

50 *"'don't go any further into this case.' Period.":* OVAL 741–002, June 23, 1972, White House Tapes, Richard Nixon Presidential Library and Museum, Yorba Linda, California.

50 *"he pulls the dumbest trick that anybody could pull and loses the presidency":* Interview with Richard Helms by John Bross, Office of the Historian, Central Intelligence Agency, December 14, 1982.

Chapter Two: James Schlesinger, William Colby, and Gerald Ford

54 *"infighting consequent upon the arrival of each new director":* Alexander Cockburn, "Politicize the CIA? You've Got to Be Kidding!," *The Nation*, December 2, 2004.

54 *"is going to stop fucking Richard Nixon":* Mel Goodman, *Whistleblower at the CIA: An Insider's Account of the Politicization of the CIA* (San Francisco: City Lights Books, 2017), p. 349.

55 *"and that was not exactly popular":* Transcript of oral history with James Schlesinger by Timothy Naftali, December 2, 2007, p. 47, Richard Nixon Presidential Library and Museum, Yorba Linda, California.

56 *"Buzhardt: Yes . . .":* OVAL 920–009, May 16, 1973, White House Tapes, Richard Nixon Presidential Library and Museum, Yorba Linda, California.

56 *"And I experienced it, both barrels":* William Colby and Peter Forbath, *Honorable Men: My Life in the CIA* (New York: Simon & Schuster, 1978), p. 339.

57 *"shall inform the Director of Central Intelligence immediately"*: Memorandum from Director of Central Intelligence Schlesinger to All Central Intelligence Agency Employees. Washington, May 9, 1973.

57 *"could survive in good working order after suffering such an instruction"*: Richard Helms with William Hood, *A Look over My Shoulder: A Life in the Central Intelligence Agency* (New York: Ballantine, 2003), p. 427.

61 *"his complicated theories that deserved further exploration"*: Colby and Forbath, *Honorable Men*, p. 334.

64 *"It's very hard to tell"*: Josh Dean, *The Taking of K-129: How the CIA Used Howard Hughes to Steal a Russian Sub in the Most Daring Covert Operation in History* (New York: Dutton, 2017), p. 319.

64 *"Colby is a disaster and really should be replaced"*: Memorandum of conversation, January 23, 1975, National Security Adviser, Memoranda of Conversations, Box 8, Gerald Ford Presidential Library, Ann Arbor, Michigan.

64 *"I've got a story bigger than My-Lai"*: Colby and Forbath, *Honorable Men*, p. 389.

64 *"distinct matters that you've gotten mixed up and distorted"*: Ibid., p. 390.

65 *"HUGE CIA OPERATION REPORTED IN U.S."*: Seymour Hersh, *New York Times*, December 22, 1974.

65 *"risen to a combustible level during the Vietnam and Watergate years, now exploded"*: Colby and Forbath, *Honorable Men*, p. 391.

66 *"nothing but a cot in it for this period"*: "Family Jewels" memo, May 16, 1973, CIA, https://www.cia.gov/library/readingroom/docs/DOC_0001451843.pdf.

67 *"Frankly we are in a mess"*: Tim Weiner, *Legacy of Ashes: The History of the CIA*, (New York: Doubleday, 2007), p. 338.

67 *"That's off-the-record!"*: Colby and Forbath, *Honorable Men*, p. 409.

67 *"uncover several assassinations of foreign officials involving the CIA"*: Ibid., p. 410.

67 *"you may have committed a crime yourself"*: Ibid., p. 385.

68 *"I believed"*: Ibid., p. 404.

68 *"thrown rather than fired at the prospective victim"*: Helms with Hood, *A Look over My Shoulder*, p. 430.

69 *"Jim, go"*: Oral history: Reflections of DCI Colby and Helms on the CIA's "Time of Troubles," September 10, 2007, CIA Oral History Archives.

69 *"Now she's left me"*: Seymour Hersh, "The Angleton," *New York Times Magazine*, June 25, 1978.

70 *"policy that Allende be overthrown by a coup"*: Cable, October 16, 1970, https://nsarchive2.gwu.edu//NSAEBB/NSAEBB8/docs/doc05.pdf.

70 *"Yes, sir"*: "Nomination of Richard Helms to Be Ambassador to Iran and CIA International and Domestic Activities, February 7, 1973" (Washington, D.C.: U.S. Government Printing Office, 1974).

71 *"for which he could or should be condemned"*: Colby and Forbath, *Honorable Men*, p. 383.

71 *"But I am satisfied that I did what I had to do"*: Colby and Forbath, *Honorable Men*, pp. 385–86.

71 *"as thoroughly ransacked as those of the Agency during these investigations"*: Helms with Hood, *A Look over My Shoulder*, p. 430.

71 *"pillaged by a foreign power"*: Oral history: Reflections of DCIs Colby and

Helms on the CIA's "Time of Troubles," Studies in Intelligence Vol. 51, No. 3, CIA.

72 *"Fidel Castro (Cuba)":* "Alleged Assassination Plots Involving Foreign Leaders: 1975 Senate Report on CIA Covert Operations to Kill Fidel Castro, Ngo Dinh Diem, and Others, Church Committee," 1975.

74 *"We are going to do some re-organizing of the national security structure":* William Colby, "Why I Was Fired from the CIA," *Esquire,* May 9, 1978.

74 *"I should have been shattered":* Ibid.

Chapter Three: George H. W. Bush, Stansfield Turner, and Jimmy Carter

79 *"THE PRESIDENT ASKS THAT YOU CONSENT":* Jon Meacham, *Destiny and Power: The American Odyssey of George Herbert Walker Bush* (New York: Random House, 2015), p. 188.

79 *"total and complete shock":* George Bush, *All the Best: My Life in Letters and Other Writings* (New York: Scribner, 2010), p. 233.

80 *"from law breaking to simple incompetence":* Meacham, *Destiny and Power,* p. 188.

80 *"I see this as the total end":* Bush, *All the Best,* p. 233.

80 *"The scars left by that experience would put me out of contention":* Ibid., p. 189.

81 *"Rumsfeld set you up, and you were a damn fool to say yes":* Ibid.

81 *"I WISH I HAD SOME TIME":* Ibid., p. 233.

81 *"as long as what he'd asked me to do wasn't illegal or immoral":* Ibid., p. 188.

82 *"It would send a message":* George Bush with Victor Gold, *Looking Forward: An Autobiography* (New York: Bantam, 1988), p. 163.

83 *"not by impersonal notices":* Ibid., p. 165.

83 *"it's tough to talk to a group of press people after two hours of cocktails":* Ibid., p. 254.

83 *"Intelligence is a demanding craft":* Bush, *All the Best,* p. 251.

84 *"fascinating subjects to get into, but just not enough time":* Ibid., p. 354.

85 *"our profession thinks you are all lying bastards":* Ibid., p. 257.

85 *"but the CIA is intact, and functioning pretty darn well":* Ibid.

86 *"plotting murder and other crimes":* Jimmy Carter, *Keeping Faith: Memoirs of a President* (Fayetteville: University of Arkansas Press, 1982), p. 147.

86 *"dumping grounds for unsuccessful candidates, faithful political partisans":* James T. Wooten, "Carter Says Ford Lags as Reformer," *New York Times,* August 12, 1976.

86 *"that he was surprised or unsurprised":* Bush, *All the Best,* p. 264.

87 *"a good background as former United Nations Ambassador and U.S. representative to China":* John Helgerson, *Getting to Know the President: CIA Briefings of Presidential Candidates: 1952–1992* (Washington, D.C.: Center for the Study of Intelligence, CIA), p. 108.

87 *"The president-elect should put his own man in the organization in whom he has confidence":* Ibid., p. 115.

88 *"They're not going to stand for it":* Ted Sorensen, *Counselor* (New York: HarperCollins, 2008), Kindle location 488.

88 *"my own personal Inspector Javert":* Ibid., Kindle location 488.

89 *"a few right-wing activists":* Ibid., Kindle location 488.

89 *"I return to private life":* Ibid., Kindle location 499.

89 *"I think it's clear":* Ted Sorensen, Press conference post-CIA Director Nomination Hearing, January 17, 1977.

90 *"I saw my career in the United States Navy flash before my eyes":* Admiral Stansfield Turner, *Burn Before Reading: Presidents, CIA Directors and Secret Intelligence* (New York: Hachette, 2005), p. 158.

90 *"The DCI job must be depoliticized":* Helgerson, John. CIA Briefings of Presidential Candidates 1952–1992. Central Intelligence Agency Library, Center for the Study of Intelligence, 1996, p. 116.

92 *"crybabies":* Stansfield Turner interview in *Newsweek*, November 21, 1977.

92 *"which was far more politically astute than my action":* Central Intelligence Agency Library, Center for the Study of Intelligence, CIA briefings of presidential candidates, p. 188.

94 *"You'd better get yourself a good lawyer":* Helms with Hood, *A Look over My Shoulder*, p. 435.

94 *"must respect and honor the Constitution and the laws of the United States":* Timothy S. Robinson, "Helms Fined $2,000 Term Suspended" *Washington Post*, November 5, 1977.

94 *"Helms will wear this conviction like a badge of honor":* Richard Helms with William Hood, *A Look over My Shoulder: A Life in the Central Intelligence Agency* (New York: Ballantine, 2003), p. 445.

95 *"The Two Oaths of Richard Helms":* Mark Lilla and Mark Moore. Case Program: The Two Oaths of Richard Helms. Harvard Kennedy School, John F. Kennedy School of Government, 1983.

96 *"It was one of those moments":* George Packer, *Our Man: Richard Holbrooke and the End of the American Century* (New York: Alfred A. Knopf, 2019), p. 49.

97 *"One thing I can say about the Shah":* Jimmy Carter remarks, November 15, 1977, State Dinner for the Shah of Iran in White House, Public Papers of the Presidents, Jimmy Carter, 1977.

97 *"an island of stability in one of the more troubled areas of the world":* Jimmy Carter remarks, December 31, 1977, Niavaran Palace Complex, Tehran.

98 *"that the CIA in the end learned nothing from SAVAK about the Shah's opposition":* Robert Jervis, *Why Intelligence Fails* (Ithaca: Cornell University Press, 2011), p. 17.

98 *"There is no serious domestic threat":* Ibid., p. 57.

99 *"Iran is not in a revolutionary or even a 'prerevolutionary' situation":* Ibid., p 45.

100 *"I was really appalled":* Zbigniew Brzezinski, *Power and Principle: Memoirs of the National Security Adviser 1977–1981* (New York: Farrar, Straus, Giroux, 1985), p. 367.

100 *"I am not satisfied with the quality of our political intelligence":* Gary Sick, *All Fall Down: America's Tragic Encounter with Iran* (Lincoln, NE: iUniverse. com, 1986), p. 90.

100 *"Thinking the Unthinkable":* U.S. Embassy Tehran, William Sullivan, cable to State Department, "Thinking the Unthinkable," November 9, 1978.

100 *"a sovereign may not save his throne":* Mohammad Reza Pahlavi, *Answer to History* (New York: Stein & Day, 1980), p. 167.

101 *"What do you propose to do":* Stuart Eizenstat, *President Carter: The White House Years* (New York: Thomas Dunne, 2018), p. 810.

102 *"and not much chance of acquiring them once his regime crumbled":* Turner, *Burn Before Reading*, p. 170.

102 *"We were just plain asleep":* Tim Weiner, "Stansfield Turner, C.I.A. Director Who Confronted Communism Under Carter, Dies at 94," *New York Times*, January 18, 2018.

106 *"there is no reason to believe that they have become less frequent over time":* Jervis, *Why Intelligence Fails*, p. 5.

Chapter Four: William Casey and Ronald Reagan

109 *"a political hack":* Bob Woodward, *Veil: The Secret Wars of the CIA, 1981–1987* (New York: Simon & Schuster, 1987), p. 8.

111 *"bankers and tycoons":* William Casey, *The Secret War Against Hitler* (Washington, D.C.: Regency Gateway, 1988), p. 7.

113 *"This is a bunch of crap":* William Casey, Hearings before the Select Committee on Intelligence of the US Senate. Nomination of Robert M. Gates to be Director of Central Intelligence: Testimony of Admiral Bobby Ray Inman. September 1991, Vol. I.

114 *Exhibit A, in his view, was a book by a journalist:* Claire Sterling, *The Terror Network: The Secret War of International Terrorism* (New York: Henry Holt, 1981).

114 *"it told me more than you bastards":* Melvin A. Goodman, *Whistleblower at the CIA: An Insider's Account of the Politics of Intelligence* (San Francisco: City Lights Books, 2017), p. 118.

114 *"CIA is slowly turning into the Department of Agriculture":* Memorandum for DCI, Deputy DCI from Robert M. Gates. Subject: Personnel. 23 September 1981. CIA Archives.

115 *"Alan, you know":* George Crile, *Charlie Wilson's War: The Extraordinary Story of How the Wildest Man in Congress and Rogue CIA Agent Changed the History of Our Time* (New York: Atlantic Monthly Press, 2003), p. 263.

116 *"Make war in Nicaragua":* Deborah Hart Strober and Gerald S. Strober, *Reagan: The Man and His Presidency* (New York: Houghton Mifflin, 1998), p. 116.

119 *"and even at home by their children":* Crile, *Charlie Wilson's War*, p. 123.

119 *"the Soviets will overpower and wear down the rebels":* Woodward, *Veil*, p. 285.

121 *"an extremist, uninhibited psychopath":* Ronan Bergman, *Rise and Kill First: The Secret History of Israel's Targeted Assassinations* (New York: Random House, 2018), p. 373.

126 *"Some strange soundings are coming from the Iranians":* Ronald Reagan, White House Diary Entry, July 17, 1985, Bethesda Naval Hospital, Ronald Reagan Presidential Library, Simi Valley, California, https://www.reagan foundation.org/ronald-reagan/white-house-diaries/diary-entry-07171985/.

126 *"Open it up":* Donald Regan, Tower Commission Report, Appendix B. "The Iran/Contra Affair: A Narrative." February 26, 1987.

126 *"the highly secret convoluted process":* Ronald Reagan (author) with Douglas Brinkley, ed., *The Reagan Diaries* (New York: HarperCollins, 2007), p. 381.

127 *liaison with foreign intelligence services was one area not covered by congressional oversight:* Woodward, *Veil*, p. 397.

128 *"The United States has not made concessions to those who hold our people in Lebanon":* Ronald Reagan, "Address to the Nation on the Iran Arms and Contra Aid Controversy," November 13, 1986.

128 *"Because I don't think a mistake was made":* Ronald Reagan, Presidential News Conference, November 19, 1986.

129 *"$12 million will be used to purchase critically needed supplies":* So-called "Diversion Memo," written by Oliver North, April 1986.

129 *"who has known him for twenty years":* H. W. Brands, *Reagan: The Life* (New York: Anchor, 2016), p. 633.

129 *"On one of the arms shipments":* Ronald Reagan and Douglas Brinkley, *The Reagan Diaries* (New York: HarperCollins, 2007), p. 453.

129 *"Certain monies," the attorney general told the press corps:* Bernard Weinraub, "Iran Payment Found Diverted to the Contras," *New York Times*, November 25, 1986.

131 *"Reagan wasn't just a lame duck, he was a dead duck," said an aide:* Author interview with Ken Duberstein, September 23, 2014.

132 *"We moved to the side of Casey's bed":* Robert Gates, *From the Shadows: The Ultimate Insider's Story of Five Presidents and How They Won the Cold War* (New York: Simon & Schuster, 1996), p. 414.

132 *"Then he was asleep, and I didn't get to ask another question":* Woodward, *Veil*, Kindle location 9025.

Chapter Five: William Webster, Robert Gates, and George H. W. Bush

137 *"No wonder":* Robert Gates, *From the Shadows: The Ultimate Insider's Story of Five Presidents and How They Won the Cold War* (New York: Simon & Schuster, 1996), p. 414.

137 *"'Take This Job and Shove It'?":* Ibid., p. 417.

140 *"with the raison d'être of the organization he was brought in to run":* Tim Weiner, *Legacy of Ashes: The History of the CIA* (New York: Anchor, 2007), p. 479.

141 *"It was a mistake":* Ronald Reagan, televised speech, Oval Office, March 5, 1987.

142 *"There is not a single Soviet soldier":* Bill Keller, "Last Soviet Soldiers Leave Afghanistan," *New York Times*, February 16, 1989.

143 *"should remain above politics, dealing solely in intelligence":* George H. W. Bush and Brent Scowcroft, *A World Transformed* (New York: Vintage, 1999), p. 21.

143 *"is, under all but the most unusual circumstances, a good formulation":* Ibid.

143 *"Gates had received his Ph.D.":* Alter, Jonathan: "The Wars Robert Gates Got Wrong," *New Yorker*, February 3, 2014.

143 *"someone capable of finding a dark lining in even the brightest cloud":* David Ignatius, "Why Bob Gates Is the Eeyore of Sovietology," *Washington Post*, May 28, 1989.

144 *"new world order":* George H. W. Bush, televised speech, September 11, 1991.

145 *"the CIA is getting rid of its Cassandra, Charlie Allen":* Michael Wines,

"Washington at Work; C.I.A. Sidelines Its Gulf Cassandra," *New York Times*, January 24, 1991.

147 *"who was prepared to work beyond any reasonable call of duty":* Mel Goodman, *Whistleblower at the CIA: An Insider's Account of the Politics of Intelligence* (San Francisco: City Lights Books, 2017), p. 277.

Chapter Six: James Woolsey, John Deutch, and Bill Clinton

154 *"jungle full of poisonous snakes":* Douglas Gartoff, "Directors of Central Intelligence as Leaders of the Intelligence Community. 1946–2005," Center for the Study of Intelligence, Central Intelligence Agency, Washington, D.C., 2005, p. 221.

159 *"Iraqi cleaning women":* Author interview with James Woolsey, March 9, 2015.

161 *"but because the agency effort was inadequate":* The Aldrich H. Ames Case: An Assessment of CIA's Role in Identifying Ames as an Intelligence Penetration of the Agency, October 21, 1994.

161 *"significant access to highly sensitive information":* CIA Inspector General Report on the Aldrich Ames Case, October 21, 1994.

161 *"Rick was just Rick":* Sandra Grimes and Jeanne Vertefeuille, *Circle of Treason: A CIA Account of Aldrich Ames and the Men He Betrayed* (Annapolis: Naval Institute Press, 2012), Kindle location 3243.

161 *"lacked the necessary":* Grimes and Vertefeuille, *Circle of Treason*, Kindle location 2966.

162 *"as a whole seems not to weigh in the balance":* Ibid., Kindle location 3047.

165 *"'This is your country'":* Taylor Branch, *The Clinton Tapes: Wrestling History with the President* (New York: Simon & Schuster, 2009), p. 241.

165 *"the 58-year-old intelligence chief is brilliant, energetic and outspoken":* Elaine Sciolino, "CIA Director Charts His Own Course," *New York Times*, September 29, 1996.

166 *in a series titled "Dark Alliance":* Gary Webb, "Cocaine Pipeline Financed Rebels: Evidence Points to CIA Knowing of High-Volume Drug Network, *San Jose Mercury News*, August 22, 1996.

171 *"In the last six weeks, he has gotten stronger politically in the region":* Testimony from John Deutch, Senate Select Committee on Intelligence, September 19, 1996.

172 *"High-risk internet sites had placed 'cookies' on the hard drives":* Britt Snider, Inspector General of the CIA, "Report of Investigation: Improper Handling of Classified Information by John M. Deutch," 1998–0028-IG, February 18, 2000, https://fas.org/irp/cia/product/ig_deutch.html.

Chapter Seven: George Tenet, Bill Clinton, and George W. Bush

173 *"dancing bear":* Tim Weiner, *Legacy of Ashes: The History of the CIA*, (New York: Random House, 2007), p. 536.

174 *"I was like a Broadway understudy":* George Tenet with Bill Harlow, *At the Center of the Storm: My Years at the CIA* (New York: HarperCollins, 2007), p. 11.

183 *"at least on the level of the* Cole, *were risk free":* The 9/11 Commission Report, July 22, 2004, p. 350, https://www.9–11commission.gov/report/.

187 *"not very crisp because we were discussing the threat every day":* Condoleezza Rice, No Higher Honor: A Memoir of My Years in Washington (New York: Crown, 2012), p. 67.

Chapter Eight: George Tenet and George W. Bush

197 *ProPublica retracted a story that Haspel:* Raymond Bonner, "Correction: Trump's Pick to Head CIA Did Not Oversee Waterboarding of Abu Zubaydah," ProPublica, March 15, 2018.

199 *the Democratic majority of the Senate Select Committee on Intelligence would issue a scathing report:* "Report of the Senate Select Committee on Intelligence Committee Study of the Central Intelligence Agency's Detention and Interrogation Program," December 9, 2014, https://www.intelligence.senate.gov /sites/default/files/publications/CRPT-113srpt288.pdf.

201 *"I'd bring back waterboarding":* Donald Trump, Republican Primary Debate, Goffstown, New Hampshire, February 6, 2016.

202 *"possesses and produces chemical and biological weapons":* George W. Bush, speech, Cincinnati, Ohio, October 2, 2007.

203 *"Political pressures cannot explain the intelligence failure":* Robert Jervis, Why Intelligence Fails: Lessons from the Iranian Revolution and the Iraq War (Ithaca: Cornell University Press, 2010), p. 135.

204 *"There's always people":* Jervis, Why Intelligence Fails, p. 133.

204 *"it could make a nuclear weapon within several months":* National Intelligence Estimate: Iraq's Continuing Programs for Weapons of Mass Destruction, October 2002, declassified July 18, 2003. https://www.cia.gov/library /readingroom/docs/DOC_0001075566.pdf.

206 *"Don't worry, it's a slam dunk!":* Bob Woodward, Plan of Attack (New York: Simon & Schuster, 2004), p. 249.

209 *"almost entirely fallacious":* Jervis, Why Intelligence Fails, p. 138.

210 *"Better intelligence would not have led to an effective policy":* Ibid., p. 3.

Chapter Nine: Porter Goss, Michael Hayden, and George W. Bush

214 *"whose face is marred by dust and sweat and blood":* Theodore Roosevelt, "Citizenship in a Republic," speech, Paris, France, April 23, 1910.

214 *"These have been eventful years":* Remarks by DCI George Tenet at Farewell Ceremony, CIA headquarters, Langley, Va., July 8, 2004.

215 *"four kinds of failures: in imagination, policy, capabilities, and management":* The 9/11 Commission Report, July 22, 2004, p. 339, https://www.9–11com mission.gov/report/.

219 *"Despite firm legal opinions":* Jose A. Rodriguez Jr. with Bill Harlow, Hard Measures: How Aggressive CIA Actions After 9/11 Saved American Lives (New York: Threshold Editions, 2012), p. 187.

219 *aired a sensational story about an Iraqi prison called Abu Ghraib:* "Court Martial in Iraq," 60 Minutes II, CBS, April 28, 2004.

220   *"the early interrogations"*: Rodriguez, *Hard Measures*, Kindle location 185.

220   *"Watch it"*: Associated Press, "Lawmaker warned CIA not to destroy tapes," NBC News, January 3, 2008.

225   *"a grasp of the lapels"*: Michael W. Hayden, *Playing to the Edge: American Intelligence in the Age of Terror* (New York: Penguin, 2016), p. 225.

225   *"exposed CIA officials and their families to retaliation from Al Qaeda and its sympathizers"*: Michael Hayden, "Director's Statement on the Taping of Early Detainee Interrogations," December 6, 2007.

226   *"CIA had waterboarded three people"*: Hayden, *Playing to the Edge*, p. 241.

226   *"He'll forever be remembered"*: Hayden, *Playing to the Edge*, p. 240.

229   *"bombing or the bomb"*: Hayden, *Playing to the Edge*, p. 291.

232   *"President Bush then granted Dagan's request"*: Ronen Bergman, *Rise and Kill First: The Secret History of Israel's Targeted Assassinations* (New York: Random House: 2018), p. 599.

Chapter Ten: Leon Panetta and Barack Obama

237   *"guarantees of humane treatment"*: Michael W. Hayden, *Playing to the Edge: American Intelligence in the Age of Terror* (New York: Penguin, 2016), p. 357.

239   *"You know my background"*: Author interview with Leon Panetta, September 21, 2018.

240   *"iron fist inside a velvet glove"*: Chris Whipple, *The Gatekeepers: How the White House Chiefs of Staff Define Every Presidency* (New York: Crown, 2017), p. 199.

240   *"So a priest and a rabbi go to a prizefight"*: Author interview with Bill Danvers, September 13, 2018.

240   *Panetta poured his own coffee into a mug marked "CIA"*: Leon Panetta and Jim Newton, *Worthy Fights: A Memoir of Leadership in War and Peace* (New York: Penguin, 2014), p. 212.

242   *"Party's over, Leon and I have a meeting"*: Ibid., p. 204.

244   *"I am living testimony to the moral force"*: Barack H. Obama, Nobel Lecture: "A Just and Lasting Peace," December 10, 2009, https://www.nobelprize.org /prizes/peace/2009/obama/lecture.

245   *In 2008, it was George W. Bush who gave the agency*: Author interview with Michael Hayden, December 17, 2014.

245   *as many strikes during Obama's first nine*: Council on Foreign Relations, https://www.cfr.org/blog/obamas-final-drone-strike-data.

246   *"Everybody thought he was in a cave"*: Jeremy Bash, *The Oath with Chuck Rosenberg*, podcast, October 30, 2019.

248   *"Hands up! Get your hand out of your clothing!"*: Joby Warrick, *The Triple Agent: The Al Qaeda Mole Who Infiltrated the CIA* (New York: Vintage, 2012), p. 8.

252   *"There is a long tradition in Washington"*: Panetta and Newton, *Worthy Fights*, p. 226.

255   *But Obama worried that it wasn't enough*: Author interview with Leon Panetta, September 21, 2018.

Chapter Eleven: David Petraeus, John Brennan, and Barack Obama

261 *"After six straight military commands":* Paula Broadwell, *All-in: The Education of General David Petraeus* (New York: Penguin, 2012), Kindle location 5952.

268 *"This technology raises profound questions":* Remarks by the President at the National Defense University, Fort McNair, Washington, D.C., May 23, 2013. https://obamawhitehouse.archives.gov/the-press-office/2013/05/23/remarks-president-national-defense-university.

271 *"exceptionally grave damage":* Adam Goldman, "Petraeus Pleads Guilty to Mishandling Classified Material, Will Face Probation," *Washington Post*, April 23, 2015.

271 *"would be just a footnote to a brilliant career":* Statement by President Obama on the Resignation of CIA Director David Petraeus, November 9, 2012. https://obamawhitehouse.archives.gov/the-press-office/2012/11/09/statement-president-obama-resignation-cia-director-david-petraeus.

277 *"potential effort to intimidate":* Dan Roberts and Spencer Ackerman, "Feinstein Accuses CIA of 'Intimidating' Senate Staff over Torture Report," *Guardian*, March 11, 2014.

278 *"A perfectly thriving state":* Michael Hayden, *The Assault on Intelligence: American National Security in an Age of Lies* (New York: Penguin, 2018), p. 193.

279 *"Gerasimov's notorious 'little green men'":* Ibid.

282 *"We know what you're doing and if you go further":* Jon Sharman, "Vladimir Putin was 'really clear' with Obama when confronted over US election hack," *Independent* (UK), December 17, 2016, https://www.independent.co.uk/news/world/americas/vladimir-putin-really-clear-barack-obama-us-election-hack-g20-cut-it-out-a7481686.html.

282 *"We've got more capacity than anybody":* Greg Miller, Ellen Nakashima, and Adam Entous, "Obama's Secret Struggle to Punish Russia for Putin's Election Assault," *Washington Post*, June 23, 2017.

283 *"The U.S. Intelligence Community (USIC) is confident":* "Joint Statement from the Department of Homeland Security and Office of the Director of National Intelligence on Election Security," October 7, 2016, https://www.dhs.gov/news/2016/10/07/joint-statement-department-homeland-security-and-office-director-national.

284 *"outside forces were doing what they could":* Glenn Simpson and Peter Fritsch, *Crime in Progress: Inside the Steele Dossier and the Fusion GPS Investigation of Donald Trump* (New York: Random House, 2019), p. 116.

284 *"the political equivalent of 9/11":* "Morell calls Russia's meddling in U.S. elections 'political equivalent of 9/11,'" December 12, 2016, https://www.politico.com/story/2016/12/michael-morell-russia-us-elections-232495.

285 *the Russian social media campaign* had *elected Trump:* James Clapper and Trey Brown, *Facts and Fears: Hard Truths from a Life in Intelligence* (New York: Viking, 2018), p. 396.

Chapter Twelve: Mike Pompeo, Gina Haspel, and Donald Trump

287 *"This story is* bullshit!*" he screamed:* Graham Lanktree, "Trump Said Inauguration Crowd Numbers Were 'Bullshit' Says Reince Priebus in New Book," *Newsweek*, February 15, 2018.

287 *"clowns out at Langley":* Jeet Heer, "Trump's War on the Intelligence Is All About Ego," *The New Republic*, January 4, 2017.

287 *"deep state":* Tyler Durden, "It's Trump vs. the Deep State vs. the Rest of Us," ZeroHedge.com, November 15, 2019.

287 *"said Saddam Hussein had weapons of mass destruction":* Statement from the Trump Transition Team, December 9, 2016.

288 *"somebody sitting on their bed that weighs 400 pounds":* Donald Trump, during first presidential debate with Hillary Clinton, Hofstra University, Hempstead, N.Y., September 26, 2016.

288 *"Do I look like someone who needs hookers?":* James Comey, *A Higher Loyalty: Truth, Lies, and Leadership* (New York: Flatiron Books, 2018), p. 258.

288 *"I think it's a disgrace":* Donald Trump, Twitter, January 11, 2017, 7:48 a.m. EST.

289 *"I want to thank everybody":* Donald Trump, remarks to the CIA, January 21, 2017.

290 *"a despicable display of self-aggrandizement":* Bess Levin, "Ex-C.I.A. Chief Blasts Trump's 'Despicable' Speech at C.I.A. Headquarters," *Vanity Fair*, January 22, 2017.

291 *"Marco Rubio will never demean our soldiers":* Michael Pompeo, Republican Caucus, Wichita, Kansas, March 5, 2016.

291 *"He's like a heat-seeking missile for Trump's ass":* Susan Glasser, "Mike Pompeo: The Secretary of Trump," *New Yorker*, August 26, 2019.

291 *"Beauty and the Beast":* Donald Trump, June 30, 2019, Seoul, South Korea.

291 *"I give him massive respect":* Glasser, "Mike Pompeo, the Secretary of Trump."

294 *"a beer salesman":* Michael Wolff, *Fire and Fury: Inside the Trump White House* (New York: Henry Holt, 2018), p. 189.

295 *"Let's fucking kill them!":* Bob Woodward, *Fear: Trump in the White House* (New York: Simon & Schuster, 2018), p. 146.

296 *"this Russia thing."* Donald Trump interview with Lester Holt, NBC News, May 11, 2017.

297 *"He was crazy, a real nut job":* Matt Apuzzo, Maggie Haberman, and Matthew Rosenberg, "Trump Told Russians That Firing 'Nut Job' Comey Eased Pressure from Investigation," *New York Times*, May 19, 2017.

297 *"I really believe that when he tells me that, he means it":* Donald Trump, aboard Air Force One, November 11, 2017.

299 *Because Putin told me:* Shane Harris, Josh Dawsey, and Carol D. Leonig, "Former White House Officials Say They Feared Putin Influenced the President's Views on Ukraine and 2016 Campaign," *Washington Post*, December 19, 2019.

300 *"North Korea best not make any more threats":* Peter Baker and Chloe Sang-Hun, "Trump Threatens 'Fire and Fury' Against North Korea if It Endangers U.S.," *New York Times*, August 8, 2017.

300 *"enveloping fire":* David Caplan, "North Korea threatens missile strike on Guam that will create an 'enveloping fire,'" ABC News, August 8, 2017.

300 *"there is No Longer a Nuclear Threat":* Donald Trump, Twitter, June 13, 2018, 4:56 a.m. EST.

300 *had called Trump a "moron":* Carole E. Lee, Kristen Welker, Stephanie Ruhle, and Dafna Linzer, "Tillerson's Fury at Trump Required an Intervention from Pence," NBC News, October 4, 2017.

302 *"quite literally a war criminal":* Jameel Jaffer, Twitter, March 13, 2018, 9:58 a.m. EST.

302 *"Gina Haspel should be prosecuted, not promoted":* Vincent Warren, March 13, 2018.

302 *"bring back waterboarding, . . . and a hell of a lot worse":* Donald Trump, Republican Primary debate, Goffstown, New Hampshire, February 6, 2016.

302 *"Torture works":* Donald Trump, Republican Primary debate, New Hampshire, February 17, 2016.

302 *"that she did not bat an eye":* Jonathan Swan, "Trump Said CIA Director Gina Haspel Agreed with Him '100%' on Torture," *Axios*, November 17, 2016.

302 *"typical, middle-class American":* Gina Haspel, Senate Select Committee on Intelligence hearing, May 9, 2018.

304 *"I've spent a lot of time with her":* Donald Trump, Gina Haspel swearing-in ceremony, May 21, 2018, McLean, Virginia.

305 *"would you warn him never to do it again?":* Jonathan Lemire, Associated Press, press conference, Helsinki, Finland, July 16, 2018.

305 *"President Putin was extremely strong and powerful in his denial today":* Donald Trump and Vladimir Putin, press conference, Helsinki, Finland, July 16, 2018.

305 *Trump thought this was "an incredible offer":* Michael McFaul, "Putin Wanted to Interrogate Me. Trump Called It 'an Incredible Offer.' Why?," *Washington Post*, July 27, 2018.

306 *"agreements":* Major General Igor Konashenkov, Russian military spokesman, July 17, 2018.

308 *"John Brennan is panicking":* Donald Trump, Twitter, May 21, 2018, 7:53 a.m. EST.

308 *"Insinuations and allegations":* Carlos Garcia, "12 Former Intelligence Chiefs Release a Statement on Trump Revoking Brennan Clearance," *The Blaze*, August 18, 2018.

309 *"It was like Pulp Fiction":* David Kirkpatrick and Carlotta Gall, "Turkish Officials Say Khashoggi Was Killed on Order of Saudi Leadership," *New York Times*, October 10, 2018.

310 *"I don't like stopping massive amounts of money that's being poured into our country":* Donald Trump, Oval Office, October 11, 2018.

310 *"If we take plastic bags and cut it into pieces, it will be finished":* Agnès Callamard, "Report of the Special Rapporteur on Extrajudicial, Summary or Arbitrary Executions: Investigation into the Unlawful Death of Mr. Jamal Khashoggi," June 19, 2019.

311 *"maybe he did and maybe he didn't!":* Donald Trump, White House, November 20, 2018.

311 *"high confidence":* Shane Harris, Greg Miller, and Josh Dawsey, "CIA Con-

cludes Saudi Crown Prince Ordered Jamal Khashoggi's Assassination," *Washington Post*, November 16, 2018.

311 *"credible evidence":* Callamard, "Report of the Special Rapporteur on Extrajudicial, Summary or Arbitrary Executions: Investigation into the Unlawful Death of Mr. Jamal Khashoggi."

311 *"the empty chair meant for CIA Director Gina Haspel":* Dick Durbin, Twitter, November 28, 2018, 12:51 p.m. EST.

311 *"no direct reporting":* Michael Pompeo, March 5, 2016, Republican Caucus, Wichita, Kansas, March 5, 2016.

311 *"I have zero question in my mind":* Bob Corker, Washington, D.C., December 4, 2018.

312 *"the antithesis of justice" and "a mockery":* Agnès Callamard, Twitter, December 23, 2019, 6:22 a.m. EST. "Bottom line: the hit-men are guilty, sentenced to death. The masterminds not only walk free. They have barely been touched by the investigation and the trial. That is the antithesis of justice. It is a mockery."

312 *"Break into the place, rifle the files":* Stanley I. Kutler, *Abuse of Power: The New Nixon Tapes* (New York: Free Press, 1997), p. 6.

313 *"they say CrowdStrike":* Donald Trump and Volodymyr Zelensky, phone call; full transcript: https://www.whitehouse.gov/wp-content/uploads/2019/09/Unclassified09.2019.pdf.

314 *"In the course of my official duties":* "Document: Read the Whistleblower Complaint," *New York Times*, September 26, 2019.

315 *"perfect":* Donald Trump, Twitter, January 19, 2020, 3:39 p.m. EST: "I JUST GOT IMPEACHED FOR MAKING A PERFECT PHONE CALL."

315 *"That's why we held up the money":* "Read Mulvaney's Conflicting Statements on Quid Pro Quo," *New York Times*, October 17, 2019.

315 *"whatever drug deal Giuliani and Mulvaney are cooking up":* Fiona Hill, testimony, House Permanent Select Committee on Intelligence, November 8, 2019.

315 *"everyone was in the loop":* Gordon Sondland, testimony, House Permanent Select Committee on Intelligence, November 20, 2019.

316 *"We used to handle them a little differently than we do now":* Donald Trump, private event at Intercontinental Hotel, New York City, September 26, 2019.

316 *"unlikely to give up all of its nuclear weapons and production capabilities":* Dan Coats, testimony, Senate Intelligence Committee, worldwide threats hearing, January 29, 2019.

317 *"Perhaps Intelligence should go back to school!":* Donald Trump, Twitter, January 30, 2019, 8:50 a.m. EST.

317 *"If Iran wants to fight":* Donald Trump, Twitter, May 19, 2019, 1:25 p.m. EST.

319 *"imminent and sinister threat":* Daniel Politi, "Claim Soleimani Targeted Due to Imminent Attack Reportedly Based on 'Razor Thin' Evidence," *Slate*, January 4, 2020.

Epilogue

321 *"We assess that the United States":* Daniel R. Coats, Director of National Intelligence, "Statement for the Record, Worldwide Threat Assessment of the

U.S. Intelligence Community, January 29, 2019" (Senate Select Committee on Intelligence), p. 21.

321 *in less than four months:* Marc Fisher, "The U.S. death toll has reached 100,000," *Washington Post*, May 27, 2020.

322 *warnings appeared frequently in the President's Daily Brief:* Michael Poznansky, "Apparently, Trump ignored early coronavirus warnings. That has consequences," *Washington Post*, March 23, 2020.

322 *Trump's original CIA briefer, Ted Gistaro:* Julian Barnes and Adam Goldman, "For Spy Agencies, Briefing Trump Is a Test of Holding His Attention," *New York Times*, May 21, 2020.

322 *the first time he'd heard of the virus:* Fox News Town Hall with President Trump at the Lincoln Memorial, Washington, D.C., May 3, 2020.

322 *Sanner's name had been revealed:* Julian E. Barnes and Adam Goldman, "For Spy Agencies, Briefing Trump Is a Test of Holding His Attention," *New York Times*, May 21, 2020.

322 *"the IC (Intelligence Community) and others did not believe":* Robert O'Brien, *Face the Nation*, CBS News, May 24, 2020.

322 *had been sounding the alarm:* Robert Delaney, "US CDC had 'very good interaction' with China after coronavirus outbreak, says director Robert Redfield," *MSN News*, May 5, 2020.

323 *Alex Azar called Trump:* Marty Johnson, "Health secretary twice warned Trump about coronavirus threat: NYT," *The Hill*, April 11, 2020.

323 *"On its face it doesn't make sense":* Author interview with Robert Gates, May 6, 2020.

323 *"this disease was more deadly":* Author interview with Senator Richard Blumenthal, May 22, 2020.

323 *John Bolton, Trump's third national security adviser, had famously abolished:* "Top White House official in charge of pandemic response exits abruptly," *Washington Post*, May 10, 2018.

324 *"The United States government might be the most":* Michael Lewis, *The Fifth Risk* (New York: W. W. Norton, 2018), p. 37.

324 *He had removed the IC inspector general:* Melissa Quinn, "The internal watchdogs Trump has fired or replaced," CBS News, May 19, 2020.

324 *"It was absolutely the worst time":* Author interview with Jeremy Bash, April 21, 2020.

325 *"They just didn't have the experience":* Author interview with Luciana Borio, May 11, 2020.

326 *pinned the blame for it on everyone else:* Andy Kroll, "As Trump Bashes China, His Administration Pays Millions to a Consulting Firm Used by the Chinese Government," *Rolling Stone*, April 16, 2020.

326 *He'd charged Barack Obama:* Nick Visser, "Trump Baselessly Accuses Obama of 'Treason'," *HuffPost*, June 22, 2020.

326 *he had accused Joe Scarborough:* Quint Forgey, "Trump promotes conspiracy theory accusing MSNBC's Joe Scarborough of murder," *Politico*, May 12, 2020.

326 *Mike Pompeo, the former CIA director, listened to every word:* Courtney McBride and Sadie German, "Pompeo Took Part in Ukraine Call, Official Says," *Wall Street Journal*, September 30, 2019.

327 *"John Wilkes Booth":* Andrew Blake, "Joe diGenova, former federal prosecutor, likens whistleblower to Lincoln's killer John Wilkes Booth," *Washington Times*, November 12, 2019.

327 *"They were all asked to do things":* Author interview with Cynthia Helms, September 17, 2018.

327 *the briefing, given annually, was abruptly canceled:* Marty Johnson, "House intelligence briefing on worldwide threat assessment delayed," *The Hill*, February 8, 2020.

327 *"I don't recall any worldwide threat briefing":* Author interview with Robert Gates, May 6, 2020.

328 *"I've received no satisfactory answer":* Author interview with Senator Richard Blumenthal, May 22, 2020.

328 *"The leaders of the intelligence community":* Author interview with Michael Morell.

328 *"President Trump may try to run the White House himself":* Chris Whipple, *The Gatekeepers: How the White House Chiefs of Staff Define Every Presidency* (New York: Crown, 2017), p. 300.

Index

Note: "LBJ" refers to Lyndon B. Johnson, and "JFK" refers to John F. Kennedy.

About the Author

Chris Whipple is an acclaimed writer, documentary filmmaker, and speaker. A former multiple Peabody and Emmy Award–winning producer at CBS's *60 Minutes* and ABC's *Primetime*, he is the chief executive officer of CCWHIP Productions. He is also a frequent guest on MSNBC and CNN, and his writing has appeared in the *New York Times*, the *Washington Post*, and *Vanity Fair*. The author, most recently, of *The Gatekeepers: How the White House Chiefs of Staff Define Every Presidency*, he was the executive producer and writer of Showtime's 2015 documentary film *The Spymasters: CIA in the Crosshairs*.